The Story of God's Chosen Family SERIES

The Story of God's Chosen Family

God Visits His Chosen Family

New Testament Study of

the Gospels and Acts

Grade 7

Teacher's Manual

Rod and Staff Publishers, Inc.
P.O. Box 3, Hwy. 172, Crockett, Kentucky 41413
Telephone: (606) 522-4348

Acknowledgments

We give thanks first to God for the Holy Scriptures, "which are able to make [our students] wise unto salvation through faith which is in Christ Jesus" (2 Timothy 3:15).

God's Word is the textbook for this course. The goal of this workbook is to instill in our children a deeper appreciation for God and His Word, to broaden their understanding of Bible facts, and to guide them toward competent study and use of the Bible for themselves.

A number of brethren worked together in writing and editing the material for this study guide. Others spent many hours reviewing the material and preparing the manuscript for publication. Ruth (Goodwin) Weaver, Edith Burkholder, Barbara Schlabach, Lester Miller, and Timothy Conley drew the illustrations.

All of the maps in this course except the one in Lesson 21 are based on Mountain High Maps® Copyright© 1993 Digital Wisdom.

The photographs in this book are used by permission of the following sources: Library of Congress (pages 30 and 128), Photri (page 104), and Bennie Hostetler (page 184). The artwork illustrating the Sanhedrin (page 190) is used by permission of Eastern Mennonite Publications.

"Thou art worthy, O Lord, to receive glory and honour and power: for thou hast created all things, and for thy pleasure they are and were created" (Revelation 4:11).

Table of Contents

TEACHER'S INTRODUCTION

Rod and Staff Bible Series Outline

The Story of God's Chosen Family (Grades 5–8)
Grade 5: God Chooses a Family
   (Old Testament—Creation to the prophet Samuel)
Grade 6: God's Chosen Family as a Nation
   (Old Testament—Saul to Malachi)
Grade 7: God Visits His Chosen Family
   (New Testament—the Gospels and Acts)
Grade 8: God's Redeemed Family—the Church
   (New Testament—Romans to Revelation)

God's Plan for His People (Grades 9, 10)
Grade 9: The Revelation of God
   (Themes and Doctrines from the Old and New Testaments)
Grade 10: The Completion of God's Plan for Man
   (More Themes and Doctrines from the Old and New Testaments)

Introductory Notes for Grade 7 Workbook

- Some information in this course not taken from the Bible itself is from *The Life and Times of Jesus the Messiah*, by Alfred Edersheim (1883). Edersheim was a converted Jew who had an extensive knowledge of Jewish history and writings. A one-volume reprint of this work is available from Christian Book Distributors, P.O. Box 7000, Peabody, MA 01961-7000. It is reasonably priced and provides a tremendous amount of background information on Jewish practices and culture in Jesus' time. Other sources of information include standard reference works, such as *The New Unger's Bible Dictionary*.

- This workbook does not follow Edersheim's conclusion that the unnamed feast in John 5:1 is a fall feast. Most harmonies of the Gospel consider this to have been a Passover. Edersheim counts three Passovers during the ministry of Christ, while this course counts four (John 2:13; 5:1; 6:4; and 13:1). This means that Christ's ministry is presented here as having been about three and a half years in length, rather than the two and a half advocated by Edersheim. This is an uncertain point, and there is no clear proof for either conclusion. But the three and a half years could fit with the prophecy in Daniel 9:26, 27.

- The time lines and other dates used in this course provide a general sequence of New Testament events. However, since opinions vary on many details, most dates should be considered approximate.

  Some dates in New Testament times are reasonably well documented. It is generally accepted that Herod the Great died in March or April of 4 B.C. Jesus was born some time before this, perhaps in 5 B.C. The fifteenth year of Tiberius Caesar, when John began his ministry (Luke 3:1), is thought to have been about A.D. 26. (Tiberius began his sole reign in A.D. 14, but he had become co-regnent prior to this.) Jesus began His ministry soon after this when He was about thirty years old (Luke 3:23). If Jesus' ministry lasted three and a half years, as is commonly thought, His crucifixion would have taken place about A.D. 30. Other established dates that provide reference points include Herod Agrippa I's death in A.D. 44 (Acts 12:23) and the destruction of Jerusalem in A.D. 70.

The Pupil's Book

Use: Workbook Versus Textbook

The pupil's book may be used as a consumable workbook or as a textbook. It is designed as a workbook, which allows the student to write answers in the book and to keep it after he completes the course. However, since most exercises are numbered or lettered, schools that prefer to reuse the books for several years may ask the students to write their answers on paper.

Chapter and Lesson Divisions

The pupil's book is divided into six chapters. Each chapter has five lessons and a review. A chapter is intended to provide work for six weeks. Chapter tests and a final test are available in a separate booklet.

This series (The Story of God's Chosen Family, Grades 5–8) follows a chronological sequence through the Bible. This workbook is a study of the Gospels and Acts. Most lessons have the following sections.

1. **Lesson Introduction**
2. **Time Line**—This supplements the lesson introduction by giving an approximate time line of a few main events in the lesson. The time line questions are intended for class discussion. The General Scope given with the time line shows the general progression of study through Luke and Acts. Students may want to keep a marker in their Bibles at this place.
3. **A. Answers From the Bible**—These exercises direct the student to Bible passages for answers. This is the core section of the course and should be completed by all students.
4. **B. Bible Word Study**—This part is intended to increase the student's understanding of unfamiliar words and terms.
5. **C. Thinking About Bible Truths**—The teacher may use these questions for class discussion or additional assignment. They are often more challenging than the other exercises. Some may be difficult for seventh grade students to answer on their own.
6. **D. Learning More About Bible Times**—This background information will help students better understand Bible facts, customs, and lands.

The Teacher's Book

Oral Review

These questions are for optional use during the class period. They provide a continual review of some main points, lessening the need to review everything before the test. If you wish, you may duplicate the questions and hand them to the students for written work or personal study.

In This Lesson

Scope

This section gives the Bible chapters or verses on which the lesson is based. Important parallel passages from other Gospels are given, but scattered individual verses used in the lesson are usually not included.

Because of time and space limitations, the lesson covers only a few key points rather than giving a thorough coverage of the whole Bible scope. This is especially true for parallel accounts given by more than one Gospel. Additional facts and themes could be drawn from the scope if time permits.

Focus

This section provides a brief outline of main events or teachings on which to focus while teaching the lesson.

Objectives

This section lists important facts or skills that the student should learn. The reviews and tests are based on these objectives.

Truths to Amplify

While one purpose of this course is to teach Bible facts, it also provides an excellent opportunity to convey spiritual truths. Several important truths in each lesson are listed for your benefit. The list is not exhaustive, nor should you feel it necessary to cover all the points mentioned. Rather, the list is for your benefit, to provide inspiration and a sense of direction. Teach as the Lord directs, with truths He has instilled in your heart.

Answer Key

A copy of the pupil's page is provided, with the answers given in colored ink. Teachers should use their own judgment when deciding whether an answer is correct. Vague or incomplete answers will not suffice. When exact answers can easily be found in the Bible, do not give credit for guesses based on the student's previous Bible knowledge. In certain cases, however, some variation is permissible.

This course calls for complete answers when long blanks are given. Some teachers might want to require students to give sentence answers for all long blanks, while other teachers might require sentence answers only when a sentence is needed for a complete answer. Teachers should tell their students what type of answer they will consider complete.

Sometimes the Answer Key gives several options for an answer or has some other directions for the teacher to consider in relation to a question. If this requires too much space to fit in the Pupil reduction, two arrows (>>) direct you to look in the margin for the additional answers or further direction.

Notes

Along the right margins are additional directions and notes that you may find interesting and helpful in teaching. The directions are in italic type, with the first line indented. The notes are preceded by bullets.

Note for Schools Outside the United States

To keep this workbook simple, metric measures have not been included in the lessons. However, the tables of measure in the back of the pupil's book give metric equivalents, and the answer key gives answers in metric units. If you normally use the metric system, tell your students to give all answers involving measure in metric.

Lesson Plans

Since this course may be used in a wide variety of settings, no detailed lesson plan is provided for each lesson. However, many schools have Bible classes two or three times a week. You may find the following suggestions helpful.

Two-Day Plan

First Day
— Read or discuss the introduction together.
— Discuss the time line and the questions provided with it.
— Read at least some of the lesson verses in class.
— Assign Part A (Answers From the Bible).

Second Day
— Discuss Part C (Thinking About Bible Truths). If possible, do this section in class. Some questions may be difficult for students to answer on their own.
— Discuss Part D (Learning More About Bible Times).
— Assign Part B (Bible Word Study) and Part D (Learning More About Bible Times). Also assign Part C (Thinking About Bible Truths) if you did not complete it in class.

Three-Day Plan

First Day
— Read or discuss the introduction together.
— Discuss the time line and the questions provided with it.
— Read some of the lesson verses in class.
— Assign some of Part A.

Second Day
— Read more of the lesson verses in class.
— Assign the rest of Part A.
— Assign Part B.

Third Day
— Discuss Part C. If possible, do this section in class. Some questions may be difficult for students to answer on their own.
— Discuss Part D.
— Assign Part D. Also assign Part C if you did not complete it in class.

Bible Memorization

Bible memorization should have an important place in a Christian school. If everyone knows a passage well, reciting it together can be a pleasant, worshipful exercise. With enough practice, any class can learn to recite Bible verses fluently and clearly. It is unfortunate when students see Bible memorization as drudgery.

Hints for Bible Memorization

1. Teachers can inspire enthusiasm for memorizing by being enthusiastic themselves about learning new verses.
2. Assign a reasonable number of verses for memorization. Students should learn only as many verses as can be effectively drilled in class. Memorizing a few verses well is better than trying to learn a large number without mastering them.
3. Select verses that students can understand and relate to. Explain the meaning of difficult passages.
4. Have short, frequent classes for Bible memorization, possibly first thing after the morning devotional or after the lunch break.
5. You may wish to copy the day's assignment onto the chalkboard, writing the passage in lines like the lines of a poem. After the students have read the first lines and recited them with their eyes closed, begin erasing the lines.
6. Group memorization is a great help. It offers variety and serves as an effective stimulant. But individual testing, both oral and written, also has its place.
7. Do not assign Bible memorization as a punishment.
8. Review previously learned verses throughout the school year. During the last few weeks of the year, the entire Bible memory program could be devoted to review.
9. Students may learn to memorize a series of verses by "counting fingers," associating each verse with a finger.
10. If you are teaching more than one grade, you may wish to assign the same memory passage to everyone in the room.

Suggested Memory Passages

The following suggestions may be helpful to you in selecting Bible passages for memorization. For each chapter in this course, three Scripture passages are given. Choice one is a passage from John, choice two is a passage from Mark or Acts, and choice three is a portion of Christ's Sermon on the Mount. There is also one thematic selection of verses suitable for the chapter being studied. From these four suggestions, choose the one you feel is best suited to your class. Divide your selected passage or theme into five or six weekly assignments. You may add or delete verses from the selections as needed.

As much as is feasible, the thematic selections have been arranged to avoid awkward transitions of person and tense. If you use these selections, you may find it helpful to type them so that the students have them all together. Typing the verses after the following pattern will make it easier for the students to memorize them line by line.

Isaiah 7:14

Therefore the Lord himself shall give you a sign;
  Behold, a virgin shall conceive,
    and bear a son,
      and shall call his name Immanuel.

Isaiah 9:6

For unto us a child is born,
  unto us a son is given:
    and the government shall be upon his shoulder:
      and his name shall be called
        Wonderful,
          Counsellor,
            The mighty God,
              The everlasting Father,
                The Prince of Peace.

Chapter One. Jesus Comes to Minister

Passage selections
  1. John 1:1–30
  2. Mark 1:1–22
  3. Sermon on the Mount—Matthew 5:1–26

Thematic selections: The Messiah Foretold
  4. Isaiah 7:14; 9:6, 7; 42:1–7; Luke 1:68–79

Chapter Two. Acceptance and Rejection

Passage selections
  1. John 5:24–47
  2. Mark 2
  3. Sermon on the Mount—Matthew 5:27–48

Thematic selections: Jesus' Compassion for Mankind
  4. Luke 4:14–21; Matthew 9:35–38; 23:37; 11:28–30; Hebrews 4:14–16

Chapter Three. Jesus Ministers to Jews and Gentiles

Passage selections
  1. John 6:26–51
  2. Mark 6:34–56
  3. Sermon on the Mount—Matthew 6:1–18

Thematic selections: Blessings on Those Who Believe
  4. Matthew 8:5–13; 9:18–29; 15:21–28

Chapter Four. Jesus Ministers in Judea and Perea

Passage selections
1. John 10:1–28
2. Mark 10:1–27
3. Sermon on the Mount—Matthew 6:19–7:6

Thematic selections: Jesus, Our Example
4. Matthew 16:24–26; John 13:12–17; Philippians 2:1–11; 1 Peter 2:20–25

Chapter Five. Jesus Completes His Work

Passage selections
1. John 17
2. Mark 15:15–39
3. Sermon on the Mount—Matthew 7:7–29

Thematic selections: "Behold the Lamb of God"
4. Genesis 22:7, 8; Isaiah 53:1–7; John 1:26–29; 19:14–18; Revelation 5:6–14

Chapter Six. God Calls a New People

Passage selections
1. John 21
2. Acts 2:1–23, 32–38
3. Sermon on the Mount—Review Matthew 5–7

Thematic selections: The Holy Spirit in the Church
4. Joel 2:28–32; John 14:16, 17; Acts 2:1–6, 14–16; 4:31–33; Romans 8:14–18

Teaching Subjective Thinking Skills

What Is Subjective Thinking?

Two basic kinds of questions are used in teaching. The most common is the objective question, which asks about a fact. This type of question tests recall and research skills, but does not necessarily test understanding. For instance, an objective question might ask how many legions of angels Jesus could have called to help Him. The student can read Matthew 26:53 and answer, "Twelve legions." However, just because he has given the fact does not guarantee that he understands his answer. He may have no idea what a legion is.

The other type of question is the subjective question, which requires the student to apply facts he has learned and draw conclusions from them. A person who thinks carefully about Matthew 26:53 will realize several things that are not stated. First, he will see that Jesus submitted to the mob in the garden because He wanted to. He had the ability to overpower them, but He did not use it. Second, Jesus could have refused to go to Calvary. Subjective questions guide the student in reaching this kind of conclusion.

Subjective thinking should not be allowed to become mere fantasy. It is based on fact and stays within the bounds of logic and reason.

Suppose you are traveling down a highway in a car. As you pass a house, you see a large, angry dog chasing a man down the driveway toward his car. What happened after you were past? The objective answer is that you do not know. However, you do have some facts that help you reach a probable conclusion. The dog was angry. The man was running to get away from him. A car was waiting at the end of the drive. You know that angry dogs can be vicious. Given these facts, which of the following is the most likely conclusion to the incident?

1. The man stops at his car to pet the dog and to praise him for being a good watchdog.

2. The dog chases the man all the way to his car, biting his leg as he frantically tries to open the door.

3. Just as the dog reaches him, the man sprouts wings and soars away to safety.

The first answer is not reasonable, given the facts you know about the situation. The second one is the most likely. The third is fantastic—men do not sprout wings. Subjective reasoning is the process that helps us reach conclusions like this.

Why Do We Need to Teach Subjective Thinking?

Everyone does some subjective thinking. However, some people have not learned to think logically and subjectively at the same time. Because of this, they often jump to wild conclusions. At other times, they reach wrong conclusions because they have not taken time to learn all the related facts. Such people need training in subjective thinking.

Other people allow the reasoning process to replace faith. They decide that they will not believe anything that they cannot reason through. Since they cannot understand Bible miracles, they refuse to believe them. This is the opposite extreme from jumping to conclusions, but it is even more serious because it destroys faith in God and His Word. Such people also need training in subjective thinking.

We must teach our students to avoid these two extremes. They must learn that faith in God and the Bible is a necessary part of the reasoning process. It is a fact that God is not tied to the same limitations that we are. On the other hand, God overrules natural laws only for special purposes, and His character always limits Him from doing evil.

A person who has learned to think properly knows that what he does today will affect his future. By applying verses such as "Love not the world, neither the things that are in the world," he realizes that television, tobacco smoking, and a host of other modern evils are wrong, even though the Bible does not specifically mention them. Subjective thinking trains a person to look at life realistically and prepares him to cope with it. As a teacher, you have an obligation to teach your students good thinking skills.

How Can We Teach Subjective Thinking?

This course includes a number of subjective questions. Seventh grade students should be able to answer some of these on their own, but they may still need some help in understanding how to reach a reasonable conclusion.

Some subjective questions in this course are multiple-choice exercises. This gives the student a starting point for his evaluation. If he thinks that two answers could be right, he must ask himself, "Which of the two is the better answer?" At first some students may not understand how a correct answer can be the wrong one, but explain that no answer is really right if a better answer is available. This is an important skill for every Christian to learn and practice.

"I am the vine, ye are the branches" (John 15:5).

CHAPTER ONE

Jesus Comes To Minister

Introduction to the New Testament
The Coming of Jesus Announced
Jesus' Birth and Childhood
John the Baptist Introduces Jesus
Jesus Begins His Ministry

For unto us a child is born,
unto us a son is given:
and the government shall be upon his shoulder:
and his name shall be called Wonderful,
Counsellor, The mighty God,
The everlasting Father, The Prince of Peace.
Isaiah 9:6

Harmony of the Gospels

For important events and teachings covered in Chapter One

Event or Teaching	Matthew	Mark	Luke	John	Location	Season
Lesson 2. The Coming of Jesus Is Announced						
The angel Gabriel appears to Zacharias.	—	—	1:5–23[1]	—	Jerusalem	
Gabriel appears to Mary.	—	—	1:26–38	—	Nazareth	
An angel appears to Joseph in a dream.	1:18–25	—	—	—	Nazareth	
The wise men see the star.	2:1–10	—	—	—	"The East"	
Lesson 3. Jesus' Birth and Childhood						
Jesus is born in Bethlehem.	1:25	—	2:1–20	—	Bethlehem	
Jesus is presented to God at the temple.	—	—	2:21–39	—	Jerusalem	
Herod tries to kill Jesus.	2:11–18	—	—	—	Judea, Egypt	
Joseph returns to Nazareth.	2:19–23	—	2:39	—	Nazareth	
Jesus talks with the teachers at the temple.	—	—	2:40–52	—	Jerusalem	
Lesson 4. John the Baptist Introduces Jesus						
John is born to Zacharias and Elisabeth.	—	—	1:5–25, 57–80	—	Judea	
John preaches and baptizes near Jordan.	3:1–12	1:1–8	3:1–18	—	Jordan Valley	
John baptizes Jesus.	3:13–17	1:9–11	3:21, 22	—	Jordan Valley	
John bears testimony of Jesus.	—	—	—	1:6–42	Jordan Valley	
Jesus confirms John's ministry.	11:2–19	—	7:18–35	—		
Herod has John beheaded.	14:1–12	6:14–29	9:7–9	—	Perea	
Lesson 5. Jesus Begins His Ministry						
Jesus is tempted in the wilderness.	4:1–11	1:12, 13	4:1–13	—	Wilderness	
Nathanael meets Jesus.	—	—	—	1:43–51		
Jesus performs His first miracle.	—	—	—	2:1–11	Cana	
Jesus cleanses the temple.	—	—	—	2:13–25	Jerusalem	Spring
Jesus talks to Nicodemus.	—	—	—	3:1–21	Jerusalem ?	
Jesus ministers in Judea.	—	—	—	3:22–30	Judea	Summer ?
Jesus ministers in Samaria.	—	—	—	4:1–42	Samaria	Late fall[2]

[1] Passages given in italics are used in the lesson.

[2] Jesus apparently visited Samaria in late fall, four months before the spring harvest.

9

Lesson 1. Introduction to the New Testament

The first two workbooks in this Bible series are a study of the Old Testament. This workbook begins a study of the New Testament.

The Jews were God's chosen family in Old Testament times. The Old Testament was God's testament, or covenant, with them. God used His covenant with the Jews to prepare the world for the coming of His Son. The New Testament is God's covenant with the church, which has become His spiritual family.

Jesus came as a Jew and lived among God's Old Testament family. But He taught a higher standard of holiness and love than the Old Testament had required. He fulfilled the Old Testament sacrifices and ceremonies by offering Himself as the perfect sacrifice for sin. And after His resurrection and ascension, Jesus established the church by sending the Holy Spirit to live in the hearts of the believers.

God had promised this better, spiritual covenant through Old Testament prophets. In Jeremiah 31:33, God had said, "I will put my law in their inward parts, and write it in their hearts; and will be their God, and they shall be my people." New Testament believers can come to God by this "new and living way" (Hebrews 10:20).

A. THE NEW TESTAMENT BOOKS

The New Testament books were written by apostles and other followers of Jesus. God inspired these men to write these books so that New Testament believers would know His will for them. We use the New Testament to guide us, just as the Jews used the Old Testament writings.

The four Gospels give Jesus' teachings, and they also record some events from His life. The Book of Acts tells how the church began and gives a few accounts from its early history.

Some New Testament books are known as epistles (letters). These books give instructions and encouragement to Christians and church leaders. God inspired the apostle Paul to write at least thirteen epistles. They are easy to identify because Paul gives his name at the beginning of each of them. Paul may have also written the Epistle to the Hebrews, but we do not know for sure since the writer did not give his name. We place Hebrews with the group of general epistles written by other apostles.

The last book in the New Testament is Revelation, written by the apostle John. Revelation contains messages from Jesus to seven churches of Asia Minor. It also includes prophetic visions that reveal some future events and give a beautiful description of the heavenly city.

This year as you study the Gospels and Acts, you will learn about the life of Christ and the beginning of the church.

The Four Gospels

Write in order the names of the four Gospels.

1. _____ Matthew _____
2. _____ Mark _____
3. _____ Luke _____
4. _____ John _____

- Under the Old Covenant, the Israelites were God's chosen people. Through Jesus, God offers salvation to all men rather than primarily to the Jews. Since the church is not a nation with civil powers, Christians are subject to the national laws of the countries in which they live, as long as these laws do not conflict with God's Word. The war against evil shifts from flesh and blood battles to spiritual battles.
- As you teach this course, consider Jesus' willingness to sacrifice His own good for the good of God's family. His miracles, His friendships, His whole life on earth point to His desire to serve rather than be served.
- You may find it helpful to make regular use of a harmony of the Gospels while teaching this course.
- An interesting reference source on New Testament Palestine is *The Moody Atlas of Bible Lands*, Moody Press, 1985.

Students should be able to say all the New Testament books from memory. Spend some time reviewing them with the students in class.

Lesson 1

In This Lesson

Focus

- The New Testament includes twenty-seven books, inspired by God and written by apostles and other followers of Jesus.
  - The New Testament books are sometimes divided into the following sections: the Gospels, the Book of History, the Pauline Epistles, the General Epistles, and the Book of Prophecy.
  - A harmony of the Gospels gives a comparison of the events recorded in the four Gospels.

- This lesson gives an overview of Palestine at the time of Christ.
  - New Testament Palestine was not the same as Old Testament Israel.
  - Herod the Great, the ruler of Palestine at Jesus' birth, was an Edomite.
  - The Greeks and Romans changed the appearance of Palestinian cities.
  - The Romans divided Palestine into districts, which included Judea, Samaria, and Galilee.
  - The map exercise includes a few places that were important in Christ's ministry. Students will need to know the location of these places for the Chapter 1 test.

10   Chapter One   Jesus Comes to Minister

The Book of History

5. _____Acts_____ is the only book of history in the New Testament.

The Pauline Epistles

 Write in order the names of the thirteen epistles written by Paul.

6. Romans	13. 1 Thessalonians
7. 1 Corinthians	14. 2 Thessalonians
8. 2 Corinthians	15. 1 Timothy
9. Galatians	16. 2 Timothy
10. Ephesians	17. Titus
11. Philippians	18. Philemon
12. Colossians	

The General Epistles

 Write in order the names of the eight general epistles.

19. Hebrews	23. 1 John
20. James	24. 2 John
21. 1 Peter	25. 3 John
22. 2 Peter	26. Jude

The Book of Prophecy

27. The New Testament book of prophecy is called _____Revelation_____.

 Memorize the New Testament books in their proper order before you take the Chapter One test. Make sure you know the correct spelling of each book and which section it belongs in.

B. THE FOUR GOSPELS

Matthew, Mark, Luke, and John wrote four accounts of Jesus' life and teachings—the four Gospels. Some events in Jesus' life were recorded by all four writers. Others were mentioned by only one or two. A comparison of the events recorded in the four Gospels is called a *harmony of the Gospels*.

A harmony of the Gospels lists events in the approximate order they happened. However, since the Gospels do not give the events in exactly the same order, it is difficult to determine for sure when some events took place. This workbook follows the general sequence of Christ's life.

The following chart shows the general plan of a harmony of the Gospels. Each chapter of this workbook includes a simple harmony of the Gospels for events covered in the lessons. If you have a more detailed harmony of the Gospels in your Bible or in a school reference book, you may find it helpful during your study this year.

 Look up key words in a concordance to find which chapters of the Gospels describe the following events. Record these chapters on the chart. The number in parentheses tells how many Gospels record the event; be sure to include all the references. The first one is done as an example. (Note: You may also use a harmony of the Gospels to find the events.)

Objectives (Answers are given in italics.)
- Students should know from memory (using correct order and spelling) the names of
  —the four Gospels. (*Matthew, Mark, Luke, John*)
  —the New Testament Book of History. (*Acts*)
  —the thirteen Pauline Epistles. (*Romans, 1 & 2 Corinthians, Galatians, Ephesians, Philippians, Colossians, 1 & 2 Thessalonians, 1 & 2 Timothy, Titus, Philemon*)
  —the eight general epistles. (*Hebrews, James, 1 & 2 Peter, 1, 2, & 3 John, Jude*)
  —the New Testament book of prophecy. (*Revelation*)

- Students should know
  —which Gospels record the birth of Christ. (*Matthew, Luke*)
  —in which three languages the title on Jesus' cross appeared. (*Hebrew [Aramaic], Greek, and Latin*)
  —the names of three important districts in Palestine. (*Galilee, Samaria, Judea*)
- Students should be able to find the following places on a map: Bethany, Bethlehem, Cana, Capernaum, Jericho, Jerusalem, Jordan River, Nazareth, Sea of Galilee.

Event	Matthew	Mark	Luke	John
1. Jesus Christ is born in Bethlehem. (2)	Chap. 1, 2		Chap. 2	
2. Wise men come to see Jesus. (1)	Chap. 2			
3. Jesus changes water to wine at Cana. (1)				Chap. 2
4. Jesus heals a man with a withered hand. (3)	Chap. 12	Chap. 3	Chap. 6	
5. Jesus feeds five thousand men. (4)	Chap. 14	Chap. 6	Chap. 9	Chap. 6
6. Jesus' countenance is transfigured. (3)	Chap. 17	Chap. 9	Chap. 9	
7. Jesus teaches at the Feast of Dedication. (1)				Chap. 10
8. Jesus gives the parable of the ten virgins. (1)	Chap. 25			
9. Jesus washes the disciples' feet. (1)				Chap. 13
10. Pilate judges Jesus. (4)	Chap. 27	Chap. 15	Chap. 23	Chap. 18, 19

C. THE SETTING OF THE NEW TESTAMENT

How Palestine Came to Be

To properly understand the events recorded in the New Testament, it is helpful to know some facts about the land of Palestine, where many of these events took place.

The old nation of Israel ceased to exist long before Jesus' birth. Jesus was not born in Israel, but in Palestine—Roman Palestine. The land remained the same, with its palm trees, hills, green valleys, and deserts; but the people ruling it had changed.

The nation of Israel (including Judah) ended in 586 B.C. when the Jews were carried captive to Babylon as a result of their sin. In 539 B.C. the Babylonians were conquered by the Persians, who allowed the Jews to return to their native land. The Persians did not allow the Jews to re-establish Israel as a Jewish nation, but they did give them some freedom to manage their own affairs.

Alexander the Great, a young ruler from Macedonia, conquered much of the civilized world around 330 B.C. Because Alexander and his successors spoke Greek, the language and culture of Palestine became steadily more Greek under their rule. Jesus understood and spoke Greek, even though His mother tongue was Aramaic (a language similar to Hebrew). Many Jews read Greek better than Hebrew, so they translated the Old Testament into Greek.

Eventually a Jewish family called the *Maccabees* arose, fought off the Greek rulers, and set up a Jewish nation again. From about 143 to 63 B.C., the Jews were free and independent. But the Maccabees' descendants mismanaged their country and began to follow the ways of the pagan Greeks. When two descendants of the Maccabees began fighting between themselves, the Romans seized the opportunity to gain control of Palestine. The Roman general Pompey conquered Jerusalem in 63 B.C.

The Romans called the land *Palestine,* which means "land of the Philistines." They put King Herod, an Idumean (Edomite), in control of Palestine. (The Edomites were descendants of Jacob's twin brother Esau.) His land included about the same area once ruled by the kings of Judah and Israel. At times the Romans sent *procurators* (governors), such as Pilate, to rule parts of Palestine. The Romans stationed groups of soldiers in major cities. A group of one hundred soldiers, called a *century*, was led by a Roman centurion.

Truths to Amplify

- The New Testament is the final authority for the New Testament church, just as the Old Testament was for Old Testament Jews. New Testament believers should not turn to the Old Testament for support of practices such as participation in war or swearing of oaths, which clearly violate New Testament principles. With the change of covenants has come a change in God's requirements for His people.
- Palestine, as Jesus knew it, was no longer the Old Testament "land of Israel." Neither was it the same as modern Palestine. Grade 7 students will benefit from an understanding of Palestine and its position in Middle Eastern affairs at the beginning of the first century.
- Christ's relationship to the Romans provides an example for the Christian's relationship to the state. Jesus taught against oppression, injustice, war, carnal indulgence, and many other Roman practices. Yet He taught respect for Roman civil authority. He had no desire to become involved in civil affairs, as He was falsely accused of doing (Luke 23:2; John 19:12).

12   Chapter One   Jesus Comes to Minister

With the Romans came new Roman laws and the Latin language. The Romans built new cities, roads, and aqueducts. Greek and Roman cities looked different from the old Jewish cities. They had wide, paved streets laid out in an orderly design. Public squares, parks, and new stone buildings added to the beauty of the cities.

Jerusalem, the Jews' capital city, became a show place under the Romans. Herod rebuilt the temple for the Jews. He also built a fortress, which he named Antonia, beside the temple. A palace on the west side of town became one of King Herod's many dwellings.

Not all the Roman contributions in Palestine were improvements. In Sebaste (Samaria), Herod built a temple dedicated to Augustus Caesar and idol worship. In many cities, the Greeks and Romans built public baths, theaters, and stadiums for open-air sports. The foreign rulers tried to appease both Jews and pagans (idol worshipers).

Street Scene in Jerusalem

1. Using a concordance, find an occasion when Jesus spoke with and helped a Greek person in need. (Describe the occasion and give the reference.) _____
   Jesus healed the daughter of a Greek woman (Mark 7:25–30).

2. In which three languages did the title on Jesus' cross appear? (See John 19:19, 20.) _____
   Hebrew (Aramaic), Greek, and Latin

3. The Romans built good roads to help them keep order in the land. The people could travel freely, and because the Roman Empire was so big, they could trade with more people than ever before. How could these advantages of Roman rule help the cause of the kingdom that Jesus announced?
   The Gospel spread rapidly over Roman roads and trade routes. With order in the land, people could travel freely and Jesus' teachings were carried from place to place.

4. Jesus could not approve of everything the Romans did, yet He respected the rulers. Look up *Caesar* in a concordance to find the following references.   or Luke 20:25
   a. A reference where Jesus said that taxes should be paid to Caesar   Matthew 22:21, Mark 12:17,
   b. A reference where Jesus was falsely accused of refusing to pay taxes to Caesar   Luke 23:2

Roman Divisions of Palestine

Roman Palestine included Galilee in the north, Samaria in the middle, Judea (sometimes spelled *Judaea*) in the south, and other Roman districts around these three. Judea was the most important Jewish region. Here lay Jerusalem, only 34 miles south of Samaria, 16 miles west of Jericho, and 35 miles southeast of Joppa.

5. On the map of Palestine on page 13, use colored pencils to lightly shade Galilee green, Samaria yellow, and Judea orange. The dotted lines show the approximate boundaries of these regions. If you need help, check the maps in the back of your Bible or in a Bible atlas.
   (Galilee should be colored green, Samaria yellow, and Judea orange.)

New Testament Places

 The shaded box contains names of places that were important in the life of Christ. Write each name in the correct blank on the map. The lettered clues may help you. If you need additional help, find the names on a map, or use a concordance to find the reference for the clue.

Bethany
Bethlehem
Cana
Capernaum
Jericho
Jerusalem
Jordan River
Nazareth
Sea of Galilee

A. Jesus was born here.
B. Jesus lived here as a boy and young man.
C. Jesus was baptized here.
D. Jesus performed His first miracle here.
E. Jesus lived here much of the time that He was in Galilee, especially during the winter.
F. Here Jesus stilled a storm.
G. Jesus visited Zacchaeus here.
H. Jesus raised Lazarus to life here.
I. Jesus was crucified outside this city.

14

Lesson 2. The Coming of Jesus Is Announced

About four thousand years had passed since Adam and Eve had fallen into sin. Almost four hundred years had passed since the last prophets had spoken to Israel. Had God forgotten His people and His promises to them?

No; God was deeply interested in His people. He was greatly concerned about their spiritual needs. And the time had almost come when He would send His own Son to earth to make a way for them to return to Him.

God's people had waited a long time for the Messiah. But very few people were ready for Him when He came. Almost nobody expected Him to come as He did.

Would the Messiah be born in the king's palace? Would He come through an important family in Jerusalem? Would trumpets be blown throughout Palestine to announce His arrival?

No; God used simple yet wonderful ways to announce the coming of His Son. God did not send His angel to the wealthy and powerful, but to Zacharias, an aged priest; to Mary, a young virgin; and to Joseph, a poor carpenter. God placed a guiding star in the heavens for all the world to see, yet only a few wise men recognized its significance. And after the Messiah had come, God sent His angelic host to herald the message, not to rich Jewish rulers, but to lowly shepherds.

Why did God reveal His plan to such people? God had chosen to send His Son to humble, sincere seekers of truth.

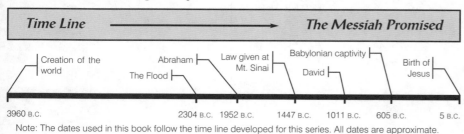

Time Line ⟶ The Messiah Promised

Creation of the world | Abraham | The Flood | Law given at Mt. Sinai | Babylonian captivity | David | Birth of Jesus

3960 B.C.   2304 B.C. 1952 B.C.   1447 B.C.   1011 B.C.   605 B.C.   5 B.C.

Note: The dates used in this book follow the time line developed for this series. All dates are approximate.

Using the Time Line

1. Jesus was born about the year _____5 B.C._____ .
2. This was about (a) _____600_____ years after the Babylonian captivity and (b) _____1442_____ years after the giving of the Law at Mount Sinai.

A. ANSWERS FROM THE BIBLE

🍇 *To complete these exercises, first study the Bible passages that are given. Fill in the short blanks with words. Whenever possible, use exact words from the Bible. Write complete answers for the questions with long blanks. For multiple-choice questions, circle the letter of the correct answer.*

God Foretells His Great Plan

Most of the Old Testament speaks of God's chosen people, the Jews. God gave His Law to them and told them how to worship Him. They were His chosen family.

God had a special purpose for His chosen people. He planned that through this family His Son would come to

Be sure your students understand that B.C. dates are counted backward from the approximate year of Christ's birth. If the years had been calculated correctly, the day of Christ's birth would be the first day of A.D. 1. (There is no year 0.) However, it has been determined that Christ was born several years earlier than was thought at the time the dates were established; thus Christ was born about 4 or 5 B.C.

Lesson 2

Oral Review

These questions are for optional use during the class period. If you wish, you may duplicate the questions and hand them to the students for written work or personal study. The numbers in brackets tell which lessons are being reviewed. Answers are given in boldface.

1. Name the New Testament books in order. (Be sure you know the correct order and spelling.) [L. 1] **Matthew, Mark, Luke, John, Acts, Romans, 1 & 2 Corinthians, Galatians, Ephesians, Philippians, Colossians, 1 & 2 Thessalonians, 1 & 2 Timothy, Titus, Philemon,**

Hebrews, James, 1 & 2 Peter, 1, 2, & 3 John, Jude, Revelation
2. Which Gospels record Christ's birth? [L. 1] **Matthew, Luke**

In This Lesson

Scope: Scattered Old Testament Prophecies; Matthew 1:1–2:10; Luke 1:1–38

Focus

• God foretold His plan of sending His Son to redeem mankind.
  —The plan was announced throughout the Old Testament.

earth. He would come as the Messiah (the Anointed One), who would save men from their sins. He would make it possible for all men to become part of God's spiritual family through the new covenant.

God wanted His people to know of this plan. After Adam and Eve sinned, and throughout Old Testament history, God sent messages about the Messiah who would come to earth.

🍇 *Read the following Old Testament prophecies that refer to Jesus' coming, and fill in the missing information. Some blanks need more than one word.*

1. (Genesis 3:15) After Adam and Eve sinned, God foretold that the woman's "seed" (the Messiah) would bruise the _____head_____ of the serpent (Satan). This meant that the Messiah would destroy Satan's power.

2. (Genesis 22:15, 18) In God's message to Abraham, He referred to the Messiah as "thy (a) _____seed_____," who would bless (b) "_____all the nations_____ of the earth."

3. (Deuteronomy 18:18) Through Moses, God foretold that the Messiah would be a great (a) _____Prophet_____ who would speak unto the people "all (b) _that I shall command him_ _____."

4. (Psalm 16:10) David prophesied that the Messiah would be God's (a) "_____Holy_____ _____One_____," whom God would not suffer to see (b) _____corruption_____. This refers to the resurrection of the Messiah's body. (Note: The Hebrew word translated *hell* in this verse often means "the grave.")

5. (Psalm 118:22) In this verse God refers to the Messiah as "the (a) _____stone_____ which the builders (b) _____refused_____." He would become "the (c) _head stone of the corner_ _____."

6. (Isaiah 42:1) In God's message through Isaiah, He referred to the Messiah as His (a) _servant (or elect)_. God's (b) _____spirit_____ would be upon Him, and He would bring judgment to the (c) _____Gentiles_____.

7. (Malachi 4:2) In His message through Malachi, the last Old Testament prophet, God said that the Messiah would arise as "the (a) _____Sun of righteousness_____ . . . with (b) _____healing_____ in his wings."

God's Plan Includes All People

Because the Jews were God's special family, they began to think of themselves as the only people God loved. Many of them became self-righteous and looked down on non-Jews. They did not understand that God loved all people and not just His special family. They did not remember that when God called Abraham and his descendants to carry out His plan, that plan included all mankind. The Messiah would come to the earth through the Jews, but He would provide salvation for all men.

Some of the verses above speak of the Messiah's ministry and blessing to all men. The following are a few more Old Testament verses that show this.

8. According to Genesis 12:3, how many families of the earth would be blessed through the Messiah? _all families_

9. According to Psalm 86:9, how many nations would worship God? _all nations_

10. a. According to Isaiah 49:6, how far would the Messiah's salvation reach? _to the end of the earth_

    b. To whom would He be a light? _the Gentiles_

—The plan is for everyone.
- God announced the coming of the Messiah to both Jews and Gentiles.
  —God sent an angel to Zacharias, Mary, and Joseph.
  —God sent a star to guide the wise men to Jesus.
- People had various ideas about the coming Messiah, but many of these ideas were not accurate.
- The Jewish world of Jesus' time included Hebrew Jews and Greek Jews.
  —The Pharisees were very traditional Hebrew Jews.
  —The Greek Jews, or Grecians, spoke Greek and

followed Greek ways. They were more open to the Gospel.
  —The Galileans were Hebrew Jews, but they tended to live more simply than the Jews of Judea.
- Jesus came to ordinary people.

Objectives
- Students should know
  —how God's Old Testament people knew about the Messiah. (*God had sent many prophecies about the coming Messiah.*)
  —for whom God sent the Messiah. (*all people*)
  —to what two people the angel Gabriel appeared,

16   Chapter One   Jesus Comes to Minister

God Breaks a Long Silence

The Bible gives no record of God speaking directly to His people for about four hundred years after Malachi. Then suddenly God broke the long silence! God sent the angel Gabriel to Zacharias the priest. Gabriel told Zacharias that he and his wife would soon have a son who would be the forerunner of the Messiah. You will read more about the angel's message and John's birth in Lesson 4.

Luke 1:8–11

11. Where was Zacharias when the angel appeared to him?   in the temple of the Lord

12. What were the people doing while he was there?   They were praying.

God Sends a Message to Mary

About six months after Gabriel's appearance to Zacharias, God sent the angel to Nazareth. There Gabriel appeared to a young woman named Mary and told her that she would be the mother of the Messiah.

What kind of woman was Mary? What special qualities did she have that caused God to choose her to be the mother of His Son? The Bible does not give specific answers to these questions, but it does tell a few things about Mary that reveal her character.

Luke 1:26–38

13. The angel told Mary that she would have a son whose name would be _____ Jesus _____. He would also be called the _____ Son _____ of the _____ Highest _____.

14. In verse 35, God said that this child would be called the _____ Son _____ of _____ God _____.

15. Mary could not understand how the angel's message could be fulfilled. In spite of this, what did she say that shows she believed God would fulfill His word?   "Be it unto me according to thy word."

- In many ways, Mary was an ordinary woman like thousands of other Jewish women of her time. However, we can see that she had an unquestioning faith and was willing to submit to God's plan for her life. God can do much with people that have these qualities, even if they are not considered great by man.

God Reveals His Plan to Joseph

At first Joseph did not understand God's plans for Mary and himself. But in a dream, an angel told Joseph to take Mary as his wife. Joseph obeyed God's command.

Matthew 1:18–23

🍇 *The angel gave Joseph two names that the coming Messiah would be called. Write each name and the reason it was given.*

16. _____ Jesus _____   "He shall save his people from their sins." (Jesus means "Saviour.")

17. _____ Emmanuel _____   This name means "God with us."

God Sends a Star to Guide the Wise Men

God used a different method to send a message about the coming Messiah to some wise men in the East. He helped them to realize that a special star in the sky was heralding the Messiah's birth. These wise men went to look for the new King. The Bible does not say whether the star first appeared before Christ's birth or afterward. But it is possible that the wise men were among the first to know that the time of the Messiah had come.

See star note on the next page.

and where he appeared to each. (*Gabriel appeared to Zacharias in the temple at Jerusalem; he appeared to Mary in Nazareth.*)

—how Mary showed that she believed Gabriel's message. (*She said, "Be it unto me according to thy word."*)

—why the names *Jesus* and *Emmanuel* were given to the Messiah. (*He was called Jesus because "he shall save his people from their sins." Emmanuel means "God with us."*)

—how the wise men knew that the Messiah had been born. (*They saw His star.*)

—what *Messiah* means, and which Greek word has the same meaning. (*the Anointed One; Christ*)

—how the Hebrew Jews of the East were different from the Greek Jews of the West. (*The Hebrew Jews spoke Hebrew, strictly kept Jewish traditions, and were generally wealthy. The Greek Jews spoke Greek, followed Greek practices, worked in common trades, and were generally more open to the Gospel.*)

—what group of people lived in the area where Jesus grew up. (*the Galileans*)

Truths to Amplify

- This lesson introduces God's plan for Jesus on the earth. Jesus did not come to live among wealthy or famous people. The people of Galilee (humble

Matthew 2:1–10

18. The wise men went to Jerusalem to search for the new Messiah they were sure had just been born. What may have been their reason for going to Jerusalem rather than to another city of Judea? (Sample answers) Jerusalem was the center of Jewish life and worship, so the wise men may have expected the Messiah to be born there. >>

19. Apparently no one in Jerusalem knew about Jesus' birth. How did the priests and scribes know where to look for Jesus? The Old Testament Scriptures (Micah 5:2) foretold that He would come from Bethlehem.

20. We do not know who the wise men were or from what country they came. Most likely they were Gentiles with a knowledge of the true God. How can we tell that God wanted the wise men to find Jesus? The star appeared to them and guided them to Jesus.

21. The Jewish teachers should have known the prophecy of the star just as well as the wise men. What may have been the reason they failed to realize that a special star was heralding the Messiah's birth?

    a. They thought King Herod was the Messiah, so they did not look for a star.

    (b) They were not prepared for the Messiah's coming, so God did not reveal His birth to them.

    c. God withheld this knowledge from them because He knew they would try to kill the child.

    d. The star was never visible in Palestine, so they did not find out about it.

B. BIBLE WORD STUDY

Find Messiah *in a Bible dictionary and complete these exercises.*

1. a. Write the meaning of *Messiah.* the Anointed One

    b. *Messiah* is a Hebrew word. What Greek word has the same meaning? Christ

Write a word from each verse that fits the definition.

    seed 2. Offspring; descendant (Genesis 3:15)

    espoused 3. Engaged to be married with a binding agreement that could be broken only by divorce (Matthew 1:18)

Or perhaps they did not know where to look and expected the Jewish religious leaders to know where He had been born. Since the temple was at Jerusalem, they would have expected the leaders to be there.

- Some people think the wise men saw the planets Jupiter, Mars, and Saturn, all lined up, shining as one big star. This happens only rarely, and it is thought to have happened two years before Jesus' birth. However, if the wise men were observant enough to see the new star, they would probably also have noticed the three planets converging. Besides, the star apparently disappeared and only reappeared after the wise men left Jerusalem. It then appeared to go before them and to stop over the place where Jesus was—actions that would hardly be possible for the converging of the planets to accomplish. It seems more likely that God created a special sign in the sky to reveal the coming of the Messiah to any who were watching. To seek a natural explanation for every supernatural event reveals a lack of faith in God's power.

Hebrew Jews) provided just the right setting for His work and teachings.

- Why did Jesus come to the common people? Jesus came to help needy people—those who were willing to be helped. The well-off were often self-sufficient and did not sense their need of help. Jesus said that the healthy do not need a doctor, and that He did not "come to call the righteous, but sinners to repentance" (Matthew 9:13).

privily (PRIHV uh lee)	4. Secretly; privately (Matthew 1:19)
incense	5. A sweet-smelling mixture burned as an offering (Luke 1:9)
hail	6. Greetings; a word used as a salutation (Luke 1:28)

C. THINKING ABOUT BIBLE TRUTHS

Ideas About the Messiah

Read the following verses, and describe what each person or group expected the Messiah to do or be.

The Jews

The Jews had some very strong opinions about what the Messiah would be like when He came, and what He would do for them. The disciples, in spite of their close association with Jesus, seemed to share these ideas.

1. Acts 1:6 (Compare with John 6:15.) _____
   The Jews expected the Messiah to restore the kingdom of Israel.

The Samaritans

The Samaritans' opinion of the Messiah's work may have been closer to the truth than that of most Jews. Because of this, they were quicker to accept the Gospel after Christ's death than many Jews were.

2. John 4:25–29 _____
   The Samaritan woman expected the Messiah to tell them all things, or to be all-knowing.

Simeon

There were only a few people who had a true understanding of the Messiah's work. Simeon was one of these. So was Anna, who is also mentioned in Luke 2.

3. Luke 2:25–33   (Sample answer) Simeon and a few others expected the Messiah to be the Saviour of
   the world and a light to lighten the Gentiles.

John the Baptist

John also understood, at least in part, what the Messiah's work would be. In these verses he mentions what Jesus would do.

4. Mark 1:6–8 _____
   John said that Jesus would baptize people with the Holy Ghost.

Jesus

Jesus knew why He came, and He freely talked about it with His disciples. But they did not seem to fully understand His purpose for coming until after the outpouring of the Holy Spirit.

5. John 3:17 (Compare with Matthew 1:21 and John 12:47.) _____
   Jesus said that He came to save the world.

D. LEARNING MORE ABOUT BIBLE TIMES

Hebrew Jews

By the time Jesus came to earth, Jews had scattered to most parts of the known world. In the east they spoke Hebrew or Aramaic. Many of these conservative Hebrew Jews were wealthy merchants, jewelers, and money lenders. Their religion was a closely guarded and complicated set of traditions. They did not make many converts. The priests at Jerusalem, the scribes, and the Pharisees were Hebrew Jews.

Read the reference, and then circle the letter of the best answer.

1. (Matthew 23:5–8) What was one problem of the Hebrew Jews that Jesus pointed out?
   a. They did their good works to be seen of men.
   b. They did not teach their children the Law.
   c. They did not make many converts.

2. (Matthew 23:24–27) The Pharisees were Hebrew Jews. Jesus criticized them for
   a. wearing comfortable clothes and eating good food.
   b. not obeying their Roman governors.
   c. being clean on the outside and unclean within.

3. (Matthew 19:21) The rich young ruler was a Hebrew Jew. Jesus told him to
   a. be baptized for the remission of sins.
   b. sell his goods and share his money with the poor.
   c. read the Scriptures.

Greek Jews

Many western Jews spoke Greek, and they lived and thought like Greek people. Unlike the Hebrew Jews, many Greek Jews did not have much money. They lived in cities and worked in common trades. Using a Greek translation of the Bible, they made many converts. They met every Sabbath in synagogues to discuss the Scriptures. Greek Jews are called Grecians in the Bible.

4. Most Jews who became Christians were Greek-speaking Jews. Why might Hebrew Jews have found it harder to accept the Gospel than Greek Jews? (Choose *all* the correct answers.)
   a. Their wealth stood in the way.
   b. Their religious prejudice stood in the way.
   c. Their pride stood in the way.
   d. Their language stood in the way.

The Galileans

North of Judea and Samaria lay a small Jewish community called Galilee. The Jews of Galilee were Hebrew Jews, but they lived more simply than many Jews of Judea. Most of them were farmers and fishermen. They were not as strict about keeping the extra details that the Pharisees had added to the Law, and they tended to be more honest and sincere. The Jews of Judea despised them and ridiculed the dialect they spoke.

5. What did God show the world by allowing Jesus to grow up in Galilee? (Choose the best answer.)
   a. Jesus came to save only the Galileans.
   b. God dwells among the sincere and lowly.
   c. God did not want Jesus to know about the Pharisees' extra laws.

6. (Matthew 26:73) How did the maid at the high priest's house know that Peter was from Galilee?
   She recognized him by his Galilean accent.

Multiple-choice questions that give more than one correct choice require more thought than those that give only one. To aid in grading, you may want to consider each choice as a separate item to be either chosen or eliminated.

20

Lesson 3. Jesus' Birth and Childhood

Why did Jesus come to earth?

From the beginning, God wanted to have fellowship with man. God created man in His own likeness. He gave man a spirit so that man could communicate with Him, and a will so that man could choose to love and obey Him. But when Adam and Eve sinned, they spoiled their relationship with God.

After the Fall of man, God began to reveal His plan for bringing man back to Him. He would send His Son as a man to live among men. His Son would walk and talk with men as

men walk and talk with one another. He would be an example for men and would teach them God's will. Most important, He would die as a sacrifice for their sins to make it possible for them to renew their relationship with God.

Jesus was part of God, and He was with God at the Creation. The Bible says that Jesus made all things. Jesus, the Creator, was coming to live among the men He created! His body was just like ours, but His inner being was God.

God waited until the time was exactly right. Then He sent His Son to the earth.

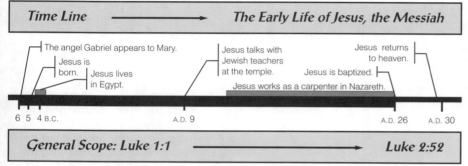

Time Line ⟶ **The Early Life of Jesus, the Messiah**

The angel Gabriel appears to Mary. | Jesus talks with Jewish teachers at the temple. | Jesus returns to heaven.
Jesus is born. | Jesus lives in Egypt. | Jesus is baptized.
Jesus works as a carpenter in Nazareth.

6 5 4 B.C.   A.D. 9   A.D. 26   A.D. 30

General Scope: Luke 1:1 ⟶ **Luke 2:52**

Note: All dates used in this course are approximate. The thick black section of the bar represents the time span covered in this lesson. The gray bars represent specific periods during this time span.

Using the Time Line

1. If Jesus was born in late 5 B.C., about how old was He when He visited the temple in early A.D. 9? (Compare your calculation with Luke 2:42.) _about twelve years old_

2. About how old was He at His baptism? (Compare with Luke 3:23.) _about thirty years old_

3. About how long was Jesus' ministry? _about 3 1/2 years_

A. ANSWERS FROM THE BIBLE

The Birth of Christ

Important things often take place without people realizing it at the time. The day that Jesus was born probably seemed ordinary to most people of Palestine. The shepherds tending their flocks around Bethlehem were ordinary men, doing what they had always done. The people at the inn probably did not worry about the young couple who needed to spend the night in a stable. It might have been a common place to stay when all the rooms were filled.

- You may want to spend some time discussing the doctrine of the Trinity with your class as an introduction to this lesson. Emphasize that even though we cannot understand how one God can be three Persons, we believe this because the Bible tells us it is so. For a background study on the subject, see the section "The Trinity" in the book *Doctrines of the Bible*.

- Josephus and other ancient historians record additional information on Herod the Great and his descendants.

- It is generally accepted that Herod died around the Passover of 4 B.C., and it is obvious that some time passed between Christ's birth and Herod's death. If the accepted date of Herod's death is correct, Christ must have been born by 5 B.C. or, at the latest, during the first weeks of 4 B.C.

Exercise 1 presents an opportunity to teach your students how to calculate a time span that crosses from B.C. into A.D. See the directions and an illustration on page 31.

- The time lines used in this book place Jesus' baptism in the fall of A.D. 26 and His crucifixion in the spring of A.D. 30. All dates are approximate.

Lesson 3

Oral Review

1. Name the thirteen Pauline Epistles in order. [L. 1] **Romans, 1 & 2 Corinthians, Galatians, Ephesians, Philippians, Colossians, 1 & 2 Thessalonians, 1 & 2 Timothy, Titus, Philemon**

2. At the end of the Old Testament period, God did not speak directly to His people for about four hundred years. Who received a message from God that broke this silence? [L. 2] **Zacharias**

3. What do the names *Jesus* and *Emmanuel* mean? [L. 2] **Jesus means "He shall save his people from their sins." Emmanuel means**

"God with us."

4. What is the meaning of *Messiah*? What Greek word has the same meaning? [L. 2] **the Anointed One; Christ**

5. What group of people lived in the area where Jesus grew up? [L. 2] **the Galileans**

In This Lesson

Scope: Matthew 2:11–23; Luke 2; John 1:1–18

Focus

- Jesus was born in Bethlehem.
  —God used a heathen emperor (Caesar Augustus) to help fulfill the prophecy of Micah 5:2.

How could these ordinary men and women have guessed that two thousand years later, millions of people would still be talking about what happened that night!

Luke 2:1–20

1. God had foretold that the Messiah would come from Bethlehem (Micah 5:2), yet Mary and Joseph lived at Nazareth. How did God use a heathen emperor to fulfill this prophecy? _____
   Caesar Augustus passed a decree requiring everyone to return to his ancestral city for a tax registration. Since Joseph was of David's lineage, he took his wife to Bethlehem.

2. Jesus was born in a stable, and His first bed was a manger. Why might God have chosen to have His Son born in such a lowly setting? (Choose the best reason.)
   (a.) To show us that no one is too poor or too humble to come to Jesus for salvation
   b. So that King Herod would not find out where Jesus was born and try to kill Him
   c. To show the Jews that God no longer loves rich and important people

🍇 *Briefly explain how each of the following took part in the events surrounding Jesus' birth.*

3. The angels _The angels announced Christ's birth to the shepherds._
   _____

4. The shepherds _The shepherds went to Bethlehem to see Jesus. Then they told everyone they met_
   what had happened.

Jesus Is Taken to Jerusalem

According to Leviticus 12, Jesus would have been forty days old when His parents took Him to Jerusalem to present Him to the Lord. Their offering of two birds indicates that they were poor. The regular offering for those who could afford it was one lamb and one pigeon or turtledove (Leviticus 12:6, 8).

Luke 2:21–40

5. How did Simeon know that Jesus was the Messiah? _The Holy Spirit revealed it to him._
   _____

6. What was Anna's reaction when she saw Jesus? _(See Luke 2:38.) "She . . . gave thanks likewise_
   unto the Lord, and spake of him to all them that looked for redemption in Jerusalem."

Jesus' Escape

King Herod was a very jealous ruler. He was determined to destroy any threats to his throne. When the wise men came to Jerusalem to inquire about the Messiah, he asked them to come back and tell him where the young child was, pretending that he wanted to worship Him too. Then he planned to kill Him. But God warned the wise men in a dream not to go back to Herod. He also warned Joseph of the danger that Jesus was in and told him to take his family to Egypt.

Matthew 2:13–23

7. How did Herod feel when the wise men did not return? _____
   He was exceeding wroth. (He also felt mocked by the wise men.)

8. a. What did Herod decide to do when he saw that the wise men were not going to return? _____
   He decided to kill all the babies that were two years old and under.

   b. What does this show us about Herod? _____
   (Sample answer) Other lives did not mean as much to him as his own position.

—Jesus was born among the poor, in a lowly stable.
—Angels proclaimed Christ's birth to shepherds.
- The Bible tells little about Jesus' earthly life before His baptism.
  —He was taken to Egypt to escape King Herod's wrath.
  —The Bible records the names of His four earthly (half) brothers.
  —Jewish history indicates that education was important to first-century Jews, but the Bible is almost silent on Jesus' education. (John 7:15 suggests that He probably had very little formal education.)

—Jesus' visit to the temple when He was twelve years old shows His early interest in His heavenly Father's work.
- Jesus was both Son of God and Son of man.

Objectives
- Students should know
  —how a heathen king's decree helped to fulfill a prophecy about Jesus' birth. (*Caesar required everyone to register for taxation in his ancestral city. Joseph took Mary to Bethlehem, the city of David, where Jesus was born.*)
  —who came to see Jesus the night He was born. (*the shepherds*)

9. List three Old Testament prophecies from this passage that were fulfilled because of King Herod and his family.   *(Any order)*

   a.   "Out of Egypt have I called my son." _____

   _____

   b.   "In Rama was there a voice heard, lamentation, and weeping, and great mourning, Rachel weeping
   for her children, and would not be comforted, because they are not."

   c.   "He shall be called a Nazarene." _____

   _____

After Herod died, Mary and Joseph returned to Palestine. At God's command they moved back to Nazareth, where Jesus lived until He was grown.

Jesus' Earthly Family

Jesus' most important relationship was with God, His real Father. But Jesus' relationships with His mother Mary and His legal earthly father Joseph were also important. Through Mary and Joseph, Jesus had a right to the throne of David.

The Bible gives the names of Jesus' (half) brothers, but it does not tell us much about Jesus' other earthly relatives. However, a careful comparison of Matthew 27:56, Mark 15:40, and John 19:25 seems to indicate that Mary had a sister named Salome, who was the wife of Zebedee. Using these verses, the relationships shown on the following chart seem probable.

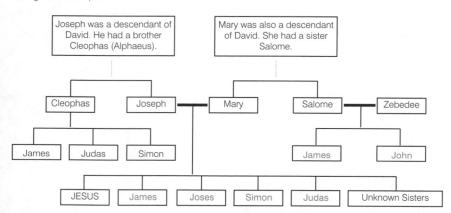

10. In the chart of Jesus' family, fill in the names of Jesus' four brothers, using Matthew 13:55, 56. We do not know the names of Jesus' sisters, but Matthew 13:56 indicates that He had more than one.

11. If this chart is correct, at least two of Jesus' first cousins were His disciples. Use Matthew 4:21 to fill in the names of the two sons of Salome and Zebedee.

12. At first Jesus' brothers did not believe on Him (John 7:5). After His resurrection, Jesus showed Himself to His brother (a) _____James_____ (1 Corinthians 15:5–7). This brother became an apostle and a leader of the church at Jerusalem. He wrote the general epistle of (b) _____James_____.

• Old Testament saints could hardly have understood how the Messiah would fulfill these prophecies. Perhaps they did not even recognize them as prophecies. Hosea 11:1 appears to point back to the Exodus rather than forward to the Messiah. The weeping mentioned in Jeremiah 31:15 was partially fulfilled when the Babylonians killed and took captive many Jews. And the prophecy of Jesus being a Nazarene is even more veiled. Apparently it refers to Nazarenes being despised (compare John 1:46 with Isaiah 53:3), or to the Hebrew word for *Nazareth,* which means "Branch." Nevertheless, in looking back we can see how all three prophecies were fulfilled in the events surrounding Christ's birth. How many prophecies concerning the future will be understood only after Christ's second coming?

—who was king of Palestine when Jesus was born. (*Herod the Great*)

—how Herod tried to destroy Jesus. (*He killed all the babies in Bethlehem that were two years old or younger.*)

—how many (half) brothers Jesus had. (*four*)

—what indicates that by age twelve, Jesus' understanding far exceeded that of other boys His age. (*The Jewish teachers were astonished at His understanding and answers.*)

—what Jesus answered when His mother asked why He had dealt thus with them. ("*Wist ye not that I must be about my Father's business?*")

—which two names of Jesus refer to His humanity and deity. (*Son of man, Son of God*)

Truths To Amplify

• Jesus not only lived as a human being on the earth; He lived as *ordinary* humans do. Seventh grade students should realize that Jesus knows about the life they experience, for He lived through childhood and adolescence.

At the same time, the dignity of Jesus' walk among men needs to be preserved. He was tempted in all points as we are tempted, but was without sin (Hebrews 4:15). Even while He had a human body, He was the Son of God, with divine attributes.

13. Jesus' other brothers apparently became believers too (Acts 1:14). His brother ___Jude___ wrote the last epistle of the New Testament.

Jesus' Education

The Bible does not tell us whether Jesus attended school. The Jewish leaders considered Jesus unlearned (John 7:15), but they may have meant that He had not studied the Law at one of the schools of the rabbis, as Paul had (Acts 22:3).

We do know that the Jews considered school very important for children (especially boys) above six years old. Jewish writings indicate that during the period immediately after Christ's life on earth, every Jewish town had a synagogue school. It was unlawful for Jewish fathers to move their families into areas where their children could not go to school. From these facts, it seems quite likely that Jesus studied at the synagogue of Nazareth along with other boys.

Jewish teachers often held their classes outdoors for fresh air and light. They tried to make the subjects interesting for their students, and they shortened the classes in hot weather. Children sat on the ground or stood. They learned to do accurate work and practice good morals. Until they were ten years old, they learned only from the Scriptures.

Jewish children memorized many Scripture passages. Each child started with a "birthday text," which was a Scripture verse beginning or ending with the letters of his name. From childhood on, he repeated his birthday text at least once a day.

A Jewish School

Jesus considered the Scriptures to be very important. If He had the privilege of attending school, He no doubt enjoyed the time spent in studying and memorizing the Scriptures. However, Jesus' understanding far exceeded what a human teacher could have taught Him. He increased in the wisdom that is from above, for He Himself was from above.

Matthew 22:29–32

14. When the Sadducees questioned the resurrection, Jesus told them they erred because they did not know ___the Scriptures (nor the power of God)___.

15. What Scripture passage did Jesus quote to them? _____
    ___"I am the God of Abraham, and the God of Isaac, and the God of Jacob."___

- Cited from Exodus 3:6.

About His Father's Business

Every spring large and happy groups of people walked south from Galilee to Jerusalem for the Passover feast. Carrying blankets and food, they camped by the wayside. So large were the groups that when Jesus was twelve years old, His parents walked a whole day before they discovered that He was missing.

Luke 2:41–52

16. This passage tells us all we know for sure about Jesus' childhood and youth. In this glimpse of His early life, we see Him eagerly discussing things pertaining to His Father's business. What indicates that even at this age, Jesus' wisdom far exceeded that of other Jewish boys?
    a. His parents looked for Him three days before finding Him in the temple.
    b. Jesus was asking questions about the Holy Scriptures.
    c. The Jewish teachers were astonished at His understanding and answers.
    d. His mother asked, "Son, why hast thou thus dealt with us?"

First, sketch a time line and divide it into fourteen segments. Next, from left to right, label the first segment 5 B.C., the next segment 4 B.C., and so on down to 1 B.C. Then, begin with A.D. 1, A.D. 2 and so on, up to A.D. 9. There is no year 0. With the span clearly divided, you can now proceed to count from late 5 B.C. to early A.D. 9, a total of approximately 12½ years. (There is only one year from a given date in 1 B.C. to the same date in A.D. 1. Likewise, similar dates in 2 B.C. and A.D. 2 are three years apart, and so forth.)

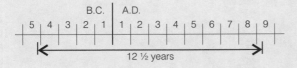

24   Chapter One   Jesus Comes to Minister

17. What question did Jesus ask that shows He knew Joseph was not His actual father? _____

    "Wist ye not that I must be about my Father's business?"

18. How did Jesus honor His earthly parents, even though He was the Son of God? (2:51) _____

    Jesus was subject (obedient) to them.

19. During His years of childhood and youth, "Jesus increased in _____ wisdom _____ and _____ stature _____, and in _____ favour _____ with _____ God _____ and _____ man _____."

This is the last we read of Jesus until He was about thirty years old. We do not know what He said and did during these years. Probably He helped Joseph with his carpenter work. (See Matthew 13:55 and Mark 6:3.) It seems quite likely that Joseph died before Jesus began His ministry, because the Gospels do not mention Joseph after this.

B. BIBLE WORD STUDY

Read these verses in their context to determine the meaning of the italicized words. Circle the letter of the correct ending. If you need help, you may use a Bible dictionary.

1. Herod *inquired diligently* about where to find Jesus (Matthew 2:7, 16). This means that he
   a. thought carefully in his own mind.
   b. put much effort into finding out.
   c. asked at random.

2. When Joseph heard that Archelaus was king in Judea, he was afraid to go *thither* (Matthew 2:22). This means he was afraid to go
   a. close.
   b. to that place.
   c. from that place.

3. Jesus would grow up to be called a *Nazarene* (Matthew 2:23). This was because He
   a. did not cut His hair.
   b. had taken a vow.
   c. lived in Nazareth.

4. As a boy, Jesus sat in the temple and spoke with the *doctors* (Luke 2:46). These doctors
   a. were men who studied and taught the Old Testament Law.
   b. attended the sick who came to Jerusalem for the Passover.
   c. lived in the temple and spent all their time praising God.

5. When Mary questioned Jesus about making them search for Him, He asked, "*Wist ye not* that I must be about my Father's business?" By this He meant,
   a. "Without you, must I not be about My Father's business?"
   b. "Do you not wish that I be about My Father's business?"
   c. "Did you not know that I must be about My Father's business?"

C. THINKING ABOUT BIBLE TRUTHS

Jesus—the Son of God and Man

Since God was Jesus' Father and Mary was His mother, Jesus was both God and man. He had the mind and power of God, but His body had many of the same limitations that our bodies do.

As a man, Jesus often used examples from everyday life in His preaching.

Tell what Jesus said about the following common items. Try to remember without checking the reference, and then read the verses to verify your answer.

1. Salt (Matthew 5:13) _____
   Salt that has lost its flavor is worthless as a seasoning. ("Ye are the salt of the earth.")

2. Lilies (Matthew 6:28) _____
   Lilies do not toil (labor) or spin (make their clothes).

3. Sparrows (Matthew 10:29) _____
   God sees each sparrow that falls to the ground (even though man places little value on sparrows).

4. Tares (weeds) among wheat (Matthew 13:30) _____
   Tares and wheat grow together, but they are separated at harvest.

5. A hen with chicks (Matthew 23:37) _____
   A hen gathers her little ones under her wings.

Jesus, growing up in the village of Nazareth, learned about ordinary people. At times He found Himself among noisy crowds. He attended weddings and funerals. He saw how government officials cheated and oppressed the people. He saw the harshness of money lenders, the luxuries of the rich, and the misery of the poor. He felt compassion for sick and needy people, such as the two blind men sitting beside the road.

Matthew 20:30–34

6. By what two names did the blind men call Jesus? (Either order)
   a. Lord
   b. Son of David

7. Match the two names the blind men used to the following descriptions of Jesus.
   a. Son of God Lord
   b. Son of man Son of David

8. Now match the names "Son of God" and "Son of man" to the following characteristics of Jesus.
   a. His humanity gave Him sympathy and compassion for human needs. Son of man
   b. His deity gave Him power to cure diseases. Son of God

D. LEARNING MORE ABOUT BIBLE TIMES

King Herod

 Read this story before doing the matching exercise.

While the Maccabees (mentioned in Lesson 1) ruled Judea, they subdued the Edomites (Idumeans). The Edomites were descendants of Esau. The Maccabees forced all the Edomites to adopt the Jewish religion. One of these Edomite "Jews," Antipater, rose to power in Palestine before Jesus' time.

Antipater turned against the Maccabean rulers of Judea and welcomed the invading Romans in 63 B.C. The Romans made Antipater the ruler of Palestine.

Antipater's son Herod made friends with the Roman ruler, Mark Antony. Herod succeeded his father as ruler of Palestine and was twice crowned king by the Romans.

After Herod became king, he divorced his wife Doris and sent her away with his oldest son. Herod then married Mariamne, a Maccabean princess. He hoped this would improve his relationship with the Jews.

King Herod reigned for thirty-two years. He built magnificent forts, aqueducts, theaters, and public buildings. He planned Roman-style cities at Caesarea, Sebaste (Samaria), Beirut, Damascus, Antioch, and Rhodes. His greatest achievements were the Jewish temple and surrounding buildings at Jerusalem. Because of his long reign and his influence on Palestine, Herod is often known as Herod the Great. However, he was a cruel and headstrong man. Very few people liked him.

Herod's sister Salome turned him against Mariamne, his Maccabean wife. Even though Herod loved Mariamne, he finally grew suspicious of her and had her murdered. He also murdered her two sons, her brother, her grandfather, and her mother.

In an attempt to kill Jesus, Herod ordered the killing of all the little children of Bethlehem that were two years old or younger. Just before his death, he killed his oldest son. Finally, mentally confused and suffering great pain, he realized that he was going to die. He ordered that at his death, a large number of Judean leaders should be killed. He thought that this would cause the Jews to mourn instead of rejoicing over his death. But no one carried out his orders. Herod died a hated man, and his three sons ruled in his stead. The Bible mentions several of his descendants.

 Write the letter of the correct ending for each sentence.

_f_	1. Herod and the other Edomites	a. welcomed the invading Romans to Palestine.
_a_	2. Herod's father	b. were sent away by Herod after he became king.
_c_	3. The Romans	c. gave Antipater and Herod positions of power.
_i_	4. Mark Antony,	d. built magnificent buildings.
_b_	5. Doris and her son	e. hated and feared Herod.
_d_	6. In many cities, Herod	f. were descendants of Esau.
_j_	7. After he divorced Doris, Herod	g. turned Herod against Mariamne.
_g_	8. Salome, Herod's sister,	h. ordered the killing of many innocent people.
_h_	9. In his old age, Herod	i. became Herod's friend.
_e_	10. The people of Palestine	j. married Mariamne, a Maccabean princess.

27

Lesson 4. John the Baptist Introduces Jesus

In Lesson 2, you briefly studied how the angel Gabriel appeared to Zacharias while he was serving in the temple. Zacharias was married to Elizabeth, who was a relative of Mary, the mother of Jesus. In this lesson you will read more about what Gabriel said and the results of his message.

In the great temple compound at Jerusalem, the priests began their work before the sun came up. Because there were more priests than were needed at one time, they were divided into twenty-four groups. Each group served in the temple for one week. Then they would return to their homes while the other twenty-three groups each served their week.

Each morning the priests on duty cast lots to decide who would perform the various daily services. The most important lot determined which priest would enter the holy place and offer incense upon the golden altar. Since a priest who had offered incense was not usually included in this lot again, he would have this special privilege only once in his lifetime.

While the chosen priest was inside the temple, offering incense, the rest of the priests and anyone else who had come to worship prayed outside. They waited there until the priest returned from offering the incense.

Perhaps the most important day in Zacharias's life was the day when the lot to offer incense fell on him. It was a special day, not only for Zacharias, but for the Jews and for all people.

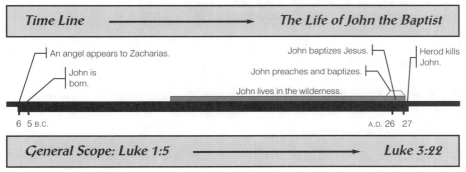

Time Line ⟶ **The Life of John the Baptist**

An angel appears to Zacharias.

John baptizes Jesus.

Herod kills John.

John is born.

John preaches and baptizes.

John lives in the wilderness.

6 5 B.C.   A.D. 26 27

General Scope: Luke 1:5 ⟶ **Luke 3:22**

Note: All dates used in this course are approximate. The thick black section of each bar represents the time span covered in the lesson. Gray bars represent specific periods.

See the explanation in Lesson 3 (page 31) about calculating a time span that crosses from B.C. into A.D. A simpler way to calculate, using number 2 as an example, is to add the number of years B.C. (5) to the number of years A.D. (26), then subtract one from the sum. From 5 B.C. to A.D. 26 is thirty years. However, since we do not know the time of year John was born and when he began his ministry, this calculated age is only approximate.

Using the Time Line

1. About what year did John begin preaching? <u>about A.D. 26</u>
2. About how old was he? <u>about thirty years old >></u>

A. ANSWERS FROM THE BIBLE

About four hundred years before Christ, the prophet Malachi had written, "Behold, I will send my messenger, and he shall prepare the way before me" (Malachi 3:1). God planned that this messenger, John the Baptist, would be a forerunner of the Messiah. Almost a year and a half before Jesus was born, the angel Gabriel appeared to Zacharias to announce John's birth.

Lesson 4

Oral Review

1. Name the books of the New Testament. (Be sure you know the correct order and spelling.) [L. 1] **Matthew, Mark, Luke, John, Acts, Romans, 1 & 2 Corinthians, Galatians, Ephesians, Philippians, Colossians, 1 & 2 Thessalonians, 1 & 2 Timothy, Titus, Philemon, Hebrews, James, 1 & 2 Peter, 1, 2, & 3 John, Jude, Revelation**

2. Name three important districts of Palestine. [L. 1] **Galilee, Samaria, and Judea (from north to south)**

3. How did God's people know about the Messiah? [L. 2] **God had sent many messages throughout the Old Testament.**

4. The Jews thought that the Messiah would be only for themselves. God wanted them to understand that He would be for . . . [L. 2] **all people, including the Gentiles.**

5. How did Herod the Great try to destroy Jesus? [L. 3] **He killed all the babies in Bethlehem that were two years old or younger.**

6. How many brothers did Jesus have? [L. 3] **four**

7. Jesus came as the Son of ——— and the Son of ———. [L. 3] **(Either order) God, man**

28   Chapter One   Jesus Comes to Minister

John's Miraculous Birth

Luke 1:5–22

1. Why did Zacharias and Elizabeth not expect that they would ever have children? (Choose two answers.)

   a. They were very poor.
   c. They did not want to have children.
   (b.) They were old.
   (d.) Elizabeth could not have children.

2. The altar of incense stood in the holy place of the temple. When Zacharias stayed in the temple longer than normal, no one entered to see if something was wrong because

   a. they were too busy praying to notice that he had not returned.
   b. they often waited a long time for the priest who burned incense.
   (c.) only the officiating priest could enter the temple while the incense was being offered.
   d. God had sent a message telling them to leave Zacharias alone.

3. Zacharias's response to the angel's message (Luke 1:18) was most similar to

   (a.) Sarah's response in Genesis 18:10–12.
   b. Hagar's response in Genesis 16:7–14.
   c. Hannah's response in 1 Samuel 1:17, 18.

4. Before Samson was born, an angel told his mother that he would be a Nazarite. John the Baptist may have been a Nazarite too. What part of the Nazarite vow was John the Baptist to fulfill? (Compare with Numbers 6:1–5.)   He was not to drink any wine or strong drink.

5. a. To what Old Testament prophet was John compared?   Elias (Elijah)

   b. What was John to prepare?
      He was to prepare the way of the Lord. (He was to prepare people for Jesus' coming.)

6. Zacharias asked the angel for a sign that his words would come true, but God had already given him a sign. What was this sign?

   a. God had given him a son.
   (c.) God had sent an angel to him.
   b. God had made him a priest.
   d. God had heard his prayers.

7. How was Zacharias punished for not believing what the angel said?
   He could not speak until the child was born (and apparently he could not hear—Luke 1:62).

John the Baptist was filled with the Holy Spirit from his birth. We are not told anything about John's boyhood years, except that he "grew, and waxed strong in spirit, and was in the deserts till the day of his shewing unto Israel" (Luke 1:80). His parents may have died before he began his ministry, since they were quite old when he was born.

Jesus and John were close relatives. Their younger years were spent in entirely different environments, each suited for the calling that God had given him to fulfill.

John's Ministry and Message

John the Baptist lived in the wilderness near the Dead Sea and along the Jordan River Valley. He baptized people in the Jordan River, perhaps at several locations. As the son of a priest, he was qualified to be a priest. But instead of serving as a priest under the Old Testament Law, he helped prepare the Jews for the New Covenant.

In This Lesson

Scope: Matthew 3:1–17; 11:2–19; 14:1–12; Mark 1:1–11; 6:14–29; Luke 1:5–25, 39–80; 3:1–22; 7:18–35; 9:7–9; John 1:6–42

Focus

• God sent John the Baptist as the forerunner of Jesus.
   —John's birth was miraculous.
   —His message was, "Repent ye: for the kingdom of heaven is at hand. . . . Bring forth therefore fruits meet for repentance."
   —His simple lifestyle enhanced his message by showing his light esteem for earthly things. It also reminded Israel of Elijah and other great prophets of old.
   —John introduced and exalted Jesus.
   —He reluctantly baptized Jesus "to fulfil all righteousness."
   —Herod Antipas ordered John's death after John rebuked him for marrying his brother's wife.
• The Trinity—God the Father, God the Son, and God the Holy Spirit—were all present at Jesus' baptism.

Objectives

• Students should know
   —why it was hard for Zacharias to believe that he

Matthew 3:1–12

8. Even though John the Baptist lived in the wilderness, he became well known. How do we know this?   The people of Jerusalem and all Judea went out to hear him.

9. John's message was
   a. "Repent ye: for the kingdom of heaven is at hand."
   b. "Listen to my voice, for I am the prophet Esaias."
   c. "Bring forth fruits for a true and holy sacrifice."
   d. "Be baptized, and turn to Abraham your father."

10. What did John the Baptist eat? What did he wear? _____
    He ate locusts and wild honey. He wore clothes made from camels' hair, and a leather belt.

11. John's simple lifestyle strengthened his message by showing that he
    a. was the prophet Elijah.
    b. believed the Messiah would also wear coarse clothing.
    c. considered the things of God more important than the things of this world.

12. By saying that he was not fit to carry Jesus' shoes, John tried to
    a. impress people with his own humility.
    b. show Jesus' greatness to the people.
    c. teach the Pharisees how to treat Jesus.
    d. humble himself so that in due time he might be exalted.

John Baptizes Jesus

Matthew 3:13–17

13. Jesus did not need to repent, for He had no sin. Why did He say He should be baptized? _____
    "Suffer it to be so now: for thus it becometh us to fulfil all righteousness."

14. Suggest a good reason why John did not want to baptize Jesus.   _____
    (Sample answer) He recognized that Jesus was greater than he was.

15. At Jesus' baptism, God was present in three Persons. How was each of these Persons manifest?
    a. God the Father   God the Father said, "This is my beloved Son, in whom I am well pleased."
    b. God the Son   Jesus was there in person.
    c. God the Holy Spirit   The Holy Spirit descended upon Jesus in the form of a dove.

John 1:35–42

16. Two disciples of John the Baptist were Andrew and John (the writer of the Gospel). What moved them to follow Jesus?   John's exclamation: "Behold the Lamb of God!"

17. Whom did Andrew bring to Jesus?   Simon Peter (his brother)

Map labels: Mediterranean Sea; Nazareth; Bethabara ? (Bethany beyond Jordan); John may have baptized at several places along the Jordan River.; Aenon ?; Jericho; Jerusalem; Wilderness of Judea; Dead Sea; The Jordan Rift Valley; 0   20 miles; 0   30 km

would have a son. (*He and his wife were old and had not been able to have children.*)
—which Old Testament prophet John the Baptist was compared to. (*Elijah*)
—where John the Baptist lived before he began his ministry. (*in the wilderness*)
—what John ate and wore. (*He ate locusts and wild honey. He wore clothes made from camels' hair, and a leather belt.*)
—what John preached. ("*Repent ye: for the kingdom of heaven is at hand.*")
—why John did not want to baptize Jesus. (*He knew Jesus was greater than he was.*)
—how God the Father and God the Holy Spirit

manifested themselves at Jesus' baptism. (*God the Father said, "This is my beloved Son, in whom I am well pleased." The Holy Spirit descended upon Jesus in the form of a dove.*)
—how John the Baptist died. (*Herod beheaded him at the request of his wife and her daughter.*)
—what group of Jews lived in the desert and practiced strict communal living. (*the Essenes*)
• Students should be able to give a synonym or definition for each of these words.
—rabbi (*master or teacher*)
—Christ (*the Anointed One [Messiah]*)
—publican (*a tax collector*)

Jesus said John the Baptist was the "Elijah" whom prophets of long ago had said would come before the Messiah (Matthew 17:10–13). Jesus also called John the greatest among them that are born of women (Luke 7:28).

Matthew 11:18, 19

Many Jews came to hear John preach, and later many of them also flocked after Jesus. However, there were many others who criticized both of them and would not accept their words.

18. Apparently John fasted frequently. When he did eat, his food was locusts and wild honey. He probably seldom ate regular meals with others. What evil thing did the Jews say about him? _____
   "He hath a devil."

19. Jesus ate regular meals with His friends, and sometimes He ate with sinners. How did the Jews still criticize Him?   "Behold a man gluttonous, and a winebibber, a friend of publicans and sinners."
   _____

| The Winding Jordan River | Possible Site of Jesus' Baptism |

The Jordan River measures about 90 to 100 feet wide, and varies from around 3 to 10 feet deep. It flows through the Zor, the floodplain of the Jordan, which varies in width from about 1/4 mile to 2 miles. The total distance from the Sea of Galilee to the Dead Sea is 65 miles, but the Jordan River twists and turns for 135 miles between these two bodies of water.

John's Death

John was not afraid of men. He rebuked sin wherever he saw it, even in Herod. In the end, this was why he was killed. But his work was accomplished, for he had done what God had sent him to do—to prepare the Jews for the coming of the Messiah. (Note: This Herod was Herod Antipas, the son of Herod the Great.)

Mark 6:14–29

20. What sin had Herod Antipas committed that John rebuked him for? _____
   He had married his brother's wife.

Truths to Amplify

- Jesus did not live like an ascetic. He spent His time among people, eating and sleeping in the towns of Palestine.
- John's ministry was of a different nature. He lived a lonely, ascetic life. Grade 7 students do not need to decide which kind of life is best for us today. Rather, they need to learn from the positive examples of both Jesus and John. Both Jesus and John held little esteem for the things of this world. Both preached repentance. Both pointed to the coming Judgment Day. They both followed God's plan for their lives, even though that led them to different lifestyles.
- John began what Jesus finished. Both played important parts in the calling together of God's new family.

21. Herod refused to kill John at first, even though his wife wanted him to. In a short paragraph, explain how Herod's wife and her daughter managed to have Herod order John's death. _____

   (Sample answer) Her daughter danced at Herod's birthday party and pleased him so much that he promised to give her anything she wanted. The mother told her to ask for John's head, and Herod was too ashamed to back down on his promise.

B. BIBLE WORD STUDY

1. The New Testament was written in Greek, but a few non-Greek words were used. Some of these non-Greek words are interpreted in the Bible. Find the following words in John 1:38–42, and give the Bible's interpretation of them.
   a. Rabbi ___Master___
   b. Messias ___the Christ___
   c. Cephas ___a stone___
2. The word *Christ* is also used in these verses. Find its meaning in a Bible dictionary. _____
   anointed (the Anointed One)
3. In Matthew 11:18, 19, people were described as *winebibbers*, *gluttonous*, and *publicans*. Find the meaning of each of these words.
   a. winebibber ___one who drinks too much wine___
   b. glutton ___one who eats too much___
   c. publican ___a tax collector___

C. THINKING ABOUT BIBLE TRUTHS

1. John preached that all men needed to repent. According to Matthew 3:8, 9, what excuse did he say the religious Pharisees and Sadducees should not make? _____
   He said they should not think, "We are Abraham's children."
2. Read John 1:29. Under God's Old Covenant with Israel, God required the sacrifice of a lamb as a temporary covering for sin. Under God's New Covenant with the Christian church, a Lamb was also sacrificed.
   a. Who is that Lamb? ___Jesus Christ___
   b. What more can He do than the lamb sacrificed in the Old Testament? _____
      He can take away the sin of the world.
3. Immediately after Jesus' baptism, Satan tempted Him. Satan wanted Jesus to serve him. How does this prove that Satan does not have the good of mankind at heart? _____
   (Sample answer) If Jesus had served Satan, He could not have saved man.
4. What was probably the reason for the Jews' criticism of both John and Jesus? _____
   Both John and Jesus taught things that the Jews did not want to accept.

D. LEARNING MORE ABOUT BIBLE TIMES

Who Were the Essenes?

John the Baptist was not the only person who lived in the wilderness. In lonely settlements around the Dead Sea, other men lived in simple communities. People called them Essenes (eh SEENZ).

When a man or boy joined the Essenes (there were few Essene women), he received three things—a pickax, an apron, and a white garment. He used the pickax to dig. He wore the apron while taking baths. (Essenes took a bath before every meal.) And the white garment was to remind him to keep himself pure at all times.

Essenes had strict laws about food. They ate little (nothing on the Sabbath), and only special foods prepared by special priests were served. They considered their meals to be sacrifices to God.

All Essene property was held in common. The Essenes made fearful vows to tell each other everything about themselves and to keep their teachings secret from outsiders. Because many Jews had corrupted the true worship, they did not worship or sacrifice at the temple. Instead, they worshiped God while facing the rising sun.

For many years people knew very little about the Essenes. But along with the discovery of the Dead Sea Scrolls, which the Essenes had hidden in caves, came a wealth of information about the Essenes themselves.

John the Baptist lived more like the Essenes than Jesus did, but neither of them followed or taught the doctrines of the Essenes. Jesus worshiped at the temple, even though not everything done there was right. And Jesus rebuked those who rejected God's plan and tried to earn their own salvation.

 For many years some people thought that John the Baptist might have been an Essene. Compare Matthew 3:1–6 with the information in this section, and list three ways that John the Baptist was different from the Essenes. (Sample answers. Other details from the section could be given.)

1. John did not wear a white garment.
2. John's food was not prepared by special priests.
3. John did not keep his teachings secret.

33

Lesson 5. Jesus Begins His Ministry

After John baptized Jesus, the Holy Spirit led Jesus into the wilderness to be tempted. Following this period of fasting and temptation, He apparently returned to the Jordan River, where John was baptizing. Here Jesus met a number of His future disciples before He returned to Galilee.

In Galilee Jesus attended a wedding at Cana, a town a little north of Nazareth. Jesus began His ministry here by performing His first miracle.

Jesus was never selfish. His miracles were not for Himself, but for others. However, the selfish Jewish leaders could not understand Jesus' compassion. From the beginning of His ministry, Jesus exposed their hypocrisy and thus threatened their positions of power and prestige. Because of this, they rejected Him. Their hatred toward Him began in the period covered by this lesson and intensified during His years of ministry. Eventually their malice drove them to demand that He be crucified.

- The Gospels focus primarily on the message of salvation rather than on the details of Jesus' life. Because of this, the Gospels sometimes group events as they relate to Jesus' teachings, rather than in strict chronological order. Since this course focuses on the events of Jesus' life as well as His message, it follows Jesus' activities as nearly in chronological order as possible. A good understanding of Jesus' life and ministry should help prepare grade 7 students to receive Jesus' message when God calls them personally.

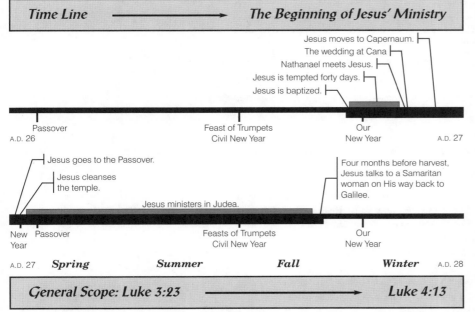

Time Line ⟶ The Beginning of Jesus' Ministry

Jesus moves to Capernaum.
The wedding at Cana
Nathanael meets Jesus.
Jesus is tempted forty days.
Jesus is baptized.

Passover — Feast of Trumpets / Civil New Year — Our New Year
A.D. 26 — A.D. 27

Jesus goes to the Passover.
Jesus cleanses the temple.
Jesus ministers in Judea.
Four months before harvest, Jesus talks to a Samaritan woman on His way back to Galilee.

New Year — Passover — Feasts of Trumpets / Civil New Year — Our New Year
A.D. 27 *Spring* *Summer* *Fall* *Winter* A.D. 28

General Scope: Luke 3:23 ⟶ Luke 4:13

Note: The time lines in this course show the general sequence of events in Jesus' ministry and the approximate seasons in which they took place. Events for which no season is given are arranged between those that can be placed with more accuracy.

Using the Time Line

1. What event in Jesus' life took place just before His forty days of temptation? His baptism ✓
2. In what season was the Passover? in the spring ✓
3. Did Nathanael meet Jesus before or after the wedding at Cana? before the wedding ✓

Lesson 5

Oral Review

1. Name the twenty-seven New Testament books in order. (Be sure you know how to spell them correctly.) [L. 1] **Matthew, Mark, Luke, John, Acts, Romans, 1 & 2 Corinthians, Galatians, Ephesians, Philippians, Colossians, 1 & 2 Thessalonians, 1 & 2 Timothy, Titus, Philemon, Hebrews, James, 1 & 2 Peter, 1, 2, & 3 John, Jude, Revelation**

2. What three languages were in common use in Palestine in New Testament times? [L. 1] **Hebrew (Aramaic), Greek, and Latin.**

3. To what two people did the angel Gabriel appear? Where did he appear to each? [L. 2] **Gabriel appeared to Zacharias in the temple at Jerusalem; he appeared to Mary in Nazareth.**

4. How did Mary show that she believed Gabriel's message? [L. 2] **She said, "Be it unto me according to thy word."**

5. Who was king of Palestine when Jesus was born? [L. 1, 3] **Herod the Great**

6. What was the message of John the Baptist? [L. 4] **"Repent ye: for the kingdom of heaven is at hand."**

34   Chapter One   Jesus Comes to Minister

A. ANSWERS FROM THE BIBLE

Jesus was baptized by John when He was about thirty years old. Even before this He was the perfect Son of God, but His baptism was the turning point in His life. Before this He was considered the son of Joseph, the carpenter of Nazareth. Now He was taking up the role for which He had come to earth. The years of preparation were almost over.

Jesus Is Tempted in the Wilderness

Satan had persuaded Adam and Eve to sin and forsake God. Now he tried the same thing with Jesus. He knew that if he could entice Jesus to sin, Jesus' purpose in coming to the earth would be defeated.

Matthew 4:1–11

1. List the three things that Satan asked Jesus to do.
   a. turn stones into bread
   b. jump from the pinnacle of the temple
   c. fall down and worship him
2. What did Jesus do each time that Satan tempted Him to do wrong? _____
   He quoted a verse from the Bible.

After Jesus was tempted in the wilderness, He apparently returned to where John was baptizing and preaching. Here John pointed out Jesus as the Messiah, and two of his disciples followed Jesus to talk with Him. One of these was Andrew, who brought his brother Peter to Jesus. The next day Jesus called Philip. Philip found Nathanael and told him that they had found the Promised One (John 1:35–45).

Nathanael Meets the Son of Man

Nathanael was not impressed when Philip told him about Jesus. But he did go with Philip to talk to Him, and he quickly changed his mind when he met Jesus.

John 1:43–51

3. Nathanael wondered if any good thing could come out of Nazareth, but he did not explain why he said this. Evidently he felt that Jesus could not be the Messiah because He came from Nazareth. Choose the statement that gives the best reason for Nathanael to say this.
   a. Nazareth was a wicked city, and no godly people lived there.
   (b) The prophets had foretold that the Messiah would be born in Bethlehem, but Jesus came from Nazareth.
   c. He thought John the Baptist was the Messiah and that they should not look for someone else.
   d. He expected the Messiah to come from his home town, Cana, and not from Nazareth.
4. Why did Nathanael change his mind so quickly about Jesus? _____
   Jesus knew things about him that an ordinary man could not have known.
5. Nathanael's statement to Jesus, "Thou art the Son of God," was correct, and Jesus did not deny it. However, what did Jesus call Himself in His response? (1:51) _____
   the Son of man

7. Why did John not want to baptize Jesus? [L. 4]
   He knew Jesus was greater than he was.

In This Lesson

Scope: Matthew 4:1–12; Mark 1:12, 13; Luke 4:1–13; John 1:43–4:42

Focus

• Before beginning His ministry, Jesus faced temptation and overcame it by quoting the Scriptures.
• Jesus, the Son of man, began to reveal Himself as the Son of God.
   —Jesus revealed Himself to Nathanael as one who knows all things, converting Nathanael from doubter to believer.
   —Jesus revealed His power to His disciples by His miracle at Cana, increasing their faith in Him.
   —Jesus revealed His authority as the Son of God by cleansing His Father's house.
   —Jesus revealed Himself as Saviour of the world to Nicodemus.
   —Jesus revealed Himself as greater than John the Baptist, and John readily acknowledged this.
   —Jesus revealed Himself to the Samaritans as one who loves all people.

Jesus Performs His First Miracle in Cana

Nathanael himself came from Galilee. His home village, Cana, was built among gardens and orchards on a hill overlooking fertile plains. One writer says that around the village of Cana grew the best pomegranates in Palestine. Jesus and His disciples went to a wedding in Cana three days after Jesus talked to Nathanael. Mary, the mother of Jesus, was invited too.

John 2:1–11

6. a. What did Mary show by the fact that she told Jesus about

   the wine running out?   (Answers may vary slightly.)

   Mary had faith in Jesus.

   _____

   b. What did Mary show by what she told the servants? ____

   Mary respected Jesus' authority.

   _____

7. What effect did Jesus' miracle of turning water to wine have on His disciples? _____

   They believed on Jesus.

Jesus Cleanses the Temple

After attending the wedding at Cana, Jesus' mother and brothers went with Him to Capernaum. (Joseph may have died before this time.) A number of Jesus' disciples were from this fishing town near the Sea of Galilee.

Peter, Andrew, James, and John all eventually left their nets to follow Jesus. At this point they were with Jesus part of the time, but they also continued their fishing business.

John 2:12–17

8. Why did Jesus leave Capernaum soon after He arrived there with His family? _____

   He went to the Passover in Jerusalem.

When Jesus came to Jerusalem, He found much evil in the temple. All Jews had to pay a yearly temple tax in Hebrew shekels. But since the Jews came from many countries, they had many different kinds of money. Greedy men sat in the temple courts and made a large profit through changing other money to Hebrew shekels.

All around the temple courts stood bazaars of the family of Annas, the rich and corrupt high priest. Here worshipers were charged high prices for the animals they needed for their sacrifices. Those who brought their own animals had to pay an examiner to inspect each animal before it could be sacrificed.

Many worshipers at the temple were sincere followers of God. No doubt they were grieved by the corruption they saw there. Most grieved of all was Jesus.

9. Make a list of the things Jesus did in cleansing the temple. _____

   (The list should include most of the following points.) He made a scourge of small cords. He drove out the moneychangers and those who sold animals. He drove out the animals. He poured out the changers' money. He overthrew their tables. He told those who sold doves to take them out of the temple.

- The lesson mentions Capernaum as being Peter and Andrew's hometown. This is based on references in the Gospels of Jesus going to Peter's house when He was obviously in Capernaum. Yet John 1:44 specifically mentions Bethsaida as the city of Andrew and Peter. No one is certain how to piece this together. It is possible that they moved from one city to the other, or that they were born in one and later moved to the other. Another possibility is that Bethsaida was a suburb of Capernaum. To further complicate the issue, it appears that there were two towns called Bethsaida, one close to Capernaum and the other east of the Sea of Galilee.

- The Bible does not say that Jesus used the scourge on the men. He may have made it to drive out the sheep and oxen (John 2:15). He sent out those

Objectives

- Students should know
  - what three things Satan tempted Jesus to do. (*turn stones into bread, jump from the pinnacle of the temple, fall down and worship him*)
  - how Jesus overcame Satan's temptations. (*He quoted the Scriptures.*)
  - who asked, "Can there any good thing come out of Nazareth." (*Nathanael*)
  - how Jesus convinced Nathanael that He was no ordinary man. (*Jesus showed that He knew all about him before they met.*)
  - what effect Jesus' miracle at Cana had on His disciples. (*It helped them to believe on Him.*)
  - why Jesus had authority to cleanse the temple. (*He is the Son of God.*)
  - what Jesus told Nicodemus He had come to do for the world. (*save it*)
  - what John the Baptist said when Jesus gained popularity. ("*He must increase, but I must decrease.*")
  - how Jesus showed the Samaritans that He loves all people. (*He spent two days teaching the Samaritans. He talked with a Samaritan woman.*)
  - why Jesus' disciples were surprised that He would talk with a Samaritan. (*The Jews despised the Samaritans.*)

10. Not just any man could have driven the merchants and moneychangers from the temple. With what authority did Jesus do this? (Clue: Think about whom He said the temple belonged to.) ___
    with the authority of the Son of God

11. a. Jesus' actions reminded the disciples of a Hebrew Scripture passage. Use a concordance to find this verse in the Old Testament. Then copy the verse and its reference. _____
    "For the zeal of thine house hath eaten me up; and the reproaches of them that reproached thee are fallen upon me" (Psalm 69:9).

    b. What word in the first part of this verse describes what Jesus felt? __zeal__

Jesus Talks to Nicodemus

Soon after the Passover, Nicodemus wanted to talk with Jesus. Nicodemus was a Pharisee and apparently a member of the Sanhedrin, the council that ruled the Jews. He came at night, perhaps so that no one would see him.

John 3:1–18

12. What reason did Nicodemus give for believing that Jesus came from God? _____
    No one could do such miracles unless God was with him.

Jesus explained to Nicodemus that it is impossible for a man to see the kingdom of God unless he is born again. Nicodemus found this difficult to understand. He thought Jesus meant that a man would need to experience a second natural birth, but Jesus was talking about a spiritual birth.

13. Jesus also explained to Nicodemus why God had sent Him to earth. He told Nicodemus that He had not come to (a) ____condemn____ the world. Instead, He had come so that the world could be (b) ____saved____. But Jesus also told Nicodemus that the only way to escape being condemned by God was to (c) ____believe____ in the Name of Jesus, the Son of God.

Jesus Becomes More Popular Than John

John was the forerunner of Jesus. When Jesus came, John stepped into the background and allowed Jesus to do His work. However, for a short while the work of John and Jesus overlapped.

John 3:22–30

14. John the Baptist and Jesus' disciples both baptized in Judea. This caused some conflict among John's disciples. What did John say that shows he did not mind that Jesus was becoming more famous than himself? "He must increase, but I must decrease."

15. How would you describe John's attitude? _____
    (Sample answer) He was humble.

Jesus Loves Everyone

Many Jews detoured Samaria by traveling along the eastern side of the Jordan River. They hated the Samaritans, just as the Samaritans hated the Jews. But Jesus loved everyone, including the Samaritans. The Bible says, "He must needs go through Samaria."
Traveling on foot was tiresome, and Jesus was weary by the time He reached the Samaritan city of Sychar. He sat down to rest on the edge of Jacob's well. To the west, Mount Gerizim and Mount Ebal rose above the valley. Ruins on Mount Gerizim marked the site where a Samaritan temple had once stood.

who sold doves by simply telling them to go (2:16). One thing is certain: as the Son of God, Jesus had authority to take whatever action was necessary to cleanse His Father's house.

If your students have center-column references in their Bibles, you may want to teach them how to use the center column to find cross-references such as this one.

• Part D in this lesson includes details on the conflicts between Jews and Samaritans to help students better understand Jesus' dealings with the Samaritans.

Truths to Amplify

• Jesus is our example in resisting temptation. He "was in all points tempted like as we are, yet without sin" (Hebrews 4:15).

• Honest seekers of truth quickly recognize who Jesus is when He reveals Himself to them. Nathanael and the Samaritan woman illustrate this. But those who reject the truth, such as the merchants in the temple, see Jesus only as a threat to their freedom and ambitions.

• Jesus met the needs of those who were rejected by the religious leaders of His time. Are we willing to "do justly, and to love mercy" (Micah 6:8), even if it brings us into disfavor with others?

It appears from Jesus' words in John 4:35 that He visited Samaria four months before the spring harvest. Men would need to wait for the grain harvest, but Jesus knew the time to gather the spiritual harvest of souls had already come. He challenged His disciples, "Lift up your eyes, and look on the fields; for they are white already to harvest."

 Choose only the best answer for each of the following.

John 4:1–12

16. By spending time in Samaria and teaching the people there, Jesus taught His disciples that
    a. the Jews were superior to the Samaritans.
    b. the Samaritans were superior to the Jews.
    c. all men are of equal worth in God's sight.
    d. the Samaritans were more in need of salvation than the Jews were.

17. A human body needs water to stay alive. Similarly, a soul needs the water of life (the Word of God) to live. It is evident that the Samaritan woman did not understand that Jesus was offering her the water of life because
    a. she wondered where Jesus would get the water He offered, since He had nothing with which to draw it.
    b. she was surprised that Jesus would ask a Samaritan for a drink of water.
    c. she thought that natural water was the only gift God had given to man.
    d. she did not know that His disciples had gone to the city to buy bread.

John 4:27–30

18. What finally convinced the woman that Jesus was the Messiah (the Christ)?
    a. He asked her for a drink of water.
    b. He offered her a drink of living water.
    c. He talked to her, even though she was a Samaritan and He was a Jew.
    d. He knew the details of her past life without having been told.

19. The disciples were Jews. Why was it hard for them to comprehend that Samaritans could also believe in Jesus and become part of God's family?
    a. The Samaritans were sinners, but the Jews were not.
    b. The Jews hated the Samaritans and presumed that God hated them too.
    c. God had never accepted anyone into His family who was not born a Jew.
    d. They thought the Samaritans did not know that there was a God.

B. BIBLE WORD STUDY

1. Jesus recognized Nathanael as a sincere Israelite. What words did He use to describe Nathanael as an honest and sincere man? (John 1:47)   _a man "in whom is no guile"_

2. The pots at the wedding feast each held approximately 20 to 30 gallons. This was from 2 to 3 _____firkins_____ apiece (John 2:6).

3. Jesus made Himself a *whip* of strong cords. With this _____scourge_____ He drove the animals out of the temple (John 2:15).

4. The temple had become a place to buy and sell. But Jesus did not want His Father's house to be a
   _____house_____ ___of___ _____merchandise_____ (John 2:16).

5. John the Baptist came to *bear witness* of Jesus. What does this expression mean? (See John 3:26, 28. Choose the best definition.)
   a. To swear that something is true
   (b.) To tell the truth or the facts about something
   c. To see something happen

6. The word *whence* appears several times in the Scripture passages of this lesson (John 1:48; 2:9; 4:11). After reading these verses, write a definition of *whence* in your own words. Check a dictionary to see if you are correct. ___"from where," "from what place," or "out of where"___

C. THINKING ABOUT BIBLE TRUTHS

Jesus—Our Example in Resisting Temptation

1. In Matthew 4:1–11 Jesus was tempted by Satan. What method did Jesus use to overcome Satan and his temptations that we can still use today? ___He quoted the Scriptures.___

2. First John 2:16 mentions three ways that we are tempted to sin. Write one of these ways to match each description given below.
   a. _____the lust of the flesh_____ This kind of temptation uses the desires and passions of our bodies to tempt us to commit sin. Satan tempted Jesus in this way by appealing to His physical hunger.
   b. _____the pride of life_____ This kind of temptation prompts us to try to be someone important and looked up to, even if it means doing something wrong to achieve this. Satan tempted Jesus to desire power as a great worldly king and to gain admiration by jumping off the pinnacle of the temple.
   c. _____the lust of the eye_____ This kind of temptation makes us want to do or wear things that will attract attention and make others admire or envy us. It can also cause us to covet things that we see. Satan tempted Jesus to seek attention and to desire the kingdoms that he showed Him.

3. Read Hebrews 4:14–16.
   a. How do we know that Jesus understands our temptations? _____
      ___He was tempted in all points as we are, so He understands all the temptations we face.___
   b. What does He want us to do when we are tempted to sin? ___He wants us to come to the throne of___
      ___grace (through prayer) and ask for help in time of need (when we are tempted).___

D. LEARNING MORE ABOUT BIBLE TIMES

The Despised Samaritans

The Jews and Samaritans hated one another. Read the following information to find reasons why.

The Samaritans date back to the time of the Assyrians. The Assyrians took most of the Israelites into captivity and sent in foreigners to colonize the land. The Israelites who remained in the land married these foreign pagans. Their descendants became the Samaritans, and their religion became a mixture of Jewish and pagan beliefs.

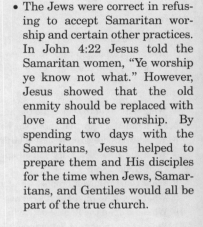

Some Samaritans were alarmed to see the Judean Jews return from Babylon and reestablish proper Jewish worship in Jerusalem. They tried to stop Nehemiah from rebuilding the walls of Jerusalem, but they failed. Other Samaritans offered to help, but the Jews would not allow them to do so.

The Samaritans built their own temple on Mount Gerizim. Later, to please their Greek rulers, the Samaritans turned their temple over to the worship of Zeus (ZOOS), a Greek god. The Jews burned down the Samaritan temple and built a dam to flood its site.

The Samaritans rebuilt their temple and returned to keeping the Law of Moses. But ill feelings between the Jews and Samaritans increased.

The Jews used signal fires to direct pilgrims traveling from Galilee to Jerusalem. The Samaritans lit false signal fires to confuse them. At times they also ambushed and robbed pilgrims. Once they scattered bones in the Jews' temple at Jerusalem to defile it. In response, the Jews refused to recognize the Samaritans as Jews and avoided them as much as possible.

The Samaritans, like the Jews, believed in the coming of a Messiah. They believed in a resurrection and life after death. After Pentecost, some Samaritans were more ready to believe the Gospel than many Jews were.

Several hundred Samaritans live at Shechem (Nablus) today. They have an old copy of the Law, and the Samaritan high priest offers a lamb during the Passover.

1. Why did Samaritans dislike the Jews? <u>The Jews once burned the Samaritan temple. They also</u> <u>refused to recognize the Samaritans as Jews. >></u>

2. Why did Jews dislike the Samaritans? <u>The Samaritans mixed idol worship with their worship of</u> <u>God. They made trouble for Jewish pilgrims and defiled the temple in Jerusalem. >></u>

• The Jews were correct in refusing to accept Samaritan worship and certain other practices. In John 4:22 Jesus told the Samaritan women, "Ye worship ye know not what." However, Jesus showed that the old enmity should be replaced with love and true worship. By spending two days with the Samaritans, Jesus helped to prepare them and His disciples for the time when Jews, Samaritans, and Gentiles would all be part of the true church.

Answers may vary slightly.

40

Chapter One Review

A. ORAL REVIEW

 Be sure you know the answers to these questions. Answer as many as you can from memory. If you need help, you may check the reference or lesson numbers given in brackets.

Where >>

1. Where was Jesus born? [Luke 2:4–7]
2. Where did Jesus grow up? [Matthew 2:23]
3. Where did John the Baptist live before he began his ministry? [Luke 1:80; Lesson 4]

What >>

4. What nations of the earth did the Messiah come to bless? [Lesson 2]
5. What did Mary say that shows she believed Gabriel's message? [Luke 1:38]
6. What two Gospels record Jesus' birth? [Lessons 1–3]
7. What did Jesus ask Mary and Joseph when He was twelve that shows He knew He is the Son of God? [Luke 2:49]
8. What Old Testament prophet was John the Baptist compared to? [Luke 1:17]
9. What was John the Baptist's message? [Matthew 3:2]
10. What did John the Baptist eat? What did he wear? [Matthew 3:4]
11. What three things did Satan tempt Jesus to do? [Matthew 4:3–10]
12. What name did Jesus call Himself in reference to His humanity? [John 1:51]
13. What effect did Jesus' miracle at Cana have on His disciples? [John 2:11]
14. What three languages were commonly used in Palestine at the time of Christ? [John 19:20]

Why >>

15. Why was it hard for Zacharias to believe that he would have a son? [Luke 1:7]
16. Why did Herod the Great have the little children of Bethlehem killed? [Matthew 2:16]
17. Why did John feel that he should not baptize Jesus? [Matthew 3:14]
18. Why were Jesus' disciples surprised that He would talk with a Samaritan? [John 4:9; Lesson 5]

Bible Words >>

 Give a synonym or definition for each italicized word.

19. Jesus was called *Emmanuel*. [Matthew 1:23]
20. People called Jesus *Rabbi*. [John 1:38]
21. Some people found fault with Jesus for being a friend of *publicans*. [Lesson 4]
22. Jesus made a *scourge* to cleanse the temple. [Lesson 5]

For You to Study >>

23. Be prepared to write the names of the New Testament books, using the correct order and spelling. [Lesson 1]

1. in Bethlehem
2. in Nazareth
3. in the deserts (wilderness)
4. all nations
5. "Be it unto me according to thy word."
6. Matthew, Luke
7. "Wist ye not that I must be about my Father's business?"
8. Elias (Elijah)
9. "Repent ye: for the kingdom of heaven is at hand."
10. He ate locusts and wild honey. He wore clothes made from camels' hair, and a leather belt.
11. turn stones into bread, jump from the pinnacle of the temple, and fall down and worship him
12. Son of man
13. It helped them believe on Him.
14. Hebrew (Aramaic), Greek, and Latin
15. He and his wife had not had any children, and they were now old.
16. He did this in an effort to destroy Jesus.
17. He knew Jesus was greater than he was.
18. The Jews despised the Samaritans.
19. "God with us."
20. Master
21. tax collectors
22. whip
23. (Review New Testament books in class as needed. Be sure the students know how to spell the names correctly.)

B. WRITTEN REVIEW

Places in Palestine

 Match the following descriptions with the names on the right. You may check a map or Bible atlas if you need help. Be prepared to label each place on a map of Palestine. You will not use all the names.

__j__ 1. The city where Gabriel appeared to Mary   a. Jerusalem

__e__ 2. The town where Jesus attended a wedding   b. Jericho

__h__ 3. The region where Jesus talked with a woman at a well   c. Bethlehem

__k__ 4. A city by the Sea of Galilee that Jesus often visited   d. Judea

__i__ 5. What the Romans called the land of Israel   e. Cana

__a__ 6. The city where Jesus talked with the Jewish teachers   f. Egypt

__g__ 7. A region in northern Palestine   g. Galilee

__c__ 8. The city where Jesus was born   h. Samaria

__b__ 9. The city near the Jordan River and the Dead Sea   i. Palestine

__d__ 10. The region between the Mediterranean Sea and   j. Nazareth
         the Dead Sea   k. Capernaum

People of Palestine

 Match each description with the name of a person or group. You will not use all the names.

__e__ 11. The king of Palestine when Jesus was born   a. shepherds

__f__ 12. Saw the angel Gabriel in the temple   b. Messiah

__j__ 13. Wealthy, strict Jews who lived in the east   c. wise men

__b__ 14. The Hebrew name for the Anointed One promised by God   d. John the Baptist

__c__ 15. Knew by a star that the Messiah had come   e. Herod the Great

__k__ 16. Jews who worked at common trades and lived in the west   f. Zacharias

__i__ 17. Lived in simple communities and observed strict rules   g. Nathanael

__a__ 18. Heard angels praising God when Jesus was born   h. Old Testament prophets

__d__ 19. Rebuked Herod Antipas for his sin   i. Essenes

__h__ 20. Wrote about the coming Messiah   j. Hebrew Jews

                                            k. Greek Jews

How

 Write answers to these questions. Do as many as you can from memory. If you need help, you may check the reference given in brackets.

21. How did Jesus astonish the Jewish teachers when He was twelve? [Luke 2:46, 47] _____
    by His understanding and answers

22. How did God the Father and the Holy Spirit manifest themselves at the baptism of Jesus the Son?
   [Matthew 3:16, 17] God the Father said, "This is my beloved Son, in whom I am well pleased." The
   Holy Spirit descended upon Jesus in the form of a dove.

23. How did Jesus overcome Satan's temptations? [Matthew 4:4, 7, 10] by quoting the Scriptures

24. How did Nathanael become convinced that Jesus was no ordinary man? [John 1:47–50]
     He was convinced when he saw that Jesus knew all about him, without having met him.

25. How did Jesus show the Samaritans that He loved all people? [John 4:4, 27–42]
     He spent two days teaching the Samaritans. (He talked with a Samaritan woman.)

Who Said It?

🍇 *Name the person who said the following, and finish each quotation. Check the reference only if you need help.*

_____Jesus_____ 26. "Wist ye not that I must be about my ____Father's____ business?" [Luke 2:49]

_____Nathanael_____ 27. "Can there any good thing come out of ____Nazareth____?" [John 1:46]

_____Jesus_____ 28. "Make not my ____Father's____ house an house of merchandise." [John 2:16]

_____Jesus_____ 29. "For God sent not his Son into the world to condemn the world; but that the world through him might be ____saved____." [John 3:17]

_____John (the Baptist)_____ 30. "He must increase, but I must ____decrease____." [John 3:30]

"I am the vine, ye are the branches" (John 15:5).

CHAPTER TWO

Acceptance and Rejection

Come unto me, all ye that labour
and are heavy laden, and I will give you rest.
Take my yoke upon you, and learn of me;
for I am meek and lowly in heart:
and ye shall find rest unto your souls.
For my yoke is easy, and my burden is light.
Matthew 11:28–30

Harmony of the Gospels

For important events and teachings covered in Chapter Two

Event or Teaching	Matthew	Mark	Luke	John	Location	Season
Lesson 6. Jesus' Fame Spreads						
Jesus heals a nobleman's son.	—	—	—	4:46–54 [1]	Cana	Late fall [2]
Jesus is rejected at Nazareth.	—	—	4:16–30	—	Nazareth	
Jesus moves to Capernaum.	4:13–16	—	4:31, 32	—	Capernaum	
Jesus calls four disciples.	4:18–22	1:16–20	5:1–11	—	Capernaum	
Lesson 7. Jesus Serves the Galileans						
Jesus performs miracles at Capernaum.	8:14–17	1:21–34	4:31–41	—	Capernaum	
Jesus prays in a desert place.	—	1:35–37	—	—	Desert place	
Jesus preaches throughout Galilee.	4:23–25	1:36–39	4:42–44	—	Galilee	
Jesus cleanses a leper.	8:2–4	1:40–45	5:12–16	—	Galilee	
Jesus heals a man sick of the palsy.	9:2–8	2:1–13	5:17–26	—	Capernaum	
Lesson 8. The Sabbath and the Pharisees						
Jesus heals an impotent man.	—	—	—	5:1–47	Jerusalem	Spring [3] ?
The disciples pick grain on the Sabbath.	12:1–8	2:23–28	6:1–5	—		Spring [4]
Jesus heals a man with a withered hand.	12:9–14	3:1–6	6:6–11	—		
Jesus heals by the Sea of Galilee.	12:15–21	3:7–12	—	—	Sea of Galilee	
Lesson 9. Jesus Calls Believers						
Jesus calls Matthew (Levi).[5]	9:9–13	2:14–17	5:27–32	—	Galilee	
Jesus chooses twelve disciples.	10:1–4	3:13–19	6:12–16	—	Galilee	
Sermon on the Mount (first part)[6]	5:1–48	—	6:17–36	—	Galilee	
Lesson 10. Jesus Instructs His Followers						
Sermon on the Mount (last part)	6:1–7:29	—	6:37–49	—	Galilee	

---

[1] Passages given in italics are used in the lesson.

[2] Jesus performed this miracle soon after returning to Galilee from His visit in Samaria. This was apparently in late fall or early winter, four months before the spring harvest.

[3] Most sources consider the unnamed feast of John 5 to be a Passover. Edersheim considered it a fall feast.

[4] This account obviously took place during spring harvest. Luke 6:1 might refer to a Sabbath soon after Passover.

[5] The time of Matthew's call and feast is uncertain. It is included in the lesson on Jesus calling believers, even though this is probably not the correct chronological order.

[6] This follows the order given in Luke. Matthew places the sermon earlier in Jesus' ministry. Jesus may have given these teachings on more than one occasion.

45

Lesson 6. Jesus' Fame Spreads

In this chapter you will see how Jesus faced both popularity and opposition as people started to take more and more notice of Him. Those whom He helped loved Him, but some of His teachings threatened the corrupt Jewish leaders. Because of this, Jesus received much opposition in spite of the good that He did.

"Not many wise men after the flesh, not many mighty, not many noble" are called to become part of God's family (1 Corinthians 1:26). Rather, God chooses men of low estate so that "no flesh should glory in his presence."

Jesus left the self-righteous Jews of Judea and returned to Galilee. Among the common farmers and fishermen of Galilee, Jesus found many people who believed in Him.

In this first part of Jesus' ministry, He was unknown to most people. He did not have a large crowd of followers. He traveled alone, unattended by His disciples, teaching and healing the people. He was fulfilling a prophecy of Isaiah—that a great light would spring up in Galilee (Matthew 4:12–17).

The events of this lesson mark the beginning of Jesus' popularity. But His popularity brought with it opposition from those who should have known Him best.

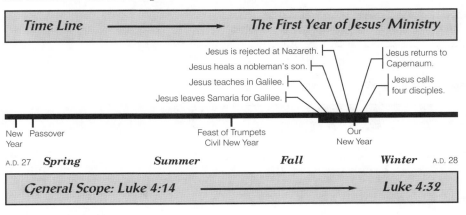

Using the Time Line

1. In what season did Jesus leave Samaria and return to Galilee?   in late fall (or early winter)

2. Number these events in the order in which they happened.

   4   Jesus returns to Capernaum.

   2   Jesus heals a nobleman's son.

   3   Jesus goes to Nazareth.

   1   Jesus leaves Samaria for Galilee.

Lesson 6

Oral Review

1. Name three important districts of Palestine. [L. 1] **Galilee, Samaria, Judea**

2. Who spoke each of these languages: Latin, Greek, Hebrew? [L. 1] *Latin*: **the Romans,** *Greek*: **the Greeks and many other people,** *Hebrew*: **the Jews**

3. To what two people did the angel Gabriel appear? Where did he appear to each? [L. 2] Gabriel appeared to Zacharias in the temple at Jerusalem; he appeared to Mary in Nazareth.

4. What indicates that by age twelve, Jesus' understanding and wisdom far exceeded that of other boys His age? [L. 3] **The Jewish teachers were astonished at His understanding and answers.**

5. Where did John the Baptist live before he began his ministry? [L. 4] **in the wilderness**

6. What was Jesus' first miracle? [L. 5] **changing water to wine at Cana**

7. Jesus told Nicodemus that He had come to ——— the world rather than to condemn it. [L. 5] **save**

46 Chapter Two   Acceptance and Rejection

A. ANSWERS FROM THE BIBLE

Jesus' Popularity in Galilee

In Lesson 5, you read how Jesus stopped and talked to a Samaritan woman at the well of Sychar. After two whole days in Samaria (most Jews would have hated to spend one night there), Jesus traveled on to Galilee. He paid a second visit to Cana.

 To complete these exercises, first study the Bible passages that are given. Fill in the short blanks with words. Whenever possible, use the exact words from the Bible. Write complete answers for the questions with long blanks. For multiple-choice questions, circle the letter of the correct answer.

John 4:43–54

1. Why did the Galileans believe in Jesus? <u>They had seen Jesus' miracles at the feast of the Passover.</u>

2. A nobleman came all the way from Capernaum to Cana (about 15 to 20 miles) to ask Jesus to heal his son. What did Jesus imply that the nobleman would have to see before he would fully believe on Him? <u>"signs and wonders" (a miracle)</u>

3. The nobleman did not understand the power of the Son of God. To heal his son, he thought Jesus would need to <u>come to his house</u>.

4. How did Jesus show the nobleman that His power was greater than what he thought? _____
<u>He healed the nobleman's son from where He was.</u>

5. Who else believed in Jesus after seeing His power to heal the sick? <u>the nobleman's household</u>

Luke 4:14, 15

The Book of Luke skips over the events that took place between the temptation of Jesus and His return to Galilee. But these verses in Luke show how the Galileans reacted to Jesus' works and teachings.

6. Jesus wanted everybody to hear the Good News and join God's kingdom. What method did Jesus use to spread the Good News throughout Galilee? <u>Jesus taught in the synagogues.</u>

7. How did these Galileans react to Jesus' teachings? <u>They glorified Him.</u>

Jesus' Rejection in Nazareth

In His travels, Jesus returned to His hometown. The people of Nazareth were probably not surprised to see Him stand up in the synagogue service and read the Scriptures. He may have done this before. But now that He was becoming famous, they wanted to hear what He would say to them.

Luke 4:16–21

8. Jesus read to them from Isaiah 61 (Esaias). What did He tell them about this prophecy? <u>"This day is this scripture fulfilled in your ears." (They were hearing the fulfillment of this Scripture passage.)</u>

9. Why would Jesus' statement have startled the people of Nazareth?
   (a.) Jesus was claiming that these verses in Isaiah were written about Him.
   b. Jesus was claiming that He was Isaiah the prophet.
   c. They had never heard these verses before and did not know that they were in Isaiah.
   d. Jesus spoke to them in Latin instead of Hebrew or Greek.

In This Lesson

Scope: Matthew 4:13–25; Mark 1:14–20; Luke 4:14–32; 5:1–11; John 4:43–54

Focus

- This lesson examines various responses to Jesus' teaching.
  - Most Galileans accepted Jesus during the early part of His ministry.
  - The nobleman sought healing for his son and gained greater faith in Jesus.
  - The people of Nazareth refused to accept Jesus as more than Joseph's son. They became angry with Jesus when He rebuked their lack of faith.
  - The people of Capernaum were astonished at Jesus' doctrine and power.
  - Peter, Andrew, James, and John willingly left all to follow Jesus.
  - Peter recognized His own sinfulness when He witnessed Jesus' power in supplying the large catch of fish.
- Synagogue worship included studying the Scriptures and praying, but not offering sacrifices.

Jesus knew the hearts of the people of Nazareth. He knew that they were hoping to see Him perform some of the miracles they had heard about. Most of these people had known Jesus and His family for a long time. They did not believe that a son of Joseph the carpenter could be a great prophet and miracle worker.

Luke 4:22–30

10. Jesus told the people of Nazareth that prophets are not _____accepted_____ in their own country.

11. Why could Jesus not work many miracles in Nazareth? (Compare this account with the one recorded in Matthew 13:54–58.) __because of their unbelief__

12. Jesus used miracles performed by the prophets Elijah (Elias) and Elisha (Eliseus) as examples. Both of these miracles were done for the benefit of Gentiles. Why did the people of Nazareth become so upset at the illustrations Jesus gave?

   a. Jesus was telling them that He would do miracles only for Gentiles.

   b. Jesus was implying that they were Gentiles.

   (c.) Jesus was implying that believing Gentiles receive more of God's blessings than unbelieving Jews do.

13. What did the people that Jesus had grown up with try to do with Him? _____

   They tried to throw Him over the brow of a hill.

14. Why was Jesus able to walk away from them?   (Sample answer) The power of God was with Him.

Jesus' Move to Capernaum

After leaving the people of Nazareth, Jesus moved to Capernaum. Here Jesus made His home in the fresh, lakeside climate along the shore of the Sea of Galilee. Capernaum, built on a slope along the lake, lay only two miles from the Jordan River's entrance. Snow-capped Mount Hermon stood on its northeastern horizon.

Both Jews and Gentiles lived in Capernaum. Many Jews in Capernaum, such as Jairus and the nobleman whose son Jesus healed, were friendly toward Jesus. The Gentiles also listened to His teaching. Some of them, such as the centurion whose servant Jesus healed, also became believers in Jesus.

Capernaum made a good home for Jesus. Not only did He find eager listeners among the people of Capernaum, but He could also reach many travelers. Several important roads met at Capernaum. The Great Trunk Road—the main road between Egypt and Mesopotamia—passed right through the town.

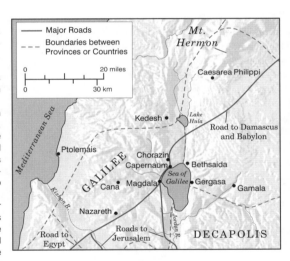

Galilee at the Time of Christ

Objectives

- Students should know
  - what miracle Jesus did for a nobleman from Capernaum. (*Jesus healed his son without going to his house.*)
  - how Jesus spread the Good News throughout Galilee. (*He traveled about and taught in the synagogues.*)
  - why Jesus' stories of Elijah and Naaman offended the people of Nazareth. (*These stories were about Gentiles who received God's blessings rather than the Jews.*)
  - what the people of Nazareth tried to do to Jesus after He preached to them. (*throw Him over the brow of a hill and kill Him*)
  - why Jesus moved to Capernaum. (*The people of Nazareth did not accept Him; whereas many people in Capernaum did.*)
  - what occupation Peter, James, and John had before Jesus called them. (*They were fishermen.*)
  - when Peter confessed that he was a sinful man. (*when Jesus caused him to catch a multitude of fish*)
  - how synagogue worship differed from temple worship. (*Sacrifices were offered at the temple, but not at synagogues.*)
  - the meaning of *amend.* (*recover*)

Luke 4:31, 32

15. How did the people of Capernaum feel about Jesus' doctrine? _____

    They were astonished because Jesus taught with power (authority).

Jesus' Willing Followers

Many people flocked to hear Jesus and to watch Him perform miracles. But many of these were just curiosity seekers. Jesus wanted friends and followers that He could depend on to stay with Him even when He was unpopular. He needed men who would be willing to suffer for Him and to spend their lives spreading the Gospel.

Mark 1:16–18

16. What did Peter and Andrew need to do to become fishers of men?   follow Jesus

_____

Mark 1:19, 20

The night before Jesus' called the fishermen might have been a stormy one. Their nets were broken and needed to be washed. In spite of its dangers and the hard work involved, fishing was perhaps the best-paying job in the area. Zebedee was a fairly well-to-do fisherman, with his own boat. His two sons and hired hands worked for him.

17. What does James and John's willingness to leave their father show about how they felt toward Jesus' work?   They saw the "fishing of men" as

    something more important than making money.

_____

Luke 5:1–11

These verses add a few details that the passage in Mark does not record.

18. Peter had probably been there when Jesus performed other miracles. He had certainly heard about them if he had not seen them. Why did this miracle make such an impression on him?
    a. He had not slept the night before and was quite tired and easily impressed.
    b. Peter thought that Jesus might do more such miracles for him if he followed Him.
    c. It involved him personally, and he knew how much power it took to perform it.
    d. He knew that Jesus was not a fisherman and did not know much about fish.

19. Peter's reaction to this miracle is noteworthy.
    a. What did Peter do when he saw the miracle that Jesus had performed? _____
       He fell down at Jesus' knees.
    b. What did he say?   "Depart from me; for I am a sinful man, O Lord."

_____

20. The Bible does not indicate that Jesus said anything to Peter about his sins on this occasion. Why might Peter have reacted in this way to the miracle?
    a. He was afraid that Jesus would not help him catch more fish if he did not repent of his sins.
    b. He felt guilty because he knew it was wrong to be a fisherman.
    c. The miracle made him realize that Jesus also knew all of his sins.
    d. All of the above are true.

Truths to Amplify
- The Galileans definitely accepted Jesus more readily than the Judeans did. Jesus was popular in Galilee for some time. But Jesus did not minister just to be popular. He did His Father's will and spoke the truth, regardless of the consequences. When this cost Him the admiration of His friends, He steadfastly kept on working for man's salvation.
- Strangely enough, the Galileans of Nazareth who knew Jesus best were the least responsive to His teachings. Grade 7 students could profit from discussing in class why this was the case.

B. BIBLE WORD STUDY

Match the words with their meanings. You will not use all the meanings.

e	1. Nobleman (John 4:46)	a.	edge or top
c	2. Amend (John 4:52)	b.	catch of fish
h	3. Physician (Luke 4:23)	c.	recover
a	4. Brow (of a hill) (Luke 4:29)	d.	scribe
f	5. Doctrine (Luke 4:32)	e.	government official
j	6. Gennesaret (Luke 5:1)	f.	teaching
i	7. Launch (Luke 5:4)	g.	the Mediterranean Sea
b	8. Draught (DRAHFT) (Luke 5:9)	h.	doctor
		i.	put out or start
		j.	another name for the Sea of Galilee

C. THINKING ABOUT BIBLE TRUTHS

Fishers of Men

Matthew 28:19, 20

1. Jesus wanted His disciples to learn how to "fish" for men. What men were they to fish for? ____
   They were to fish for men of all nations.

2. How were the disciples to do this "fishing"? _____
   They were to teach all nations (and baptize the believers).

The "Fish"

Complete the following sentences.

John 8:33–36

3. Many Jews of Jesus' time did not recognize their need to be set free. They claimed that they were
   free already, but this was not true.
   a. Politically, the Jews were under the control of _the Romans_ . (See Lesson 1.)
   b. Spiritually, the Jews were under the control of _Satan (sin)_ .
4. a. According to these verses, who would have set the Jews free? _the Son (Jesus)_
   b. Would this have brought them spiritual or political freedom? _spiritual freedom_
   c. Which freedom is the most important, spiritual or political? _spiritual freedom_

1 Corinthians 1:21–25

5. Fish usually do not want to be caught. Often men do not want to believe in the Gospel either.
   These verses tell us that the preaching of Christ was a (a) _stumblingblock_ to the Jews and
   (b) _foolishness_ to the Greeks (Gentiles). However, to those who did believe and allowed
   the Gospel to "catch" them, the preaching of Christ was (c) _____
   "the power of God, and the wisdom of God" .

D. LEARNING MORE ABOUT BIBLE TIMES

The Synagogue in Jesus' Time

The Jews began meeting in synagogues long before Jesus' time. In 586 B.C., Nebuchadnezzar and his army had captured Jerusalem and destroyed the temple. Jews who all their lives had gathered at the temple suddenly had no place to offer sacrifices and to worship God.

Scattered throughout Babylon, Persia, and the Greek world, Jews began gathering in small groups for worship. These groups came to be called *synagogues*. (*Synagogue* is derived from a Greek word that means "to gather together.") Synagogue congregations could not offer sacrifices, because the Law required that sacrifices be offered at the temple (or tabernacle). But they could study the Scriptures and pray.

Synagogue congregations kept the Jewish faith alive until Jesus' day. At first these groups probably gathered in homes, as the exiled Jews did at Ezekiel's house (Ezekiel 8:1). Eventually special buildings were constructed in which to meet every Sabbath (our Saturday). Synagogue services continued to be held even after some Jews returned to Judah and restored the temple sacrifices and worship.

Men sat on the main floor of the synagogue. Women sat on a balcony or behind a screen.

The Jewish elders sat on a high platform along one end of the synagogue, facing the congregation. Behind them, scrolls of the Law lay in a closet, which was often called the ark. The seats of the elders became known as Moses' seat. (See Matthew 23:2.)

The regular Sabbath services in a synagogue included Bible reading, Bible instruction, and prayer. Special services were held on Monday and Thursday, which were market days, for those coming from a distance.

Yehudah Goes to the Synagogue

Some of the sentences in the following story contain errors. Find the sentences with errors, and explain why each is wrong.

1. As always on Sunday morning, Yehudah prepared for the synagogue service. _____
   The Sabbath was on Saturday, not Sunday.

2. Later, Yehudah entered the En-Karim synagogue and sat with his family. _____
   Since the women sat separately, Yehudah would have sat only with his father and any brothers.

3. Several men sat in front on what Yehudah knew as Moses' seat. (Correct)

_____

4. A silver cloud of smoke rose from the altar, where a lamb was being sacrificed. _____

   Sacrifices were not made in a synagogue. People came to read the Law and to pray. _____

5. Yehudah listened while Rabbi Nathan ben Isaac explained a passage of the Scriptures. _____

   (Correct) _____

6. Yehudah hurried outside after the service. He could barely wait to help his father haul firewood

   this beautiful afternoon.   They would never have hauled firewood on the Sabbath. _____

52

Lesson 7. Jesus Serves the Galileans

Two things directed Jesus' actions: His love for God and His love for people. Because He loved God, Jesus always did what was right. Because He loved people, He did everything He could to help them—to free them from sin and to give them peace and joy.

The Jewish leaders did not love others as Jesus did. One example of their lack of love was their treatment of lepers.

God had given instructions about leprosy when He gave laws to the Israelites. He did not want people with leprosy to mingle with those who did not have it. Leprosy in the Old Testament typified sin. But God always loved the lepers themselves. As soon as their leprosy went away, they were to be received back into their homes and towns as ordinary people.

The Jewish leaders did not understand God's laws about leprosy. They went to outrageous extremes to separate themselves from lepers. By doing so, they sinned against God and man and became worse than the lepers themselves.

Jewish rabbis warned people to stay at least 6 feet away from lepers. They said that with a wind blowing, 100 feet was barely enough. One rabbi boasted of not eating an egg bought on a street on which a leper had passed. Another said he always threw stones at lepers to keep them a safe distance away.

Imagine the shock these self-righteous people felt when Jesus walked up to a leper and touched him!

Jesus loved the lepers, just as He loved everyone else. He healed them and welcomed them into God's family. But in doing so, He aroused the wrath of His fellow Jews.

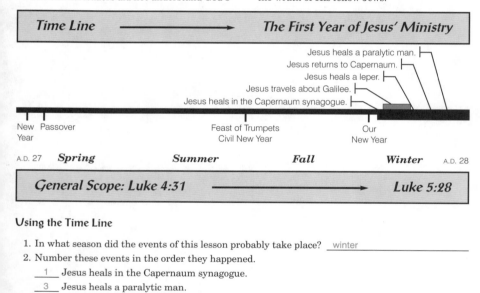

Time Line ⟶ *The First Year of Jesus' Ministry*

Jesus heals a paralytic man.
Jesus returns to Capernaum.
Jesus heals a leper.
Jesus travels about Galilee.
Jesus heals in the Capernaum synagogue.

New Year   Passover   Feast of Trumpets   Our
                          Civil New Year   New Year

A.D. 27   *Spring*   *Summer*   *Fall*   *Winter*   A.D. 28

General Scope: Luke 4:31 ⟶ *Luke 5:28*

Using the Time Line

1. In what season did the events of this lesson probably take place?   winter
2. Number these events in the order they happened.
   <u>1</u> Jesus heals in the Capernaum synagogue.
   <u>3</u> Jesus heals a paralytic man.
   <u>2</u> Jesus travels about Galilee.

Lesson 7

Oral Review

1. Jesus came as the Son of —— and the Son of ——. [L. 3] **God, man**
2. How did King Herod try to destroy Jesus? [L. 3] **He killed all the babies in Bethlehem that were two years old or younger.**
3. What was the message of John the Baptist? [L. 4] **"Repent ye: for the kingdom of heaven is at hand."**
4. How did Jesus show the Samaritans that He loves all people? [L. 5] **He spent two days teaching the Samaritans. (He talked with a Samaritan woman.)**
5. What miracle did Jesus do for a Galilean nobleman? [L. 6] **Jesus healed his son without going to his house.**
6. Why did Jesus move to Capernaum? [L. 6] **The people of Nazareth did not accept Him, but many people in Capernaum did.**
7. Why did Jesus' stories of Elijah and Naaman offend the people of Nazareth? [L. 6] **These stories were about Gentiles who received God's blessing rather than the Jews.**
8. How did synagogue worship differ from temple worship? [L. 6] **Sacrifices were offered in the temple, but not at synagogues.**

A. ANSWERS FROM THE BIBLE

Jesus Proves His Authority

In the last lesson Jesus called Peter, Andrew, James, and John to be His disciples. Soon after this, Jesus and His disciples attended a service in the synagogue at Capernaum.

Mark 1:21–28

1. The scribes were Jewish scholars who recopied and studied the Scriptures. In what way was Jesus' teaching different from theirs? <u>Jesus taught with authority.</u>

2. Who at the synagogue that day knew that Jesus is the Son of God?
   a. the scribes and Pharisees
   (b.) an unclean spirit (demon) within a man
   c. a man possessed with an unclean spirit (demon)
   d. Peter's mother-in-law

3. "Hold thy peace" literally meant "Be muzzled!" What is the only authority powerful enough to command evil spirits to be quiet or to come out of men? <u>the authority of God</u>

4. Jesus always refused to allow the evil spirits to speak about Him or to tell people who He was. Why might Jesus not have wanted the demons to testify about Him?
   a. He did not want the Roman rulers or the scribes and Pharisees to find out who He was.
   b. He was afraid people would find out He was God's Son if He let the demons speak.
   (c.) He did not need or want the testimony of demons.

Jesus Heals in Capernaum

After the synagogue service, Jesus and His friends entered Peter's house. Apparently Peter's mother-in-law lived in the same house as Peter and his wife did. She was sick with a fever.

Mark 1:29–34

5. How did Peter's mother-in-law show good manners and gratitude to Jesus for healing her? <u>After her healing, she served Jesus and the disciples.</u>

6. The Sabbath ended when the sun went down. Then, while lights were being lit throughout Capernaum, "all the city" gathered at Peter's house, bringing the sick to be healed. What might be the reason they waited until sundown instead of bringing them earlier? <u>The Jewish leaders forbade healing on the Sabbath.</u>

7. What did the demons know that the crowd of people did not? <u>that Jesus was the Son of God</u>

Jesus Finds Strength for Service

Jesus is God. He is one with the Father. But while He lived on earth, Jesus was also a man, with many of the same physical limitations that other men have. He became tired and hungry, just like other men. He often took time to pray to God for help and strength to do His day's work.

• After Jesus called the fishermen to be His disciples, He took them back to their hometown of Capernaum to begin His work. This followed God's usual requirement that people begin working for Him at home. Those who cannot live for God and be a good testimony at home are not ready to work for Him elsewhere.

In This Lesson

Scope: Matthew 8:1–4, 14–17; 9:1–8; Mark 1:21–2:13; Luke 4:31–44; 5:12–26

Focus
• This lesson gives examples of Jesus' mercy and service to needy people.
  —Jesus healed a demon-possessed man in the Capernaum synagogue.
  —Jesus healed Peter's mother-in-law of her fever.
  —Jesus ministered to "all the city" who had gathered, by casting out devils and healing the sick.
  —Jesus healed a leper during His travels around Galilee.
  —When a man sick of the palsy was let down through the roof, Jesus forgave his sins and healed his body.

Objectives
• Students should know
  —why Jesus always told evil spirits to be quiet when they testified that He was the Son of God. (*He did not need or want the help of Satan.*)
  —what family relation of Peter's Jesus healed. (*Peter's mother-in-law*)
  —how we know that prayer was important to Jesus. (*At times He rose early or stayed up all night to pray.*)

54   Chapter Two   Acceptance and Rejection

Mark 1:35–39

8. How do we know that this time of prayer was important to Jesus? _____

    Jesus rose early, "a great while before day," to go out to pray.

9. Instead of going back to Capernaum, where everyone was looking for Him, Jesus went on to other towns in Galilee with His disciples. This shows us that
    a. Jesus was afraid of the people of Capernaum.
    b. Jesus was not seeking popularity and the praise of men.
    c. Jesus loved the people in other parts of Galilee more than the people of Capernaum.
    d. Jesus did not realize that the people of Capernaum were looking for Him.

Jesus Cleanses a Leper

Most of the Jews feared leprosy more than they feared death, because a leper was an outcast, hated by everyone. They did not dare to go close to a leper because of the danger of catching leprosy. But Jesus did not fear leprosy and was just as ready to heal a leper as anyone else.

Mark 1:40–45

10. Jesus helped sick people because   He had compassion on them (He loved them)

    _____ .

11. The Jews were still under the Old Testament Law during the time Jesus lived. While He was on earth, He was careful to respect the Law of Moses (but not all the extra laws the Pharisees had invented). Jesus told the cleansed leper to show himself to the priest. By obeying Jesus, the man who had been cleansed
    a. would be kept safe from getting leprosy again.
    b. was making sure he was rid of all the leprosy.
    c. was also respecting the Law of Moses.

12. When the man who had been cleansed went to the priests, it showed them that
    a. it was their responsibility to cleanse him.
    b. Jesus respected the Law of Moses.
    c. all lepers should be cleansed.

13. Jesus did not want the leper to tell others about his healing. Jesus wanted to
    a. avoid doing too many miracles.
    b. make sure only the right kind of people told about His miracles.
    c. be known more for the truths He preached than for His miracles.

14. The leper told many people what Jesus had done. This made things difficult for Jesus because
    a. great crowds of people came just to watch Him do miracles.
    b. people were upset because He had healed a leper.
    c. too many people found out about Him.

Jesus Shows Mercy

The common people of Galilee loved Jesus and believed that He was sent by God. But the Jewish leaders became suspicious of Him. They were upset about Jesus' disregard for their man-made rules.

—what moved Jesus to heal the sick. (*His compassion*)
—why Jesus sent the leper He had healed to the priest. (*The Law of Moses required a priest to certify that a healed leper was clean.*)
—what two things Jesus did for the man sick of the palsy. (*He forgave his sins and healed him.*)
—what Jesus did to a man lowered through a roof to prove that He could forgive sins. (*He healed him.*)

• Students should know the definitions of the following words.
  —ministered (*served*)
  —divers (*various*)
  —noised (*heard or spread*)
  —palsy (*paralysis; partial or complete loss of ability to move or feel*)

Truths to Amplify
• True acts of mercy do not meet the world's approval. Satan is cruel and vengeful. He knows that Jesus' acts of mercy lead toward the salvation of souls. Therefore he opposes them wherever he can.
• Point out the difference between superficial mercy and true mercy. Superficial acts of mercy include material assistance such as food and clothing drives, disaster relief, and other programs for the needy *that are not geared toward bringing people to*

Mark 2:1–13

15. Jesus was probably standing in the interior gallery of a well-to-do home in Capernaum. Making a hole in the roof did not involve actual damage, only the removal of clay tiles. By taking this risk of making themselves look foolish, the sick man's friends proved something about themselves, something Jesus could see. What was it? _____
    They had faith in Jesus. (They also had love and concern for their friend.)

16. The Jews thought sick people were always guilty of sin. They told sick people to repent. What did Jesus say to the man who was sick of the palsy before healing him? _____
    "Son, thy sins be forgiven thee."
    _____
    _____

17. What did Jesus show by forgiving the man's sins before He healed him? _____
    that forgiveness of sins was more important than healing

18. How did Jesus prove to the scribes that He had power to forgive sins?   by healing the man
    _____

The Jews used the flat roofs of their houses for many activities. Stairs on the outside of the house permitted people to climb up without entering the house.

repentance and conversion. True mercy—the kind Jesus showed to the people of Palestine—is not focused upon the physical, but upon the spiritual needs of men. True mercy includes material assistance (James 2:14–16), but it does not see material aid programs as ends in themselves (Matthew 4:4).

56 Chapter Two Acceptance and Rejection

B. BIBLE WORD STUDY

Write the letter of a synonym for the word or words in italics. Choices may be used more than once or not at all. All references are from Mark.

<u>e</u> 1. Jesus *straightway* entered the synagogue (1:21).

<u>b</u> 2. A man with an *unclean spirit* cried out (1:23).

<u>e</u> 3. And *forthwith* when they left the synagogue, Jesus and His disciples went to Simon's house (1:29).

<u>e</u> 4. Simon's mother-in-law was sick, and *anon* they tell Him of her (1:30).

<u>h</u> 5. After Jesus healed her, she *ministered* unto them (1:31).

<u>j</u> 6. Jesus healed many who had *divers* diseases (1:34).

<u>g</u> 7. Jesus *suffered* not the devils to speak (1:34).

<u>a</u> 8. Jesus straitly *charged* the cured leper not to tell any man (1:43).

<u>d</u> 9. It was *noised* that Jesus was in the house (2:1).

<u>f</u> 10. They brought a man sick of the *palsy* (2:3).

a. commanded
b. demon
c. eventually
d. heard; spread
e. immediately
f. paralysis; partial or complete loss of ability to move or feel
g. permitted
h. served
i. strange
j. various

• *Straightway* (Mark 1:21), *forthwith* (1:29), and *anon* (1:30) are all translated from the same Greek word. Mark uses this word as often as all the other New Testament writers combined.

C. THINKING ABOUT BIBLE TRUTHS

God's Love for Man

God loves all men. Because of His love for man and His hatred for sin, God sent His Son to provide a way for anyone to be delivered from sin. So it is no surprise that Jesus ministered to the needs of men during His earthly ministry. Jesus' compassion on the sick, the lonely, the downcast, and the repentant sinners proves how much God cares about our everyday needs.

1. From each of the following verses in the Book of Mark, write *in your own words* something that Jesus said or did which proves that He loves man.
   a. Mark 1:23–26 He cast unclean spirits out of people.
   b. Mark 1:41 He touched a leper.
   c. Mark 2:5 He forgave sins.
   d. Mark 2:15 He ate with publicans and sinners.
   e. Mark 4:37–39 He calmed a storm that threatened to sink the ship.
   f. Mark 5:35, 41, 42 He raised people from the dead.
   g. Mark 6:34 He taught the people many things.
   h. Mark 8:1–8 He fed hungry people.

2. God showed His love for man through His Son. According to 1 John 4:9, it was because of God's love that He sent His Son into the world, that we might live through Him .

3. Read 1 John 3:1. Because of God's love, He made it possible for all mankind to become _____ sons of God .

D. LEARNING MORE ABOUT BIBLE TIMES

Sickness in Bible Times

Sick people know they need help. Jesus said, "They that are whole need not a physician; but they that are sick" (Luke 5:31). Many sick people believed on Jesus and were healed. A few common sicknesses are described below.

A common sickness in Jesus' time was malaria. Mosquitoes that spread the disease lived in swamps and in irrigated gardens around cities. Malaria caused high fever and usually death. Other types of **fevers** were also common.

People with heart, liver, or kidney problems were often afflicted with a symptom called **dropsy**. Their bodies slowly filled with fluid until they died.

Infections of the brain or spinal cord caused **palsy**. People with palsy often became paralyzed in their arms and legs, and sometimes they lost their speech or hearing.

Blindness was a common physical problem in the Middle East. Bright sunlight, heat, dust, and unclean living habits brought on eye infections that caused blindness.

Physicians used oil and wine to clean wounds, and they used herbs to treat sickness.

Look up the references and tell what disease Jesus healed in each of these cases.

1. The centurion's servant (Matthew 8:5–13) <u>palsy</u>
2. Peter's mother-in-law (Mark 1:30, 31) <u>fever</u>
3. Bartimaeus (Mark 10:46–52) <u>blindness</u>
4. A Pharisee's guest (Luke 14:1–4) <u>dropsy</u>

Jesus' Ministry in Galilee

Jesus traveled about Galilee, healing people and teaching in the synagogues. Sometimes He traveled outside Galilee, into Gentile territory. But He returned to Galilee as His home base.

From the following information, find names for the blank spaces on the map below.

1. Jesus' boyhood home (Matthew 2:19–23)
2. A widow's son raised to life (Luke 7:11–17)
3. Water changed to wine (John 2:1–11)
4. Peter's mother-in-law healed (Matthew 8:5, 14, 15)
5. A blind man healed (Mark 8:22–26)
6. A Syrophenician woman's daughter healed (Matthew 15:21–28)
7. Peter's great confession (Matthew 16:13–20)

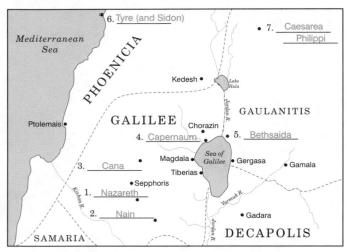

Galilee at the Time of Christ

59

Lesson 8. The Sabbath and the Pharisees

During the second year of His ministry, Jesus was very popular with the common people. But Jewish leaders were already starting to oppose Jesus and His teachings. Before the year was over, they were making plans to kill Him.

The longer Jesus taught and ministered to people, the more the Jewish leaders disagreed with Him. They thought Jews should live to keep the Law. Jesus lived to help people.

The conflict between Jesus and the Jewish leaders became especially noticeable when He helped people on the Sabbath. God had given the Israelites commandments about keeping the Sabbath. But the Jews had added hundreds of their own rules and interpretations to the commandments of the Law. These rules became a central part of the Jews' religion. The Jewish leaders, and especially the Pharisees, were upset when Jesus did not obey their rules. They did not want to understand when He tried to show them God's true purpose for the Sabbath.

Because the extra Sabbath laws violated God's purpose for the Sabbath, Jesus could not please the Jews and obey God's will at the same time. As God's Son, Jesus had the authority to say what should be done on the Sabbath. But Jesus did not become involved in long arguments with the Jews over the Sabbath. He fulfilled God's will by simply continuing to do good to everyone, every day. Many of the common people were glad for His ministry.

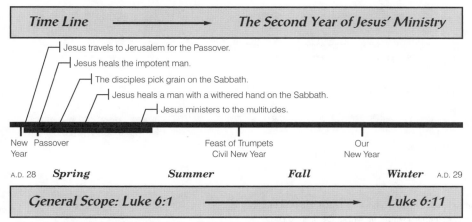

Time Line ⟶ **The Second Year of Jesus' Ministry**

Jesus travels to Jerusalem for the Passover.
Jesus heals the impotent man.
The disciples pick grain on the Sabbath.
Jesus heals a man with a withered hand on the Sabbath.
Jesus ministers to the multitudes.

| New Year | Passover | | Feast of Trumpets Civil New Year | Our New Year | |
| A.D. 28 | *Spring* | *Summer* | *Fall* | *Winter* | A.D. 29 |

General Scope: Luke 6:1 ⟶ **Luke 6:11**

Note: Some people think the feast mentioned in John 5 was a fall feast rather than the Passover. This workbook follows the more common chronology on this question, but neither argument can be proved.

Using the Time Line

1. During which season did grain ripen in Palestine? <u>spring</u>
2. According to the time line (and the order of events in the Gospels), did Jesus heal the man with the withered hand before or after His disciples plucked grain? <u>after</u>

Lesson 8

Oral Review

1. Which Gospels record Christ's birth? [L. 1] **Matthew, Luke**
2. Why did Mary wonder how she could be the mother of the Messiah? [L. 2] **She was not married.**
3. Who were Jesus' brothers? [L. 3] **James, Joses, Simon, and Judas**
4. Where did Jesus go immediately after He was baptized? [L. 5] **into the wilderness to be tempted by Satan**
5. How did Jesus overcome Satan's temptations? [L. 5] **He quoted the Scriptures.**
6. What did the people of Nazareth try to do to Jesus after He preached to them in their synagogue? [L. 6] **They tried to throw Him over the brow of a hill and kill Him.**
7. Why did Jesus always tell evil spirits to be quiet when they testified that He is the Son of God? [L. 7] **He did not need or want Satan's help.**
8. What moved Jesus to heal the sick? [L. 7] **He had compassion on them.**

At Bethesda helpless lying,
For relief and healing sighing
Neither living, neither dying,
Lay a beggar in despair,

     Till one day a seeking Saviour
     Spoke a word of love and favor,
     "Friend, arise and do not waver,
     I have come to give you life."

        Hear the Voice of Hope come winging,
        Setting stifled hearts to singing,
        Holy peace and purpose bringing:
        "I have come to give you life!"

           —Margaret Penner Toews
          From *Five Loaves and Two Small Fish*

A. ANSWERS FROM THE BIBLE

After spending about four months in Galilee, Jesus and His disciples went up to Jerusalem for the feast of the Passover. This was the second Passover since Jesus' baptism and marked the beginning of the second full year of His ministry.

Healing on the Sabbath Day

Jesus' disregard for the man-made Sabbath regulations probably infuriated the Pharisees more than anything else He did. However, Jesus showed that it is God's will for man to always do good—even on the Sabbath.

John 5:1–16

1. In order to be healed, the sick man seemed to think Jesus would need to
   a. tell him to get up and walk.
   b. tell someone to help him.
   c. help him get into the water.

2. The healed man carried his bed on the Sabbath Day because
   a. he had confidence in the Person who told him to carry it.
   b. he did not know it was the Sabbath Day.
   c. he did not care about the Sabbath Day.

3. Jesus used the example of the man's healing to teach him an important truth. He told him
   a. to be careful not to get sick again because his sickness would be worse the second time.
   b. his infirmity had been sent as a punishment for his sinfulness.
   c. the punishment for sinning would be worse than the infirmity from which he had been healed.

Choose all the correct answers for number 4.

4. The Law of Moses was given for the good of God's people. The fact that the Jews were offended by what Jesus had done on the Sabbath shows that they
   a. did not understand Moses' Law.
   b. did not understand how God's people were to help each other.
   c. understood the Sabbath better than Jesus did.
   d. liked their own rules better than God's rules.

In This Lesson

Scope: Matthew 12:1–21; Mark 2:23–3:12; Luke 6:1–11; John 5

Focus

- Jesus addressed the issue of God's will concerning keeping the Sabbath.
  —Jesus healed on the Sabbath because it is right to do good on the Sabbath. (It is sin when one fails to do the good that he could. See James 4:17.)
- Jesus reproved the Pharisees for not recognizing Him as being Lord of the Sabbath and greater than Moses.
  —Jesus defended the disciples' right to pluck grain on the Sabbath to satisfy their hunger. He said that the Sabbath was made for man, and not man for the Sabbath.
  —The Pharisees criticized Jesus and rejected His teaching about the Sabbath. They considered their rules more important than Jesus' teachings. Instead of repenting at Jesus' reproof, they turned against Him and sought to kill Him.
  —After the Jewish leaders rejected Him, Jesus ministered to the multitudes of common people and Gentiles who followed Him.
  —A brief study of sample Jewish Sabbath laws shows how burdensome they had become and why Jesus openly rejected them.

Reproving the Pharisees

John 5:17–47 records a discourse between Jesus and the Pharisees, in which Jesus tried to explain to them why He had the authority to ignore the man-made Sabbath laws. However, the Pharisees were not willing to listen to Jesus. Instead, they looked for a way to kill Him.

John 5:17–20, 31–47

5. How did Jesus know that God approved of what He was doing when He healed people on the Sabbath Day? __He had seen God the Father do good on the Sabbath Day. (See 5:19, 20. Give credit__ __for reasonable answers that show clear thinking.)__

6. Jesus told the Pharisees that He was not just making these claims Himself. He pointed out that (a) ___John (the Baptist)___ had told them who He was. Also the (b) ___works___ that He did were evidence of who He was. They also had the evidence of (c) ___God (the Father)___, who had spoken at His baptism and had been speaking through Him ever since. Besides all this, the (d) ___Scriptures___ also testified of Him. However, the Pharisees refused to accept these evidences because they did not have God's love within them.

7. The Pharisees proudly claimed to be followers of Moses. But Jesus told them that their belief in Moses made them more accountable to God for rejecting Him. This was because
   (a.) Moses had written about the Messiah (Jesus), yet the Pharisees refused to accept Jesus' words.
   b. Moses was the Messiah, but the Jews had failed to realize it.
   c. Moses had never written about the coming Messiah.

Plucking Grain on the Sabbath

It is obvious that this event took place during the spring, when the grain was ready for harvest. Some people think that "the second sabbath after the first" (Luke 6:1) refers to the first or second Sabbath after the Passover.

Matthew 12:1–8

8. The Old Testament does not forbid the picking and eating of grain on the Sabbath. Why did the Pharisees believe it was unlawful? (If you need help, read the lesson introduction again.)
   (a.) The Pharisees were obeying extra laws that they had made.
   b. The Pharisees did not have personal copies of the Law of Moses. Therefore they did not know exactly what the Law said.

9. How did Jesus prove to the Pharisees that God's Law is to be used for the people's good?
   a. Jesus quoted a passage from the Book of Leviticus.
   (b.) Jesus used the example of David and the shewbread.

10. Jesus quoted the Scripture passage, "I will have mercy, and not sacrifice." How would a good understanding of this teaching have kept the Jews from condemning the guiltless?
    a. If the Jews had understood this Scripture passage, they would have stopped sacrificing animals and started being kind to people.
    (b.) If the Jews had understood this Scripture passage, they would have known that God wanted them to have compassion for the needs of others rather than an overemphasis on detailed laws.

11. Jesus had the authority to say what was lawful on the Sabbath because He was ___Lord___ of the Sabbath.

Objectives
- Students should know
  —why the Pharisees were upset when Jesus healed on the Sabbath. (*He was ignoring their Sabbath laws.*)
  —why Jesus had authority to say what was lawful on the Sabbath. (*He was Lord of the Sabbath.*)
  —what kind of deeds Jesus said were lawful on the Sabbath. (*good deeds*)
  —what law of God the Pharisees broke by trying to stop Jesus from healing on the Sabbath. (*God's law requiring them to show mercy and love*)
  —how Jesus found strength to do His work. (*He spent much time in prayer.*)

—which Old Testament prophet foretold that the Gentiles would trust in Jesus. (*Isaiah*)
—when the Jewish Sabbath began and ended. (*It began at sunset on Friday and ended at sunset on Saturday.*)
—what Jesus meant when He said, "The sabbath was made for man, and not man for the sabbath." (*God meant the Sabbath for man's refreshment, not as a burden to him.*)

62 Chapter Two Acceptance and Rejection

Healing a Withered Hand on the Sabbath

Matthew, Mark, and Luke all record another Sabbath incident immediately after the account of the disciples plucking grain. In Matthew and Mark, it could appear that both of these events took place on the same Sabbath, but Luke states that they occurred on different Sabbaths. We must remember that only a few of Jesus' many works are recorded in the Gospels. (See John 20:30, 31; 21:25.) This next recorded incident may have occurred on the next Sabbath, or on a Sabbath later in the spring or summer of Jesus' second year of ministry.

Jesus could have tried to please the unbelieving Jews by observing all their unnecessary rules. But as the Light of the world, He had come to expose sin and error rather than to help cover it up. He took this opportunity to try to help them to see their mistake. But again, they hated Him so much that they paid no attention to what He said.

Luke 6:6–12 (Matthew 12:9–14; Mark 3:1–6)

12. What did the scribes and Pharisees think Jesus might do to the man with the withered hand?
They thought Jesus might heal the man on the Sabbath.

Instead of healing the man immediately, Jesus asked the scribes and Pharisees if it was lawful to do good on the Sabbath (Mark 3:4). He pointed out that they themselves considered it lawful to care for animals on the Sabbath, and asked, "How much then is a man better than a sheep?" (Matthew 12:11, 12).

13. Why did Jesus look on these self-righteous men in anger? (Mark 3:5) _____
He was grieved at the hardness of their hearts.

14. What did Jesus teach them by not waiting till the following day to heal the man?
    a. Jesus taught them that all rules made by man are bad, and that each person should decide for himself what God wants him to do.
    (b) Jesus taught them that God's laws of mercy and love are more important than the unreasonable rules they had added.

15. In Matthew 12:12, Jesus gave the true meaning of God's Law regarding the Sabbath. He said, "It is lawful to do well on the sabbath days
_____."

16. How were the Pharisees breaking God's Law by trying to forbid Jesus to heal the man's hand?
    (a) The Pharisees were breaking the part of God's Law about showing mercy and love to other people.
    b. The Pharisees did not believe that God wanted sick people to be healed.

17. Instead of admitting their sinful attitudes and repenting, the Pharisees opposed Jesus even more strongly. How did they feel, according to Luke 6:11? _____
They were filled with madness.

18. Where did Jesus find strength to keep on teaching as He faced men who were seeking to destroy Him? Jesus spent many hours in prayer alone with God.
_____

Ministering to the Multitudes

By now the Pharisees hated Jesus so much that they also condemned the good deeds He did on the other days of the week. Because of their counsel against Him, Jesus withdrew to the Sea of Galilee (perhaps to the far side, which was Gentile territory) for a while (Mark 3:7). But at this time Jesus was still popular among the common people, and great crowds followed Him wherever He went.

Truths to Amplify

- As the Son of God, Jesus had every right to challenge the perverted Sabbath laws. The Jews' problem went beyond the keeping of the Sabbath—it involved a self-righteous religion that shut out anyone who was not part of their race and culture. In response to Jesus' message of love and mercy, the Pharisees condemned Him and associated Him with the devil. In this context we have the prophecy that "he shall shew judgment to the Gentiles" and "in his name shall the Gentiles trust."

- Although Jesus needed to reprove the Jewish leaders' abuse of authority, He always upheld the proper use and respect for authority. He told His disciples to give even the corrupt leaders the respect due to their position (Matthew 23:1–3). The only valid reason for refusing to obey leaders is when obedience to them would violate a higher law. In such cases, "we ought to obey God rather than men" (Acts 5:29).

- We must maintain proper attitudes toward present-day applications of Scriptural principles. History shows that churches who make no practical applications soon lose the Scriptural principles. However, those who allow applications to become an end in themselves also lose the principles, and all that remains is a form of godliness void of power. "Whether therefore ye eat, or drink, or whatsoever ye do, do all to the glory of God" (1 Corinthians 10:31).

Lesson 8. The Sabbath and the Pharisees   **63**

Matthew 12:14–21

19. From the context of these verses, Jesus evidently withdrew into Gentile territory. What three verses in the Old Testament did this fulfill? *(Use a concordance to find the reference. Esaias is the Greek form of Isaiah.)*   Isaiah 42:1–3

20. a. According to Matthew 12:14–21, what would Jesus do for the Gentiles? _____

    He would show judgment to the Gentiles.

    b. What would the Gentiles do with Jesus? _____

    The Gentiles would trust in His Name.

Reeds were used for writing. When they cracked, they were crumpled up and thrown away. Wicks of flax carried the flame of Jewish lamps. When they became so small that the flame died out and they only smoked, people snuffed them out and destroyed them. This prophecy compares the people Jesus worked with to such reeds and flax.

21. The prophecy foretold that the Gentiles would trust Jesus because He would treat people with

    a. severity and partiality.

    (b.) justice and gentleness.

B. BIBLE WORD STUDY

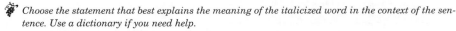

Choose the statement that best explains the meaning of the italicized word in the context of the sentence. Use a dictionary if you need help.

1. A multitude of *impotent* folk were at the pool of Bethesda (John 5:3).

    (a.) The crowd consisted of people who were feeble and sick.

    b. The group included people who were angry at Jesus for healing on the Sabbath.

    c. The crowd were people who were unable to restrain themselves.

2. Jesus pointed out that the priests could *profane* the Sabbath without being guilty (Matthew 12:5).

    a. The priests were allowed to swear on the Sabbath Day.

    (b.) The Law allowed priests to do physical work on the Sabbath Day in performing ceremonies.

    c. The priest could perform unholy ceremonies on the Sabbath Day without being punished.

3. On the Sabbath Day, Jesus healed a man who had a *withered* hand (Luke 6:6).

    a. The man's hand had been cut off in an accident.

    b. The man's hand had changed color because of age.

    (c.) The man's hand was shriveled and dry.

4. The Pharisees held a *council* against Jesus after He healed on the Sabbath Day (Matthew 12:14).

    (a.) The Pharisees gathered together to discuss what to do with Jesus.

    b. The Pharisees asked the Romans for advice on what to do with Jesus.

    c. The Pharisees gathered to pray about what to do with Jesus.

5. The Pharisees *communed* with each other to decide what to do about Jesus (Luke 6:11).

    a. The Pharisees held a Communion service at the synagogue.

    b. The Pharisees wrote letters to each other to get advice.

    (c.) The Pharisees talked the matter over with each other.

C. THINKING ABOUT BIBLE TRUTHS

The Sabbath

Jesus refused to be bound by the unnecessary rules of the self-righteous Pharisees, but He always kept God's Law in the way that God had intended for it to be kept. As God's Son, He knew better than any other man what God's will was for the Sabbath.

1. When and how did God establish the very first Sabbath? _____
   God established the Sabbath at the end of the first week by resting from His work of creating all things.

2. Read Exodus 31:12–17.
   a. Why did God want His people to set one day apart from their normal routine? _____
      It was to be a sign of the covenant between God and His people.
   b. What did God say that His people should not do on the Sabbath?   work

3. a. Read Isaiah 58:13, 14. Why did God want His people to rest from their work and from seeking their own pleasures and goals on the Sabbath? _____
      God wanted them to keep it as a holy day and to delight in Him.
   b. Were the Pharisees' extra rules for the Sabbath a help in fulfilling God's purpose for the Sabbath? Give a reason for your answer.   No. (Sample reasons) Instead of helping people
      delight in God's will on the Sabbath, the extra rules burdened people and kept the Sabbath from
      being the blessing that God had intended. Many people whom the Pharisees condemned for
      breaking the Sabbath were actually innocent in God's sight.

4. The Old Testament Law required the priest to perform certain ceremonies on the Sabbath. The Pharisees allowed this temple work because they believed the temple was more important than the Sabbath. What did Jesus prove to them by saying, "In this place is one greater than the temple"? (Matthew 12:5, 6)   If the temple was greater than the Sabbath and Jesus was greater than
   the temple, then He was greater than the Sabbath. Therefore He had the right to say how God should
   be honored on the Sabbath.

Some of these questions may be difficult for seventh grade students. Do these exercises together in class if possible.

D. LEARNING MORE ABOUT BIBLE TIMES

The Jews' Sabbath

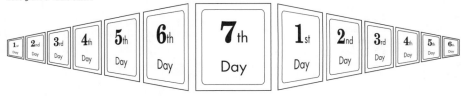

Jewish Beliefs About the Sabbath

During the centuries just before and after Christ, Jewish rabbis wrote down many traditions regarding the Sabbath. These rules, along with Jewish traditions on many other subjects, were compiled into books that are still considered important by modern Orthodox Jews. Some of these traditions were written by rabbis after the time of Christ, but many were already being practiced during Jesus' ministry. This section discusses a few examples of the Jewish rules concerning the Sabbath.

The Jews believed that the week consisted of six days. The Sabbath was not really considered part of the week. It was an extra day, a day of joy and rest when one avoided work and engaged in activities that made the day a pleasure. Since the Jews counted days from sunset to sunset, the Sabbath began at sunset on Friday evening and ended at sunset on Saturday evening.

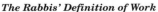

A Jewish leader announced the beginning of the Sabbath when the sun went down. He blew a ram's horn three times and then laid it down. It was now the Sabbath, and unlawful to carry anything.

The Rabbis' Definition of Work

The rabbis listed thirty-nine main categories of work that were not permitted on the Sabbath Day. Some of these were sowing seed, plowing, reaping, binding sheaves, threshing, sifting, grinding, kneading, baking, shearing wool, spinning, weaving, tying a knot, undoing a knot, sewing two stitches, hunting, killing, skinning, preparing hides, cutting leather, writing two letters of the alphabet, building, lighting or putting out a fire, and carrying belongings from place to place outside the home. Each of the thirty-nine main kinds of work had an almost infinite number of interpretations and applications.

For instance, anything to do with agriculture, such as picking a blade of grass, was considered sinful. Cutting off a mushroom was doubly sinful because that might cause another one to spring up in its place. Chairs could be lifted from one place to another, but not dragged, lest they plow furrows in the soil.

Fishing on the Sabbath fell under the sin of harvesting. Rolling wheat kernels came under the sin of sifting. Rubbing the end of a stalk of wheat made one guilty of threshing. Bruising a stalk of wheat fell under the sin of grinding.

Carrying liquids on the Sabbath was restricted to a mouthful of milk, a cup of wine, and as much oil as it takes to anoint one's littlest toe. Nothing useful could be carried, such as two horsehairs that could be made into a snare for birds, or a scrap of paper big enough to be used as a customs receipt, or enough ink with which to write two letters of the alphabet, or a fragment of pottery big enough to use for stirring coals.

The rabbis considered it a sin to heal on the Sabbath. Helping the sick or wounded was allowed only if life was in danger. The only medicines permitted for use on the Sabbath were those that would keep a wound from getting worse.

A person was not allowed to examine his clothing before putting it on because he might be tempted to commit the sin of squashing an insect with his finger. Neither was he allowed to read after dark on the Sabbath, because he might be tempted to commit the sin of moving his lamp.

- The pupil's book gives only a few examples of Jewish Sabbath laws. See Appendix 17 in *The Life and Times of Jesus the Messiah* for additional ones. In this appendix, Edersheim notes, "Through 64½ folio columns in the Jerusalem [Talmud], and 156 double pages of folio in the Babylon Talmud does the enumeration and discussion of possible cases drag on." No wonder Jesus said, "Woe unto you also, ye lawyers! for ye lade men with burdens grievous to be borne" (Luke 11:46).

Exceptions to the Rules

As the rabbis multiplied the number of Sabbath rules, it became increasingly difficult to keep all of them. To make them more bearable, exceptions were made in certain cases. Often these exceptions illustrate how ridiculous the system of Sabbath rules had become.

The rabbis said that on the Sabbath it was permissible to walk only inside one's home or a distance not more than 2,000 cubits away from home. This was called a "sabbath day's journey" (Acts 1:12). But if a wire or a rope was stretched out from one's dwelling place, it was considered as part of the dwelling, and one could count 2,000 cubits from the end of it. If, on the day before the Sabbath, articles of food were placed at 2,000 cubit intervals, one could keep walking from one to another. Each item of food was considered to mark a temporary "home."

All the Sabbath laws were supposedly based on the Scriptures. But besides these "Scriptural" commands, the rabbis also had rules that they admitted were not directly in the Bible. They enforced these rules to show due respect for the Sabbath and to prevent people from being led in the direction of sin. Examples of this kind of Sabbath rule include the following rules in case of a house fire on the Sabbath. The owner could rescue scrolls of the Scriptures, enough food to last through the Sabbath, and the clothes that he was wearing. While rescuing clothes from a burning house, the owner could put on one garment, take it outside and remove it, reenter the house to put on another garment, walk outside and take it off, reenter the house, and so forth.

1. At what time of day did the Sabbath begin and end? __at sunset__

2. When Jesus' disciples plucked and ate grain on the Sabbath, which of these laws did they disregard? __the laws against harvesting, sifting, and threshing__

3. Which other Sabbath rules described above did Jesus openly disregard? _____
   Jesus healed the sick on the Sabbath, and He told a man to carry his bed.

4. Which Sabbath laws do you think would have been especially difficult to obey? _____
   (Answers will vary.)

5. Jesus rebuked those who insisted on keeping the extremely detailed Sabbath rules by saying, "The sabbath was made for man, and not man for the sabbath" (Mark 2:27).

   a. Considering God's original purpose for the Sabbath, how had He meant it to be a day for the service of man? __It was to be a day for the refreshment of man, both physically and spiritually.__

   b. How did the Pharisees make the Sabbath a day for man to serve? _____
   They made it burdensome with all their rules. Men actually had to "work" to keep it.

67

Lesson 9. Jesus Calls Believers

Life was no longer what it had once been for the Jews of Palestine. Now they were under Roman power, and the Romans ruled Palestine with a strong hand.

The Jews' ideas often clashed with the Romans' ideas. Even the Jews' glorious temple at Jerusalem bore the marks of Roman domination. Godless King Herod, who built it, also built an amphitheater in Jerusalem. He placed a golden vine (the symbol of Israel) over the temple's holy of holies. He also placed a golden eagle (the symbol of Rome, and a "graven image") over the temple's main gate. For these and similar deeds, the Jews hated the Romans. Above all, they hated paying Roman taxes.

To collect their taxes, Roman officials placed publicans (tax collectors) along main roads and on bridges. All who passed by had to stop, let the publican look at their things, and pay whatever tax he demanded. The Romans did not care how much the publican charged, as long as they received the amount they wanted.

Many publicans were dishonest. They overcharged and mistreated people. The Jews hated them with a passion. Publicans who were Jews were put out of the synagogue. Many of their fellow Jews thought it sinful to pay them money.

Jesus loved the publicans just as much as He loved anyone else. He wanted everyone to enjoy a life of true righteousness as He taught in the Sermon on the Mount. Some publicans were glad to hear about this new life and wished to repent. Jesus could help these true seekers more than He could help the self-righteous, proud Pharisees, who thought they did not need to repent.

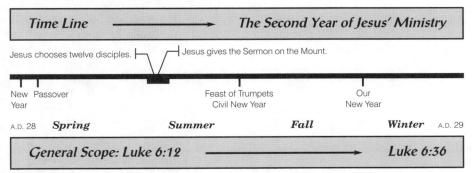

Note: It is uncertain when Christ called Matthew (Levi) and when Matthew served his feast. These events are covered in this lesson with the call of the twelve disciples, but they are not necessarily in chronological order.

Using the Time Line

1. Did Jesus choose His twelve disciples before or after He gave the Sermon on the Mount? _____
   before

2. We do not know for sure when these events took place, but if the time line above is correct, they happened during which season? summer

Lesson 9

Oral Review

1. The Jews thought that the Messiah would be only for themselves. God wanted them to understand that He would be for . . . [L. 2] **all people, including the Gentiles.**

2. What did John the Baptist eat and wear? [L. 4] **He ate locusts and wild honey. He wore clothes made from camels' hair, and a leather belt.**

3. How did God the Father and God the Holy Spirit manifest themselves at Jesus' baptism? [L. 4] **God the Father said, "This is my beloved Son, in whom I am well pleased." The Holy Spirit descended upon Jesus in the form of a dove.**

4. How did Jesus spread the Good News in Galilee? [L. 6] **He traveled about and preached in the synagogues.**

5. After Jesus healed a leper, what did He tell him to do? [L. 7] **Jesus told him to go and show himself to the priest.**

6. Name two things Jesus did for the man sick of the palsy. [L. 7] **He forgave his sins and healed him.**

A. ANSWERS FROM THE BIBLE

Jesus Calls a Publican

Walking along the seashore in Galilee, Jesus found Himself among the busy traffic on the Roman road that ran from Damascus to Egypt. Beside the road stood the hated tax booths. Pack animals had to stop there. All packs were opened. Men and boys fourteen years old and upward had to pay a tax. Women above twelve years of age did likewise. There was a tax on every axle that passed the booth, a tax on pedestrians, a tax on wheels, a tax for using bridges, and a tax on a vast variety of goods being transported.

Jesus saw the activity at the booth. He understood the muttered curses, the lifted eyebrows, and the sly passing of money under tables. But Jesus also saw Levi (Matthew), a Jewish publican who was ready for a new life.

Tax Collector at Work

Mark 2:14–17

1. Why was it most unusual in the Jews' eyes for Jesus to ask Levi to follow Him? (If you need help, read the lesson introduction again.) <u>Levi was a publican (tax collector).</u>
   <u>The Jews hated publicans and considered them to be</u>
   <u>sinners.</u>

2. What did Levi do that shows he had great faith in Jesus? _____
   <u>Levi left his business and followed Jesus.</u>

3. What did other publicans and sinners do that shows their confidence in Jesus? _____
   <u>Many publicans and sinners followed Jesus and ate with Him.</u>

4. What did the scribes and Pharisees say when they saw Jesus eating with Levi and his friends?
   <u>"How is it that he eateth and drinketh with publicans and sinners?"</u>

5. Jesus replied, "They that are (a) <u>whole</u> have no need of the (b) <u>physician</u>, but they that are (c) <u>sick</u>: I came not to call the (d) <u>righteous</u>, but (e) <u>sinners</u> to repentance."

6. In Jesus' answer to the Pharisees, who were the "whole," who were the "sick," and who was the "physician"? <u>The "whole" were the Pharisees, the "sick" were the publicans and sinners, and the</u>
   <u>"physician" was Jesus.</u>

Jesus Calls the Twelve Disciples

Jesus had many disciples, but out of these He now chose twelve to be His close companions. These twelve He called apostles. The Bible also refers to them as the twelve disciples. From now on their time with Him was a period of training for the great work of establishing and leading the church.

Luke 6:12–16

7. Jesus spent the entire night in prayer before He chose the twelve disciples. Why might He have done this? <u>(Sample answer) Choosing the apostles was a very important matter. These men would</u>
   <u>be the ones that would establish the church after He was gone, and He wanted to be sure that the</u>
   <u>choice was God's will.</u>

- The first three Gospels all place Matthew's call and his feast immediately after the healing of the man lowered through a house roof. However, if the three accounts are compared, Matthew 9 seems to indicate that the raising of Jairus's daughter took place on the day of Matthew's feast. Mark and Luke record the raising of Jairus's daughter somewhat later.

  One possible explanation is that some time passed between Jesus' call to Matthew and Matthew's feast, and that the Gospels record his feast immediately after his call to keep the two incidents together. The important point is not the exact order of events, but that Matthew answered the call by forsaking his old life and following Jesus.

- Note that Jesus is looking at this from the perspective of the Pharisees. In His eyes the Pharisees were as needy as anyone else.

---

7. Whose laws were the disciples disobeying when they plucked grain on the Sabbath to eat? [L. 8] **the laws of the scribes and Pharisees**

8. Why did Jesus have the authority to say what was lawful on the Sabbath? [L. 8] **He was Lord of the Sabbath (and the Son of God).**

In This Lesson

Scope: Matthew 5:1–44; 9:9–13; Mark 2:14–22; 3:13–19; Luke 5:27–39; 6:12–36

Focus

- Jesus came to call people to a new life of righteousness. His call was heard by those who felt their need.

—Jesus called Matthew the publican.
—Jesus called twelve apostles to help Him.
—Jesus instructed the multitudes.
—In the Sermon on the Mount, Jesus established a higher standard of righteousness for His followers than that of the Law of Moses.

8. Write the names of the twelve disciples (as given in Luke 6:13–16) and memorize them.

a. _____Simon Peter_____   g. _____Matthew_____

b. _____Andrew_____   h. _____Thomas_____

c. _____James_____   i. _James the son of Alphaeus_

d. _____John_____   j. _____Simon Zelotes_____

e. _____Philip_____   k. _Judas the brother of James_

f. _____Bartholomew_____   l. _____Judas Iscariot_____

9. The list of disciples given in Mark 3:16–19 is slightly different. Apparently the Thaddaeus in Mark's list was the same man as the one Luke calls (a) _Judas the brother of James_. Matthew was also called (b) _____Levi_____ , at least before he was a disciple (compare Matthew 9:9 and Mark 2:14). Some people also think that Bartholomew was the same man as Nathanael (John 1:45; 21:2), but this is not certain.

10. The apostles helped Jesus establish the Christian church by

   (a.) spreading Jesus' teachings.

   b. making sure that Jesus went to many towns.

   c. bringing many people to hear Jesus.

The Sermon on the Mount

   God gave the Old Testament Law, speaking from Mount Sinai. Jesus gave new laws, also speaking from a mountain. His laws called people to a new life of righteousness. They are called the Sermon on the Mount.

   This marked the beginning of a new era in the life of the apostles. The principles that Jesus taught them in the Sermon on the Mount were the foundation of the church they would eventually help to establish in Jesus' Name.

Matthew 5:1–12

11. Jesus outlined His teachings in ten statements (5:3–12). About fifteen hundred years earlier, God had also outlined His teachings for Israel in ten statements. God's ten Old Testament statements (the Ten Commandments) emphasized the things the Israelites were not to do. Jesus' ten New Testament statements (the Beatitudes) emphasize

   a. what happens when one disobeys.

   (b.) the blessings of obedience.

   c. the foolishness of living in sin.

12. Read Matthew 5:17. Jesus did not come to break the laws God had given His Old Testament family. He came to fulfill them and to strengthen them. For example, Jesus strengthened one Old Testament teaching by

   (a.) including the sin of being angry in the command not to kill (Matthew 5:21, 22).

   b. saying that one cannot add one cubit onto one's stature (Matthew 6:27).

   c. teaching about the birds not sowing or reaping (Matthew 6:26).

13. Jesus was more obedient to the spirit of the Law of Moses than the Pharisees were because He

   a. dressed according to Old Testament rules.

   b. preached more about the Law.

   (c.) had genuine love for all men.

• Note that Nathanael is mentioned among the apostles in John 21:2. However, the lists that give all twelve apostles do not use this name. It is quite possible that he, like Levi, can be identified with one of the names in Luke 6:13–16. Bartholomew is the most likely candidate (though perhaps not the only one). Nathanael is mentioned only in John, whereas John never mentions Bartholomew. In addition, both Nathanael and Bartholomew are associated with Andrew.

Objectives

• Students should know

   —why the Jews disliked the publicans. (*They were tax collectors, and they often overcharged the people.*)

   —which apostle was a tax collector before Jesus called him. (*Levi, who was also called Matthew*)

   —the meaning of *disciple* and of *apostle*. (*disciple: one who follows another to learn from him; apostle: one who is sent with a message*)

   —what Matthew's other name was. (*Levi*)

   —why Jesus was criticized when He went to Levi's house. (*Levi was a publican and was considered a sinner.*)

   —the names of the twelve disciples. (*Simon Peter, Andrew, James, John, Philip, Bartholomew, Matthew, Thomas, James the son of Alphaeus, Simon Zelotes, Judas the brother of James, Judas Iscariot*)

   —what we call Jesus' sermon of new laws recorded in Matthew 5–7. (*the Sermon on the Mount*)

   —what we call the ten points Jesus gave near the beginning of the Sermon on the Mount. (*the Beatitudes*)

   —what Jesus told His followers to do for their enemies. (*He told them to love their enemies, bless them, and pray for them.*)

14. What name do we give to the new laws that Jesus gave on the mountain? __the Sermon on the__ __Mount ("The Beatitudes" is also an acceptable answer, since the Scripture reference for this section__ includes only the first part of the Sermon.)

Matthew 5:21, 22, 33, 34, 38, 39, 43, 44

15. Instead of saying, "Thou shalt not kill," Jesus said, "Whosoever is (a) _____angry_____ with his (b) _____brother_____ without a cause shall be in (c) _____danger_____ of the (d) _____judgment_____."

16. Instead of saying, "Thou shalt not forswear thyself," Jesus said, (a) "_____Swear_____ not at (b) _____all_____."

17. Instead of saying, "An eye for an eye and a tooth for a tooth," Jesus said, "(a) _____Resist_____ not evil: but whosoever shall (b) _____smite_____ thee on thy right cheek, turn to him the (c) _____other_____ also."

18. Instead of saying, "Love thy neighbour, and hate thine enemy," Jesus said, " _____ __"Love your enemies, bless them that curse you, do good to them that hate you, and pray for them__ __which despitefully use you, and persecute you" (Matthew 5:44)__ _____ _____."

19. a. To what group of people did God give the Old Testament Law? _____
      __the children of Israel_____

    b. For whom are the New Testament laws given? _____
      __all people (However, only born-again believers can understand them and live by them.)__

B. BIBLE WORD STUDY

Choose the best meaning for the words in italics. You may use a dictionary or Bible dictionary.

1. Jesus found Levi sitting at the *receipt of custom* (Mark 2:14). Levi was
   (a.) charging taxes.   b. changing money.   c. keeping Jewish traditions.

2. Jesus had many *disciples* among the crowds who followed Him (Luke 6:13). A disciple is one who
   a. is a close friend.
   b. leaves his home to follow another.
   (c.) follows another to learn from him.

3. Jesus called twelve men to follow Him and named them *apostles* (Luke 6:13). An apostle is
   (a.) one who is sent with a message.
   b. a ruler over an assembly of people.
   c. a disciple of an important teacher.

4. Jesus said, "Till heaven and earth pass, *one jot or one tittle* shall in no wise pass from the law, till all be fulfilled" (Matthew 5:18). *One jot or one tittle* means
   a. a section or a title.   b. a large or small law.   (c.) the smallest letter or mark.

5. Jesus warned against calling another person *Raca*, an Aramaic term of contempt (Matthew 5:22). This term means
   a. lazy and sluggish.   (b.) empty and worthless.   c. proud and lofty.

—for whom Jesus gave the Sermon on the Mount. (*He gave it for His followers, and indirectly for all people; but only born-again believers can understand and obey it.*)

- Students should be able to name at least three Old Testament commands that Jesus changed in the Sermon on the Mount. (*The following points are covered in this workbook.*)
  —"Thou shalt not kill." (*Changed to: "Whosoever is angry with his brother without a cause shall be in danger of the judgment."*)
  —"Thou shalt not forswear thyself." (*Changed to: "Swear not at all."*)
  —"An eye for an eye, and a tooth for a tooth."

(*Changed to: "Resist not evil: but whosoever shall smite thee on thy right cheek, turn to him the other also."*)
  —"Love thy neighbour, and hate thine enemy." (*Changed to: "Love your enemies, bless them that curse you, do good to them that hate you, and pray for them which despitefully use you, and persecute you."*)

Truths to Amplify

- The Sermon on the Mount is the heart of Jesus' teaching. However, it does not include the New Testament plan of salvation. Jesus' redemptive work was not yet finished when He preached this sermon.

C. THINKING ABOUT BIBLE TRUTHS

Jesus—a Friend of Sinners

1. According to Matthew 11:19, Jesus was called a friend of publicans and sinners. Why was He not embarrassed about this? Jesus was not proud. He loved the publicans and sinners. He saw more sincerity in the publicans and sinners than in the self-righteous upper-class Jews.

2. Jesus said He came to call sinners to repentance.
   a. Did this include the Pharisees? (See Romans 3:23.) yes
   b. Which were more likely to repent, the Pharisees or the publicans? Why? the publicans, because they understood that they were sinners

3. What kind of "righteousness" drives people away from Jesus? (See Romans 10:3.) self-righteousness (man's own "righteousness")

4. The twelve men whom Jesus chose were called disciples at first, and later they were called apostles. Why? They were called disciples, or followers, while they were following Jesus. After He appointed them apostles, they became bearers of the Gospel, witnesses of what they had experienced.

5. If Jesus came to fulfill the Old Testament Law, why did the Pharisees accuse Him of not keeping it? See Matthew 12:1–8 and Mark 7:1–13. The things the Pharisees accused Jesus of not keeping were not mentioned in the Law. They were rules the Pharisees themselves had added.

D. LEARNING MORE ABOUT BIBLE TIMES

Jesus' Apostles

Write the correct name in each blank to identify Jesus' apostles. If you need help, you may use a Bible dictionary or a concordance.

1. Andrew was Peter's brother.
2. James was the first apostle to lose his life for preaching the Gospel.
3. John was "the disciple whom Jesus loved."
4. (Simon) Peter received a new name from Jesus that means "rock."
5. Judas the brother of James was called Thaddaeus in Matthew's Gospel.
6. Philip brought Nathanael to Jesus.
7. Matthew (Levi) was a publican before Jesus called him.
8. Thomas was often called Didymus (twin).
9. Simon Zelotes was a Zealot (rebel) before coming to Jesus.
10. James the son of Alphaeus was called "the less" to distinguish him from another disciple.
11. Judas Iscariot served as the disciples' treasurer.
12. Bartholomew is possibly the disciple who was also called Nathanael.

Without Jesus' death on the cross and the coming of the Holy Ghost, no one could put the Sermon on the Mount into practice. Only with the teachings of the rest of the New Testament is the Sermon on the Mount complete.

- The Sermon on the Mount is not just a philosophical collection of high ideals, as the world supposes. It is God's truth to be lived out in real life by true believers. The principles Christ gave in the Sermon on the Mount are simple, yet only those who have been born again can understand their full meaning.

72 Chapter Two Acceptance and Rejection

Fishing

Some of Jesus' closest friends were fishermen, and He used stories of fishermen in His preaching. On one occasion, He preached from a fishing boat.

1. Which four of Jesus' close friends were fishermen? (Clue: Check *fishers* and *nets* in a concordance.) Simon Peter, Andrew, James, and John

Fish was a favorite meat for the people of Palestine. They gladly paid two or three times as much for fish as they paid for beef or mutton.

2. On what occasion does the Bible record that Jesus ate fish? (Check *fish* in a concordance.) _____
   when He appeared to the apostles in the upper room

Fishing With a Small Cast Net

Fishermen on the Sea of Galilee fished with lines, with round nets made to cast into the water, and with seine nets.

3. Which one of Jesus' disciples fished with a line? (Check *hook* in a concordance.) Peter (Matthew 17:26, 27)

4. What did he catch? a fish with a piece of money in its mouth

A fisherman could use a small net along the shore without a boat. However, nets cast into shallow water often collected trash, and the fisherman could not drag his nets through large areas of water.

A seine net was dragged between two boats. After spreading the net in a large loop, the fishermen pulled the net and the fish into their boats.

Seine Net Fishing

5. Did Jesus' disciples cast small nets from the shore, or larger nets from boats? (If you need help, check *nets* in a concordance.) Most accounts indicate that they cast nets from boats. But they may have also cast small nets from the shore at times.

Fishing boats on the Sea of Galilee usually held only four people. A few held more, but even they were small and not very seaworthy. The Sea of Galilee, lying 700 feet below sea level, is warm. When warm air rises from the Sea of Galilee and meets cold winds coming in from the Mediterranean Sea, sudden storms come up. Violent storms are still common on the Sea of Galilee.

Mending Nets

6. How did Jesus miraculously save His disciples' ship? (Check *storm* in a concordance.) _____
   He calmed the sea in a storm.
   _____
   _____
   _____

- Jesus probably ate fish many times. He served fish to the five thousand, to the four thousand, and to His disciples after His resurrection.

73

Lesson 10. Jesus Instructs His Followers

Jesus preached the Sermon on the Mount soon after He called the twelve apostles. He probably directed it to them to show them what He would expect of His followers in the church that they would help to establish. However, Matthew 5:1 seems to indicate that other people besides the apostles were also present.

Many people today try to discredit the Sermon on the Mount. They do not want to believe that God wants them to practice the doctrines that Jesus taught in it. But Jesus said that those who hear and do His teachings are wise, and that those who do not obey them are foolish (Matthew 7:24–26). Most of the principles in the Sermon on the Mount are also mentioned in the Epistles, so we know that the apostles and the early church believed that they were to be practiced.

The Sermon on the Mount gives practical instructions that are easy to understand. It deals with many everyday situations, and it tells us how we should react to them. Jesus practiced these teachings Himself. He is our perfect example.

In the last lesson we looked at the first section of the Sermon on the Mount. This lesson will cover the rest of it.

General Scope: Luke 6:37 ⟶ *Luke 6:49*

A. ANSWERS FROM THE BIBLE

Instructions About Almsgiving

Sometimes newspapers show pictures of someone giving a sum of money to help a good cause. People who want others to know how much they give have not learned the lesson that Jesus taught His followers in these verses.

Matthew 6:1–4

1. a. If people want to have credit from God for their giving, they must <u>give in secret</u>
   <u>   </u>.

   b. Otherwise the only reward that they will receive is the praise of <u>   men   </u>.

Instructions About Prayer

Jesus was not impressed with people who did things to be seen of men. It is not always wrong to pray in public or in groups, but it is always wrong to pray merely to be seen by others.

Matthew 6:5–18

 Choose two answers for number 2.

2. Jesus warns against using vain repetitions in prayer. The person who prays the same words over and over again
   (a.) thinks that God needs to be persuaded to answer his prayer.
   b. shows that God is hard of hearing.
   c. impresses God with his spirituality.
   (d.) proves he does not have faith that God will answer him.

Lesson 10

Oral Review

1. Name the twenty-seven New Testament books in order. [L. 1] **Matthew, Mark, Luke, John, Acts, Romans, 1 & 2 Corinthians, Galatians, Ephesians, Philippians, Colossians, 1 & 2 Thessalonians, 1 & 2 Timothy, Titus, Philemon, Hebrews, James, 1 & 2 Peter, 1, 2, & 3 John, Jude, Revelation**

2. Why did John not want to baptize Jesus? [L. 4] **He knew that Jesus was greater than he was.**

3. What effect did Jesus' miracle at Cana have on His disciples? [L. 5] **It helped them to believe on Him.**

4. How did Jesus find strength to do His work? [L. 8] **He spent much time in prayer.**

5. Why were the Pharisees so upset when Jesus healed on the Sabbath? [L. 8] **He was ignoring their Sabbath laws.**

6. Why did the Jews dislike the publicans? [L. 9] **They were tax collectors, and they often overcharged the people.**

7. Name the twelve disciples. [L. 9] **Simon Peter, Andrew, James, John, Philip, Bartholomew, Matthew, Thomas, James the son of Alphaeus, Simon Zelotes, Judas the brother**

3. Jesus taught a prayer to His disciples in verses 9–13. This prayer is sometimes called the Lord's Prayer or the Model Prayer and is a good example or pattern for us to follow when we pray. The following principles are all found in this prayer. Number them in the order that they occur in the prayer. The first one is done for you.

    __8__ a. Acknowledging God as the all-powerful Lord, to whom all glory belongs (6:13)

    __1__ b. Acknowledging God as our Father (6:9)

    __2__ c. Acknowledging God's holiness (6:9)

    __6__ d. Asking for God's forgiveness (6:12)

    __3__ e. Asking for God's kingdom to be fully established (6:10)

    __5__ f. Asking God to supply our natural needs in life (6:11)

    __7__ g. Asking to be delivered from temptation and evil (6:13)

    __4__ h. Asking for God's will to be accomplished in the lives of men (6:10)

4. The Lord's Prayer says, "Forgive us our debts, as we forgive our debtors." This means that
   a. God will not forgive our sins if anyone owes us money.
   (b.) God will not forgive the sins we commit if we refuse to forgive the wrongs others do to us.
   c. God will always forgive us our sins, no matter how we feel about other people.
   d. God expects us to lend our money to others without expecting to be repaid.

5. The same people who loved to pray on the street corners also had ways of showing people when they were fasting, making it seem as if they were doing something very difficult to serve God. Jesus told His followers that they should (a) _anoint their heads and wash their faces_

   _____

   so that no one would see when they fasted. Then God would (b) ___reward___ them.

Instructions About Material Possessions

Every person owns some things. This is not wrong, but these possessions should not be so important to us that they interfere with our love for God. Instead, we should use them to bring honor and glory to God. Jesus did not have many earthly possessions—He did not even have a home—but He was happy and content without them. He did not allow things, or the desire for things, to control Him. In these verses He tried to help His followers learn how to relate to their possessions.

Matthew 6:19–34

6. When we own something that is dear to us, it becomes our treasure. Many things can happen to earthly treasures—they break, are stolen, or wear out. Jesus told His followers to accumulate heavenly treasures rather than earthly treasures because in heaven treasures are safe. We can lay up treasures in heaven by
   (a.) seeking the things of God rather than earthly things.
   b. putting all our money in the bank instead of spending it.
   c. putting large sums of money in the offering.
   d. giving away all the money and things we own so that no one can steal them.

7. Verse 24 in this section states, "Ye cannot serve God and mammon." This means that when we allow the desire for material things to control us, we will not be able to ___serve God___ .

of James, Judas Iscariot

8. For whom did Jesus give the Sermon on the Mount? [L. 9] **all people (but more specifically, all true believers, since only those who are born again can understand and obey them)**

In This Lesson

Scope: Matthew 6:1–7:29; Luke 6:37–49

Focus
• Jesus gave instruction in the Sermon on the Mount about
   —giving.
   —prayer.
   —material possessions.
   —brotherhood relationships.
   —approaching God.
   —the Golden Rule.
   —identifying false Christians.
• Jesus taught with an authority that astonished the people. As the Son of God, He had both the wisdom and the right to expound truths both new and old.

Objectives
• Students should know
   —how God wants us to give our alms. (*in secret*)
   —what using vain repetitions in prayer means.

8. What lesson about material things can we learn from the birds? _____

   God will supply our needs, so we should not worry about them.

   _____

9. The Christian's first priority is not to provide for his earthly needs or to gain material riches, but
   rather to seek the kingdom of God and His righteousness . If we do this, God
   will take care of the other things we need.

Instructions About Brotherly Relationships

Everyone faces the temptation to be critical of others. It is easy to see the faults of others and overlook our own, but Jesus expects something different from His followers.

Matthew 7:1–6

10. What will happen to a person who harshly judges (criticizes) another? _____

    He will also be harshly judged (criticized).

11. Why is it so much easier to see the faults in others than it is to see our own faults? _____

    (Sample answer) We tend to excuse our own wrongdoing, but we hold others accountable for theirs.

    _____

12. a. What is the difference between a mote and a beam? _____

    A beam is a log or large plank, and a mote is a small speck.

    b. Why might Jesus have used such an illustration? to show us how easy it is to pick out little
    faults in others while we are overlooking big faults in our own lives

Instructions About Approaching God

God loves His children even more than earthly fathers love their children. It should not surprise us that God wants to do good things for His children, and that He wants us to come to Him when we have a need.

Matthew 7:7–11

13. God invites His children to (a) ___ask___, (b) ___seek___, and (c) ___knock___
    when they have a need. The usual way to do this is by (d) ___praying___.

Instructions About the Golden Rule

Matthew 7:12 is often called the Golden Rule. According to the last part of this verse, the Golden Rule summarizes the teaching of the entire Old Testament.

Matthew 7:12–14

14. How does following the Golden Rule help us to treat others as we should? Generally we want oth-
    ers to treat us fairly and kindly, so we will treat others this way if we follow this rule.

    _____

Instructions About False Christians

The church has been plagued from the very beginning with those who claim to be following God and yet are not true Christians. The Bible contains a number of warnings against such people, and it tells us how to recognize them.

In this section Jesus also shows His disciples how to avoid the judgment that will come upon such people.

- To keep this point balanced, also note verses such as 2 Thessalonians 3:10 and 1 Thessalonians 4:11.

(*saying words repeatedly without true meaning*)
—the implication of the statement, "Forgive us our debts, as we forgive our debtors." (*God will not forgive us if we refuse to forgive others.*)
—what Jesus told His disciples to do when they fasted. (*anoint their heads and wash their faces*)
—how we lay up treasures in heaven. (*by seeking heavenly things rather than earthly*)
—what Jesus meant by the statement, "Ye cannot serve God and mammon." (*We cannot serve God if we allow the desire for material things to control us.*)
—what will happen to the person who harshly criticizes another. (*He will also be harshly judged [criticized].*)

[*criticized*].)
—the difference between a *beam* and a *mote*. (*A beam is a log or large plank; a mote is a small speck.*)
—how following the Golden Rule helps us to treat others as we should. (*Generally we want others to treat us kindly and fairly, so we will treat others this way if we follow this rule.*)
—why the people were astonished at Jesus' teachings in the Sermon on the Mount. (*He taught with authority, and not as the scribes taught.*)

Matthew 7:15–29

15. Jesus states that many people who call Him Lord are not true Christians, even though they may prophesy, cast out devils, and do other wonderful works. Why is it not safe to judge a person's Christianity by such works?

    a. Everyone who prophesies in Jesus' Name is a true prophet, even if he does not do miracles.

    (b.) They may be doing such works by Satan's power.

    c. Their outward appearance shows that they are ravening wolves.

16. How are true Christians different from false prophets and hypocrites? (Sample answers) They produce good fruit (7:16–18). They do God's will (7:21). They hear and do Christ's teachings (7:24, 25).

17. Why were the people so astonished at Jesus' teachings?
    He taught with authority, and not as the scribes taught.

B. BIBLE WORD STUDY

All the words in this exercise are used in the Sermon on the Mount. Choose the best ending to illustrate the meaning of the italicized words.

1. Jesus taught that we are not to *do alms* before men, but rather in secret. We should not

    a. pray for show, but rather in private.

    b. put ointment on a wound when others are watching.

    (c.) show others how much money we give to God.

2. The heathen pray using *vain repetitions*, but God's people are not to do this. They should not

    a. stand in the street corners and pray loud prayers so that all will hear.

    (b.) repeat the same words over and over again without meaning it from their hearts.

    c. pray in a language that they do not understand.

3. Earthly treasures are *corrupted* by moths and rust. This means that

    a. earthly things are usually made poorly or tainted by moths and rust.

    b. earthly things should be preserved from moths and rust.

    (c.) all earthly things will eventually decay or be destroyed.

4. No man can serve both God and *mammon*. Mammon can include

    (a.) money and material things.

    b. many kinds of warm-blooded animals.

    c. evil men and evil spirits.

5. Jesus talked about a man who had a *mote* in his eye. He probably had

    a. a big stick in his eye.

    b. an insect in his eye.

    (c.) a speck of dirt in his eye.

6. The Bible says many things against people who are *hypocrites*. This is because they

    (a.) pretend to be something that they are not.

    b. have beams of wood in their eyes.

    c. do not know what is right and what is wrong.

Truths to Amplify

• The Sermon on the Mount is highly practical. It deals with issues that seventh graders face in their everyday experiences. Even students who have not yet reached the age of accountability can use the principles taught in the Sermon on the Mount as ideals. However, students should be taught that these principles can never be fully reached without God's help. When God's time is right, the Holy Spirit awakens within a young person an awareness that his natural heart is carnal and that he cannot attain to God's standard of righteousness by himself. Students should not be pressured to make a decision before this time.

Lesson 10. Jesus Instructs His Followers **77**

C. THINKING ABOUT BIBLE TRUTHS

Figures of Speech in the Sermon on the Mount

Jesus often used parables and figures of speech in His teaching. In this section He used both similes and metaphors to teach lessons to His followers. In a short paragraph, explain what Jesus meant by each of the following figures of speech. Be sure to read the context in which the term is used so that you understand it better. All references are from Matthew.

1. A hungry wolf dressed in a sheepskin (7:15) (Individual answers. Discuss the deception and danger involved. It is critical that true Christians discern those who are false before they cause great damage to the flock.)

2. People compared to fruit trees (7:16–20) (Individual answers. Discuss the difference between works and fruit with the students. Note that Jesus considered it safe to evaluate a person by his fruit, but not by his works.)

3. A man building a house on a rock (7:24, 25) (Individual answers. Discuss the importance of doing what Jesus taught. Those who hear but neglect or refuse to obey are more accountable than those who have no opportunity to hear.)

4. A man building a house without a foundation (7:26, 27) (Individual answers. Discuss the importance of laying a good foundation before the storms strike. The foolish man's house may have appeared just as good as the wise man's house, but its true character was quickly revealed when it was tested.)

D. LEARNING MORE ABOUT BIBLE TIMES

Fasting

The Jews observed certain days of the year as special days for fasting. The most important fast was the Day of Atonement, which is called "the fast" in Acts 27:9. God had commanded the Israelites to "afflict their souls" on this day (Leviticus 23:27). During the Babylonian captivity, the Jews added other days of public fasting. For example, they fasted on the seventeenth day of their fourth month because on that day Nebuchadnezzar had captured Jerusalem. Besides these general fasts, the Jews often fasted in private.

Seventh grade students should be familiar with similes and metaphors, but you might want to review the terms. Discuss these questions in class if they seem too difficult for your students to answer on their own.

When observed properly, public and private fasting helped the Jews to remember lessons from their history and to mourn for sin. However, too often fasting was done merely as public display rather than because of godly sorrow. Jesus told of a Pharisee who thought fasting twice a week made him better than other people (Luke 18:12). Jesus taught against the wrong kind of fasting, but He also encouraged its right use.

Tell why these people fasted.

1. Hannah (1 Samuel 1:5–7)   Hannah had no children (and Elkanah's wife vexed her about it).

2. David (2 Samuel 12:15–17)   His son was very sick (and God had said the child must die because of David's sin).

3. Ezra (Ezra 10:6)   He mourned for the sins of his people.

Three people in the Bible fasted for forty days. Read the references and name them.

4. Exodus 34:27, 28   Moses
5. 1 Kings 19:8, 9   Elijah
6. Matthew 4:2   Jesus

Earlier in this lesson you studied what Jesus taught about fasting in the Sermon on the Mount. Answer these questions about other teachings of Jesus on fasting.

7. Jesus did not establish regular days of fasting for His disciples. Rather, He taught by example that one should fast when there is a need for it. While Jesus was on earth, His disciples did not fast as often as some other Jews. When did Jesus say that His disciples would fast? (Matthew 9:15)   after He was no longer with them

8. Jesus taught that prayer and fasting could strengthen a person and prepare him for God's service. What work did Jesus say was possible only by prayer and fasting? (Matthew 17:18–21)   casting out devils such as the one the boy had

79

Chapter Two Review

A. ORAL REVIEW

 Be sure you know the answers to these questions. Answer as many as you can from memory. If you need help, you may check the reference or lesson numbers given in brackets.

What >>

1. What were Peter, Andrew, James, and John doing when Jesus called them? [Mark 1:16–20]
2. What moved Jesus to heal the sick? [Mark 1:40, 41]
3. What kind of deeds did Jesus say were lawful on the Sabbath? [Matthew 12:12]
4. What law of God were the Pharisees breaking when they tried to stop Jesus from healing on the Sabbath? [Matthew 12:7, 12; Lesson 8]
5. What Old Testament prophet foretold that Gentiles would trust in Jesus? [Matthew 12:17–21]
6. What did Jesus mean when He said, "The sabbath was made for man, and not man for the sabbath"? [Mark 2:27; Lesson 8]
7. What was Matthew's other name? [Lesson 9]
8. What do we call Jesus' sermon of new laws that is recorded in Matthew 5–7? [Lesson 9]
9. What do we call the ten points Jesus gave at the beginning of the Sermon on the Mount to outline His teachings? [Lesson 9]
10. What did Jesus tell His disciples to do when they fasted? [Matthew 6:16–18]
11. What did Jesus mean by the statement, "Ye cannot serve God and mammon"? [Lesson 10]
12. What is the difference between a mote and a beam? [Lesson 10]

When >>

13. When did Peter confess that he was a sinful man? [Luke 5:4–8]
14. When did the Jewish Sabbath begin? When did it end? [Lesson 8]

How >>

15. How did Jesus spread the Good News in Galilee? [Luke 4:14, 15]
16. How did synagogue worship differ from temple worship? [Lesson 6]
17. How do we know that prayer was important to Jesus? [Mark 1:35; Luke 6:12]
18. How did a man who could not walk get through a crowd to Jesus? [Mark 2:3, 4]
19. How did Jesus tell His followers to treat their enemies? [Matthew 5:44]
20. How does God want us to give our alms? [Matthew 6:3, 4]
21. How can we lay up treasures in heaven? [Matthew 6:20; Lesson 10]
22. How does following the Golden Rule help us to treat others as we should? [Matthew 7:12; Lesson 10]
23. How was Jesus' teaching different from that of the scribes? [Matthew 7:29]

1. They were fishing (and mending their nets).
2. His compassion for them
3. good deeds
4. God's law requiring them to show mercy and love
5. Isaiah
6. God meant the Sabbath for man's refreshment, not as a burden to him.
7. Levi
8. the Sermon on the Mount
9. the Beatitudes
10. anoint their heads and wash their faces
11. We cannot serve God if we allow the desire for material things to control us.
12. A beam is a log or large plank, and a mote is a small speck.
13. after Jesus performed the miracle of the great catch of fish
14. It began at sunset on Friday and ended at sunset on Saturday.
15. He traveled about and preached in the synagogues.
16. Sacrifices were offered at the temple, but not at synagogues.
17. At times He rose early in the morning (or stayed up all night) to pray.
18. He was lowered through a hole in the roof.
19. He told them to love their enemies, bless them, and pray for them.
20. in secret
21. by seeking the things of God rather than the things of the earth
22. Generally we want others to treat us fairly and kindly, so we will treat others this way if we follow this rule.
23. Jesus taught with authority.

80   Chapter Two   Acceptance and Rejection

Bible Words   >>

 Give a definition for each italicized word. If you need help, review Part B in Lessons 6–10.

24. The boy began to *amend* when Jesus spoke to his father.
25. Peter's mother-in-law *ministered* to Jesus.
26. Jesus healed those with *divers* diseases.
27. It was *noised* that Jesus was in the house.
28. Jesus healed a man sick of the *palsy*.
29. The heathen use *vain repetitions* in their prayers.

24. recover
25. served
26. various
27. heard; spread
28. paralysis; partial or complete loss of ability to move or feel
29. words repeated without true meaning

B. WRITTEN REVIEW

People of Palestine

 Match the following persons or groups with the sentence endings that describe them.

f	1. The people of Nazareth	a. felt grateful and showed hospitality.
h	2. The scribes	b. showed himself to the priests.
a	3. Peter's mother-in-law	c. are ones who are sent with a message.
b	4. The leper	d. learned that Jesus could heal from a distance.
g	5. The man sick of the palsy	e. were tax collectors.
d	6. The nobleman	f. tried to throw Jesus over the brow of a hill.
j	7. Levi	g. was forgiven and healed by Jesus.
e	8. Publicans	h. did not think Jesus could forgive sins.
i	9. Disciples	i. are followers.
c	10. Apostles	j. was a former tax collector.

Write the names of Jesus' twelve disciples. If you need help, see Luke 6:14–16. Be sure you know these names from memory for the test.

11. Simon Peter
12. Andrew
13. James
14. John
15. Philip
16. Bartholomew
17. Matthew
18. Thomas
19. James the son of Alphaeus
20. Simon Zelotes
21. Judas the brother of James
22. Judas Iscariot

Teachings of Jesus

These are three of the commandments which Jesus changed in the Sermon on the Mount. Write the changes that He made to each. If you need help, see Matthew 5:21–48.

23. "Thou shalt not kill."   Changed to: "Whosoever is angry with his brother without a cause shall be in danger of the judgment."

24. "An eye for an eye, and a tooth for a tooth."   Changed to: "Resist not evil: but whosoever shall smite thee on thy right cheek, turn to him the other also."

25. "Love thy neighbor, and hate thine enemy."   Changed to: "Love your enemies, bless them that curse you, do good to them that hate you, and pray for them which despitefully use you, and persecute you."

🍇 *Finish these sentences. If you need help, review Lesson 10 and Matthew 6 and 7.*

26. God will forgive us our debts as we   forgive our debtors .

27. The person who harshly judges (criticizes) others   will also be harshly judged (criticized) .

Why

🍇 *Write answers for the following questions. Answer as many as you can from memory. If you need help, you may check the reference or lesson numbers given in brackets.*

28. Why did Jesus' stories of Elijah and Naaman offend the Jews of Nazareth? [Luke 4:25–28; Lesson 6]   Jesus showed by these stories that believing Gentiles receive more of God's blessings than unbelieving Jews do.

29. Why did Jesus always tell unclean spirits to be quiet when they testified that He was the Son of God? [Lesson 7]   Jesus did not need or want Satan's help.

30. Why were the Pharisees upset when Jesus healed on the Sabbath Day? [Lesson 8]   He was ignoring their Sabbath laws.

31. Why did Jesus have the authority to say what was lawful on the Sabbath? [Matthew 12:8]   He was Lord of the Sabbath (and the Son of God).

32. Why did the Jews criticize Jesus when He went to Levi's house for a feast? [Mark 2:15–17]   Levi was a publican and was considered a sinner.

"I am the vine, ye are the branches" (John 15:5).

CHAPTER THREE

Jesus Ministers to Jews and Gentiles

Miracles in Galilee

Jesus Teaches in Parables

Believers and Unbelievers

Jesus—the Bread of Life

Jesus Goes to the Gentiles

For I came down from heaven,
not to do mine own will, but the will of him that sent me.
And this is the Father's will which hath sent me,
that of all which he hath given me I should lose nothing,
but should raise it up again at the last day.
And this is the will of him that sent me, that every one
which seeth the Son, and believeth on him, may have everlasting life:
and I will raise him up at the last day.

John 6:38–40

Harmony of the Gospels

For important events and teachings covered in Chapter Three

Event or Teaching	Matthew	Mark	Luke	John	Location	Season
Lesson 11. Miracles in Galilee						
Jesus heals the centurion's servant.	8:5–13[1]	—	7:1–10	—	Capernaum	
Jesus raises a widow's son.	—	—	7:11–17	—	Nain	
Jesus forgives a sinful woman.	—	—	7:36–50	—	Pharisee's house	
Grateful women care for Jesus' needs.	—	—	8:1–3	—		
Jesus' friends think He is too busy.	—	3:20, 21	—	—		
The scribes and Pharisees accuse Jesus.	12:22–45	3:22–30	11:14–36	—	Galilee	
Jesus claims the faithful as His family.	12:46–50	3:31–35	8:19–21	—		
Lesson 12. Jesus Teaches in Parables						
The sower	13:1–23	4:1–20	8:4–15	—	Capernaum[2]	
The tares	13:24–30, 36–43	—	—	—	Capernaum	
The seed growing to maturity	—	4:26–29	—	—	Capernaum	
The mustard seed	13:31, 32	4:30–32	13:18, 19	—	Capernaum	
The leaven hidden in meal	13:33	—	13:20, 21	—	Capernaum	
The hidden treasure in a field	13:44	—	—	—	Capernaum	
The pearl of great price	13:45, 46	—	—	—	Capernaum	
The net full of fish	13:47–50	—	—	—	Capernaum	
Lesson 13. Believers and Unbelievers						
Jesus stills the tempest.	8:23–27	4:35–41	8:22–25	—	Sea of Galilee	
Jesus heals the demoniac of Gergesa.	8:28–34	5:1–20	8:26–39	—	Gergesa	
Jesus heals a woman and raises Jairus's daughter.	9:18–26	5:21–43	8:41–56	—	Capernaum	
Jesus is rejected at Nazareth again.	13:53–58	6:1–6	—	—	Nazareth	
Lesson 14. Jesus—the Bread of Life						
Jesus feeds the five thousand.	14:13–21	6:30–44	9:10–17	6:1–14	Near Bethsaida	Spring[3]
Jesus walks on the water.	14:22–33	6:45–52	—	6:15–21	Sea of Galilee	Spring
Jesus condemns hypocrisy.	15:1–20	7:1–23	—	—		
Jesus teaches about bread from heaven.	—	—	—	6:22–71	Capernaum	
Lesson 15. Jesus Goes to the Gentiles						
Jesus heals a Greek woman's daughter.	15:21–28	7:24–30	—	—	Near Tyre/Sidon	
Jesus heals in Decapolis.	15:29–31	7:31–37	—	—	Decapolis	
Jesus feeds the four thousand.	15:32–39	8:1–9	—	—	Desert place	
The Pharisees demand a sign.	16:1–4	8:10–12	—	—	Magdala	
The leaven of the Pharisees	16:5–12	8:13–21	—	—	Sea of Galilee	

---

[1] Passages given in italics are used in the lesson.

[2] After giving the parables in Mark 4, Jesus left for the other side of the lake (Mark 4:35). Soon He returned to His home base of Capernaum (Matthew 9:1), where He had left the multitude (Luke 8:40).

[3] See John 6:4. The Passover was in early spring.

85

Lesson 11. Miracles in Galilee

Nowhere did Jesus do more miracles than in Galilee. The humble people believed in Jesus, and He rewarded their faith by performing miracles for them that unbelievers did not see.

Imagine going to the funeral of a boy and walking toward the cemetery with his body—and then seeing Jesus suddenly raise him back to life! Imagine seeing crippled people whom Jesus had healed, standing up and walking. How would you have felt while eating bread and fish that Jesus had multiplied from five loaves and two small fish to feed five thousand men! With the disciples, the Galileans looked on and wondered, "What manner of man is this?"

Jesus loved people. He gladly performed miracles that helped them to believe in Him and His words, but He never did miracles for show or public praise. When the proud, scornful Pharisees demanded a sign, Jesus would not grant their request. Likewise, when Herod Antipas wanted Him to perform a miracle as if He were a circus actor, Jesus refused again.

Jesus came to bring men back to God, and each miracle that He did helped to fulfill God's purpose for Him.

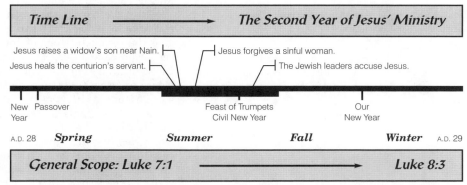

Time Line ⟶ **The Second Year of Jesus' Ministry**

Jesus raises a widow's son near Nain. ⊢
Jesus heals the centurion's servant. ⊢
⊣ Jesus forgives a sinful woman.
⊣ The Jewish leaders accuse Jesus.

New Year   Passover   Feast of Trumpets Civil New Year   Our New Year

A.D. 28   *Spring*   *Summer*   *Fall*   *Winter*   A.D. 29

General Scope: Luke 7:1 ⟶ **Luke 8:3**

Note: The events in this lesson cannot be placed in an exact season. They are given in their approximate order. See the note following the time line in Lesson 12.

Using the Time Line

1. a. According to Luke 7:11, where did Jesus go the day after He healed the centurion's servant?
      to Nain
   b. What miracle did He do there?   He raised a widow's son.

2. According to Luke 8:1, what did Jesus do during this period of His ministry that may have taken several months?   He preached in every city and village.

Lesson 11

Oral Review

1. What is the meaning of *Messiah*? What Greek word has the same meaning? [L. 2] **the Anointed One; Christ**
2. Which two brothers of Jesus wrote books of the New Testament? [L. 3] **James and Jude**
3. Why did Jesus have authority to cleanse the temple? [L. 5] **He is the Son of God.**
4. How do we know that prayer was important to Jesus? [L. 7] **He rose early in the morning, before it was day, to spend time in prayer.**
5. What was the apostle Matthew's other name? [L. 9] **Levi**
6. What do we call the ten points Jesus gave at the beginning of the Sermon on the Mount to outline His teachings? [L. 9] **the Beatitudes**
7. How does following the Golden Rule help us to treat others as we should? [L. 10] **Generally we want others to treat us fairly and kindly, so we will treat them this way if we follow this rule.**
8. What is the difference between a *mote* and a *beam*? [L. 10] **A beam is a log or large plank, and a mote is a small speck.**

A. ANSWERS FROM THE BIBLE

A Gentile With Faith

The Roman centurion was a Gentile, but he had many Jewish friends in Capernaum. Apparently he understood and respected the Jewish beliefs, for he did not want Jesus to defile Himself by entering his house. The centurion was sure that Jesus could heal his servant without being present. Jesus marveled at his insight.

To complete these exercises, first study the Bible passages that are given. Fill in the short blanks with words. Whenever possible, use exact words from the Bible. Write complete answers for the questions with long blanks. For multiple-choice questions, circle the letter of the correct answer.

Matthew 8:5–13

1. The Roman centurion was not a descendant of Abraham. He did not belong to God's Old Testament family. In spite of this, he had more _____faith_____ than any Jew that Jesus had met in Palestine.

2. Jews did not ordinarily visit Gentiles. What did Jesus say that shows He was willing to enter a Gentile's house to heal the centurion's servant?   "I will come and heal him." (8:7)
   _____

3. The centurion said that he and Jesus were similar in that both were under a higher authority and
   a. had soldiers under them.
   b. were centurions.
   c. could heal others without being present.
   d. had authority to give orders.

4. By saying this, the centurion meant that Jesus
   a. should send a servant to heal the man.
   b. could simply order that the man be healed.
   c. should listen to his orders.
   d. should tell him what to do.

Galileans With Faith

Luke 7:11–17

Following the Galilean tradition, the mother of the young man walked ahead of the stretcher, mourning loudly. Wailing and lamentation arose from the many people who were with her. Barefoot youths carried the stretcher, changing often so that all would get a turn.

5. When Jesus saw the widow weeping for her son,
   a. He wished someone could help her.
   b. He comforted her and raised her son.
   c. He reproved her for her lack of faith.
   d. He wished that her son had not died.

6. The Galileans responded rightly to Jesus' miracle. They
   a. asked Jesus to teach them.
   b. followed Jesus back to Jerusalem.
   c. dried their tears to sing and pray.
   d. feared and glorified God.

Various Responses to Jesus and His Miracles

The last two sections show good responses to Jesus' miracles. This section shows both good and bad responses to Jesus and His miracles.

• Some reference books make an issue of the differences between Matthew 8:5–13 and Luke 7:2–10. Perhaps the two accounts should be combined to give the complete story of the centurion and Jesus. Perhaps the centurion sent the Jewish elders to Jesus first, then sent some friends (as in Luke 7), and finally came himself (as in Matthew 8). We should not allow such seeming discrepancies to shake our faith in the inerrancy of the Bible, but rather admit that we do not understand how all the Bible details fit together.

In This Lesson

Scope: Matthew 8:5–13, 12:22–50; Mark 3:20–35; Luke 7:1–17, 36–50; 8:1–3, 19–21

Focus

• Various people responded differently to Jesus and His miracles.
   —The Roman centurion believed that Jesus could speak the word and heal his servant from a distance. Jesus commended his faith as an example for others to follow.
   —The people of Nain feared and glorified God after seeing Jesus raise the widow's son.
   —The woman who anointed Jesus' feet proved her love for God and her sorrow for sin. In response, Jesus granted her the greatest miracle of all—forgiveness of sins.
   —Some women whom Jesus had healed showed their gratitude by following Jesus and ministering to His needs.
   —The multitudes who saw the dumb man healed asked, "Is not this the son of David?"
   —The Pharisees condemned Jesus and accused Him of doing miracles by the devil's power.
   —Jesus' earthly family and some of His friends tried to divert His attention from His work.

Luke 7:36–50

In Luke 7:47, 48, Jesus performed the greatest miracle of all. Notice the difference between the Pharisee's and the woman's response to Jesus. This shows how different their attitudes toward Him were.

7. Which of these is the most likely reason Simon the Pharisee invited Jesus for a meal?

   a. He thought highly of Jesus.

   (b.) He was curious about what Jesus taught.

   c. He was sure Jesus was a prophet.

   d. He felt guilty about his sins.

Washing a Guest's Feet

8. (Choose three answers.) Simon showed his lack of appreciation for Jesus by

   (a.) not giving Him water to wash His feet.

   b. not speaking to Him.

   c. not giving Him good food.

   (d.) not greeting Him with a kiss.

   e. inviting Him with a group of sinners.

   (f.) not anointing His head with oil.

9. Jesus used this opportunity to teach Simon a lesson about love and forgiveness. Why did Simon love Jesus less than the woman did?

   (a.) The woman saw herself as a great sinner, and Simon did not see his need; therefore he was not forgiven.

   b. He knew that he was more sinful than the woman was and thought that Jesus would not forgive Him.

   c. He had fewer sins than the woman, so he did not need to be forgiven as she did.

   d. He was a man, and she was a woman.

10. The greatest miracle that Jesus could do for anyone was to forgive his sins. But every time that Jesus forgave sins, it stirred up turmoil in the minds of Jewish leaders who witnessed it. Why? (If you need help, read Mark 2:6, 7.)

   a. The Jewish leaders thought they were the only people who could forgive the sins of others.

   (b.) Because only God can forgive sins, Jesus proved that He is God each time He forgave sins. The scribes and Pharisees thought this was blasphemy.

   c. The scribes and Pharisees taught that sinners could never be forgiven.

   d. The scribes and Pharisees were jealous because they had wanted Jesus to forgive their sins too, and He did not.

Luke 8:1–3

Most of the people whom Jesus healed were grateful. The women in these verses found a practical way to show their gratitude as Jesus traveled through the cities and towns, preaching the glad tidings of the kingdom of God.

11. What miracle had Jesus done for these women?   _He had healed them of evil spirits and infirmities._

• This lesson discusses God's power manifested in miracles. We must not think every miracle is automatically from God, for many miracles have also been performed by Satan's power. (See Exodus 7:11, 12 for one example.) However, those who sincerely wanted to know the truth could tell that Jesus' miracles were from God. They were done for God's glory, they were in perfect accord with the Word of God, and the miracle worker lived a life of holiness. Such miracles contrast sharply with Satan's "signs and lying wonders" (2 Thessalonians 2:9), even though undiscerning observers often fail to recognize the difference.

Objectives

• Students should know

  —how the Roman centurion proved his faith. (*He asked Jesus to heal his servant without coming to his house.*)

  —how Jesus helped the widow of Nain. (*He raised her son.*)

  —why Simon the Pharisee loved Jesus less than did the woman who washed Jesus' feet. (*The woman saw herself as a great sinner, and Simon did not see his need; therefore he was not forgiven.*)

  —why the scribes and Pharisees were upset when Jesus forgave someone's sin. (*They knew that only God could forgive sins, but they refused to acknowledge Jesus as God.*)

  —what Mary Magdalene and other women did for Jesus. (*They cared for His needs.*)

  —who thought Jesus was doing too much for His own good. (*His friends*)

  —by whose power the Pharisees accused Jesus of doing miracles. (*Satan's*)

  —the definition of *centurion* and of *bier*. (*centurion: captain of one hundred soldiers; bier: stretcher*)

Truths to Amplify

• Which is easier, telling a crippled man to rise up and walk, or telling a man that his sins are forgiven? Not only did Jesus ask this question (Luke 5:23), but He

12. How did these women show their gratitude to Jesus? _They followed Him and ministered unto Him_
    out of their substance (served Him from their own goods).

13. The name *Magdalene* probably indicates that Mary Magdalene was from Magdala, a town on the
    western shore of the Sea of Galilee. What did Mary Magdalene and other women do for Jesus at
    His death? (Mark 16:1) _They brought spices with which to anoint His body._

Mark 3:20, 21

At times Jesus was so busy doing good things for others that He had almost no time for Himself. If He wanted
to be alone to pray, He had to do it at night when everyone else was sleeping. The Bible says that sometimes
Jesus and His disciples hardly had time to eat because of the crowds that followed them.

14. Jesus' friends wanted to get Him away from the crowds because
    a. they did not want the crowds to be helped.
    b. they thought Jesus was doing too much for His own good.
    c. they wanted to receive Jesus' attention.
    d. they were afraid of what the Jews might do to Jesus.

15. According to Matthew 9:36, what moved Jesus to spend so much time helping people? _____
    He was moved with compassion for the multitudes, who were like sheep without a shepherd.

Matthew 12:22–26

The scribes and Pharisees could have learned much from the Roman centurion and others who had faith in
Jesus. Unlike these true believers, the scribes and Pharisees refused to acknowledge that Jesus is the Son of
God. They looked for faults in Him and falsely accused Him of being a sinner. In these verses they made one of the
worst accusations that anyone could make against God's Son.

16. The place where Jesus healed this man was probably somewhere in Galilee. Even though the
    people around Him had probably seen Him perform miracles before, they were especially
    impressed by this one. Who did the people think Jesus was when they saw the miracles He did?
    the Son of David (in other words, the Messiah)

17. The scribes and Pharisees had probably come to look for ways to discredit Jesus' work. What
    did they say about Him to try to counteract the feelings of the other people who had seen the
    miracle? _They said that He was casting out devils by Satan's power._

18. The Pharisees did not deny that Jesus did miracles, nor that the miracles were good.
    But they said He must be doing them with the power of the devil. How did Jesus prove their rea-
    soning wrong? _He explained that if Satan cast out devils, he would be fighting against himself._

Matthew 12:46–50

Most (or all) of Jesus' earthly brothers and sisters did not believe in Him at this time. Perhaps they were even trying to hinder His work by coming to talk to Him. This may have prompted Jesus to make a comparison between
His disciples and His family as He did here.

19. What was Jesus busy doing when His family wanted to talk with Him? _____
    He was talking to the people.

20. Who belongs to Jesus' family? _all those who do God's will_

also amply demonstrated that He had the power to
do both.

• The purpose of Jesus' miracles was to lead men into
an understanding of the greatest and most miraculous work: the salvation of men's souls and their
deliverance from sin. Jesus did not do miracles to
flaunt His power, to win a following, or to make a
name for Himself. Everything He did was to help
men find liberty from their sin and become children
of God.

• Modern-day miracle workers who do not have a good
purpose for performing their acts do not follow
Jesus' steps.

B. BIBLE WORD STUDY

 Write the letter of the correct definition or synonym for each italicized word. Use a dictionary if necessary.

__d__ 1. Jesus' friends thought He was *beside Himself* for spending so much time with the people (Mark 3:21).

__g__ 2. A Roman *centurion* told Jesus about his servant who was sick (Matthew 8:5).

__e__ 3. The centurion's servant was *grievously tormented* with his disease (Matthew 8:6).

__b__ 4. Jesus touched the *bier* of the widow's son in Nain (Luke 7:14).

__f__ 5. Jesus *sat at meat* in the Pharisee's house (Luke 7:37).

__i__ 6. A woman poured *ointment* on Jesus feet (Luke 7:38).

__h__ 7. Jesus told a story about a *creditor* (Luke 7:41).

__a__ 8. One debtor owed five hundred *pence* (Luke 7:41).

__c__ 9. Women who followed Jesus ministered unto Him of their *substance* (Luke 8:3).

a. pennies
   (See note below.)

b. stretcher

c. goods

d. out of His mind

e. seriously ill

f. ate a meal

g. captain of one
   hundred soldiers

h. moneylender

i. perfume

Note: Our English Bibles use *penny* for the Roman coin *denarius.* One *denarius* was the normal daily wage of a common laborer.

C. THINKING ABOUT BIBLE TRUTHS

Wrong Responses to Miracles

Miracles were not new to the Jews. The Old Testament contains many accounts of miracles performed by God's prophets. The scribes and Pharisees knew that ordinary men could not perform miracles. However, they did not want to accept the fact that Jesus had come from God, so they tried to prove that His miracles were from another source.

 Read the verses in parentheses and answer these questions.

1. (Acts 7:51, 52) The way the Jews treated Jesus was nothing new in the history of the Jewish people.
   a. Whom else had the Jews mistreated in the past? _the prophets_
   b. Whom were they actually resisting when they did these things? _the Holy Spirit (God)_

2. (John 10:31–33) The leading Jews steadfastly refused to admit that Jesus' miracles were from God. If they had admitted this, they would also have had to believe Him when He told them that He is God.
   a. What sin did the Jews claim that Jesus was guilty of committing? _blasphemy_
   b. What did they try to do to Him? _They tried to stone Him._

Be sure the students read and understand the note on pence (denarii). One Roman denarius (called penny in the King James Bible) was the common daily wage (Matthew 20:2). It was a silver coin worth much more than our modern penny.

3. (Acts 14:8–13) The people of Lystra did not realize that Paul and Barnabas received their power to do miracles from God.

    a. Whom did these people think that Paul and Barnabas were? _____

       gods in the likeness of men (Jupiter and Mercurius)

    b. What did the people decide to do because of the miracle Paul and Barnabas did? _____

       They decided to offer a sacrifice to them.

4. (2 Thessalonians 2:9–12) Not all miracles are from God, nor is every miracle worker from God. These verses refer to a man who uses Satan's power to do miracles and deceive people.

    a. What kind of people will be deceived by the miracles that come from Satan? _____

       those who do not believe the truth

    b. All of Satan's miracles are a _____lie_____ and are intended to _____deceive_____ people rather than to help them. They glorify man rather than God. In contrast, a miracle from God will lead people to truth, will meet the real needs of man, and will glorify God. Knowing these differences can help us to properly evaluate a miracle.

D. LEARNING MORE ABOUT BIBLE TIMES

Did It Happen in Galilee?

Jesus spent most of His early ministry in Galilee, teaching and doing miracles. The following list reviews some of the miracles covered so far in this workbook. Write yes or no for each miracle to tell whether Jesus performed it in Galilee. Read the references and check the map if you need help.

  yes   1. Jesus turns the water into wine (John 2:1–11).

  yes   2. Jesus heals the nobleman's son (John 4:46–54).

  yes   3. Jesus supplies a great catch of fish for the disciples (Luke 5:4–10).

  yes   4. Jesus heals a man with an unclean spirit at a synagogue (Mark 1:21–28).

  yes   5. Jesus heals Peter's mother-in-law (Mark 1:29–31).

  yes   6. Jesus cleanses a leper (Mark 1:39–45).

  yes   7. Jesus heals a man sick of the palsy (Mark 2:1–12).

  no   8. Jesus heals an impotent man (John 5:1–9).

  yes   9. Jesus heals the centurion's servant (Matthew 8:5–13).

  yes   10. Jesus raises a widow's son (Luke 7:11–17).

91

Lesson 12. Jesus Teaches in Parables

Like springing grass and flowers, the crowd of Jesus' followers grew during His second year of ministry. Some Galileans became faithful disciples. But the interest of others blossomed only for a time, and then it withered away like the flowers.

Among the crowd of followers were scribes and Pharisees from Jerusalem. Critically they listened to Jesus, hoping to catch Him saying something with which they could find fault. Jesus knew that in their hearts they were not interested in the truth. No matter how clearly He taught, they would not believe. So He taught in parables (stories with lessons). Those who were interested in the truth would understand. But those who wanted to live in darkness would not understand the meanings and would be less able to find fault with Jesus' teaching.

All who met Jesus needed to make a choice. Either they believed in Him and His message, or they rejected Him. Their choice depended on whether they really wanted to believe God or whether they were determined to take their own selfish way.

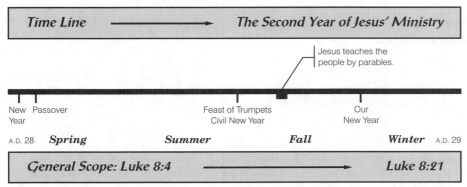

Time Line ⟶	The Second Year of Jesus' Ministry

Jesus teaches the people by parables.

New Year / Passover   Feast of Trumpets Civil New Year   Our New Year

A.D. 28   *Spring*   *Summer*   *Fall*   *Winter*   A.D. 29

General Scope: Luke 8:4 ⟶	Luke 8:21

Note: It is difficult to date the events during the second year of Jesus' ministry. Jesus' disciples plucked grain on a Sabbath during the spring harvest (Mark 2:23), but the next event that can be dated with certainty is the feeding of the five thousand the next spring (John 6:4). The events between these two springs can only be spaced out in their approximate order. However, the fact that half the parables in this lesson mention the sowing of seed suggests that Jesus may have given them during the fall, when grain was planted.

Using the Time Line

1. During what season did the Jews plant their barley and wheat?   <u>fall</u>
2. What suggests that Jesus might have given the parables in this lesson during this season?   _____
   <u>Half the parables in this lesson mention planting seed.</u>

Lesson 12

Oral Review

1. What was the first miracle that Jesus did, and where did He do it? [L. 5] **He turned water into wine at the town of Cana.**
2. Why did Jesus always stop evil spirits from telling people who He was? [L. 7] **He did not need or want Satan's help.**
3. When did the Jewish Sabbath begin? When did it end? [L. 8] **It began at sunset on Friday and ended at sunset on Saturday.**
4. Name the twelve disciples. [L. 9] **Simon Peter, Andrew, James, John, Philip, Bartholomew, Matthew, Thomas, James the son of Alphaeus, Simon Zelotes, Judas the brother of James, Judas Iscariot**
5. How does God want us to give our alms? [L. 10] **in secret**
6. What did Jesus mean by the statement, "Ye cannot serve God and mammon"? [L. 10] **We cannot serve God if we allow the desire for material things to control us.**
7. Why did Simon the Pharisee love Jesus less than did the woman who washed Jesus' feet? [L. 11] **The woman saw herself as a great sinner, and Simon did not see his need; therefore he was not forgiven.**

92 Chapter Three Jesus Ministers to Jews and Gentiles

A. ANSWERS FROM THE BIBLE

The events in this lesson took place on the shore of the Sea of Galilee. Jesus sat in a boat to teach these parables (Jewish teachers usually sat). From the boat, He spoke to a great crowd of people who had gathered. Some of these people were true seekers, but many were merely curious about Jesus. Others were hostile toward Him and were there to find fault.

The Parable of the Sower

Galilee was a rural community with many farmers. All the people in the crowd that day probably either had seen someone plant a field of grain or had done it themselves. They may have been able to watch a sower from where they stood listening to Jesus.

Matthew 13:1–9, 18–23

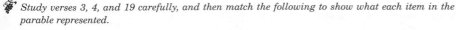 *Study verses 3, 4, and 19 carefully, and then match the following to show what each item in the parable represented.*

d	1. The sower	a.	God's Word
a	2. The seed	b.	the heart of the listener
c	3. The fowls of the air	c.	Satan
b	4. The ground	d.	someone speaking God's Word

The four types of soil in this parable illustrate four types of hearts that people have. The way a person responds when he hears the Gospel indicates what type of heart he has. Only those who have an honest and good heart, such as that illustrated by the fourth type of soil, will produce spiritual fruit.

5. The wayside was probably the edge of a path or road on which people walked. It was so hard that seeds could not put down roots and grow. The wayside represents a person who
   a. has never had the opportunity to hear God's Word.
   (b) listens so carelessly to God's Word that it cannot penetrate his heart to take root there.
   c. would like to listen to God's Word but is too busy with other things to take time for it.

6. The seed that fell on stony ground started to grow, but the new plants did not last long. Their roots could not penetrate deeply enough into the stony soil to receive the moisture they needed to stay alive when the sun became hot. This soil represents a person who
   (a) is attracted by God's Word, but loses interest as soon as he faces tests and hard times.
   b. is too busy to listen to those who try to tell him God's Word.
   c. has never heard God's Word, and so is unable to respond to it.

Use caution when considering parable interpretations from commentaries and other reference books. Many commentators teach that the kingdom parables support the state church system or the modern church system, where sinners and "Christians" remain in the congregation together. They feel that God will sort out His true followers from the wicked on the Day of Judgment. But Jesus clearly stated that "the field is the world" (not the church). Therefore, the parables depict the Christian's life "in the midst of a crooked and perverse nation" (Philippians 2:15). Many passages, such as 2 Corinthians 6:14–18; 1 Corinthians 5:1–13; and John 17:14–17, stress the need for purity in the church.

8. How did the centurion prove his faith in Jesus? [L. 11] **He asked Jesus to heal his servant without coming to his house.**

In This Lesson

Scope: Matthew 13:1–53; Mark 4:1–34; Luke 8:4–18

Focus
- This lesson is a study of the first series of parables recorded in the Gospels.
- Jesus taught the people and the disciples in parables
  —so that the disciples could understand.
  —so that those who had already turned from the truth would not understand.

- Jesus used parables to explain truths about the kingdom of heaven.
  —In spite of the small beginning of the church, the message of salvation has brought peace to thousands and has had a major influence on the world.
  —We must be willing to give up everything else to be part of God's kingdom.
  —Not everyone who appears to be part of the kingdom of heaven will necessarily be ready to enter heaven at the judgment.
  —Those who are part of the kingdom will want to share their blessings with others so that they too can be part of the kingdom.

7. The seed that fell on the thorny ground also started to grow, but the plants were soon choked out by thorns. This soil represents a person who
   a. turns from God's Word when he is persecuted for his faith or faces other trials.
   b. has such a prickly character that other Christians do not want to be around him.
   c. is genuinely interested in God's Word, but is so busy with other things that he has no time for it.

8. Some of the seed fell on good ground. This seed grew and the plants produced fruit. This soil represents a person who
   a. hears God's Word, studies it, and allows it to change his life.
   b. considers himself good because he has studied the Bible for many years.
   c. becomes a farmer and raises many crops for the Lord.

9. Some of the seed that fell on good ground brought forth a hundredfold, some sixtyfold, and some only thirtyfold. According to this,
   a. God plants better seed in some people than He does in others.
   b. all Christians will be productive in their Christian lives, although not in equal amounts.
   c. God loves some of His children more than He does the rest.

The Parable of the Tares

The parable of the tares is the first of the "kingdom parables." God's kingdom on earth is made up of God's children. It does not include any of Satan's servants.

Matthew 13:24–30, 36–43

The tares of which Jesus spoke were probably a kind of grass that grew in Palestine. They looked very similar to wheat when they were growing, but they could be identified when they bore fruit. The roots of the tares intertwined with the roots of the wheat. This is why the householder was afraid his servants would root up the wheat if they pulled out the tares. Tare seeds were poisonous to man and to many kinds of animals.

10. Tell who or what each of these represents in the parable of the tares.
    a. the sower ___the Son of man (Jesus)___
    b. the field ___the world___
    c. the good seed ___the children of the kingdom (Christians)___
    d. the tares ___the children of the wicked one (sinners)___
    e. the enemy ___the devil (Satan)___
    f. the harvest ___the end of the world___
    g. the reapers ___the angels___

11. When will the children of God be separated from the rest of the people? ___at the end of the world___

12. What will finally happen to the "tares" and the "wheat"? ___
    The tares will be cast into a furnace of fire (hell) and the wheat will be gathered into the barn (heaven).___

Objectives
- Students should know
  —the main lesson of the parable of the sower. (*People respond differently to the Gospel, depending on what type of heart they have.*)
  —what the seed and the ground represent in the parable of the sower. (*the seed: God's Word; the ground: the hearts of those who hear God's Word*)
  —what the field represents in the parable of the tares. (*the world*)
  —how the kingdom of heaven is like the pearl in the parable. (*One must give up everything to enter the kingdom.*)
  —why Jesus taught in parables. (*so that only those who believed would understand*)
  —the meaning of *parable*, of *tares*, and of *leaven*. (*parable: a short story that illustrates a truth; tares: poisonous weeds; leaven: yeast*)
  —what scribes did. (*copied books and kept records*)

94 Chapter Three   Jesus Ministers to Jews and Gentiles

Other Kingdom Parables

The kingdom parable given above and the six given below all begin with the words "The kingdom of heaven is like," or similar words. Jesus may have given the parable recorded in Mark 4 at a different time, but it is similar to the others and fits well in this list. These seven parables teach various truths about God's kingdom.

13. Fill in the blanks. Be prepared to discuss the meanings of the parables in class.
    a. Mark 4:26–29   The kingdom of God (heaven)   is compared to a man planting seed without knowing how it will grow.
    b. Matthew 13:31, 32   The kingdom of heaven is compared to _____ a grain of mustard seed (which grew into a great plant) .
    c. Matthew 13:33   The kingdom of heaven is compared to _____ leaven (which a woman hid in meal) .
    d. Matthew 13:44   The kingdom of heaven is compared to _____ treasure hidden in a field .
    e. Matthew 13:45, 46   The kingdom of heaven is compared to _____ a merchant man seeking goodly pearls >> .
    f. Matthew 13:47–50   The kingdom of heaven is compared to   a net .

Interpreting the Kingdom Parables

Not everyone interprets the kingdom parables exactly the same. The exercises below will help you understand some lessons from them. Some of the parables could probably teach additional lessons.

Mark 4:26–29

14. We cannot see a plant grow, yet we know that it does because it becomes taller over a period of time. When we compare this to the kingdom of heaven, it shows us that the kingdom of heaven
    a. will continue to grow and expand, even though we may not think any progress is being made.
    b. includes all men in every place, even if we cannot see any growth in their lives.
    c. is invisible and cannot be recognized by men.

Matthew 13:31–33, 44–52

15. In verses 31 and 32, Jesus compared the kingdom to a grain of mustard seed, one of the smallest kinds of seeds. Yet this small seed often grows into a plant from 10 to 15 feet tall. In verse 33 the kingdom is compared to leaven (yeast). A small amount of leaven will cause a large amount of flour to rise. Both of these illustrations teach that
    a. Christians should always use leaven and mustard in their baking.
    b. the kingdom of heaven will have a tremendous influence on the world, even though it had a small beginning.
    c. by the end of time, almost everyone in the world will be part of the true church.

A pearl of great price is a better answer, but the structure of the sentence will probably lead most students to the first answer.

- The interpretations given in numbers 14–18 are not the only ones possible, but they are ones that the pupils should be able to understand with little help. You will want to discuss these questions together in class to make sure the students have some understanding of the parables. However, do not confuse the students with too many different possible interpretations. Avoid using the parables to speculate about end-time events.

- We cannot really say that the kingdom is invisible, because the members of the kingdom are seen and can usually be identified.

Truths to Amplify

- It is important for the students to understand that parables have certain limitations. Parables should not be used as the foundation for a doctrine, nor should an application be made for every detail. Most parables can be interpreted several ways to teach more than one truth, but we should avoid creating a complicated interpretation that needs every detail of the parable to support it. A correct interpretation of a parable will be supported by other Scripture passages.

16. In verses 44–46, the kingdom of heaven is compared to a treasure and to a pearl of great price. In both cases, the man who wanted to buy it needed to sell everything that he owned to raise enough money. This shows us that

   a. to become part of the kingdom of heaven, we need to be willing to give up everything else.

   b. it is possible to buy our way into the kingdom of heaven if we have enough money.

   c. only those who sell all their possessions and give the money to the church can become part of the kingdom of heaven.

17. In verses 47–50, Jesus compared the kingdom of heaven to a net. From these verses we can see that

   a. not everyone who appears to be part of the kingdom of heaven is actually ready to enter heaven.

   b. like the fish in a net, there are people in the kingdom of heaven who do not want to be there but who cannot get away.

   c. there will be both good people and sinners in heaven.

18. A person who is instructed in the kingdom of heaven is someone who has a true knowledge of the kingdom by becoming part of it. According to verse 52, such a person has a collection of treasures containing both old and new things that he brings forth. This means that a person who is part of the kingdom of heaven

   a. will become well-to-do and have an abundance of money and material possessions.

   b. must give away all his possessions so that he may remain in the kingdom.

   c. will share his treasures with others so that they may also enjoy such blessings.

B. BIBLE WORD STUDY

Match the following meanings with the words from Matthew 13 on the right.

d	1. A large number of people (13:2)	a. anon
e	2. A short story that illustrates a truth (13:3)	b. gnash
g	3. To become thick, fat, or dull (13:15)	c. householder
a	4. Immediately; right away (13:20)	d. multitude
f	5. Poisonous weeds (13:25)	e. parable
c	6. The head of a family (13:27)	f. tares
h	7. Yeast (13:33)	g. wax gross
b	8. To grind (the teeth) in rage or pain (13:42)	h. leaven

Use the tables of measure inside the back cover to complete this exercise.

9. The *measure* mentioned in verse 33 was called a *saton* in Greek, or a *seah* in Hebrew.

   a. About how much did one saton (seah) equal in English (or metric) measure?

     1 peck (9 liters)

   b. In modern measure, about how much meal did the woman leaven? 3 pecks, or ¾ bushel
                                          (27 liters)

• *Anon* was also used in Lesson 7. It is repeated here for review.

Teachers in countries that normally use the metric system should tell students to give all answers involving measurements in metric.

Twenty-eight liters is also correct, since the tables of measure show that 3 seahs equal 1 ephah, which equals about 28 liters. The figures in the tables of measure are approximate.

C. THINKING ABOUT BIBLE TRUTHS

Why Did Jesus Use Parables?

Jesus did not tell parables simply for the sake of telling stories. Each of His parables taught an important truth.

Matthew 13:10–17

 Choose all *the correct answers for number 1.*

1. After the parable of the sower, Jesus' disciples asked Him why He spoke in parables. According to verses 11–13, Jesus spoke in parables so that
   a. all men would understand.
   b. those who understood some spiritual truth would understand more.
   c. the rich would understand and the poor would not.
   d. those who were blind and deaf to spiritual truth would not understand.
   e. only those who sincerely wanted to understand would understand.

2. According to verses 10–17, which one of the following is *not* true?
   a. If a person had no interest in the truth, Jesus allowed him to remain ignorant.
   b. It was possible for someone to hear the truth without understanding it. To such people, the parables were just interesting stories.
   c. Jesus wanted to conceal the truth from all His listeners, so He spoke in parables.
   d. Jesus taught in parables so that those who had already rejected the truth would fail to understand His teaching.

3. What did Jesus say that indicates He thought His disciples should be able to understand the parables? <u>"It is given unto you to know the mysteries of the kingdom of heaven" (Matthew 13:11).</u>
   <u>(Other answers are possible.)</u>

4. Find the reference in Isaiah that Jesus' parables fulfilled. (Clue: Use a center-column reference Bible, or check *perceive* or *convert* in a concordance.) Reference in Isaiah: <u>Isaiah 6:9, 10</u>

5. The disciples were blessed above many others because they had the privilege of hearing Jesus explain God's truths to them. Who else desired this privilege but did not receive it? <u>_____</u>
   <u>righteous men and prophets of Old Testament times</u>

D. LEARNING MORE ABOUT BIBLE TIMES

The Scribes

The early kings of Judah had scribes to write their letters, record their decrees, and keep their financial records.

1. What service did Shaphan the scribe do for King Josiah in 2 Chronicles 34:18? <u>He read the Book of the Law to him.</u>

- Point out that even though we cannot hear Jesus teach, we have many blessings that the Old Testament saints did not. Today we have the complete Word of God, and Christians have the indwelling Spirit as their teacher (John 16:13).

King Hezekiah gave his scribes additional work besides keeping official records. He had them recopy books and write down stories and proverbs.

2. Whose proverbs did Hezekiah's scribes copy? (Proverbs 25:1) _Solomon's_

Ezra was a scribe. After he returned to Judea, scribes filled an important role in the preservation of the Jews' faith. The scribes retained a high respect for the Law, even when some priests began to neglect parts of it. However, the scribes placed so much emphasis on their interpretation of the Law that the true meaning was often lost.

The Jews called the scribes doctors and teachers.

3. Where did the scribes meet in Jerusalem? (Luke 2:46) _in the temple_

In Jesus' time, the scribes enjoyed the honors that people gave them. They liked to be called rabbi (master). They taught that a person should help a scribe before he helped his own father.

4. For what did Jesus criticize the scribes in Mark 12:38–40?
   Jesus criticized the scribes for their love of long clothing, salutations, and important seats to be seen of men. He also criticized them for devouring widows' houses (oppressing widows) and for making long prayers for show.

The scribes not only copied the Scriptures but also made it their business to interpret and teach the Jewish laws. They taught laws specifically given in the Old Testament, laws based on Old Testament examples, and laws that they had added "for safety's sake." The detailed laws of the scribes governed every detail of life.

5. The laws below are a few of the ones taught by the scribes. Circle the letters of the three that actually came from the Old Testament.
   a. Thou shalt wash both hands before eating food.
   (b.) Thou shalt love the LORD thy God.
   c. Thou shalt eat no egg laid on the Sabbath.
   d. Thou shalt not plug a leak nor wipe a wound on the Sabbath.
   (e.) Thou shalt not covet thy neighbor's house.
   (f.) Thou shalt not bear false witness.
   g. Thou shalt not eat the bread of Gentiles.

98

Lesson 13. Believers and Unbelievers

According to Mark 4:35, the first two events in this lesson took place on the evening of the same day that Jesus spoke the parables of the last lesson. On the following day, Jesus healed the woman with an issue and raised Jairus's daughter.

During this second year of ministry, Jesus had many followers. However, in the coming months more and more people would turn against Him. The Jewish leaders had already rejected Him, and the Galileans had to decide what they would do.

In the meantime Jesus kept on doing good. He taught the people and performed miracles. Everywhere He went, He found people who needed His help.

Sometimes Jesus went far out of His way to help someone in need. Jesus and His disciples crossed a stormy lake to help a man who was so bound by Satan that he was unable to come to Jesus and ask for help.

But Jesus could not help everyone. Some people, such as the people of Nazareth and some Jewish leaders, had no faith in Him at all. They refused to receive His teachings or to believe that His power to work miracles came from God. From such people Jesus turned sadly away. Because of their unbelief, they missed great blessings that God wanted to give them.

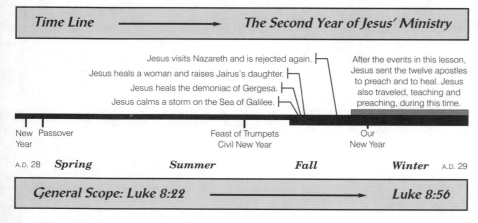

Using the Time Line

🍇 *Check a Bible dictionary for the answers to these questions.*

1. The first three events listed on the time line took place within twenty-four hours. When did the Jewish day start? at sundown

2. Probably Jesus stayed in Nazareth for several days so that He could be there over the Sabbath Day and preach in the synagogue. What day of our week was the Jewish Sabbath? on Saturday

Lesson 13

Oral Review

1. How did a heathen king's decree help fulfill a prophecy about Jesus' birth? [L. 3] **Caesar required everyone to register in his ancestral city. Joseph took Mary to Bethlehem, the city of David, where Jesus was born.**

2. Why did Jesus sometimes rise very early in the morning? [L. 7] **to spend time alone in prayer**

3. Why was Jesus criticized when He went to Levi's house for a feast? [L. 9] **Levi was a publican and was considered a sinner.**

4. What will happen to the person who harshly judges (criticizes) another? [L. 10] **He will also be harshly judged (criticized).**

5. What did Mary Magdalene and other women do for Jesus? [L. 11] **They took care of His needs. (They also prepared His body for burial.)**

6. Why did the scribes and Pharisees always become upset when Jesus forgave someone's sins? [L. 11] **They knew that only God could forgive sins, but they refused to admit that Jesus is God.**

7. In the parable of the sower, what does the seed represent? the ground? [L. 12] *the seed:* **God's Word;** *the ground:* **the hearts of those who hear God's Word**

A. ANSWERS FROM THE BIBLE

Jesus Calms a Storm

Capernaum was crowded with people who had come to watch Jesus perform miracles. Many who had listened to His parables earlier that day had not understood them. They were more interested in seeing Him "perform" than in hearing His words.

Jesus was tired after the long, wearisome day. Perhaps He wanted to get away from the multitudes for a while. Perhaps He knew that His disciples needed a change too. Jesus also knew that across the lake someone needed Him. But even by boat He could not shake off the crowd entirely—some of them followed Him in other boats. Perhaps one reason God sent the storm was to give Jesus the privacy He wanted on the other side of the lake. The storm also served to strengthen the disciples' faith.

> Loud and wild the storm was blowing,
> And the waters overflowing
> And the weary boatmen rowing
> On the wild and stormy crest.
>
> Lo! In fear and faithless error,
> "Master! Save us!" they in terror
> Cried to Him, the Burden-Bearer,
> And He spoke His "Peace, be still."
>
> *Hear the Voice of Hope come winging,*
> *Setting stifled hearts to singing,*
> *Holy peace and purpose bringing*
> *When He speaks His "Peace, be still."*
>
> —Margaret Penner Toews
> From *Five Loaves and Two Small Fish*

Mark 4:35–41

1. What did Jesus do that shows He was a man, with a body like other men? _____

   Jesus fell asleep while the boat was crossing the lake.

2. What did Jesus do that shows He is God, with authority like that of God the Father? _____

   Jesus calmed the wind and the waves.

3. a. What shows that the disciples believed Jesus could help them?   They woke Him from sleep.

   b. What shows that Jesus did more than they had expected Him to do? _____

      They said, "What manner of man is this, that even the wind and the sea obey him?"

4. What shows that Jesus thought the disciples should have reacted differently to the storm than they did?   He rebuked them for their fear and lack of faith.

Jesus Visits the Gadarenes

Jesus left the crowds in the evening (Mark 4:35), so it was probably night when He reached the other side. Coming by moonlight to the far side of the Sea of Galilee would not have been most people's choice. The far side of the sea was lonely and rocky. Steep cliffs rose from the water. Caves and rock chambers cut from the cliffs sheltered the bones of the dead. Here Jesus and His disciples came face to face with the forces of evil.

Note: It is not certain exactly where this miracle took place. The Gadarenes (Mark 5:1; Luke 8:26) are also called Gergesenes in Matthew 8:28. The map in this lesson shows Jesus traveling to Gergesa, a Gentile town across the lake from Magdala.

Mark 5:1–20

Circle the letters of all the correct answers. (Note: All multiple-choice exercises in this lesson have either two or three correct answers.)

5. When Jesus and His disciples reached the far side of the Sea of Galilee, they met a man
   a. who fed a herd of swine.
   (b.) who dwelt among the tombs.
   (c.) with an unclean spirit.
   (d.) who could not be tamed.

---

8. Define these terms: *parable, tares, leaven.* [L. 12]
   parable: **a short story that teaches a truth;**
   tares: **poisonous weeds;** *leaven:* **yeast**

In This Lesson

Scope: Matthew 8:18–34; 9:18–26; 13:54–58; Mark 4:35–6:6; Luke 8:22–56

Focus

• Each individual must make a decision about Jesus. In this lesson some believed while others remained unbelievers.
   —Jesus calmed a storm, thus strengthening the disciples' faith.

—When Jesus visited the Gadarenes, the demoniac ran to Jesus, experienced deliverance, and desired to follow Him. In contrast, the other Gadarenes considered themselves better off without Jesus.

—Jairus and the afflicted woman revealed their faith by going to Jesus with their needs. The crowd of mourners at Jairus's house laughed Him to scorn.

—Jesus returned to Nazareth and found a continued lack of faith there.

100 Chapter Three   Jesus Ministers to Jews and Gentiles

6. The name *Legion* meant
   a. that the man had many devils.   c. that the man was a soldier.
   b. a multitude.   d. a legend.

7. Jesus cast out the devils, but He had mercy on the man. Those who knew the man realized that he had been miraculously changed when they saw him
   a. sitting and properly dressed.   c. in his right mind.
   b. singing and praising God.   d. no longer cutting himself and crying out.

8. How did the herd of swine react when the devils entered into them? _____
   They ran violently down a steep place into the sea.

9. The people in the cured man's town seemed to be afraid
   a. of Jesus' almighty power.
   b. of the man whom Jesus healed.
   c. of Jesus' disciples.
   d. that Jesus' presence might bring more losses besides the swine.

10. The cured man helped in the kingdom of God by
    a. accompanying Jesus on His travels to give his testimony to the crowds.
    b. telling his friends and relatives what Jesus had done for him.
    c. going back to his own village to live.
    d. letting people see his changed life.

11. Suggest a good reason why Jesus did not let the man stay with Him. (Sample answer) The testi-
    mony of the healed man would do the most good for those who had known him while he was pos-
    sessed. Also, he might have attracted so many curious people that he actually would have hindered
    Jesus' ministry.

Jesus in Capernaum Again

Jesus and His disciples returned to Capernaum immediately after the Gadarenes begged Him to leave. The crowd was still waiting for Him there. It appears that He was surrounded by curious people before He even left the seashore. But in the crowd were two people who had been anxiously awaiting His return.

Mark 5:21–43

12. Jairus did not seek Jesus' help until his daughter was at the point of death. From the information given about Jairus in these verses and from what you studied in previous lessons, what might have been his reason for not coming sooner to ask Jesus to heal his daughter? (Sample answer) He
    was a ruler of the synagogue and held an important office. He would be putting his position in danger
    by going to Jesus for help after the scribes and Pharisees had charged that Jesus did miracles by
    Satan's power.

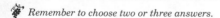 *Remember to choose two or three answers.*

13. Before Jesus did a miracle for them, both Jairus and the sick woman believed that
    a. Jesus could do the healing they desired.
    b. they would find the solution to their problems in Jesus.
    c. they would need to ask for help before they received it.
    d. Jesus wanted to help them.

• It is possible that Jesus attended Matthew's feast when He returned to Capernaum, and then went from there to Jairus's house. (See Matthew 9:9–13, 18.) The exact chronological order of the events in Matthew 9; Mark 4, 5; and Luke 5, 8 is difficult to determine.

Number 12 might be difficult for some students. Discuss this question in class if possible.

Objectives

• Students should know how the following persons showed their faith in Jesus.
  —Jairus (*He asked Jesus to heal his daughter, and trusted Him after he heard that his daughter had died.*)
  —the woman with an issue (*She touched the hem of Jesus' garment to be healed.*)
  —the man who was called Legion (*He asked to be with Jesus after he was healed, yet he obeyed Jesus' command to return home.*)
• Students should know how the following persons showed a lack of faith in Jesus.
  —the disciples in a storm (*They were greatly afraid, even though Jesus was with them.*)
  —the Gadarenes who came to see what Jesus had done (*They asked Jesus to leave.*)
  —the people of Nazareth (*They refused to believe that Jesus is the Son of God.*)
• Students should know
  —what the man called Legion was doing when the men of his country came to see what Jesus had done. (*He was sitting, clothed, and in his right mind.*)
  —why Jesus was not accepted in Nazareth. (*The people knew Him and His family and refused to recognize Him as the Son of God.*)
  —why Jesus could not do many miracles in

14. Jesus already knew who had touched Him. By asking the woman to say what she had done, He
    - (a) gave all those present the opportunity of witnessing this miracle.
    - (b) showed that no one could be healed by His power without Him knowing it.
    - (c) helped her to publicly confess her faith in Him.
    - d. showed disapproval for the way that she had sought healing.

We can only imagine how Jairus felt as he waited. Jesus could not move quickly because of the crowd, and the encounter with the woman had delayed Him some more. Jairus must have feared that by now they would be too late. At this point some messengers came to Jairus and confirmed his fear by telling him that his daughter had died.

15. The messengers told Jairus not to bother Jesus, since his daughter was already dead. What does this show about their faith?   <u>They did not believe that Jesus could help a dead person.</u>

16. The parents of the girl apparently did not think Jesus could bring their daughter back to life. When He did, they were   <u>astonished with a great astonishment</u>.

17. Jesus commanded the parents of the girl not to tell anyone about the miracle He had performed for them. However, He must have known that they would not be able to keep it a secret, since so many people knew that she had died. For what reason might Jesus have given this command?
    <u>(Sample answer) He may have given this command so that He would not be mobbed by the crowd of</u>
    <u>sightseers in Capernaum and so that He would be able to leave the town before they found out about</u>
    the miracle.

Jesus Returns to Nazareth

After raising Jairus's daughter, Jesus left Capernaum. He no longer made that town the center of His activities. The growing opposition of the Pharisees made His stay there difficult.

Early in Jesus' ministry, He had visited His hometown, Nazareth. The Nazarenes had been offended when He pointed out that He was better accepted in other towns than in Nazareth. On this visit, Jesus gave the people of Nazareth another chance to accept Him as the Son of God.

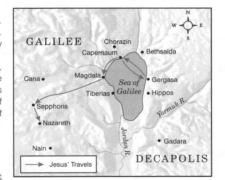

Mark 6:1–6

🍇 *Remember to choose two or three answers.*

18. The Nazarenes may have known nothing about Jesus' miraculous birth. (It had happened in a faraway town, thirty years before.) They were surprised and offended at Jesus' works because they judged Him by
    - (a) His mother.
    - (b) His brothers and sisters.
    - c. His wisdom.
    - (d) His occupation.
    - e. His miracles.
    - f. His righteous life.

19. Jesus could not do mighty works in Nazareth because <u>of the people's unbelief</u>

Nazareth. (*The people did not believe on Him.*) —what body of water is also called the Sea of Chinnereth. (*Sea of Galilee*)

- Students should know the meaning of each of the following words.
  —damsel (*girl*)
  —fetters (*chains to bind the feet*)
  —legion (*multitude*)

Truths to Amplify

- The events of this lesson are not closely related, yet one common theme runs through them. As Jesus continued to do miracles and to teach the people, the question of who He was came more clearly into

focus. People needed to make a choice either to believe on Him or to reject His claims.

- The disciples marveled at Jesus' control of the weather. Their lack of faith turned into wonder at this heretofore unknown dimension of Jesus' power. Although their faith had been small, they nevertheless would believe.

- The demon-possessed man called Legion and the Gadarenes both recognized Jesus' power. The delivered man chose Jesus' presence, but the others rejected it.

- The woman with an infirmity certainly believed as she reached out and touched Jesus' garment. Jairus believed, even when news reached him that his

B. BIBLE WORD STUDY

Match the words with their meanings. All references are from Mark.

b	1. Annoyed; displeased; distressed	a.	pluck (5:4)
j	2. Chains to bind feet	b.	offended (6:3)
f	3. Commotion; uproar	c.	asunder (5:4)
i	4. Crowd; throng	d.	pray (5:17, 23)
g	5. A girl	e.	scorn (5:40)
c	6. Into pieces; apart	f.	tumult (5:38)
e	7. Mockery; contempt	g.	damsel (5:39)
h	8. Power; goodness	h.	virtue (5:30)
d	9. To request urgently; beseech	i.	press (5:30)
a	10. To pull or tear	j.	fetters (5:4)

C. THINKING ABOUT BIBLE TRUTHS

Setting Captives Free

The man called Legion was controlled by demons. The woman with an issue of blood was a captive of her disease. Jairus's daughter was a captive of death, and the Nazarenes were captives of their unbelief. Jesus was able to free three of these, but He was powerless to do anything for the Nazarenes.

1. Both the cured man and the Gadarenes made a choice.

   a. How did the Gadarenes show that they preferred to live in spiritual darkness rather than to be set free by Jesus? They asked Jesus to leave their country.

   b. How did the cured man show that he preferred the opposite? He asked to go with Jesus.

2. The woman with an issue of blood thought she could be set free from her "captivity" without anyone knowing about it. Did this show a weakness or a strength in her faith? Explain your answer. This showed strength of faith because she believed Jesus' power was great enough to heal her without direct contact. But her fear of publicly requesting healing from Jesus also revealed some weakness in her faith. >>

3. Jairus wanted Jesus to come and lay hands on his daughter and heal her. A little while before, a Roman centurion had asked Jesus to heal his servant without even seeing him. Which of these two had the greater faith? Explain your answer. Probably the centurion had greater faith, since he felt that Jesus could just say the word and his servant would be healed.

4. Jesus was not able to set the Nazarenes free from their captivity. What did they lack that most of the other "captives" in this lesson had? The Nazarenes did not have any faith in Jesus.

Some students may find it difficult to answer all the following questions on their own. If possible, discuss at least numbers 1–4 in class.

The answer could be either strength or weakness, depending on the explanation. Accept any reasonable answer. (Matthew 14:36 records the healing of many others in this way, perhaps from her example.)

However, do not discredit Jairus. It took quite a bit of faith on his part to come to Jesus too, even though it appears to have been a last resort. Jesus honored the faith he had, and used the opportunity to increase his faith.

• In every other case, faith was involved. Although the dead girl could not exercise faith, she would not have been raised if her father had not had enough faith to go to Jesus on her behalf.

daughter had passed away. The watching multitude did not believe as they laughed at Jesus.

• The people of Nazareth chose sight rather than faith. They trusted what they saw and understood naturally, rather than accepting the obvious supernatural power of Jesus. This is the same mistake modern men make who claim to believe only what can be explained scientifically.

The more that people insist on a natural explanation for what they believe, the more difficult it is to explain Christ's life. It can be understood only as people choose, by faith, to accept His claims.

5. Jesus did not always heal people in the same way. In the following list, find contrasts in the healing of the woman who touched Jesus' hem and the daughter of Jairus. Arrange them in two lists, matching the contrasting pairs of points.

She came to Jesus.	She was aware of what was happening.
Jesus went to her.	She was unaware of what was happening.
The crowd was shut out.	She touched Jesus.
She was in the midst of a crowd.	Jesus touched her.

The Woman With an Infirmity

a. She came to Jesus.

b. She was in the midst of a crowd.

c. She was aware of what was happening.

d. She touched Jesus.

The Daughter of Jairus

e. Jesus went to her.

f. The crowd was shut out.

g. She was unaware of what was happening.

h. Jesus touched her.

D. LEARNING MORE ABOUT BIBLE TIMES

The Sea of Galilee

Much of Jesus' ministry took place in Galilee near the Sea of Galilee. Jesus sometimes used it as a highway, crossing it by boat. Many of His disciples came from the area around the Sea of Galilee. Capernaum, where Jesus made His headquarters, was on the northern shore of the lake.

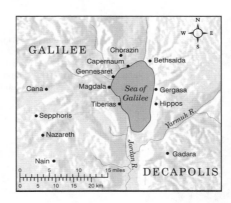

1. The Sea of Galilee is a relatively small body of water that is actually a lake rather than a sea. Use the map scale to calculate its greatest length (north and south) and width.
   a. length: 13 miles (21 km)
   b. width: 8 miles (13 km)
2. The Bible uses various names for the Sea of Galilee. Read the following references and find the name used in each verse.
   a. Numbers 34:11 Sea of Chinnereth
   b. Matthew 4:18 Sea of Galilee
   c. Luke 5:1 Lake of Gennesaret
   d. John 21:1 Sea of Tiberias

104   Chapter Three   Jesus Ministers to Jews and Gentiles

The Sea of Galilee was important to the economy of Galilee. It supplied food and jobs for many people. A number of the disciples were fishermen before Christ called them.

Many of the boats on the Sea of Galilee were small. Boats such as the one pictured in the foreground on the right were intended to hold only about four people. It was dangerous to be too far from shore in these boats when the weather became stormy, as it often did on this lake.

3. Some of Jesus' disciples were probably quite well-to-do, since fishing was one of the better jobs in Galilee. Apparently at least some of them owned their own boats. (See Luke 5:3, 11.) One of them may have owned a boat large enough to hold _____thirteen_____ or more people (Luke 8:22). However, Jesus or His disciples may have borrowed or rented this larger boat.

4. Jesus performed a number of miracles around the Sea of Galilee. Earlier in this lesson Jesus calmed a storm that was threatening to sink the boat He was in. On another occasion He _walked on the sea (water)_ _____ (Matthew 14:25).

- This reference does not specifically state that all twelve disciples were with Jesus. However, all twelve were with Him when He fed the five thousand (Luke 9:12), and they apparently all left in the same boat (Mark 6:45). Jesus joined them after walking on the water (Mark 6:51).

The Sea of Galilee is the lowest freshwater lake in the world. It is below sea level in the Jordan River Valley and is surrounded by higher land and hills. The high hills and the sudden temperature changes that are common in the area cause the sudden storms for which the Sea of Galilee is noted. In Jesus' time, a number of cities and villages were located along the northern and western shores of the lake, but the hills on the east were too steep for settlement.

The Sea of Galilee

5. Look up the *Sea of Galilee* in a Bible dictionary. (Check under "Galilee, Sea of.")
   a. How far below sea level is the surface of the lake?
      about 700 feet (213 m) >>
   b. How deep is it at the deepest spot?
      about 150–165 feet (46–50 m) >>

Answers will vary slightly, depending on which reference book is used.

105

Lesson 14. Jesus—the Bread of Life

Jesus had become popular. Crowds flocked to hear Him, especially after He miraculously fed five thousand people. But Jesus knew that some were following Him for the wrong reasons. Many in the crowds had little desire to understand who He was or to learn more of God's will. Some saw Him as a kind of magician. Others wanted to make Him a king and overthrow the Romans.

If Jesus had been like many men, He would have let the crowds cheer Him and bring Him fame. But Jesus was not seeking an earthly following. Even though He knew that it would turn many people away, He spoke God's words and plainly pointed out sin. Jesus knew that only the truth could deliver people from sin and bring them into God's spiritual family.

Jesus did not let His popularity change His message. He had come to seek and to save those who were lost. He did miracles to make it easier for people to believe His teaching, not to entertain them. But when Jesus said that He is the spiritual bread from heaven, many of His followers left Him.

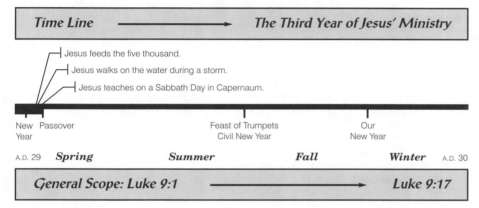

Time Line ⟶ **The Third Year of Jesus' Ministry**

Jesus feeds the five thousand.

Jesus walks on the water during a storm.

Jesus teaches on a Sabbath Day in Capernaum.

| New Year | Passover | Feast of Trumpets Civil New Year | Our New Year |

A.D. 29 **Spring**   **Summer**   **Fall**   **Winter** A.D. 30

General Scope: Luke 9:1 ⟶ **Luke 9:17**

Using the Time Line

1. Before what major Jewish feast did the events of this lesson take place? (Compare your answer with John 6:4.)   the Passover
2. Which of the events on the time line did Jesus do the night after He fed the five thousand? (Notice the order of the events, and think about which could be done at night. If you need further help, read Matthew 14:21–34.)   He walked on the water during a storm.

A. ANSWERS FROM THE BIBLE

The Feeding of the Five Thousand

Between the events of the last lesson and this one, Jesus sent out His disciples in pairs to preach repentance and heal the sick. The disciples had returned just before the events of this lesson began. Jesus wanted to take them away from the crowd for some rest and fellowship. The crowds were still thronging them, and it was

• The feeding of the five thousand is one of the few events of Jesus' ministry that is recorded in all four Gospels. This provides an important link between the Gospel of John and the other Gospels.

Lesson 14

Oral Review

1. How did King Herod try to destroy Jesus? [L. 3] **He killed all the babies in Bethlehem that were two years old or younger.**
2. How did Jesus answer His mother's question when she and Joseph found Him talking to the teachers at the temple? [L. 3] **"Wist ye not that I must be about my Father's business?"**
3. Instead of repaying "an eye for an eye, and a tooth for a tooth," how did Jesus say we should respond if someone mistreats us? [L. 9] **"Resist not evil: but whosoever shall smite thee on thy right cheek, turn to him the other also."**
4. What did Jesus do for the widow of Nain? [L. 11] **He raised her son back to life.**
5. Why did Jesus teach in parables? [L. 12] **so that only those who believed would understand**
6. In the parable of the tares, what does the weedy grain field represent? [L. 12] **the world**
7. What was the man called Legion doing when the men of his country came to see what Jesus had done? [L. 13] **He was sitting, clothed, and in his right mind.**
8. Why could Jesus not do as many miracles at Nazareth as He did in other places? [L. 13] **The people of Nazareth did not believe in Him.**

106   Chapter Three   Jesus Ministers to Jews and Gentiles

impossible for Jesus and the disciples to be alone or to rest where they were.

According to Matthew 14:13, Jesus had also just heard about John the Baptist's death. The sadness this brought Him may have given Him another reason for seeking rest and quietness at this time. But, like usual, it was difficult for Jesus to get away from the crowd. When they saw Him leaving by boat, some people guessed where He was going and ran around the northern end of the lake to meet Him on the other side. As the crowd traveled, it became larger and larger. By the time the people reached the place where Jesus went ashore, the crowd had swelled to about five thousand men, besides women and children.

Mark 6:30–36

1. Jesus had wanted to be by Himself, but the people flocked after Him. Instead of sending them away, He
   a. was thankful for the chance to demonstrate His power to them.
   b. hid on the mountain so that they could not find Him.
   c. was moved with compassion toward them and taught them many things.
   d. left them with the disciples and went out alone to pray.

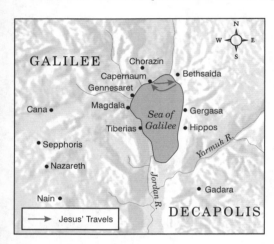

Jesus sat down with His disciples on a mountain slope near Bethsaida. There He taught the multitude many things and cured the ones in need of healing. It was a spring day just before the Passover, and the hills around the Sea of Galilee were green with grass.

2. As afternoon passed into evening, the disciples began to think about the crowd's need for food. They knew that most of the people had not brought food along when they hurried around the lake to meet Jesus on the other side. What did they suggest that Jesus do? _____
They suggested that He send the multitude away to buy food.

John 6:5–14

Jesus was never at a loss for what to do. He knew how He would supply food for the crowd. But He also saw an opportunity to teach His disciples another lesson.

3. Jesus wanted Philip to learn that
   a. one should always come prepared.
   b. it is not wise to draw a multitude into the wilderness.
   c. people are more interested in food than in sound teaching.
   d. God is always able to supply every need.

Andrew told Jesus that one boy had five loaves and two small fish. But he added, "What are they among so many?" He must have realized that Jesus was planning to do something with the boy's food, but he could not see how it would help much.

In This Lesson

Scope: Matthew 14:13–15:20; Mark 6:30–7:23; Luke 9:10–17; John 6

Focus
- Jesus desired rest for Himself and His disciples. But when crowds followed Him, He had compassion on them and taught them many things.
- Jesus fed the five thousand with five loaves and two fish.
- Jesus refused to be made an earthly king or to let a desire for fame distort His message.
- Jesus taught the disciples trust during a storm on the lake.
- Jesus taught that He is the spiritual Bread of Life from heaven.
- After Jesus' teaching on spiritual bread, many of His disciples turned away from Him.

Objectives
- Students should know
  —what Jesus used to feed the five thousand. (*five loaves and two fish*)
  —what Jesus taught His disciples by using common food to feed the five thousand. (*God can do much with little, ordinary things.*)
  —what the people wanted to do to Jesus after He fed the five thousand. (*make Him king*)

4. Number the following events in the correct order to show how Jesus met the multitude's need. The comments in italics give some lessons that we can learn from this miracle.

    __2__   a. Jesus gave thanks for the food. *(Jesus demonstrated thankfulness.)*

    __5__   b. All those present ate until they were filled. *(God can provide all we need.)*

    __3__   c. Jesus gave the bread and fish to His disciples. *(Every good gift comes from God.)*

    __6__   d. Jesus told His disciples to gather the leftovers. *(God wants us to avoid wasting food.)*

    __4__   e. The disciples distributed the food to the multitude. *(God uses men to help meet needs.)*

    __1__   f. Jesus told His disciples to make the people sit down in groups. *(God is orderly.)*

5. Barley bread was one of the simplest foods in Galilee. Ordinarily barley was considered animal feed. Only the poor used it for food. By using the boy's bread and fish to feed the multitude, when He could just as easily have given bread from heaven, Jesus showed that

    (a.) God can use ordinary things to do great works.

    b. God feeds only those who cannot afford regular food.

    c. God does not like the food of the rich.

    d. the people were not worthy of better food.

6. The men who saw Jesus perform this miracle said, "This is of a truth that prophet that should come into the world." They were thinking of a prophecy God had given through Moses. Read Deuteronomy 18:15, 18. In these verses God had said the prophet would come from

    a. the north.   (c.) among the people.

    b. Galilee.   d. the tribe of Benjamin.

John 6:15; Matthew 14:22, 23

The excited multitude wanted to crown Jesus king. They did not know that He was already a king. Nor were they really interested in His teachings. Rather, they saw the potential advantages of having a king with such tremendous miracle-working powers.

7. How did the multitude plan to make Jesus king?   by force

Jesus still wanted to have some time alone. He sent the multitude away and told the disciples to take the boat and return to the other side of the lake without Him.

8. What did Jesus do when He was finally alone?   Jesus went up into a mountain to pray.

Jesus Walks on the Water

That night a great wind began to sweep across the lake. Looking across the waters, Jesus could see the disciples toiling to bring their boat to shore (Mark 6:48). Jesus left the mountain and went to help them.

Matthew 14:24–33

9. The disciples could not see Jesus well enough to recognize Him. What was He doing that caused them to think that He was a spirit?   walking on the water

10. Peter sometimes spoke and acted before he thought things through. What shows that he had not considered everything before he stepped out of the boat?

    When Peter saw the strong wind, he was filled with fear.

Discuss the lessons in italics as time permits.

- Point out that in spite of Peter's weaknesses, he did exercise faith in Jesus by leaving the boat and by calling on Him for help. How many of us would have left the boat?

—what the disciples did when Jesus entered the boat after walking on the water. (*worshiped Him*)

—what the Pharisees rejected to keep their traditions. (*the commandments of God*)

—what Jesus taught that turned many people away from Him. (*that He is the Bread of Life from heaven*)

—who continued to follow Jesus after many others left Him. (*His twelve disciples*)

—the meaning of *fourth watch.* (*the last Roman watch of the night, lasting from about 3:00 A.M. to 6:00 A.M.*)

Truths to Amplify

- The occasion of Jesus' feeding of the five thousand is well remembered. Jesus showed mercy upon the multitude by giving them bread and fish to eat. But passing out bread and fish was far from Jesus' main work. What we may not remember so well is what Jesus did first when He saw the multitude. "And Jesus, when he came out, saw much people, and was moved with compassion toward them, because they were as sheep not having a shepherd: and he began to teach them many things" (Mark 6:34).

- Jesus taught by word and action. It is Jesus the teacher whom we want to see. Jesus did miracles to teach something about Himself. In feeding the five

108   Chapter Three   Jesus Ministers to Jews and Gentiles

11. What did the disciples do and say after Jesus and Peter were in the boat? _____
    They worshiped Him saying, "Of a truth thou art the Son of God."

The Pharisees Oppose Jesus

Even though Jesus had openly performed a great miracle by feeding the five thousand, the Pharisees still did not believe on Him. Jesus was not the kind of Messiah they were looking for. Worse yet, He did not keep the extra rules they had made. Since He did not fit their idea of what God expected of men, they concluded that He must be a sinner. In their opinion, His miracles were just further proof that He received His power from Satan.

John 6:24–27

12. Jesus told the people that they followed Him because they   ate of the loaves and were filled
    _____.

13. Jesus said they should not labor for natural food, but rather for that which _____ endureth _____
    unto _____ everlasting _____ _____ life _____.

Mark 7:1–13

This incident also took place soon after the feeding of the five thousand.

14. Many sick people came to Jesus to be healed when He returned to Capernaum (Mark 6:54–56).
    But the Pharisees and scribes who came from _____ Jerusalem _____ began to criticize Jesus again.

15. Why did the Jews criticize Jesus' disciples? _The disciples ate with unwashen hands._
    _____

16. Jesus and His disciples kept the laws God had given to Moses. But the Pharisees thought they
    should also keep _the traditions of the elders_____.

17. Jesus condemned the Pharisees for rejecting the commandment of God in order to keep _____
    the commandments of men
    _____.

18. Jesus gave one example of how the Pharisees placed their rules above God's commandments.
    Through Moses, God had given the command, "Honour thy _____ father _____ and thy
    _____ mother _____." But the Pharisees said that if someone dedicated his possessions as a gift,
    which they called _____ Corban _____, to the temple, he did not need to care for his parents.

Spiritual Bread From Heaven

John 6:30–35

The people who were present at the feeding of the five thousand found Jesus again at Capernaum on the Sabbath Day (John 6:59). Jesus knew that the main reason they were interested in Him was that He had fed them in the desert by a miracle. He warned them not to labor for the meat that perishes, but for the meat that lasts for eternity. They did not understand Him when He tried to explain to them what He meant by this. Instead, they asked Him for a sign to prove who He was.

19. Jesus knew that another miracle would not help them believe. Instead, Jesus said that He would
    (a.) give Himself to provide life for the world.
    b. give them the true teachings of Moses.
    c. give them higher ideals to live by.
    d. give them a constant supply of bread.

- Edersheim gives more details regarding this practice. The Jewish leaders permitted a person to free himself from his responsibility to his parents by claiming to devote to God the possessions that he should have used for parental care. Worse yet, he could indefinitely postpone the actual giving of the gift, and thus continue to benefit from it himself.

thousand, Jesus taught about trusting in God for our needs. By walking on the water, He taught about God's power. No doubt other lessons were taught by these events as well. (For a sample of lessons taught in the feeding of the five thousand, see the italicized comments in number 4.)

- Jesus was more willing to lose friends than to neglect the work He came to do. Not only did He lose friends, but He also gained enemies. But Jesus never expressed resentment against His enemies. They were like the enemies of Christians today—enemies who hate the righteous example that reveals their wickedness. The Pharisees were lovers of darkness because their deeds were evil. While teaching the accounts of Jesus and His enemies, call special attention to Jesus' nonresistant example.

Many People Turn Away

The people did not understand what Jesus was telling them because they were more interested in what He could do for them physically than spiritually. Most of them were interested in bread they could eat, not in spiritual bread.

John 6:66–69

20. Because of His teaching about spiritual bread, Jesus
  a. became more popular.
  b. lost many of His disciples.
  c. was able to do many more miracles.
  d. was able to help the Pharisees understand the truth.

21. Jesus asked the twelve disciples what they planned to do. Outspoken Peter answered for them all. By his answer we know that they
  a. thought Jesus' words were too difficult.
  b. were seriously considering leaving Him too.
  c. were still not certain who Jesus was.
  d. believed that eternal life could be found through Jesus' teaching.

B. BIBLE WORD STUDY

 Write a short definition or a synonym for the italicized word or phrase in each sentence. Use a dictionary or Bible dictionary if you need help.

Sample answers are given for 1–4.

1. A great *company* came to see Jesus at the place where He had gone to rest (John 6:5).
   crowd; multitude; group of people

2. Jesus *constrained* His disciples to take a boat to the other side so that He could pray alone (Matthew 14:22). _required; compelled_

3. The people *took shipping* to look for Jesus (John 6:24). _took a boat; went sailing_

4. The Pharisees kept the *traditions* of the elders (Mark 7:3). _practices handed down_

 Use the following information to answer question 5.

In Roman times people divided the night into four watches.
—first watch: *from 6:00 P.M. to 9:00 P.M.*
—second watch: *from 9:00 P.M. to midnight*
—third watch: *from midnight to 3:00 A.M.*
—fourth watch: *from 3:00 A.M. to 6:00 A.M.*

5. About what time of the night did the disciples see Jesus walking on the Sea of Galilee? (Matthew 14:25) _sometime between 3:00 A.M. and 6:00 A.M._

 Answer the following questions.

6. In Jesus' time, a day's wage for a common laborer was one Roman denarius (called a penny in our Bibles). How many days would one man have needed to work to buy "two hundred pennyworth of bread"? (John 6:7) _two hundred days_

7. The disciples rowed about 25 or 30 furlongs before they saw Jesus walking on the water (John 6:19). Approximately how far is this in modern measure? (Use the tables of measure inside the back cover.) about 3 miles (about 5 km)

C. THINKING ABOUT BIBLE TRUTHS

Spiritual Food

1. Read John 4:31–34. What did Jesus consider more important than eating? _____
   to do God's work of helping people find salvation

2. Read Job 23:12. Job realized that spiritual food was more important than natural food. What did Job consider to be his spiritual food? the words of God's mouth

3. Read John 6:35, 51. Who is the living bread (the One who can supply all our needs) that came down from heaven? Jesus

4. We cannot listen to Jesus' sermons in the same way people did when they followed Him in Galilee. List at least two ways Christians today can receive spiritual food from God. (Sample answers)
   by reading the Bible, by listening to the preaching of God's Word, by believing Jesus' words

D. LEARNING MORE ABOUT BIBLE TIMES

Bread From Heaven

Use the clues below to fill in this puzzle. If necessary, use a concordance to find the reference of the verse or incident.

Across

1. Jesus said, "I am the bread of life: he that cometh to me shall never ——."

4. "This is that bread which came down from heaven: not as your fathers did eat ——, and are dead."

6. The Pharisees were displeased because the —— did not wash their hands before eating bread.

7. "This is the bread which cometh down from heaven, that a man may eat thereof, and not ——."

9. "The bread of God is he which cometh down from heaven, and giveth —— unto the world."

In the margin:

• The furlong measurement (the Greek *stadion*) used in the New Testament is sometimes confused with the English furlong. This confusion seems to stem from the King James Version rendering of the Greek word *stadion* (approximately 606 feet) as *furlong*, since the English furlong was only slightly longer (660 feet). This Bible series uses the 606 feet equivalent, which was the approximate length of the stadion according to Bible reference sources such as the *New Unger's Bible Dictionary* and *Davis Dictionary of the Bible*.

Keep the discussion of Part C on a level that your students can understand. The important point is that Jesus (and His Word) provides spiritual life and nurture, just as natural food provides physical nutrition.

A. ANSWERS FROM THE BIBLE

Jesus' Trip Through Gentile Territory

The map on this page shows the approximate route that Jesus and the apostles traveled during the events in this lesson. As far as we know, this was the farthest that Jesus ever traveled outside Jewish territory. During this trip Jesus and His disciples traveled approximately 125 miles. It would have taken them about a week to travel this distance if they had stopped only for the nights. Since Jesus also spent time doing miracles and teaching the Gentiles, they may have spent a month or more in their travels before returning to the northern coast of the Sea of Galilee.

1. Jesus traveled to the borders of Tyre and Sidon, through Decapolis to the Sea of Galilee, and on to Magdala (Dalmanutha) and Bethsaida (Mark 7:24, 31; 8:10, 22). The map shows a possible route that He may have taken after leaving Capernaum. Beginning with Chorazin, list in order the names of seven towns or cities that were on the route that is shown.

   a. _____Chorazin_____
   b. _____Kedesh_____
   c. _____Tyre_____
   d. ____Caesarea Philippi____
   e. _____Hippos_____
   f. _____Magdala_____
   g. _____Bethsaida_____

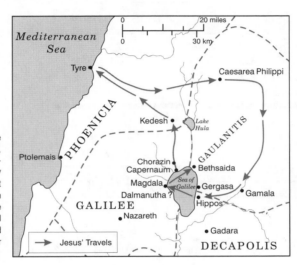

The Woman of Canaan

When Jesus spoke to this Gentile woman who lived near Tyre and Sidon, He implied that the Jews were God's children and the Gentiles were merely "dogs." To us, that sounds unfriendly. But Jesus wanted to help this heathen woman learn something about God. He wanted her to know that the God of Israel is the true God for all nations. He wanted her to accept the "Jewish" God as her personal God before He helped her.

Matthew 15:21–28

2. Jesus told the woman that it was not right to cast the children's meat to the dogs. What did the woman say that shows she understood that the God of Israel was merciful enough to help her, a Gentile, in spite of what Jesus said? _____
   She said, "Truth, Lord: yet the dogs eat of the crumbs which fall from their masters' table."

3. How did Jesus reward this Gentile woman's faith? _He healed her daughter._____
   _____

112

Lesson 15. Jesus Goes to the Gentiles

In Lesson 14, we studied how the Galileans made their choice to turn against Jesus. Only the twelve disciples and a few others continued to follow Him. But when the Jews turned their backs on Jesus, He went to other people who were glad to receive Him.

After the Sabbath at Capernaum when many of the Jews abandoned Him, Jesus visited the Gentiles.

First Jesus and a few of His disciples traveled west to the borders of Tyre and Sidon. There Jesus hoped to stay hidden in a house for a while. But it was impossible. News of His presence soon spread.

The same thing was true when Jesus traveled east and south to the Gentile territory of Decapolis. There the Gentiles flocked to see Him in crowds almost as large as the Jewish crowds had been. Later, some of these Gentiles may have become part of the Christian church.

Jesus did not receive as much opposition from the Gentiles as He did from the Jews. When He crossed the lake for a stop at Magdala, the Pharisees again came to find fault with Him.

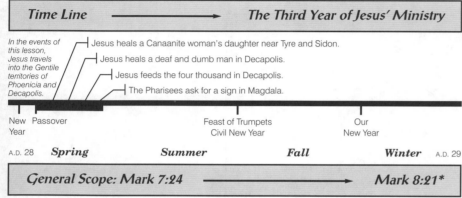

Time Line ⟶ **The Third Year of Jesus' Ministry**

In the events of this lesson, Jesus travels into the Gentile territories of Phoenicia and Decapolis.

Jesus heals a Canaanite woman's daughter near Tyre and Sidon.

Jesus heals a deaf and dumb man in Decapolis.

Jesus feeds the four thousand in Decapolis.

The Pharisees ask for a sign in Magdala.

New Year — Passover
Feast of Trumpets / Civil New Year
Our New Year

A.D. 28   *Spring*   *Summer*   *Fall*   *Winter*   A.D. 29

General Scope: Mark 7:24 ⟶ **Mark 8:21***

* Note: Luke does not record the events of this lesson.

Using the Time Line

1. What Jewish feast took place just before or during the time covered by this lesson?
   the Passover

2. The Gospels do not record that Jesus attended this feast. Where do the Gospels say Jesus traveled about this time? (See the lesson introduction and the time line note.) _____
   He traveled among the Gentiles.

- The last chapters of Matthew and Mark are much more similar than the earlier portions of these books. Beginning with Matthew 14:1 and Mark 6:14, these two Gospels give most of the same events in the same order. Luke and John do not mention the events covered in this lesson. However, Luke gives details about the Perean ministry that the others omit, and John records what Jesus taught and did in Jerusalem. Together, the four Gospels provide a well-balanced account of Jesus' life and ministry.

Lesson 15

Oral Review

1. How did God the Father and God the Holy Spirit manifest themselves at Jesus' baptism? [L. 4] **God the Father said, "This is my beloved Son, in whom I am well pleased." The Holy Spirit descended upon Jesus in the form of a dove.**

2. What do we call Jesus' sermon of new laws recorded in Matthew 5–7? [L. 9] **the Sermon on the Mount**

3. How do we lay up treasures in heaven? [L. 10] **We seek the things of God rather than the things of the earth.**

4. Who thought Jesus was doing too much for His own good? [L. 11] **His friends**

5. What job did scribes do for Old Testament kings? [L. 12] **They copied books and kept records.**

6. How did the woman with an issue prove that she had faith in Jesus? [L. 13] **She touched the hem of Jesus' garment.**

7. By using a few loaves and fishes to feed the five thousand, what did Jesus teach His disciples? [L. 14] **God can do much with little, ordinary things.**

8. After feeding the five thousand, how did Jesus teach the people not to be wasteful? [L. 14] **He had the disciples gather up all the leftovers.**

A. ANSWERS FROM THE BIBLE

Jesus' Trip Through Gentile Territory

The map on this page shows the approximate route that Jesus and the apostles traveled during the events in this lesson. As far as we know, this was the farthest that Jesus ever traveled outside Jewish territory. During this trip Jesus and His disciples traveled approximately 125 miles. It would have taken them about a week to travel this distance if they had stopped only for the nights. Since Jesus also spent time doing miracles and teaching the Gentiles, they may have spent a month or more in their travels before returning to the northern coast of the Sea of Galilee.

1. Jesus traveled to the borders of Tyre and Sidon, through Decapolis to the Sea of Galilee, and on to Magdala (Dalmanutha) and Bethsaida (Mark 7:24, 31; 8:10, 22). The map shows a possible route that He may have taken after leaving Capernaum. Beginning with Chorazin, list in order the names of seven towns or cities that were on the route that is shown.

   a. _____Chorazin_____
   b. _____Kedesh_____
   c. _____Tyre_____
   d. _____Caesarea Philippi_____
   e. _____Hippos_____
   f. _____Magdala_____
   g. _____Bethsaida_____

The Woman of Canaan

When Jesus spoke to this Gentile woman who lived near Tyre and Sidon, He implied that the Jews were God's children and the Gentiles were merely "dogs." To us, that sounds unfriendly. But Jesus wanted to help this heathen woman learn something about God. He wanted her to know that the God of Israel is the true God for all nations. He wanted her to accept the "Jewish" God as her personal God before He helped her.

Jesus' Travels

- Jesus may have traveled farther north than the route shown on the map.
- There may have been more than one Bethsaida near the Sea of Galilee. (The literal meaning of Bethsaida is "house of fishing.")

Matthew 15:21–28

2. Jesus told the woman that it was not right to cast the children's meat to the dogs. What did the woman say that shows she understood that the God of Israel was merciful enough to help her, a Gentile, in spite of what Jesus said? _____

   She said, "Truth, Lord: yet the dogs eat of the crumbs which fall from their masters' table."

3. How did Jesus reward this Gentile woman's faith?   He healed her daughter.
   _____

In This Lesson

Scope: Matthew 15:21–16:12; Mark 7:24–8:21

Focus

- Jesus left Galilee for a while and traveled through Gentile territory.
  —Jesus traveled to Phoenicia and helped a Syrophoenician woman.
  —In Decapolis Jesus healed a deaf and dumb man and fed the four thousand.
  —Jesus briefly visited the Jewish territory around Magdala (Dalmanutha), where the Pharisees found fault with Him.
  —Jesus and His disciples crossed the Sea of Galilee

again on their journey to Bethsaida. On the way, Jesus warned His disciples to beware of the leaven (doctrine) of the Pharisees.

Objectives

- Students should know
  —how the Syrophoenician woman proved her faith in Jesus. (*She continued to ask Jesus for help.*)
  —what Jesus taught His disciples by helping the Gentiles. (*God loves everyone, and everyone who has true faith can receive God's blessing.*)
  —what the Gentiles of Decapolis did when they saw Jesus' miracles. (*They glorified the God of Israel.*)
  —how the group of four thousand was probably

4. The disciples had wanted to send the woman away. Like other Jews of their time, they probably abhorred Gentiles and avoided contact with them as much as possible. What did Jesus teach His disciples by healing the Gentile woman's child? _____

   that God's mercy was not only for the Jews

The Deaf and Dumb Man

After healing the Gentile woman's daughter, Jesus and His disciples traveled to Decapolis, a Gentile region extending south and east of the Sea of Galilee (see the map on page 113). The region received its name because of its ten independent cities. (In Greek, *deka* means "ten," and *polis* means "city.") Although many Jews lived in Decapolis, most of its population was heathen. On His journey, Jesus did more miracles for Gentile people.

Mark 7:31–37

5. What did the people of Decapolis think Jesus should do to the deaf and dumb man to heal him?

   put His hands on him

6. This man, who was probably a Gentile, might have been uncertain about Jesus. What did Jesus do to heal him, which may have strengthened his faith? Name at least three things. _____

   (Any three) He put His fingers into his ears, He spit, He touched his tongue, He looked up to heaven,
   He sighed, and He said, "Ephphatha" (Be open).

7. See Matthew 15:30, 31. Whose God did the Gentiles glorify for the miracles Jesus did? _____

   the God of Israel

Jesus Feeds the Four Thousand

Because of their similarities, it is easy to forget that the feeding of the five thousand and the feeding of the four thousand were two separate events. However, as you compare them closely, you will see that in a number of ways the two occasions were distinctly different.

Mark 8:1–9

8. Compare the feeding of the five thousand with the feeding of the four thousand. The account of the feeding of the five thousand is found in Mark 6:30–44.

   a. How long had the multitude been with Jesus?
      5,000: one day   4,000: three days

   b. How much food was available?
      5,000: five (barley) loaves and two fish   4,000: seven loaves and a few fish

   c. Where did the people sit?
      5,000: on the green grass   4,000: on the ground

   d. Who passed out the food?
      5,000: the disciples   4,000: the disciples

   e. How much food was left?
      5,000: twelve baskets   4,000: seven baskets

9. What two kinds of food seem to have been common in the region of Galilee? bread and fish

- Although it is not evident in our English Bibles, the Gospel writers used different Greek words in referring to the baskets for collecting the leftovers from the four thousand and from the five thousand. The twelve baskets (Greek *kophinos*) were wicker baskets that could easily be carried by hand. But the seven baskets (Greek *spuris*) were larger storage baskets that were sometimes large enough to hold a man (Acts 9:25). It is significant that Jesus kept this distinction when He referred to the two events in Matthew 16:9, 10 and Mark 8:19, 20.

different from the five thousand that Jesus had fed earlier. (*Quite likely the four thousand were Gentiles and the five thousand were Jews.*)

—how much food was left after Jesus fed the four thousand. (*seven baskets full*)

—why the Pharisees asked for a sign from heaven. (*They wanted to find fault with Jesus.*)

—what Jesus meant by the leaven of the Pharisees and the Sadducees. (*their false doctrine*)

—how the Jews were to treat Gentiles according to the Old Testament Law. (*kindly*)

Truths To Amplify

- Jesus showed mercy to the Gentile neighbors of the Jews, which was altogether in line with God's plans for the Christian church. Years later, the early church gradually came to understood that God's new family was to include more than just Abraham's flesh-and-blood descendants.

- Grade 7 students may profit from a class discussion on some of the following prophecies concerning the Gentiles: Genesis 22:18, Isaiah 9:2, Isaiah 49:6, Isaiah 60:3, Hosea 2:23, and Ephesians 3:6.

10. The four thousand who gathered around Jesus may have been mostly Gentiles. The previous time, the crowd had been Jewish. What did Jesus show by doing these very similar miracles for two very different groups of people?   (Sample answer) Jesus cares about the needs of all people.

The Pharisees Demand a Sign

From Decapolis, Jesus crossed the Sea of Galilee to the coasts of Magdala (called Dalmanutha in Mark 8:10). It is not certain whether this refers to the town of Magdala just west of the lake or to some other place. (See the map on page 113.) When the Pharisees heard that Jesus was back in Jewish territory, they came and demanded that He show them a sign from heaven.

Matthew 16:1–4

11. The Gentiles of Decapolis had glorified the God of Israel when they saw Jesus' miracles. Were the Pharisees seeking a sign so that they could also glorify God, or did they want to find fault with Jesus?   They wanted to find fault with Jesus.

12. Since the Pharisees could read the signs of the sky to determine the weather, Jesus implied that they should also be able to read   the signs of the times   . In other words, they should have known that Jesus had come from God and that they should follow Him.

13. Jesus had just shown many signs to the Gentiles, but the only sign that He planned to give to the Pharisees and Sadducees was that of   the prophet Jonah   .

14. Through His miracles, Jesus had already given many signs to the Jews. But the Jewish leaders had ignored them and attributed the miracles to Satan's power. Jesus told them that requiring more signs was proof that they were part of "a   wicked   and   adulterous   generation."

The Leaven of the Pharisees and Sadducees

Leaving Magdala, Jesus and His disciples crossed the Sea of Galilee again to Bethsaida. (See the map on page 113.) On the way across the lake, Jesus warned the disciples about the leaven of the Pharisees and of the Sadducees. Jesus was referring to the false doctrine of the Pharisees, and not to natural bread. But the disciples misunderstood His warning. They thought Jesus was rebuking them for forgetting to bring bread.

Matthew 16:5–12

 *Choose four answers. Be sure to read verse 12 carefully.*

15. In these verses, Jesus was telling His disciples that
   a. they should never buy bread from the Pharisees and Sadducees.
   b. He could provide for all their needs, just as He had met the needs of the multitudes.
   c. because they did not trust Him to provide for their needs, they had little faith.
   d. if they had enough faith, He would always provide their food by miracles.
   e. they should avoid the teachings of the Pharisees and Sadducees.
   f. the doctrine of the Pharisees and Sadducees was dangerous.

- God did not give signs to unbelievers. He did speak three times from heaven to give testimony that Jesus was His Son. However, none of these was in the presence of Christ's enemies, who would not have believed no matter what signs He had given them.

- This sign was fulfilled in Christ's death and resurrection. Compare Matthew 12:39, 40.

B. BIBLE WORD STUDY

From the list on the right, choose the best meanings for the words and phrases in italics as they are used in the following verses.

g 1. "It is not *meet* to take the children's bread" (Matthew 15:26).

c 2. "They bring unto him one that was deaf, and had an *impediment* in his speech" (Mark 7:32).

a 3. "He *charged* them that they should tell no man" (Mark 7:36).

h 4. "A great deal they *published* it" (Mark 7:36).

b 5. "[They] were *beyond measure* astonished" (Mark 7:37).

e 6. "*Divers* of them came from far" (Mark 8:3).

f 7. "It will be *foul* weather" (Matthew 16:3).

d 8. "The sky is red and *lowring*" (Matthew 16:3).

a. commanded
b. exceedingly
c. handicap; defect
d. overcast; threatening
e. some; various ones
f. stormy
g. suitable; right
h. told; proclaimed

- Numbers 3 and 6 review words from Lesson 7.

C. THINKING ABOUT BIBLE TRUTHS

Jesus and the Gentiles

1. On His journey through Gentile territory, Jesus did many miracles for people who had quite likely been idol worshipers. Later at Magdala, He refused to do a miracle as a sign for the Pharisees. What does this tell us about these Gentiles?   The Gentiles accepted Jesus and believed in Him. They had more faith in Him than many Jews did.

The following questions may be difficult for some students to answer on their own. If possible, discuss these questions in class. They could also be used as challenge or bonus questions.

2. Jesus rebuffed the Syrophoenician woman three times (Matthew 15:21–28). First He ignored her. Next He said He was sent only to needy Israelites. Finally He compared her to a dog. Why did the woman not become upset and leave?   She had faith that Jesus could heal her daughter. (Also, she humbly admitted that what He said was true, yet she saw Him as her only source of help.)

3. Jesus received hardly any opposition in heathen lands, as He did from the Jewish leaders. The Gentiles accepted Him and spread His fame far and wide. Why may it have been easier for the Gentiles to accept Jesus' teachings?   The Gentiles were not hampered by mistaken ideas about the Messiah, as the Jews were.

- One exception to the Gentiles' general receptiveness was the Gadarenes' response in asking Jesus to leave.

4. After Jesus healed the man called Legion, He told him to tell others about his deliverance. But in this lesson Jesus charged the deaf and dumb man not to tell anyone. Why might Jesus have told the one to tell and the other not to tell?   (Sample answer) When large crowds were already following Him, Jesus did not want more people to follow Him for the wrong reasons. Also, the demoniac experienced spiritual deliverance; whereas the healing that many people received was primarily physical.

D. LEARNING MORE ABOUT BIBLE TIMES

Proselyte Family at Prayer

Jews and Gentiles

In the Old Testament, God commanded the Jews to separate themselves from their heathen neighbors. He knew that if His people had close contact with the ungodly, they would find it difficult to remain holy themselves. However, God showed in various ways that He still loved the Gentiles and accepted those who had faith in Him.

During New Testament times, both Jews and Gentiles lived in Palestine. Neither group enjoyed living close to the other. To keep from losing their identity as a people, the Jews had invented many extra rules to keep themselves apart from others. They despised the Gentiles (instead of just keeping themselves pure), and the Gentiles disliked them for it. The following information will help you to understand the problem between Jews and Gentiles, and why the Jews objected when Jesus and the apostles helped Gentiles.

Gentiles had to become proselytes (converts) before the Jews would teach them about their religion. Otherwise, the Jews felt they had no right to know about God. If Gentiles asked about their beliefs, some Jews cursed them rather than giving them an answer.

Despised Children

Children born of mixed marriages between Jews and Gentiles were considered illegitimate by the Jews. Some Jews of Jesus' time believed that everything that caused the Gentiles to increase was sinful. For this reason, they refused to help any Gentile mother.

Jews did not try to put Gentiles into danger. But if they saw a Gentile in danger, some Jews believed it was wrong to help him.

God had commanded the Jews to avoid certain foods. But strict Jews of Jesus' time considered all foods touched by Gentiles to be unclean. Gentile servants could never be left alone in a room with food, lest they touch something. Even catching a whiff of Gentile wine made a Jew "unclean." When a Gentile milked a cow, Jews could not drink the milk. Neither could they enter a Gentile's house without becoming "unclean" for the rest of the day.

Gentiles set aside shady groves as places for idol worship. The Jews were correct in avoiding these places. However, some of their rules regarding these trees were extreme. Not only did they refuse to sit in the shade of such trees, but they also believed that eating bread that was baked over a fire of their branches was wrong. Even wearing a garment that was woven with a shuttle made from such a tree was considered sinful.

• The book *The Life and Times of Jesus the Messiah* (mentioned in the Teacher's Introduction) has several appendices that give interesting information such as this. Much of this information is not commonly known and will add interest to your teaching if you have time to study it.

118   Chapter Three   Jesus Ministers to Jews and Gentiles

Laws Requiring Kindness to Gentiles

Deuteronomy 10:17–19; Exodus 23:9

Earlier in this lesson you learned that Jesus spent some time ministering to Gentiles, even though He had come primarily to the Jews. This fulfilled a prophecy and helped to prepare the apostles for the time when Gentiles would be accepted as fellow believers in the church. The Jewish Christians gradually overcame their dislike for the Gentiles when they realized that the extra laws the Jewish leaders had added were not based on God's Law.

1. Which Old Testament principle in these passages would have solved most of the problems between Jews and Gentiles in Jesus' day?   They were to love strangers and not oppress them.

2. Why were the Jews commanded to be kind to the Gentiles among them?
   The children of Israel had once been strangers themselves (in Egypt).

3. According to Numbers 35:14, 15, what special right of protection did sojourners among the Israelites enjoy under the Old Testament Law?
   They had the right to enter Israel's cities of refuge if they accidentally killed someone.

4. Read Luke 2:28–32. From Simeon's prophecy, describe what Jesus was to the Gentiles.
   Jesus was a light that lightened the Gentiles by helping them to understand God.

5. Read Ephesians 3:6. God planned that in the New Testament church, Gentile believers would "be (a)   fellowheirs   [with Jewish believers], and of the same (b)   body , and partakers of his promise in (c)   Christ ."

Chapter Three Review

A. ORAL REVIEW

 Be sure you know the answers to these questions. Answer as many as you can from memory. If you need help, you may check the reference or lesson number given in brackets.

What >>

1. What was the man called Legion doing when the men from his country came to see what Jesus had done? [Mark 5:15]
2. In the parable of the tares, what does the weedy field represent? [Matthew 13:36–38]
3. What body of water has also been called the Sea of Chinnereth, the Lake of Gennesaret, and the Sea of Tiberias? [Lesson 13]
4. What did Jesus use to feed the five thousand? the four thousand? [Mark 6:41; 8:5–7]
5. What did the people want to do with Jesus after He fed the five thousand? [John 6:15]
6. What did the disciples do when Jesus entered the boat after walking on the water? [Matthew 14:33]
7. What did the Pharisees reject in order to keep their traditions? [Mark 7:9]
8. What did Jesus teach that caused many people to turn away from Him? [John 6:35, 51, 66]
9. What did Jesus teach His disciples by healing the daughter of the Gentile woman? [Lesson 15]
10. What did Jesus mean when He warned His disciples to beware of the leaven of the Pharisees and Sadducees? [Matthew 16:6–12]

How >>

11. How did these people show their faith in Jesus?
    a. the Roman centurion [Matthew 8:8]
    b. the man called Legion [Mark 5:18–20]
    c. Jairus [Mark 5:23, 36, 40]
    d. the woman with an issue [Mark 5:27, 28]
    e. the disciples after many people left Jesus [John 6:67–69]
    f. the Syrophoenician woman [Matthew 15:22–28]
12. How did these people show their lack of faith?
    a. the disciples in a storm [Mark 4:38–40]
    b. the people who saw the man healed of demons [Mark 5:14–17]
    c. the people of Nazareth [Mark 6:1–6]
13. How much food was left after Jesus fed the five thousand? the four thousand? [Mark 6:43; 8:8]
14. According to the Old Testament, how were the Jews supposed to treat the Gentiles? [Deuteronomy 10:19]

Why >>

15. Why did Simon the Pharisee love Jesus less than did the woman who washed Jesus' feet? [Luke 7:40–48; Lesson 11]

1. He was sitting, clothed, and in his right mind.
2. the world
3. the Sea of Galilee
4. five (barley) loaves and two fish; seven loaves and a few small fish
5. They wanted to make Him king.
6. They worshiped Him. (They called Him the Son of God.)
7. the commandment (Word) of God
8. He told them that He is the Bread of Life that came down from heaven.
9. He loved Gentiles as well as Jews. (Whoever has true faith, whether Jew or Gentile, will receive God's blessings.)
10. He meant that they should avoid their false doctrine.
11. a. He asked Jesus to heal his servant without coming to his house.
    b. He desired to be with Jesus, yet he obeyed His command to return home and tell what Jesus had done for him.
    c. He asked Jesus to come and heal his daughter, and he trusted Jesus even after he heard that his daughter had died.
    d. She touched the hem of Jesus' garment in order to be healed.
    e. They stayed with Jesus and believed that He had the words of eternal life.
    f. She continued to ask Jesus to heal her daughter.
12. a. They became very fearful, even though Jesus was with them.
    b. They asked Jesus to leave their country.
    c. They refused to believe in Jesus as the Son of God.
13. twelve baskets full; seven baskets full
14. kindly (They were to love them.)
15. The woman saw herself as a great sinner, and Simon did not see his need; therefore he was not forgiven.

16. Why did the scribes and Pharisees always become upset when Jesus forgave someone's sins? [Mark 2:6, 7; Lesson 11]
17. Why did Jesus teach in parables? [Matthew 13:10–13; Lesson 12]
18. Why was Jesus not accepted by the people of Nazareth? [Mark 6:1–6; Lesson 13]
19. Why could Jesus not do as many miracles in Nazareth as He did in other places? [Mark 6:5, 6]
20. Why did the Pharisees ask Jesus for a sign from heaven? [Matthew 16:1]

16. They knew that only God could forgive sins, and they refused to recognize Jesus as God.
17. so that only those who believed would understand
18. He had grown up among them, and they knew Him and His family.
19. because of their unbelief
20. They were tempting Him. (They wanted to find fault with Him.)

B. WRITTEN REVIEW

Match

Match each description with the correct person or group.

d	1. Had her son raised to life	a. the Pharisees
g	2. Was thankful to have her sins forgiven	b. Simon the Pharisee
b	3. Failed to treat Jesus as an honored guest	c. the Gentiles of Decapolis
f	4. Took care of Jesus' needs	d. a widow of Nain
a	5. Accused Jesus of casting out devils by Satan's power	e. Jesus' friends
e	6. Thought Jesus was doing too much	f. some women who followed Jesus
c	7. Glorified the God of Israel	g. a woman who washed Jesus' feet

Match each definition with a word on the right. If you need help, review Lessons 11–15.

b	8. Captain of one hundred soldiers	a. scribe
f	9. Short story that illustrates a truth	b. centurion
h	10. Weeds	c. fetters
i	11. Yeast	d. damsel
a	12. Bookkeeper; writer	e. legion
d	13. Girl	f. parable
c	14. Foot chains	g. watch
e	15. Multitude	h. tares
g	16. A part of the night	i. leaven

Parable Interpretations

Match each parable with its meaning. You will need to use one meaning twice. If you need help, review Lesson 12, Matthew 13, and Mark 4:26–29.

b	17. The parable of the sower
c	18. The parable of tares among wheat
d	19. The parable of a man planting seed without knowing how it will grow
a	20. The parable of a hidden treasure
a	21. The parable of a pearl of great price

a. The kingdom of heaven is only for those who are willing to give up all else.

b. A person responds to the Gospel in one of at least four ways.

c. The righteous and the wicked will live together in the world until Jesus returns.

d. The kingdom of heaven will continue to grow even though we may not see much progress.

Map Review

Match each place on the left with its description on the right, and then label it on the map. Review the lessons and the maps in this workbook if you need help.

f	22. Nain	a. Jesus cast demons out of a man called Legion.
a	23. Gergesa	b. Jesus fed the four thousand in this Gentile region.
e	24. Capernaum	c. Jesus fed the five thousand.
h	25. Nazareth	d. Jesus healed the daughter of a Gentile woman near this city.
c	26. Bethsaida	e. Jesus healed the woman with an issue and raised Jairus's daughter.
g	27. Sea of Galilee	f. Jesus raised a widow's son.
d	28. Tyre	g. Jesus stilled a storm and walked on the water.
b	29. Decapolis	h. Jesus was rejected by His own people.
i	30. Magdala	i. The Pharisees asked for a sign from heaven.

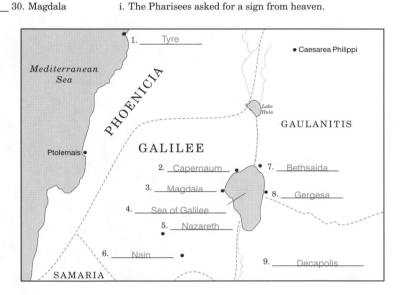

"I am the vine, ye are the branches" (John 15:5).

CHAPTER FOUR

Jesus Ministers in Judea and Perea

Who Is Jesus?

Jesus—a Servant to Mankind

Acceptance and Rejection at Jerusalem

The Perean Parables

Jesus—Stedfast in a Gathering Storm

Let this mind be in you, which was also in Christ Jesus:
Who . . . took upon him the form of a servant, and was made
in the likeness of men: And being found in fashion as a man,
he humbled himself, and became obedient unto death, even the death
of the cross. Wherefore God also hath highly exalted him,
and given him a name which is above every name: That at the name of Jesus
every knee should bow, of things in heaven, and things in earth,
and things under the earth; And that every tongue should confess
that Jesus Christ is Lord, to the glory of God the Father.
Philippians 2:5–11

Harmony of the Gospels

For important events and teachings covered in Chapter Four

Event or Teaching	Matthew	Mark	Luke	John	Location	Season
Lesson 16. Who Is Jesus?						
Jesus heals a blind man.	—	8:22–26[1]	—	—	Bethsaida	
Peter confesses Jesus as the Christ.	16:13–20	8:27–30	9:18–21	—	Caesarea Philippi	
Jesus foretells His death and rebukes Peter.	16:21–28	8:31–9:1	9:22–27	—	Caesarea Philippi	
Jesus is transfigured.	17:1–13	9:2–13	9:28–36	—	A high mountain[2]	
Lesson 17. Jesus—a Servant to Mankind						
Jesus provides temple tax money.	17:24–27	—	—	—	Capernaum	
Jesus teaches His disciples humility.	18:1–9	9:33–50	9:46–50	—	Capernaum	
Jesus talks with His earthly brothers.	—	—	—	7:1–10	Galilee	Early fall
The Samaritans reject Jesus.[3]	—	—	9:51–56	—	Samaria	
Jesus sends out seventy missionaries.	—	—	10:1–20	—		
Mary sits at Jesus' feet.	—	—	10:38–42	—	Bethany	
Lesson 18. Acceptance and Rejection at Jerusalem						
Jesus teaches at the Feast of Tabernacles.	—	—	—	7:11–8:59	Jerusalem	Early fall
Jesus heals a man who was born blind.	—	—	—	9:1–41	Jerusalem	Early fall
Jesus eats at a Pharisee's house.	—	—	11:37–54	—	Perea[4]	
Jesus journeys toward Jerusalem again.	—	—	13:22–35	—	Perea	
Jesus teaches at the Feast of Dedication.	—	—	—	10:22–42	Jerusalem	Winter
Lesson 19. The Perean Parables						
The Good Samaritan	—	—	10:25–37	—	Perea	Fall-Winter
The lost sheep and the lost coin	—	—	15:1–10	—	Perea	Fall-Winter
The prodigal son	—	—	15:11–32	—	Perea	Fall-Winter
The rich man and Lazarus[5]	—	—	16:19–31	—	Perea	Fall-Winter
The Pharisee and the publican	—	—	18:9–14	—	Perea	Fall-Winter
Lesson 20. Jesus—Steadfast in a Gathering Storm						
Jesus raises Lazarus from the dead.	—	—	—	11:1–54	Bethany	Winter
Jesus heals ten lepers.	—	—	17:11–19	—	Samaria/Galilee	
The rich young ruler questions Jesus.	19:16–30	10:17–31	18:18–30	—		
Jesus meets Zacchaeus.	—	—	19:1–10	—	Jericho	Early spring
Mary anoints Jesus' feet and head	26:6–13	14:3–9	—	12:1–11	Bethany	Early spring[6]

---

[1] Passages given in italics are used in the lesson.

[2] Possibly Mt. Hermon

[3] This follows Edersheim's order of events, but the chronology is uncertain. Some harmonies of the Gospels place Luke 9:51–10:42 after the Feast of Tabernacles.

[4] Jesus apparently spent much of His last months in Perea. (See John 10:40.) Only Luke records the Perean ministry, while John records Jesus' visits to Jerusalem during these months.

[5] This seems to be an actual account rather than a parable.

[6] John 12:1 states that this was six days before the Passover, or just before Jesus' triumphal entry into Jerusalem.

125

Lesson 16. Who Is Jesus?

In the last chapter you saw that many of the Galileans finally turned against Jesus. In this chapter you will study Jesus' life as He entered the last months of His earthly ministry. His Galilean ministry was mostly behind Him. He had just had another confrontation with the Jewish leaders at Magdala. From there He traveled north into Gentile territory again before heading south to Perea and Jerusalem.

The Jewish leaders thought that if Jesus was truly the Son of God, He should prove it by a special sign. Instead of giving them the sign they asked for, Jesus reproved them. He had already given them many signs, yet they still refused to believe in Him.

Rather than trying to explain things to people who did not want to believe, Jesus withdrew with His disciples. He had important things to reveal to them. He knew His time on earth was short. The Jewish leaders had turned against Him and were making plans to kill Him. Soon He would no longer walk on the earth. Other men would carry on the work He had begun, and He would work through them.

Jesus planned that His twelve disciples would serve as leaders in the church that He would establish. The disciples had much to learn about the church. Jesus took them aside, away from the crowds, and headed north to the city of Caesarea Philippi.

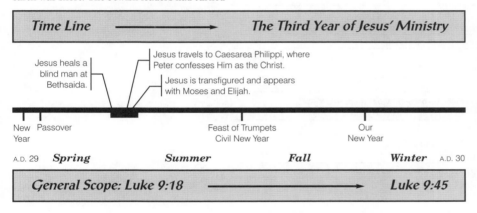

Using the Time Line

1. About how many days passed between Peter's confession of Christ and the Transfiguration? (Matthew 17:1) __six__

   • Luke 9:28 says eight. Perhaps this included part days.

2. What miracle did Jesus do the day after His Transfiguration (Luke 9:37–43)? (This course does not cover that miracle in detail.) __Jesus cast an unclean spirit out of a man's son.__

   • This miracle is not given on the time line because it is not covered in the lesson. You may want to discuss it in class or during a devotional period.

Lesson 16

Oral Review

1. To what Old Testament prophet was John the Baptist compared? [L. 4] **Elijah**
2. What did John the Baptist say when he learned that Jesus was becoming more popular than he was? [L. 5] **"He must increase, but I must decrease."**
3. What family relation of Peter's did Jesus heal? [L. 7] **Peter's mother-in-law**
4. Define *disciple* and *apostle*. [L. 9] *disciple:* **one who follows another to learn from him;** *apostle:* **one who is sent with a message**
5. Why did Simon the Pharisee love Jesus less than did the woman who washed Jesus' feet? [L. 11] **The woman saw herself as a great sinner, and Simon did not see his need; therefore he was not forgiven.**
6. How did the people of Nazareth show their lack of faith in Jesus? [L. 6, 13] **by refusing to believe that Jesus is the Son of God**
7. What did Jesus teach His disciples by healing the daughter of the Gentile woman? [L. 15] **He loved Gentiles as well as Jews. (Whoever has faith, whether Jew or Gentile, will receive God's blessings.)**
8. What did the Gentiles of Decapolis do when they

126   Chapter Four   Jesus Ministers in Judea and Perea

A. ANSWERS FROM THE BIBLE

A Blind Man

After leaving Magdala, where the Pharisees had demanded a sign, Jesus crossed the Sea of Galilee to Bethsaida. This town had been built by the Roman ruler Philip, the brother of Herod Antipas, and was also called Bethsaida-Julius. It was a Gentile town on the north side of the Sea of Galilee. The blind man may have been a Gentile.

Mark 8:22–26

 Compare the healing of the deaf and dumb man (Mark 7:32–37) with the healing of the blind man (Mark 8:22–26).

1. What did the people ask Jesus to do?
   a. deaf and dumb man: They asked Jesus to put His hand upon him.
   b. blind man: They asked Jesus to touch him.
2. Where did Jesus take the men?
   a. deaf and dumb man: Jesus took him aside from the multitude.
   b. blind man: Jesus took him out of town.
3. What did Jesus do with His hands?
   a. deaf and dumb man: Jesus put His fingers in his ears and touched his tongue.
   b. blind man: Jesus put His hands first upon him and then on his eyes.
4. What else did Jesus use to heal the men?
   a. deaf and dumb man: Jesus used spit.
   b. blind man: Jesus used spit.
5. Before healing took place, where did Jesus direct His own view or the man's view?
   a. deaf and dumb man: Jesus looked up to heaven.
   b. blind man: Jesus made him look up.
6. After the men were healed, what did Jesus ask them to do?
   a. deaf and dumb man: Jesus asked him to tell no man.
   b. blind man: Jesus asked him to neither go into the town, nor to tell it to any in the town.

Peter's Confession and Rebuke

Caesarea Philippi sat on a slope of Mount Hermon, surrounded by woods and cliffs. Out of a nearby rock wall burst a stream that was one of the main sources of the Jordan River. Perhaps Jesus and His disciples were viewing this scene when the following conversation took place.

 To complete these exercises, first study the Bible passages that are given. Fill in the short blanks with words. Whenever possible, use exact words from the Bible. Write complete answers for the questions with long blanks. For multiple-choice questions, circle the letter of the correct answer.

Matthew 16:13–20

7. The people of Jesus' time had different ideas about who He was. When Jesus asked His disciples who men thought He was, they said that men thought He might be
   (a)   John the Baptist   , (b)   Elias (Elijah)   , (c)   Jeremias (Jeremiah)   ,
   or (d)   one of the other prophets   .

saw the miracles that Jesus did? [15] **They glorified the God of Israel.**

In This Lesson

Scope: Matthew 16:13–17:13; Mark 8:22–9:13; Luke 9:18–36

Focus

- Jesus reveals Himself to honest seekers.
  - —After confronting the Pharisees at Magdala, Jesus turned again to Gentile territory.
  - —Jesus healed a blind man at Bethsaida. Some aspects of the miracle are similar to Jesus' healing of the deaf and dumb man in Decapolis. Perhaps both men were Gentiles.
  - —Jesus asked the disciples, "Whom do men say that I am?" Many Jews thought He was a former prophet risen again.
  - —Peter confessed that Jesus is the Christ, the Son of the living God. Jesus declared that He would build His church on this confession.
  - —Jesus began to foretell His death openly to His disciples.
  - —Jesus was transfigured in the presence of Peter, James, and John. He appeared with Moses and Elijah.

8. a. Which disciple knew who Jesus really is? __Peter__
   b. What did he say about Jesus? __"Thou art the Christ, the Son of the living God."__

   c. How did he know who Jesus is? __God had revealed it to him.__

9. Jesus said that upon this (a) _____rock_____ (this confession), He would build His (b) _____church_____.

10. Jesus gave the apostles the authority they would need to lead the early church. Under the direction of the Holy Spirit, they would make decisions based on the teachings He had given them. Jesus said that whatever they (a) _____bind_____ on earth would be bound in (b) _____heaven_____.

11. Jesus' work was not yet done. He had not yet died to become the Saviour of all men. He told His disciples to keep the fact that He was _____the Christ_____ a secret until His work was done.

Matthew 16:21–23

These were trying times for the apostles. They did not seem to understand what Jesus was trying to tell them. Even though they had been under Jesus' teaching for several years, their idea of what the Messiah would do was far from correct. It must have seemed as if their world was falling apart when Jesus started talking of dying.

12. Jesus began to prepare the disciples for His coming death. What shows that Peter did not understand why Jesus needed to die? __He began to rebuke Jesus for talking about being killed.__

13. Just before this, Jesus had called Peter blessed for speaking words from God. But now Jesus detected Satan's influence in what Peter said. How did Jesus show that He would not tolerate Satan's suggestions, even if they came through one of His disciples? __Jesus turned and said to Peter, "Get thee behind me, Satan: thou art an offence unto me: for thou savourest not the things that be of God, but those that be of men."__

The Transfiguration

Matthew 17:1–9

This event probably took place on Mount Hermon, which is just north of Caesarea Philippi. The three peaks of Mount Hermon are snow-covered the year around, and it would have taken at least six hours to reach them from the bottom. But the Bible does not specifically say that Jesus and His three disciples climbed all the way to the top. They may have gone only far enough up one of the slopes to be alone.

14. How was Jesus changed in the presence of Peter, James, and John? __Jesus' face shone as the sun, and His clothing became white as the light.__

15. Which made the greatest impression on the three disciples?
    a. the brightness of Jesus' face and clothing   c. the bright cloud
    b. Moses and Elijah   (d.) the voice they heard

16. The voice of God spoke to the disciples, telling them that Jesus is His Son and that they were to listen to Him. What might this have signified?
    a. Jesus spoke the same words that Moses and Elijah had spoken.
    (b.) The words that God spoke through His Son were even more important than those He had spoken through Moses and the prophets.
    c. The disciples were to stop reading the Old Testament, which had been written by Moses, the prophets, and other men.

Objectives
- Students should know
  —what direction Jesus told the blind man of Bethsaida to look. (*up*)
  —the disciples' answer when Jesus asked them who men thought He was. (*John the Baptist, Elias [Elijah], Jeremias [Jeremiah], or one of the other prophets*)
  —who Peter said Jesus is. ("*Thou art the Christ, the Son of the living God.*")
  —what Jesus said He would build on the confession that Peter made. (*His church*)
  —why Jesus rebuked Peter soon after Peter had confessed Him as the Christ. (*Jesus detected Satan's influence in Peter when Peter rebuked Him for talking about needing to suffer and die.*)
  —what pagan city, at the base of Mount Hermon, was the scene of Peter's great confession. (*Caesarea Philippi*)
  —how Jesus appeared at His Transfiguration. (*His face shone as the sun, and His clothing was white as the light.*)
  —who appeared with Jesus at His Transfiguration. (*Moses and Elias [Elijah]*)
  —what God spoke from heaven at Jesus' Transfiguration. ("*This is my beloved Son, in whom I am well pleased; hear ye him.*")

128   Chapter Four   Jesus Ministers in Judea and Perea

17. Until when did Jesus say the Transfiguration should be kept a secret? _____
    until He had risen from the dead

18. Read Luke 9:28–36 for more details on the Transfiguration, and answer these questions.

   a. What was Jesus doing when He was transfigured?   praying

   b. What did Moses, Elijah, and Jesus talk about? _____
      Jesus' decease (death) that would take place at Jerusalem

   c. What were Peter and the other disciples doing while this was happening?   sleeping

Mount Hermon—the Probable Mount of Transfiguration

B. BIBLE WORD STUDY

Match the best description to each word or phrase.

i	1. Flesh and blood (Matthew 16:17)	a. appearance
g	2. Savourest (Matthew 16:23)	b. clothing
h	3. Transfigured (Matthew 17:2)	c. death
b	4. Raiment (Matthew 17:2)	d. dirty
f	5. Tabernacles (Matthew 17:4)	e. face
a	6. Fashion (Luke 9:29)	f. tents
e	7. Countenance (Luke 9:29)	g. appreciate; be mindful of
c	8. Decease (Luke 9:31)	h. changed; transformed
		i. a human, or human abilities

Truths to Amplify

- Having heard the Pharisees' arguments and having seen many people turn away from Jesus, the disciples may have felt discouraged. In addition, Jesus began to speak of His coming suffering and death, completely contrary to their concept of the Messiah. Perhaps seeds of doubt were taking root and beginning to grow in Judas's heart. Even Peter, who gave a ringing declaration of his faith, still did not understand the real purpose of Jesus' ministry. For the special benefit of Peter and others of the leading disciples (and for the eventual benefit of all Christians), Jesus revealed Himself in heavenly glory. He appeared with Moses and Elijah, as the new lawgiver and new prophet for the New Testament church.

- That the experience on the Mount of Transfiguration had a permanent effect upon the disciples may be proven from Peter's words in 2 Peter 1:16–18. Note especially the powerful statement "we . . . were eyewitnesses of his majesty."

C. THINKING ABOUT BIBLE TRUTHS

The Disciples' Faith

One of the most important questions that faced the Jews of Jesus' time was, "Who is Jesus?" Was He a deceiver working by Satan's power, as the Pharisees claimed? Was He a great prophet of God? Or was He—could He be—the promised Messiah?

Jesus knew all the false ideas that people had about Him. He wanted His disciples to realize that He was more than just another great prophet or teacher. When He asked His disciples who they thought He was, Peter answered correctly, "Thou art the Christ [Messiah], the Son of the living God."

Jesus was pleased with Peter's response, yet He knew that His disciples' understanding and faith were still very limited.

Matthew 16:21–23

1. When Jesus began telling His disciples about His suffering and death, Peter rebuked Him. How might Peter have responded to Jesus' announcement had his trust in Jesus as the Son of God been stronger?   If Peter had completely trusted Jesus as the Son of God, he would have tried to understand why Jesus needed to die rather than trying to persuade Jesus that He should not need to suffer.

Matthew 16:24–28

After rebuking Peter, Jesus told His disciples that those who wanted to follow Him would need to suffer with Him. They would need enough faith in Him to forsake all other desires, and even their lives, to obey Him without question.

2. The disciples were hoping to gain positions of power in the earthly kingdom they expected Jesus to establish. What did Jesus say was worth more than anything else in the world?   a man's soul

The disciples were correct in believing that Jesus is the Messiah and that He would reward them for following Him. However, Jesus' kingdom and rewards are spiritual; whereas at this time the disciples were looking only for earthly benefits.

3. When will Jesus' followers receive their rewards?   when He comes in glory with His angels (at the end of the world)

Matthew 17:1–9

4. Moses, the Israelites' greatest leader, gave them the Law. Elijah, a great Israelite prophet, upheld the Law. Jesus said that He had come to fulfill the Law. Why would Moses' and Elijah's presence on the Mount of Transfiguration have reassured the disciples that Jesus is indeed the Messiah?   The disciples could feel reassured that Jesus' teaching was in full agreement with everything God had revealed to the Jews up to that point.

"Thou Art the Christ"

"Thou art the Christ!" upon this Rock,
Foundation firm and sure,
Is built the true and living church,
Forever to endure.
Though hosts of sin and wickedness
With fury may assail
Her gates of righteousness and peace,
They never shall prevail.

"Thou art the Christ!" the Son of God,
Anointed from above,
Who came to earth that we might know
Divine, redeeming love;
Who suffered shame and agony
Upon the cruel tree;
Who gave His life that we might live;
Who died to set us free.

130   Chapter Four   Jesus Ministers in Judea and Perea

D. LEARNING MORE ABOUT BIBLE TIMES

Jesus Travels North

From the shaded box, select the correct words to fill the blanks. (You may use words more than once.) The map below will help you. For numbers 4–6, check a Bible atlas map of Canaan divided among the twelve tribes.

Bethsaida	Hermon	Naphtali
Caesarea Philippi	Lake Hula	Sea of Galilee
Dan	Manasseh	Simon Peter

After leaving Magdala, Jesus and His disciples crossed the (1) ____Sea of Galilee____ by boat and came to the town of (2) ____Bethsaida____ on its northern shore. Here Jesus healed a blind man.

Next Jesus and His disciples headed north by foot. About 10 miles north of the Sea of Galilee lay a small body of water called (3) ____Lake Hula____, which was known in the time of Joshua as the Waters of Merom. Marshy lowlands surrounded this small lake, so Jesus may have followed a main road to the west of it. This land just west of the upper Jordan River had once belonged to the tribe of (4) ____Naphtali____. The road through it passed rich and fruitful highlands before turning west.

North of the small lake lay a wedge of land that had once belonged to the tribe of (5) ____Dan____. Here the road ran through a wilderness of wild oleander bushes, honeysuckle, and clematis that grew beside clear, rushing streams. These streams were the headwaters of the Jordan River.

The land northeast of the Sea of Galilee was peaceful and productive in Jesus' day. Moses had given this land to the tribe of (6) ____Manasseh____ (Joshua 13:29–32), but God's people no longer lived there. Jesus and His followers traveled to a large pagan city called (7) ____Caesarea Philippi____, which stood at the base of Mount (8) ____Hermon____. Near the city stood the temple of Pan, a false god.

Jesus and His disciples would not have felt at home in this pagan city. But here, far from the scribes and Pharisees, (9) ____Simon Peter____ made his great confession of faith in Jesus: "Thou art the Christ, the Son of the living God." About a week later, Jesus ascended a high mountain, which was possibly Mount (10) ____Hermon____, and was transfigured before Peter, James, and John.

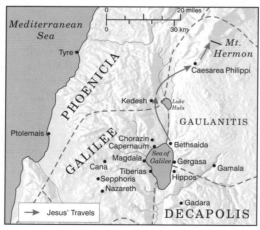

131

Lesson 17. Jesus—a Servant to Mankind

On the Mount of Transfiguration, Jesus' face shone as the sun, and His garments glowed in the radiant light. This brief glimpse of glory caused the astonished disciples to wish they could stay there forever.

Jesus knew, however, that humiliation comes before glory. Great glory would be His, but first He would need to pass through the valley of suffering. From the heights of Mount Hermon, He must descend to live among people who would misunderstand Him, hate Him, and finally crucify Him.

Jesus' journey from the Mount of Transfiguration to Mount Calvary would take Him through Galilee, where He had just been rejected by many of His former followers. From there it would take Him to Perea and then to

Judea, where He had even more enemies than in Galilee. The hatred of the Pharisees and ruling Jews toward Him would continue to increase. It would be a difficult road.

Jesus also knew He must prepare His disciples for His coming death. He knew how much they needed to grow in understanding and faith. Even as He reached the bottom of the Mount of Transfiguration, He found His disciples surrounded by people. The disciples had failed in their attempt to cast out a demon.

"O faithless and perverse generation," Jesus said, "how long shall I be with you?" After healing the boy, Jesus told His disciples they needed to pray and fast before they could cast out such demons. Then He led them back the long road to Galilee.

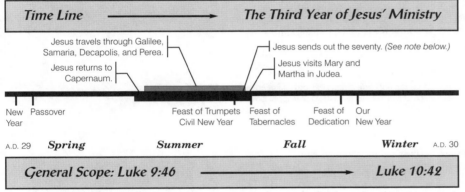

Time Line ⟶ **The Third Year of Jesus' Ministry**

Jesus travels through Galilee, Samaria, Decapolis, and Perea.

Jesus sends out the seventy. *(See note below.)*

Jesus returns to Capernaum.

Jesus visits Mary and Martha in Judea.

| New Year | Passover | | Feast of Trumpets Civil New Year | Feast of Tabernacles | Feast of Dedication | Our New Year |

A.D. 29   *Spring*   *Summer*   *Fall*   *Winter*   A.D. 30

General Scope: Luke 9:46 ⟶ **Luke 10:42**

Note: Jesus may have sent out the seventy earlier or later than shown here. The sequence of the other events is probably correct, but the exact time when each happened is not known.

Using the Time Line

1. Most events in Jesus' ministry cannot be dated exactly. However, by comparing the Gospels, we can determine a general outline of events. For example, Jesus' visit to Mary and Martha's house is not dated, but it seems quite likely that He stopped there while He was in Judea for one of the feasts. In what town did Mary and Martha live? (John 11:1) <u>Bethany</u>
2. a. During what Jewish month was the Feast of Tabernacles? (Study a Jewish calendar in a Bible dictionary.) <u>Tisri, or Ethanim</u>
   b. What month of our calendar would this be? <u>September or October</u>

- Tisri (or Ethanim) is the seventh month of the Jewish sacred calendar and the first month of the Jewish civil calendar. Before the Babylonian exile, the month was called Ethanim. After the exile it was called Tisri.

Lesson 17

Oral Review

1. Name two things Jesus did for the man sick of the palsy. [L. 7] **He forgave his sins and healed him.**
2. What kind of deeds did Jesus say were lawful to do on the Sabbath? [L. 8] **good deeds**
3. What does the Lord's Prayer mean when it says, "Forgive us our debts, as we forgive our debtors"? [L. 10] **God will not forgive our sins if we refuse to forgive others for wrongs they do against us.**
4. What did Jesus use to feed the five thousand?

[L. 14] **five (barley) loaves and two fish**
5. Who continued to follow Jesus after many people turned away from Him? [L. 14] **Jesus' twelve disciples**
6. What did the Gentiles of Decapolis do when they saw the miracles that Jesus did? [L. 15] **They glorified the God of Israel.**
7. What statement did Peter make about Christ? [L. 16] **"Thou art the Christ, the Son of the living God."**
8. Who appeared with Jesus at His Transfiguration? [L. 16] **Moses and Elias (Elijah)**

A. ANSWERS FROM THE BIBLE

Jesus' Example in Paying Taxes

Every year at the Passover, the Israelites paid a tax for the upkeep of the temple. If they could not be in Jerusalem, they usually paid it to a local tax collector who was responsible to collect it for the temple authorities. The Bible does not record that Jesus attended the Passover at the beginning of His third year of ministry. If He did not attend, this may explain why He and His disciples had not paid this tax. It was probably the local tax collector that approached Peter and asked him whether Jesus was going to pay it. There is no indication in these verses that this man was trying to trap Jesus. He was simply performing his duty.

Matthew 17:24–27

1. Jesus is the Son of God. He should not have needed to pay tax for the upkeep of God's house in Jerusalem. But Jesus paid it anyway because
   a. the Jews forced Him to pay.
   b. He was afraid of the Romans' power.
   c. He wanted to avoid offending the Jews.
   d. He owed it to God.
2. What lessons did Jesus teach Peter by miraculously providing enough money to pay the tax for both of them? (Choose three answers.)
   a. We do not need to earn tax money.
   b. God can arrange circumstances to fulfill His will.
   c. God provides for our needs if we obey Him.
   d. We should care about the needs of others, while still fulfilling our own responsibilities.
   e. Fishing with a hook is more profitable than fishing with a net.

The Disciples Learn About Being Humble

Jesus tried to prepare His disciples for His coming death, but they did not understand His words. Instead of asking Him to explain what He meant, they began arguing about which of them would have the greatest position in the kingdom they thought Jesus would soon set up. One day while they were in the house at Capernaum, Jesus spoke to them about pride and humility.

Mark 9:30–37; Matthew 18:2–4

3. The disciples did not want to tell Jesus what they had been talking about because
   a. they wanted Jesus to read their thoughts.
   b. they had been arguing selfishly.
   c. they no longer had a desire to be first.
   d. they were humble by nature and slow to speak.
4. Jesus took a child and set him in the midst of the disciples. What lesson did He teach with the child?
   a. God exalts the humble in the eyes of the world.
   b. God humbles those who desire to be great in the kingdom of heaven.
   c. Those who humble themselves will be great in God's kingdom.

John 7:1–10

Jesus' earthly brothers thought that if Jesus claimed to be from God, He should try to convince everyone by remaining in public rather than withdrawing from the crowds at times. But Jesus had no intentions of becoming great in the way that His brothers thought of greatness. He had come to serve people and to give His life as a sacrifice for sin.

5. Did Jesus' brothers really think Jesus was who He claimed to be? __no__

- John 7:5 says, "For neither did his brethren believe in him."

In This Lesson

Scope: Matthew 17:24–18:35; Mark 9:30–50; Luke 9:46–56; 10:1–24, 38–42; John 7:1–10

Focus

- Jesus taught His disciples humility and true greatness
  —by setting an example in paying tribute.
  —by teaching that the greatest ones are servants of all and by using a child to illustrate humility.
  —by refusing to show Himself to the world at the suggestion of His earthly brothers.
  —by His example in showing mercy to the Samaritans.
  —by sending out seventy missionaries to preach the kingdom of God and to heal the sick.
  —by teaching that our devotion to Him is more important than our natural service.

Objectives

- Students should know
  —where Peter found money to pay tribute for himself and Jesus. (*in the mouth of a fish*)
  —the definition of *tribute.* (*a tax*)
  —what lesson Jesus taught His disciples by using a child as an example. (*We should be humble like children.*)
  —why the Samaritans of a certain village refused to

6. Why did Jesus wait to go up to the Feast of Tabernacles until His brothers had left? (See 7:10.)

   so that He could go to the feast privately

Rejected in Samaria

Most of the Jews in Judea and Galilee had rejected Jesus. Now the Samaritans also rejected Him.

Luke 9:51–56

7. In verse 51, the phrase "received up" refers to Jesus' final work on earth, which ended with His ascension into heaven. Write the part of this verse that suggests Jesus' attitude as He set out for Jerusalem. _____

   "he stedfastly set his face"

8. Jesus decided to go through Samaria instead of detouring east across the Jordan as most Jews did. Why did the Samaritans refuse to give lodging to Jesus and His disciples? _____

   They were headed toward Jerusalem.

9. In the Old Testament, God's people as an earthly nation were to destroy their earthly enemies.
   a. Did James and John understand that Jesus was changing this? no
   b. Give a reason for your answer. _____
   They wanted to call down fire to destroy their enemies.

10. Someday God will punish those who have rejected Jesus. Why did Jesus have mercy on the Samaritans at this time? He had come to save men's lives rather than to destroy them.

Jesus Sends Out Missionaries

At some point during His closing months of ministry, Jesus sent out seventy disciples two by two. Luke records this event as happening soon after the Samaritans rejected Jesus. Some time passed before they returned, but both events are covered in this part of the lesson.

Luke 10:1–12, 17–20

11. Jesus sent out seventy disciples, two by two. What did He tell them to do? (Choose three.)
    (a) Pray that God would send laborers into His harvest.
    b. Take enough provisions for a long journey.
    (c) Preach the kingdom of God and heal the sick.
    (d) Find lodging with those who were faithful.

• James and John's response was one of retaliation. If God ruled by this principle, or even by dealing out immediate justice, no one would be spared. Someday God will judge all who persist in rejecting Him, but it is not for us who have received God's mercy to request that He shorten the day of grace for someone else.

give lodging to Jesus. (*He had steadfastly set His face to go to Jerusalem.*)

—what James and John wanted to do to the Samaritans who rejected Jesus. (*call down fire to destroy them*)

—why Jesus sent out seventy of His disciples two by two. (*to spread the Gospel*)

—what Jesus told His disciples to rejoice in. (*that their names were written in heaven*)

—why Martha became upset with her sister Mary, and what Jesus told Martha. (*Martha complained that Mary had left her to do all the work, but Jesus told her that Mary had chosen the most important thing.*)

Truths to Amplify

• Jesus' life shows what it really means to be a servant. Just after the Transfiguration, during which a small measure of His glory was revealed, Jesus faced the cross. He willingly came down from that mountaintop experience to serve needy mankind. "[He] made himself of no reputation, and took upon him the form of a servant: . . . he humbled himself, and became obedient unto death, even the death of the cross" (Philippians 2:7, 8). Jesus patiently taught His disciples the meaning of true servanthood, and thus of true greatness.

12. What were they to do when a city would not listen to their message? <u>They were to wipe off the</u> <u>dust of the city as a sign and to remind the people that the kingdom of God had come nigh unto them.</u>

13. The missionaries returned with joy because
   a. many people had been converted.
   b. no one had persecuted them.
   c. everyone had heard the message of salvation.
   d. even devils (demons) were subject to them.

14. Jesus wanted His disciples to rejoice, but not because of the power that He had given them. The greatest reason for God's children to rejoice is because
   a. their names are written in heaven.
   b. they are able to read the Bible.
   c. God speaks to them.
   d. they shine as lights in the world.

Luke 10:38–42
   When Jesus arrived in Bethany, a village near Jerusalem, He went to the home of His friends Lazarus, Martha, and Mary. This visit to Bethany may have been during the time of the Feast of Tabernacles (John 7:11–14).

15. During the Feast of Tabernacles, people stayed in shelters made of palm leaves. Perhaps Martha was busy with extra work during this time, besides her work of serving Jesus as a guest. What was her complaint? <u>She said that Mary was not helping her serve.</u>

16. Why did Jesus rebuke Martha? <u>He said she was too worried and preoccupied with her work.</u>

17. What did Jesus say about Mary? <u>He said Mary had chosen the good part, which would not be taken from her.</u>

18. What lessons can we learn from the example of Martha and Mary? (Choose two.)
   a. It is wrong to show hospitality to others.
   b. It is wrong to be more concerned about natural things than about spiritual things.
   c. If we listen to Jesus, we will not need to do our everyday household tasks.
   d. Jesus desires our devotion to Him and His Word more than our natural service.

B. BIBLE WORD STUDY

Circle the letter of each correct answer. Note how each phrase is used in its context. You may need to check the meanings of some words in a dictionary or Bible dictionary.

1. What was the *tribute money* received in Capernaum? (Matthew 17:24)
   a. a toll   b. a fine   c. a tax

2. When the disciples *held their peace* (Mark 9:34), what did they do?
   a. They refrained from quarreling.
   b. They maintained good relationships.
   c. They refrained from speaking.

Lesson 17. Jesus—a Servant to Mankind **135**

3. Jesus *stedfastly set His face* to go to Jerusalem (Luke 9:51). Which of the following best describes Him at this time?
   a. He never smiled, but walked gravely toward Jerusalem.
   b. He firmly decided to go to Jerusalem and would not let anything distract Him.
   c. He constantly looked straight ahead in the direction of Jerusalem.

4. When Jesus told the seventy to carry neither *purse nor scrip* (Luke 10:4), He meant they should take neither
   a. billfold nor writings.   b. purse nor instructions.   c. money nor a bag for food.

5. When Martha was *cumbered about much serving* (Luke 10:40), she
   a. was distracted by the burden of her work.
   b. was unable to leave her work for a short break.
   c. lacked coordination and needed Mary's steady hands to help her.

C. THINKING ABOUT BIBLE TRUTHS

True Greatness

The world's idea of greatness is different from God's measure of true greatness. God is all-powerful, all-knowing, and all-sufficient. Even the wealthiest, mightiest, and most intelligent men are as nothing in His sight. Such men are no more important to God than the lowliest person on earth. Those called great by the world often oppress others in an effort to exalt themselves. But the truly great ones are humble people who gladly obey God's Word and spend their lives serving others.

1. The disciples evidently thought that whoever is greatest (or first) should be served by others. What did Jesus tell them to do if they wanted to be first in God's sight? (Mark 9:35) _____
   He told them to be last of all and servant of all.

2. Most Jews thought the Messiah would be a great military leader who would deliver them from their bondage to the Romans. Many of them rejected Jesus because He did not fit their idea of what the Messiah would be like. But Jesus is much greater than the Messiah that the Jews were looking for.
   a. What bondage did Jesus offer to deliver the Jews from instead of the Roman bondage? (See John 8:33–36.)   their bondage to sin and Satan

   b. Why was this a greater work than the work the Jews expected the Messiah to do?   It delivered
   men from a much greater need than the other would have. (Only God Himself can do this great work.)

3. Instead of making His disciples great military leaders, Jesus told them to be like lambs in the midst of wolves. How was Jesus like a lamb in the midst of wolves in this lesson?   He did not
   retaliate against the Samaritans when they did not receive Him, but quietly went elsewhere.

4. Read Philippians 2:5–11. This passage describes Christ as the perfect example of humility and true greatness. Which of the following statements are true? (Choose three.)
   a. Christ did not consider Himself equal with God.
   b. Christ left His heavenly glory and became a servant among men.
   c. Christ humbled Himself and submitted to death on the cross.
   d. Because Christ humbled Himself, God has exalted Him above everyone else.

• The Greek word translated *cumbered* includes the idea of distraction. Thus, Martha's work not only burdened her, but it also distracted her from Jesus' teaching as well. This concept is not as definite in our English Bibles, but students should be able to determine the correct choice.

Answers for numbers 1–3 may vary slightly. Accept reasonable answers that show the student has been thinking.

D. LEARNING MORE ABOUT BIBLE TIMES

Jesus' Supporters

Many people opposed Jesus' work. But here and there, among both Jews and Gentiles, men dared to stand up for Him. Some of them made public confessions of their support.

Look up the references in the shaded box to find what each of the following people said about Jesus. Write their words and the references on the correct lines.

Matthew 16:16	Mark 9:24	John 7:46
Matthew 21:9	John 1:29	John 9:33

1. John the Baptist: "Behold the Lamb of God, which taketh away the sin of the world" (John 1:29).

2. Simon Peter: "Thou art the Christ, the Son of the living God" (Matthew 16:16).

3. The father of a boy with an evil spirit: "Lord, I believe; help thou mine unbelief" (Mark 9:24).

4. The high priest's officers: "Never man spake like this man" (John 7:46).

5. The man born blind: "If this man were not of God, he could do nothing" (John 9:33).

6. The multitude with palm branches: "Hosanna to the son of David: Blessed is he that cometh in the name of the Lord; Hosanna in the highest" (Matthew 21:9).

137

Lesson 18. Acceptance and Rejection at Jerusalem

Jewish feasts were times of joy and gladness. Jews from all over the known world crowded into Jerusalem. Judeans and Galileans mingled with these foreign Jews, many of whom had dreamed of visiting Jerusalem since childhood.

Of all their feasts, the Jews liked none better than the Feast of Tabernacles. Passover came in early spring, when the weather was still cool. Pentecost was fifty days later, after the days had become quite warm. But the Feast of Tabernacles came in early fall, when leaves began turning yellow and the air turned refreshingly crisp. The summer harvest had just been completed, and it was a time of thanksgiving and rejoicing.

God had commanded the Jews to live in booths (tabernacles) of palm leaves during the Feast of Tabernacles. The booths were to remind them of their journey through the desert and of God's loving care for them. The feast lasted seven days, during which the Jews rejoiced in God's goodness, took part in special services, and invited guests to share their meals.

The Levites' songs and chanted recitations sounded through the temple courts during the Feast of Tabernacles. The smoke of many sacrifices rose all day, to hang like a cloud over the Kidron valley.

At night, the temple buildings—made of white marble, cedarwood, and gold—reflected the light of four great candelabra (decorative candlesticks) in the temple court. The glare of torches lit pilgrims singing in the streets as the sound of hymns floated through Jerusalem.

- This lesson describes the Feast of Tabernacles as observed in Jesus' time. Some events and ceremonies, such as the pouring out of water and the use of great lights, were not specifically commanded by God in the Old Testament. Nevertheless, Jesus used the symbolism of the lights and the outpoured water to call men to Himself.
- The following sources provide additional information on the Feast of Tabernacles: *The Life and Times of Jesus the Messiah*, Book 4, Chapters 6, 7; *The Temple: Its Ministry and Services*, Chapter 14 (both by Edersheim); *New Unger's Bible Dictionary*, "Festivals."

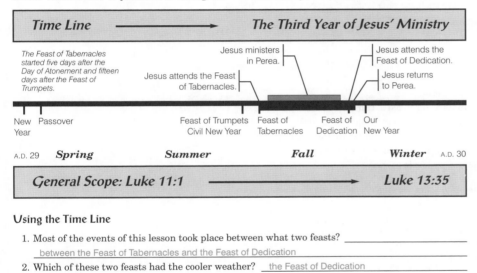

Time Line ⟶ **The Third Year of Jesus' Ministry**

The Feast of Tabernacles started five days after the Day of Atonement and fifteen days after the Feast of Trumpets.

Jesus ministers in Perea.

Jesus attends the Feast of Tabernacles.

Jesus attends the Feast of Dedication.

Jesus returns to Perea.

New Year | Passover | Feast of Trumpets Civil New Year | Feast of Tabernacles | Feast of Dedication | Our New Year

A.D. 29 *Spring* *Summer* *Fall* *Winter* A.D. 30

General Scope: Luke 11:1 ⟶ **Luke 13:35**

Using the Time Line

1. Most of the events of this lesson took place between what two feasts? _____
   between the Feast of Tabernacles and the Feast of Dedication
2. Which of these two feasts had the cooler weather? the Feast of Dedication

Lesson 18

Oral Review

1. What was Jesus' first miracle? [L. 5] **He changed water to wine at Cana.**
2. Why was Jesus criticized when He went to Levi's house for a feast? [L. 9] **Levi was a publican and was considered a sinner.**
3. Why did the scribes and Pharisees always become upset when Jesus forgave someone's sins? [L. 11] **They knew that only God could forgive sins, and they refused to admit that Jesus is God.**
4. How did Jairus show his faith in Jesus? [L. 13] **He asked Jesus to heal his daughter, and trusted Him even when he heard that his daughter had died.**
5. After Jesus fed the five thousand, what did the people want to do? [L. 14] **They wanted to make Jesus king.**
6. According to the Old Testament, how were the Jews supposed to treat the Gentiles? [L. 15] **kindly**
7. In what did Jesus tell His disciples to rejoice? [L. 17] **that their names were written in heaven**
8. What lesson did Jesus teach by using a child as an example? [L. 17] **We should be humble like children.**

138   Chapter Four   Jesus Ministers in Judea and Perea

A. ANSWERS FROM THE BIBLE

Jesus at the Feast of Tabernacles

The Feast of Tabernacles lasted seven days. Jesus was not at the temple during the first days of the feast. Jews from all parts of the country wondered why He was not at the feast, and secretly asked one another where He might be.

John 7:11–18

1. The Jews at the Feast of Tabernacles did not all have the same opinion of Jesus.
    a. How did the people disagree in their opinions about Him? _____
    Some thought He was a good man; others thought that He deceived the people.
    b. Why were they afraid to discuss the subject openly? _____
    They were afraid the Jews (Jewish leaders) would hear them.

2. Jesus went up to the temple a few days after the feast had started.
    a. What did Jesus do in the temple rather than work miracles as His brothers had suggested?
    He taught the people.
    b. Why did the Jews marvel when they heard His teaching? They were surprised that He knew letters without having learned. (He had learning without having a formal education.)
    c. From what source did Jesus say His teaching came? from God
    _____

> • Note that none of these Jews seemed to think He was the Messiah.

John 7:19, 20, 25, 26, 30–32, 44–48

The people were surprised that Jesus was able to teach unhindered in the temple. They knew that the rulers were trying to kill Him, and yet the rulers did not seem to be doing anything against Jesus.

3. After reading the verses above, choose the correct statement.
    a. The Jews threatened Jesus but did not actually want to harm Him.
    b. Those who wanted to kill Jesus followed His example of doing things in the open.
    c. The rulers did nothing to Jesus because they were not sure whether He was the Christ or not.
    (d.) The rulers were not able to capture Jesus until God chose to allow them to.
    e. The officers who were sent to capture Jesus were afraid of Him.

Myrtle Branch

🍇 *Read the following information carefully before doing the next exercise.*

Each morning during the Feast of Tabernacles, the Jews of Jesus' time observed a number of special ceremonies. Those who had gathered at Jerusalem left their booths at daybreak. In their right hands they carried bouquets of myrtle, palm, and willow branches. In their left hands they carried lemon-like citron fruits.

After gathering at the temple, the crowd split into three groups. Some stayed at the temple to observe the preparation of the morning sacrifice. Others walked to the nearby Kidron valley and cut willow branches with which to decorate the altar.

The third group formed a joyous procession following a priest with a golden pitcher. Winding down from the temple, this third group found its way to the pool of Siloam, just inside Jerusalem's fountain gate. There the priest filled his golden pitcher with water that had flowed to the pool from a nearby spring. Then the procession returned to the temple, arriving there just as the preparation of the sacrifice was being completed.

In This Lesson

Scope: Luke 11:37–54; 13:22–35; John 7:11–53; 9:1–41; 10:22–42

Focus

• When people heard Jesus, they needed to make a decision about Him. Many rejected Him, but a few received Him as the Son of God.
    —Jesus taught openly at the Feast of Tabernacles. The rulers tried to take Him, but God kept them from their purpose because it was not yet time for Jesus to lay down His life.
    —During the Feast of Tabernacles, Jesus presented Himself as the giver of living water (the Holy Spirit). Some acknowledged Him as the Prophet or the Christ, but others rejected His claims.
    —Jesus healed the blind man so that God's works would be made manifest. The Pharisees blindly refused to see this marvelous work as a confirmation that Jesus had come from God, but the man who had once been blind saw clearly who Jesus is.
    —The Pharisee who invited Jesus for a meal marveled that Jesus did not follow the detailed Jewish rules. Jesus pointed out the inner corruption that was defiling the Pharisees.
    —At the Feast of Dedication, Jesus said that the

The priest carrying the pitcher ascended the steps of the altar and poured the water into a silver basin, from where it flowed down to the base of the altar. The people rejoiced at the outpouring of the water. They considered it to be a symbol of the Holy Spirit, which God had promised to pour out on His people someday.

Immediately after this ceremony, the Levites chanted Psalms 113—118, which was known as the "Great Hallel." The crowd of worshipers responded by waving the branches in their hands, by shouting "Hallelujah!" ("Praise ye Jehovah!") and "Hosanna!" ("Save now!"), and by repeating other phrases from the Great Hallel.

John 7:37–41

On the last day of the feast, Jesus stood and spoke to the crowd. Perhaps He cried out this invitation soon after the morning ceremonies described above. The people had just observed the outpouring of spring water, and had burst forth with shouts of "Save now!" Near the end of the Great Hallel, the Levites had chanted, "Blessed be he that cometh in the name of the LORD" (Psalm 118:26). The true worshipers among the crowd recognized the significance of Jesus' words.

4. a. During the Feast of Tabernacles, a priest poured out spring _____ water _____ at the altar.

    b. On the last day of the feast, Jesus stood and proclaimed that rivers of _____ living _____ _____ water _____ would flow out of those who _____ believed _____ on Him.

    c. According to verse 39, Jesus was referring to the future work of the _____ Holy _____ _____ Spirit _____ in the lives of believers.

5. What did three different groups of people say about Jesus after hearing His words?

    a. "Of a truth this is the Prophet."

    b. "This is the Christ."

    c. "Shall Christ come out of Galilee?"

A Blind Man and Blind People

Jesus spent much time teaching while He was in Jerusalem for the Feast of Tabernacles. One day the scribes and Pharisees brought a woman who had committed adultery, and they tried to trap Jesus by the question they asked Him, hoping that He would make a rash judgment against her. But Jesus said, "He that is without sin among you, let him first cast a stone at her." The rulers were smitten with conviction, for they knew that they had also sinned.

Later Jesus taught the people, "If ye continue in my word, then are ye my disciples indeed; and ye shall know the truth, and the truth shall make you free." These words angered the Jewish rulers because they thought they knew the truth and were already free. But Jesus knew that they had closed their eyes in blindness to His teaching. The rulers became so angry with Jesus that they took up stones to kill Him, but He escaped and left the temple. As He passed through the streets, He saw a man who had been born blind.

John 9:1–7

6. The Jews wrongly believed that a special affliction was always evidence of a specific sin. What reason did Jesus give for the man's blindness? _____

    Jesus said that the man's blindness gave Him an opportunity to show God's works to the people.

7. The blind man evidently did not know much about Jesus, but he had faith in God's power. What shows that he must have believed Jesus could help him?   He obeyed Jesus' instructions.

John 9:13–16

The blind man's neighbors and friends were amazed at his healing, but they were not sure about the Man who had healed him. So they brought the man who had been blind to the Pharisees.

leaders did not believe because they were not His sheep. Those who are His sheep hear Him and follow Him.

Objectives

• Students should know

    —why some people at Jerusalem were afraid to speak openly about Jesus. (*They feared the Jewish leaders.*)

    —what Jesus said He would cause to flow from those who believe on Him. (*rivers of living water [the Holy Spirit]*)

    —what reason Jesus gave for the blindness of the man whom He healed at Jerusalem. ("*that the*

works of God should be made manifest in him")

    —why the Pharisees criticized Jesus for healing the blind man during the Feast of Tabernacles. (*Jesus healed him on the Sabbath.*)

    —what reasoning was used by the man who had been blind to prove that Jesus was not a sinner. (*God does not hear sinners; therefore, Jesus could not have performed the miracle if He had been a sinner.*)

    —who was expelled from the synagogue after Jesus healed him. (*the man who had been born blind*)

    —what the blind man did when He learned that Jesus is the Son of God. (*He worshiped Him.*)

    —what Jesus said at the Feast of Dedication that

8. The Pharisees thought that Jesus could not be of God because He had
   a. helped a blind man.   c. used clay and spittle to heal a man.
   b. healed on the Sabbath Day.   d. kept the Sabbath Day.

9. The Pharisees could not agree among themselves on
   a. how to keep the Sabbath Day.
   b. whether the man had actually been healed or not.
   c. whether or not Jesus had kept the Sabbath Day.
   d. whether Jesus was a sinner or not.

The Jewish leaders did not know what to do. They did not think that a sinner could heal a blind man, yet many of them thought Jesus must be a sinner because He had broken their laws. They questioned the man's parents, hoping to prove that the man had not really been blind. This only added evidence for the miracle. So they called in the healed man again and told him to say that God had healed him, rather than Jesus. But the man's faith in Jesus remained unshaken, and he bravely pointed out their wrong in questioning such a marvelous work of God.

John 9:30–33

10. The healed man knew that Jesus had healed him. What reasoning did he use to prove that Jesus was not a sinner as the leaders claimed? God does not hear sinners. Therefore, if Jesus had been a sinner, He could not have done such a marvelous work of God.

The Jewish leaders could not answer the man's honest reasoning, but they refused to acknowledge that Jesus had come from God. Humiliated, they responded by casting the healed man out of the synagogue.

John 9:35–41

11. The healed man had remained faithful to Jesus despite strong opposition. Jesus rewarded him by opening his spiritual eyes to further truth. What did the man do when he learned that Jesus is the Son of God? He (believed Jesus and) worshiped Him.

12. Jesus said that He had come "that they which see not might see; and that they which see might be made blind."
   a. What kind of person received spiritual sight through Jesus' ministry? _____
      sinners who repented and believed the truth
   b. What kind of person became spiritually blind through Jesus' ministry? _____
      self-righteous people who refused to believe the truth

13. Why was it so hard for Jesus to help the Pharisees? _____
    The Pharisees were blind to their own mistakes, sins, and ignorance.

Jesus at a Pharisee's House

Jesus probably spent much of His last half year of ministry in Perea. (See John 10:40.) Here the people were more friendly toward Him. It was probably in Perea that a Pharisee invited Him to a meal.

Luke 11:37–44

The Pharisees had invented long and elaborate rules about how to wash and how to say prayers over different foods before eating. They spent many hours debating where to lay the towel after washing and whether to wash their hands before or after filling a cup. Jesus could not support such a system of works that hindered the true worship of God.

caused the Jews to try to stone Him. (*He said that God was His Father, and that He and His Father are one.*)

—the definition of *blasphemy* as used in this lesson. (*falsely claiming to be God*)

—what Jewish feast was also called Hanukkah. (*the Feast of Dedication*)

Truths to Amplify

• Little by little, people formed definite opinions about Jesus as His ministry progressed. At first many had come out of curiosity to hear Him and to ask questions. But by the time of the events covered in this lesson, most people either were convinced that He was the Christ or else they hated Him for His righteous works. (Tragically, the majority took the latter position.)

• A knowledge of Jesus still entails a choice, for no accountable person can be passive about Him. Either we love Jesus and accept His great salvation, or we reject Him and hate Him for exposing our sin. (Grade 7 students may begin to sense this personal responsibility while studying the life of Jesus. Teach the truth unapologetically without putting public pressure on the maturing conscience of the child.)

14. How did Jesus' host feel when Jesus did not wash His hands before eating?   He marveled.

15. The Pharisees tried to appear righteous outwardly, but inwardly they had wrong motives. To what two things did Jesus compare them?

a.   to a cup and platter that are clean only on the outside

b.   to graves that men do not see as they walk over them

Jesus Journeys Toward Jerusalem

About two months after the Feast of Tabernacles, Jesus journeyed to Jerusalem for the Feast of Dedication.

Luke 13:22

16. What did Jesus do while traveling toward Jerusalem?   He taught in the cities and villages.

Luke 13:31–35

Herod Antipas, who had killed John the Baptist, ruled Galilee and Perea. In an attempt to quickly drive Jesus from their territory, the Pharisees of Perea told Him that Herod was seeking to kill Him. But Jesus knew that the Jewish leaders, and not Herod, were His real enemies.

17. The Jews of Jerusalem wanted to kill Jesus, yet Jesus loved them. What had He desired to do for these people?   He had wanted to gather them as a hen gathers her brood under her wings.

Jesus at the Feast of Dedication

The Feast of Dedication (Hanukkah) had its beginning after a Greek ruler named Antiochus Epiphanes (an TY uh kuhs ih PIHF uh neez) defiled the temple and made it a place to worship Zeus (ZOOS), a Greek god. Three years later, Judas Maccabeus cleansed the temple and lit its lamps again. In memory of this, the temple and all Jewish homes were lit up every year at Hanukkah.

The feast lasted for eight days. On the first evening one lamp was lit in each home, and each evening after that an additional lamp was lit. This meant that on the eighth day each household would burn eight lamps. With the lights came feasting, the giving of gifts, and family gatherings. No public mourning was allowed during the feast of Hanukkah.

John 10:22–33

18. What reason did Jesus give for the Jewish leaders' refusal to believe on Him?
    They were not of His sheep.

19. How do Jesus' sheep (the real members of God's fold) respond to Jesus?
    They hear His voice and follow Him.

20. What did Jesus say that caused the Jews to pick up stones to kill Him?
    He said that God was His Father, and that He and His Father are one.

142   Chapter Four   Jesus Ministers in Judea and Perea

B. BIBLE WORD STUDY

Fill in the blanks, using the words or phrases in parentheses as clues.

1. Jesus told the Pharisees that their inward part was full of _____ravening_____ (greed; plundering) and wickedness (Luke 11:39).

2. Jesus criticized the Pharisees for offering the tenth part of _____mint_____ and _____rue_____ (garden herbs) while neglecting more important matters (Luke 11:42).

3. Jesus said that the man had been born blind so that God's works might be made _____manifest_____ (plain; obvious) in him (John 9:3).

4. The Jews _____cast_____ _____out_____ (excommunicated) from the synagogue the man who had been born blind (John 9:34).

5. The Jews accused Jesus of _____blasphemy_____ (falsely claiming to be God) (John 10:33).

C. THINKING ABOUT BIBLE TRUTHS

Lessons From the Feasts

The Jews had a number of feasts or festivals during the year. Each of these feasts emphasized a different aspect of God's work with His people. All of them also pointed forward to the work that Jesus would do on earth. Two of these feasts were the Feast of Tabernacles and the Feast of Dedication.

1. During the Feast of Tabernacles, four large candelabra (multi-branched candle holders or lamps) burned every night in the temple court. The light of the flaming torches could be seen throughout Jerusalem. For the Jews, this symbolized the truth and revelation of their faith. Who is the fulfillment of this symbol, and how? (See John 8:12.) _____

   Jesus fulfilled this symbol by giving spiritual light to the world.

2. During the Feast of Tabernacles, the Israelites lived in temporary shelters called booths or tabernacles. The Feast of Tabernacles is also called the Feast of Ingathering (Exodus 23:16) because it took place after all the grains and fruits had been gathered in. Thus it was a time of thanksgiving for the blessings God had given. Circle the letters of the two statements that give lessons we can learn from this feast.

   (a.) The Feast of Tabernacles could be a type of the rejoicing God's children will experience in heaven after they have finished their earthly work.

   b. The Feast of Tabernacles could be a type of the rejoicing that would take place after the Messiah had driven out the Romans.

   (c.) The flimsy booths used during the Feast of Tabernacles could signify that God's people can rejoice even when their outward circumstances are not ideal or secure.

3. The Feast of Dedication was not established by God, but Jesus approved its observance by teaching in the temple during this feast. The first Feast of Dedication commemorated a time when true worship was restored in Israel. Thus it could have pointed to

   a. a time when the Jews would never be able to turn away from God.

   b. a time when God's people would stop serving Him and turn to idols.

   (c.) the time when Jesus would bring a new and better worship of God.

REMINDER: The exercises in Part C often require a greater depth of understanding than those in the other sections. When time permits, discuss Part C together in class.

• Since the Feast of Tabernacles closely followed the Day of Atonement, when the yearly sacrifice for the sins of God's people was made, it could also have been a type of the rejoicing that would follow the sacrificial death of Jesus.

D. LEARNING MORE ABOUT BIBLE TIMES

The Feast of Tabernacles

Read the references, and match each sentence with the correct ending.

____c____ 1. The Feast of Tabernacles was celebrated (Leviticus 23:34)

____d____ 2. During the Feast of Tabernacles, the Jews (Leviticus 23:39–42)

____f____ 3. The booths served (Leviticus 23:43)

____b____ 4. Services during the feast (Numbers 29:12–16)

____a____ 5. Jews kept the Feast of Tabernacles (Deuteronomy 16:13)

____g____ 6. During the feast, everyone was (Deuteronomy 16:14, 15)

____e____ 7. Ezra and Nehemiah (Nehemiah 8:13–18)

a. after the Israelites had gathered in the fruit of the land.

b. included sacrifices of animals, flour, and oil.

c. for seven days.

d. lived in booths (makeshift shelters).

e. restored the practice of keeping the Feast of Tabernacles.

f. to remind them of the Israelites' wanderings in the wilderness.

g. to rejoice in the blessings of the LORD.

The Jews' Ban

Under Old Testament Law, those who committed certain sins were to be "cut off" from the people. Originally this may have meant putting them to death. However, by Ezra's time or before, the Jews censured certain offenders by separating them from the congregation (Ezra 10:8). This action is often called "excommunication" or "placing under a ban." The Jewish leaders of Jesus' time applied the ban in three degrees of severity.

- A ban of the first degree, for small offences, lasted either seven or thirty days.
- If a person under a ban of the first degree remained unrepentant, he was put under a ban of the second degree for an additional thirty days.
- A ban of the third degree, lasting indefinitely, was for those who seriously violated Jewish law or who remained unrepentant. Ten Jewish leaders had to agree that this ban was necessary. They cursed the guilty man and sometimes proclaimed the ban by blowing on a ram's horn. A man put under the third-degree ban became unclean, like a leper. No one was permitted to touch him, eat with him, or help him.

Write true *or* false. *Correct the false statements.*

____true____ 8. The Jews cast out the man to whom Jesus had given sight. _____
_____

____false____ 9. The Jews' ban made the blind man's parents afraid of disobeying Jesus. _____
____The Jews' ban made the blind man's parents afraid of disobeying *the Jews.*____

____false____ 10. The Jewish leaders cast out (banned) the healed man because he thought he was better than they were. ____The Jewish leaders cast out (banned) the healed man be-____ ____cause *they thought they were better than he was.*____

____true____ 11. The Jews applied the ban in three degrees of severity, according to the seriousness of the deed and the offender's willingness to repent. _____
_____
_____

____true____ 12. No Jew could eat with a person under the severest ban. _____
_____

In the rewritten sentences for numbers 8–12, the corrections are in italics. The pupil's sentences may vary somewhat.

144

Lesson 19. The Perean Parables

East of Jerusalem, the hills of Judea drop sharply down to the Jordan River. In Jesus' time, the southern half of the Jordan marked a boundary between Roman districts. West of it rose the dry, rugged hills of Samaria and Judea. East of it lay Perea.

Perea was a predominantly Jewish territory governed by Herod Antipas, who had killed John the Baptist. Jesus apparently spent the winter in Perea after attending the Feast of Tabernacles. His winter was interrupted by a short trip to Jerusalem to attend the Feast of Dedication, as you saw in the previous lesson. After this feast, Jesus returned to Perea.

The Gospels tell little about what Jesus did in Perea, but Luke records many of His teachings during that period. The parables of the foolish rich man, of the great supper, of the prodigal son, of the unjust steward, and of the beggar Lazarus were probably given in Perea.

The common people loved to hear Jesus speak and thronged around Him as always. However, the Pharisees were in the crowd too, and a number of these parables seem to have been spoken directly to them.

The Perean parables are different from the parables Jesus gave earlier in His ministry. Jesus had given the earlier parables to hide the truth from those who did not believe. These later ones He gave in such a way that they could hardly be misunderstood. Some of them explicitly warned Christ's enemies that God would bring judgment upon them unless they repented.

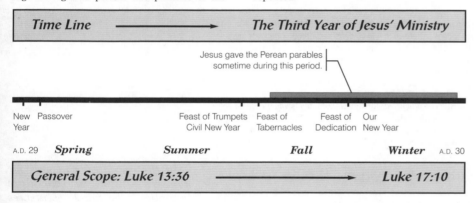

Time Line ⟶ *The Third Year of Jesus' Ministry*

Jesus gave the Perean parables sometime during this period.

| New Year | Passover | | Feast of Trumpets Civil New Year | Feast of Tabernacles | Feast of Dedication | Our New Year |

A.D. 29   *Spring*   *Summer*   *Fall*   *Winter*   A.D. 30

General Scope: Luke 13:36 ⟶ *Luke 17:10*

Using the Time Line

1. Jesus apparently spent time in Perea before and after the Feast of Dedication. During which Jewish month was this feast held? (Use a Bible dictionary.)   Chislev (Kislev)
2. Approximately which month of our year would this have been?   December (or November)

Lesson 19

Oral Review

1. Why did Jesus send the healed leper to see the priest? [L. 7] **Jesus respected the Law of Moses, which required a priest to look at a healed leper to certify that he was clean.**
2. Which apostle was a publican before Jesus called him? [L. 9] **Levi (Matthew)**
3. What will happen to the person who harshly judges (criticizes) others? [L. 10] **He will also be harshly judged (criticized).**
4. What lesson does the parable of the sower teach?

[L. 12] **People respond to the Gospel in different ways.**

5. Why was Jesus not accepted by the people of Nazareth? [L. 6, 13] **He had grown up among them and they knew Him and His family.**
6. What did Jesus say He would build on the confession that Peter made? [L. 16] **His church**
7. Why were some people at Jerusalem afraid to speak openly about Jesus? [L. 18] **They feared the Jewish leaders.**
8. Define *blasphemy*. [L. 18] **falsely claiming to be God**

Lesson 19. The Perean Parables **145**

A. ANSWERS FROM THE BIBLE

Who Is My Neighbor?

The Jews were very careful not to defile themselves outwardly. Because of this they would not help a Gentile in trouble. They taught that only fellow Jews were qualified to be the "neighbors" referred to by the Law of Moses. By restricting the term in this way, they failed to properly keep the Old Testament Scriptures.

The lawyer who asked this question was trying to justify himself with the typical reasoning used by the Jews. Jesus did not answer the lawyer's question directly. Instead, He told him a story that helped the lawyer to answer his own question.

Luke 10:25–37

1. The lawyer apparently thought he could earn the right to eternal life by doing good things. What two things did he think were necessary?

    a. <u>Love the Lord thy God with all thy heart, soul, strength, and mind.</u>

    b. <u>Love thy neighbor as thyself.</u>

Jesus told the lawyer that he had answered correctly. Jesus Himself had quoted these laws when others had asked Him which commandment was the greatest. However, the lawyer's understanding of these commandments fell far short of their full meaning. A person who loves God with all his heart, soul, strength, and mind will repent of his sin, believe in Jesus for salvation, and obey all of God's will. One who loves his neighbor as himself will care about the needs of others as much as he cares about his own and will endeavor to live peaceably with others.

2. What shows that the lawyer did not have true love for all men? _____
    <u>He tried to justify himself by asking, "Who is my neighbor?"</u>

> • He may have realized that he was not fully keeping these commandments unless *neighbor* was restricted to only a few.

3. The parable seems to indicate that the man who fell among thieves was a Jew. The priest and the Levite, who were fellow Jews, did not help him. But the Samaritan did, even though he was considered an enemy. Choose two reasons for the difference in how these men responded.

    a. The priest and the Levite could not help the man because they had temple duties to perform.
    (b.) The Samaritan had more love for his fellow men than the priest or the Levite did.
    (c.) The priest and the Levite may have been afraid that the wounded man was a Gentile.
    d. The priest and the Levite would have been defiled if they had touched the wounded man.
    e. The Samaritan thought the wounded man was a fellow Samaritan.

4. The lawyer was able to answer his own question when Jesus finished His story.

    a. Who in the story loved his neighbor as himself? <u>the Samaritan</u>
    b. Who is our neighbor? <u>any person who is in need of our help</u>

> • Notice that the lawyer avoided saying the hated name.

In This Lesson

Scope: Luke 10:25–37; 15:1–32; 16:1–31; 18:1–14

Focus

• Jesus used parables to teach basic truths to the Pharisees and others.
    —The parable of the Good Samaritan illustrates that all men are our neighbors to whom we owe our love.
    —The parables of the lost sheep, lost coin, and lost son show that all sinners are potential saints. Christians should help them find the way back to God and should rejoice when they return.

—The story of the rich man and Lazarus demonstrates the seriousness of our choices in this life. God sees and cares how we treat those around us.
—The parable of the Pharisee and the publican reveals that the sin of self-righteousness is just as evil as any other sin. One cannot be forgiven as long as he refuses to acknowledge his sin.

Objectives

• Students should know
    —who is our neighbor according to the parable of the Good Samaritan. (*any person who is in need of our help*)
    —which parable illustrates that a person can be lost

Seeking the Lost

One day when publicans and sinners came to hear Jesus, the scribes and Pharisees murmured against Him. These leaders looked down on sinners and avoided them, rather than trying to help them. They did not understand that God wants all men to be saved, or that some sinners long for deliverance. But Jesus' love went out to those whom He had come to seek and to save. In the next three parables, Jesus tried to help the self-righteous leaders see the importance of helping sinners find God. Each of these parables looks at the problem from a different perspective.

Luke 15:1–7

5. In this parable the lost sinner is represented as a lost sheep. Choose three lessons that this parable teaches.

  ⓐ It usually takes effort on the part of another person to help a sinner find the way to God.

  ⓑ Sinners can be lost through their own carelessness.

  ⓒ God's people should rejoice when a sinner finds God.

  d. It is generally the shepherd's fault that sheep are lost.

Luke 15:8–10

6. In this parable the lost sinner is represented as a lost coin. How was the lost coin different from the lost sheep? (Choose one answer.)

  a. The coin was lost on purpose, but the sheep was lost by accident.

  b. The coin was saved against its will. The sheep wanted to be saved.

  ⓒ The coin did not know it was lost. The sheep knew it was lost but was helpless to find the way home.

A Typical Sheepfold

Luke 15:11–32

The sheep and the coin were lost because of carelessness or ignorance. But in this parable, the son deliberately left the safety of his father's house. No one went looking for him, for he needed to decide to repent and return. However, his father was watching for him and was ready to welcome him home.

In this parable the younger son represents the lost sinner, the older son represents the religious Pharisees, and the father represents God.

7. What did the younger son ask his father to give him? _____

  the portion of goods that would be his when his father died

through his own carelessness. (*the parable of the lost sheep*)

—which parable illustrates God's desire to welcome repentant sinners home. (*the parable of the prodigal son*)

—who was lost besides the younger son in the parable of the prodigal son. (*the elder son*)

—which character in the parable of the prodigal son depicted the Pharisees and Jewish leaders. (*the elder son*)

—which story told by Jesus shows that we cannot change our destiny after we die. (*the account of the rich man and Lazarus*)

—why God forgave the publican in the parable but not the Pharisee. (*The publican confessed his sin and begged for mercy, but the Pharisee was proud and did not see his need for repentance.*)

Truths to Amplify

• The students should realize that true followers of God show love toward more than just those with whom they go to church. "Who is my neighbor?" is a question that we all face. The Jews thought they knew the answer—a fellow Jew. It did not occur to them that the Law of Moses could include kindness to those outside the "family" of God's chosen people. When they were uncertain whether the victim of a tragedy was a Jew or a Gentile, many Jews

8. What did the younger son do with that which he received? He gathered his possessions and took them to a far country, where he wasted his goods in riotous living.

9. Why did the younger son need to take a job feeding swine? His money was gone, and it was apparently the only job he could find. (Also, there was a famine in the land that made his predicament even worse.)

10. What shows that the younger son was paid very little or nothing for feeding the swine? He became so desperately hungry that he would have been glad to eat the pigs' food, but no one gave even that to him.

11. What is one lesson that this first part of the parable teaches us?
    a. When a person deliberately takes his own way in life, he will have to suffer the consequences.
    b. Younger sons should always stay home and work on their father's farm if they want to be happy.
    c. The younger son should have invested his money rather than spending it so foolishly.
    d. There is always joy in heaven over a sinner that repents.

The younger son repented of his sin and resolved to return to his father. However, he realized that he did not deserve to be taken back as a son. He decided to ask his father if he could become one of his hired servants.

🍇 *Choose two answers for number 12.*

12. The father saw the younger son coming while he was still "a great way off." He ran to meet him, welcoming him with a kiss. From this we can see that
    a. the father did not realize how sinful the younger son had become.
    b. God is always ready to forgive sinners who repent and turn to Him.
    c. God does not consider His children to be sinners, even if they turn their backs on Him.
    d. God is eagerly waiting for sinners to come to Him.

The father was so glad to see his son again that he gave him back all the privileges that he used to have. But the older brother was not glad to see his brother return. He refused to welcome him back home.

13. How was the elder brother like the Pharisees? (Choose *all* the correct answers.)
    a. He was not interested in helping sinners find the Father.
    b. He felt that he had always obeyed his father and deserved the father's special favor.
    c. He was upset with his father for welcoming the sinner home.
    d. Everything his father owned belonged to him, since the younger brother had already taken his share.

The Rich Man and Lazarus

This is an account of an actual happening rather than only a parable. The rich man was typical of the Pharisees of that time. Like the rich man, the Pharisees lived for themselves and often neglected to help those in need around them. Jesus used this account to give an explicit warning that those who think only of themselves will experience eternal judgment.

Luke 16:19–31

14. In the story both the rich man and Lazarus died.
    a. Where did the rich man go after he died? to hell
    b. Where did Lazarus go? to Abraham's bosom

preferred to risk not helping a Jew rather than to risk accidentally helping a Gentile. Jesus' teachings ran completely counter to this idea. He taught an undiscriminating love.

- Self-righteousness is perhaps one of the most dangerous sins. Other sins make a person feel guilty, but the sin of self-righteousness is easy to overlook and very difficult to acknowledge. The Pharisees were some of Jesus' most adamant enemies because He pricked their bubble of complacency.

- The Bible seems to indicate that the saints who died before Jesus' resurrection did not immediately go to heaven. They went to Hades, the place of departed spirits, which was separated into two parts by a great gulf (Luke 16:26). The righteous went to a place of comfort called Paradise (Luke 23:43), and the wicked were cast into a place of torment. After Jesus' resurrection, Paul speaks of Paradise as being in "the third heaven" (2 Corinthians 12:1–4). Today, Christians who are "absent from the body" are "present with the Lord" (2 Corinthians 5:6–8; Philippians 1:23).

148   Chapter Four   Jesus Ministers in Judea and Perea

15. What lessons does this story teach? (Choose three.)
   (a.) God sees and cares how we treat other people.
   b. Rich people will go to hell, but poor people will go to heaven.
   (c.) We can do nothing to change our destiny after we die.
   (d.) A miraculous sign or message will not change the mind of a person who refuses to heed the Bible.

Make sure the students understand why b is incorrect. Our eternal destiny is not determined solely by whether we are rich or poor.

The Pharisee and the Publican

Many publicans and sinners followed Jesus and found salvation. But the Pharisees despised these people and failed to see their own sin. In this parable, Jesus tried to show the Pharisees how God felt about such attitudes.

Luke 18:9–14

16. How did the Pharisee's prayer reveal his self-righteous attitude? He thanked God that he was not like other men, mentioning especially the publican who stood nearby. He also told God about the "good" things that he did for Him.

17. In what way was the publican's prayer different from the Pharisee's? He acknowledged that he was a sinner and begged for mercy. Even his appearance showed how different his attitude toward God was than the Pharisee's.

18. a. Which of the two men did God accept? the publican
    b. Why? God accepts those that humble themselves before Him and ask for forgiveness. (Because the Pharisee failed to see his own sinfulness, he neither sought nor received forgiveness.)

B. BIBLE WORD STUDY

Choose the statement that best defines the word or words in italics.

1. A certain lawyer *tempted* Jesus by asking Him a question (Luke 10:25).
   (a.) He was trying to test or prove Jesus.
   b. He was trying to deceive Jesus.
   c. He wanted Jesus to commit a sin.

2. The Samaritan traveler had *compassion* on the wounded man (Luke 10:33).
   a. He felt compelled to help him.
   b. He hoped that he could make money by helping him.
   (c.) He pitied him and felt love toward him.

3. The younger son would *fain* have filled his belly with the husks the swine ate (Luke 15:16).
   a. He could not make himself eat the husks.
   (b.) He would have been glad to eat the husks.
   c. He was forced to eat the husks.

4. The younger son wasted his *substance* with *riotous* living (Luke 15:13).
   (a.) He spent all his possessions for sinful pleasures.
   b. He gave his belongings to the poor so that they could share his pleasures.
   c. He used all his money to try to overthrow the government.

- When the King James Version of the Bible was translated, *test* and *prove* were synonyms of *tempt*.

5. The rich man *fared sumptuously* every day (Luke 16:19).
   a. He enjoyed many earthly pleasures every day.
   b. He fed a large crowd of rich friends every day.
   c. He made a lot of money every day.

C. THINKING ABOUT BIBLE TRUTHS

Right Attitudes Toward Others

The stories in this lesson show that God cares about our attitudes toward other people. The priest and the Levite, the elder son, the rich man, and the Pharisee all revealed a selfish, uncaring attitude. Jesus taught the better way of love and compassion. Those who follow Him and humbly serve others bring blessings to others and find true joy themselves.

1. People who do not love God often push others down in an attempt to exalt themselves. However, despising others is a very serious wrong that always includes pride and selfishness, and may include envy, hate, bitterness, and other sins.
   a. Read Proverbs 14:31. Who is a person indirectly reproaching when he despises someone else?
      God (his Maker)
   b. Read Philippians 2:3. How should each person consider others? _____
      Each should consider others better than themselves.
   c. What would the rich man have done differently if he had considered Lazarus in this way? ____
      (Sample answer) He would have cared for him and treated him as an honored guest.

Jesus gave many teachings on how to relate to others. The two passages below illustrate practical ways of showing proper attitudes.

Luke 14:7–9

2. What example of showing preference to others did Jesus give in this parable? _____
   A person invited to a wedding should sit down in the lowest room rather than the highest.

3. Give a practical way that you could apply the principle taught in this parable. (Think of a situation at home or at school when a choice you make affects what others receive.)   (Individual answers)
   _____
   _____

Luke 14:12–14

Often when we plan a meal or a special event, we invite our close friends or relatives. This is not wrong in itself, but it is wrong if these are the only people that we are concerned about.

4. Give a practical way that you could follow the principle taught in this parable. (Think of a way you could show this spirit without preparing a meal.)   (Individual answers)
   _____
   _____

- A literal translation of the Greek words here is "making merry brilliantly." A standard dictionary leaves the impression that the meaning should have something to do with eating. While eating is included, emphasize that the best meaning includes the rich man's general lifestyle, which was luxurious.

Discuss these questions in class. For numbers 3 and 4, discuss practical ways that students can show compassion and care for others. Point out that such caring is always costly for the giver, but the blessings to those he helps and to himself far outweigh the cost.

D. LEARNING MORE ABOUT BIBLE TIMES

The Judaizers

After Jesus' resurrection, some Pharisees and priests became Christians. They remembered the teachings of Christ and realized that He is indeed the Messiah. However, some of them thought that Christians still needed to keep the Law of Moses. Because of this, they tended to drift back into dependence on good works for salvation. These people are often called the Judaizers.

Many Judaizers may have been sincere people. They honestly felt that they were guarding the truth by insisting that Gentile believers must become Jews and fulfill the Old Testament Law. However, they misunderstood God's plan. They did not realize that the Law of Moses had done its work and that it was no longer needed. Their misunderstanding hindered God's plan instead of helping it.

1. Read Acts 15:1–5. At this time Paul and Barnabas were at Antioch, where many Gentiles had become members of the church.

   a. What did the men from Judea think the church should require of Gentile converts? _____
      They thought the Gentile converts should be circumcised and obey the Law of Moses.

   b. How did they decide to settle the dispute? _____
      The church sent Paul and Barnabas to Jerusalem to consult the apostles about the matter.

   c. What group at Jerusalem agreed that the Law of Moses must be kept? _____
      some converted Pharisees

The apostles and elders held a meeting to determine who was right. In this meeting, Peter reminded the other leaders of how God had sent him to Cornelius. There God had revealed to him that the Gentiles could be converted as they were, without becoming Jews. He also reminded them that the Jews themselves had never been able to keep the Law completely. How then could they put this burden upon the Gentiles?

2. Read Acts 15:23–29. These verses record the decision the apostles made.

   a. Did the apostles approve of what the Judaizers were doing? _no_
   b. Were the Gentiles asked to keep the Law? _no_

The Pharisees had long considered themselves the guardians of God's truth. It is little wonder that some of them tried to influence the church with their ideas. However, the Judaizers needed to learn that true doctrine is not based on man's interpretation of truth, but on God's revelation of His will. Those who seek God's Word with an honest heart will understand God's true doctrine.

About forty years after Jesus' resurrection, Jerusalem was destroyed and Jewish worship at the temple ceased. By this time many Gentiles had joined the church. Gradually the Jewish influence in the church lessened and the opposition of the Judaizers came to an end.

3. Copy a phrase from Acts 15:28 that shows God directed the church leaders in making the decision that they did. _"It seemed good to the Holy Ghost."_

- The Judaizers may have consisted mostly of converted Pharisees.

151

Lesson 20. Jesus—Steadfast in a Gathering Storm

Jesus ministered in all the major districts of Palestine while He was on earth. He taught in Judea at the beginning and end of His ministry. In between He spent much of His time in Galilee. He took trips through Samaria and visited the Gentile regions surrounding Galilee. Now He had spent most of His last winter in Perea, teaching the Jews who lived there.

All this time the opposition to Jesus' teaching was growing. Almost from the very start of His ministry, the Pharisees and Jewish leaders had opposed Him. As the novelty of His miracles wore off, the common people gradually turned against Him too. By His last winter, most of those who remained with Him did so because they were convinced that He is the Son of God. Even these close followers were beginning to realize that the Jews' hatred toward Jesus was becoming serious.

Jesus left Perea two days after He received a message that Lazarus was seriously ill. After going to Bethany to raise Lazarus from the dead, Jesus withdrew to a place called Ephraim. From there He made one last visit to His home country of Galilee, and then He set out on what He knew would be His last journey to Jerusalem. With Him went His best friends.

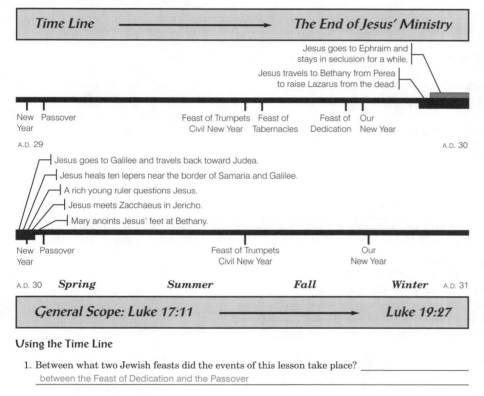

Using the Time Line

1. Between what two Jewish feasts did the events of this lesson take place? _____
   between the Feast of Dedication and the Passover

Lesson 20

Oral Review

1. How much food was left over after feeding the four thousand? [L. 15] **seven baskets full**
2. Describe the appearance of Jesus at His Transfiguration. [L. 16] **His face shone as the sun, and His raiment became white as the light.**
3. Why did the Samaritans of a certain village refuse to give lodging to Jesus? [L. 17] **He had steadfastly set His face to go to Jerusalem.**
4. Why did Jesus send people out two by two? [L. 17] **to preach the Gospel**
5. Who was expelled from the synagogue after Jesus healed him? [L. 18] **the man born blind**
6. What did Jesus say that caused the Jews to try to stone Him? [L. 18] **He said that God was His Father, and that He and His Father are one.**
7. In the parable of the prodigal son, who was lost besides the younger son? [L. 19] **the older son**
8. In the parable of the Pharisee and the publican, why did God forgive the publican but not the Pharisee? [L. 19] **The publican acknowledged his sin and begged for mercy, but the Pharisee failed to see his need for repentance.**

2. Number these events in the order they happened.

   __3__   Jesus heals ten lepers.

   __1__   Jesus raises Lazarus from the dead.

   __4__   Jesus meets the rich young ruler.

   __6__   Mary anoints Jesus' feet at Bethany.

   __2__   Jesus withdraws to Ephraim.

   __5__   Jesus meets Zacchaeus.

A. ANSWERS FROM THE BIBLE

The Resurrection of Lazarus

Jesus was spending the winter in Perea when He received an urgent plea from Judea for help. The disciples realized that Judea was a dangerous place for Jesus to go. But Jesus did not fear His enemies or allow them to hinder Him from doing God's work. He knew that the Jewish leaders could not take Him before it was God's time.

John 11:1–16

1. What message did Jesus receive in Perea? Jesus heard that Lazarus was sick.

2. Which two verses in this passage show that the disciples thought it was dangerous for Jesus to go to Jerusalem? verses 8 and 16

3. What did Jesus say was the purpose of Lazarus's sickness and death?

   Jesus said it was "for the glory of God, that the Son of God might be glorified thereby."

John 11:17–37

Jesus could have kept Lazarus from dying. He could have healed him from Perea without going to Bethany, or He could have kept him alive until He reached Bethany. But Jesus had other plans. He knew God's purpose would be better fulfilled by allowing Lazarus to die before He went to Bethany.

4. What did both Martha and Mary tell Jesus?

   a. "Whatsoever thou wilt ask of God, God will give it thee."

   (b.) "Lord, if thou hadst been here, my brother had not died."

When Jesus said that those who believe in Him will never die, He did not speak of bodily death. He spoke of the believers' inner life. A believer's soul lives with Jesus even after his body dies. At the end of the world, his body will be resurrected to live forever.

5. The Sadducees were Jews who did not believe in a resurrection. What did Martha believe?

   (a.) Martha believed that the dead would rise in the resurrection at the last day.

   b. Martha believed that Lazarus might suddenly rise at any time.

6. Even though Jesus knew that Lazarus would soon arise from the dead, He still shared the sorrow of Lazarus's family and friends. What did He do that showed how deeply He cared about human suffering and grief? He wept. (He also groaned and was troubled.)

John 11:38–46

When some of the Jews saw Jesus weeping with Mary and Martha, they wondered why He had not kept Lazarus from dying. No one seemed to realize what Jesus was about to do. Even Martha protested when Jesus asked

Some students may not have heard this explanation of verse 16. You may want to discuss this point in class. Most students should be able to find verse 8 without help.

In This Lesson

Scope: Matthew 19:16–30; 20:20–28; 26:6–13; Mark 10:17–31; 14:3–9; Luke 17:11–19; 18:18–30; 19:1–10; John 11:1–12:11

Focus

- In the face of growing danger, Jesus steadfastly carried out His purpose on earth.
  - Jesus used Lazarus's sickness and death to reveal Himself as the Resurrection and the Life, to strengthen His disciples' faith, and to bring the Jews to a decision to accept or reject Him as the Son of God.

- —After the Jewish rulers determined to kill Jesus, He went into seclusion at Ephraim.
- —Jesus apparently returned briefly to Galilee and then made His way back to Judea. Along the way He healed ten lepers, talked with a rich young ruler, and met Zacchaeus in Jericho.
- —After arriving at Bethany, Jesus attended a feast and was anointed by Mary.

Objectives

- Students should know
  - —what Jesus said was the purpose for Lazarus's sickness and death. (*It was for the glory of God, that the Son of God might be glorified thereby.*)

Lesson 20. Jesus—Steadfast in a Gathering Storm **153**

them to open the tomb. But when Jesus cried, "Lazarus, come forth," every eye must have been riveted on the dark entrance of the cave. Imagine being in the crowd when "he that was dead came forth"! No longer need they wonder what Jesus would do this time. But what would they do with Him?

7. The Jews saw evidence at Lazarus's resurrection that dead bodies can come back to life. They also saw proof that Jesus is the Resurrection and the Life and has power over death. What effect did this have on many of them? <u>Many believed on Jesus.</u>

8. Not everyone was happy that Jesus had raised Lazarus from the dead. Where did some of the Jews go with the news? <u>to the Pharisees</u>

John 11:47, 48, 53

When the Jewish leaders learned that Jesus had raised Lazarus, they resolved more firmly than ever that Jesus must be put to death. Like the apostles, the Jewish leaders seemed to realize that Jesus' work was heading toward some kind of climax. Also like the apostles, they did not understand what that climax was to be.

9. Why did the chief priests and Pharisees become alarmed and determine to put Jesus to death after hearing about Lazarus's resurrection?
   a. They believed that Jesus did not actually perform miracles, but deceived the people.
   (b.) They were afraid they would lose their position as rulers.

Jesus Returns to Galilee

Because of the rulers' decision to put Jesus to death, Jesus and His disciples could no longer travel about openly. They withdrew for a while to a town called Ephraim, near the wilderness (John 11:54). The location of Ephraim is not certain, but the map on page 154 gives a probable location.

Luke 17:11; Matthew 19:1, 2

10. It seems quite likely that these events took place on Jesus' final trip to Jerusalem. If this is correct, what route did Jesus probably take? (Also see the map on the next page.)
   (a.) Jesus traveled through Samaria to Galilee, and then returned to Jerusalem through Perea on the eastern side of the Jordan.
   b. Jesus traveled through Hebron to Beersheba, and then returned to Jerusalem by way of Bethlehem.

Jesus Heals Ten Lepers

The reference to Samaria and Galilee in Luke 17:11, 12 may mean that the village where Jesus met these lepers was on the border between Samaria and Galilee. Or it may simply mean that the village was somewhere along the path of Jesus' journey through Samaria and Galilee.

The nine Jewish lepers apparently did not mind associating with the Samaritan leper. Their common disease and their status as outcasts would have given them a mutual bond.

Luke 17:12–19

11. Why did Jesus tell the lepers to show themselves to the priests? (See Leviticus 14:2, 3, 20.) _____
   <u>The priests were required to examine a healed leper before he could be pronounced clean.</u>

- Number 9. You may want to discuss some other possibilities with your class. Much has been said about the corruption of the Jewish leaders, who were willing to kill an innocent person to keep their positions. However, Paul's early life as a Pharisee shows that some Jewish leaders may have honestly thought that Jesus was doing His miracles by Satan's power. Such men may have feared that if Jesus set Himself up as a false Messiah and involved the Jews in a war with the Romans, they would lose their place and their nation to the Romans. (However, like Paul, they could not remain both honest and ignorant indefinitely.)

  Others may have been astute enough to see that they would lose their leadership under the system of worship that Jesus was promoting. These promoted the old ways in order to maintain their status, even though they may have realized that Jesus was right.

- There is some difference of opinion about the location of Ephraim, the place where Jesus went after healing Lazarus. The map in this lesson shows the location commonly advocated by most Bible atlases, with the approximate site preferred by Edersheim as an alternative location.

- Number 10. It should be re-emphasized here that there are many things about Christ's ministry that we do not know

—why the disciples did not want Jesus to return to Judea. (*They feared the Jewish leaders.*)

—how Jesus expressed His sorrow when He saw others mourning Lazarus's death. (*He wept.*)

—what effect the raising of Lazarus had on the people of Bethany. (*Many believed on Jesus.*)

—what effect the raising of Lazarus had on the Jewish rulers. (*They determined to put Jesus to death.*)

—what the Samaritan leper did after Jesus healed him. (*He gave glory to God and thanked Jesus.*)

—why the rich young ruler decided not to follow Jesus. (*He loved his possessions too much to obey Jesus' command to sell all that he had and give*

the money to the poor.)

—what Jesus told His disciples to do to become great in His kingdom. (*serve others*)

—how Zacchaeus showed that he had truly repented. (*He said he would give half his goods to the poor and restore fourfold anything he had taken unjustly.*)

—what Jesus gave as the purpose for Mary's anointing of His feet and head. (*She did it in preparation for His burial.*)

The lepers were cleansed after they left to obey Jesus' instructions. When the Samaritan saw that he was healed, he returned to express his gratitude.

12. Jesus was disappointed that the Samaritan was the only one who returned. What did Jesus want all those whom He healed to do?
    a. He wanted them to publicly acknowledge Him as a great miracle worker.
    b. He wanted them to give glory to God.

On the Road to Jerusalem

As Jesus traveled toward Jerusalem for the feast of the Passover, He did not try to travel in secret as He had the summer before. That time He had wanted to avoid too much publicity and opposition. This time He would openly give His life for the world. Great crowds gathered around Him and went with Him toward Jerusalem.

While the group was traveling, a rich young ruler came to Jesus and wanted to know what he must do to have eternal life. The mother of James and John came to Jesus too. She wanted her sons to have high places in Jesus' kingdom. Jesus took time to show these individuals the root of their problems.

Matthew 19:16–22

13. Jesus told the rich young ruler that no one is good except God. What shows that the young ruler thought himself good? He said that he had kept all the commandments from his youth up.

14. When Jesus told the rich young ruler to sell all his possessions and give the money to the poor, the young man became sad and went away. How must he have felt about his possessions? He must have valued his possessions more highly than his spiritual life.

Matthew 20:20–28

15. To find a truly high place in His kingdom, Jesus told the disciples to serve others (become a servant).

16. Jesus Himself is the Son of God, yet He had come as the Son of man to give His life a ransom for many .

Jesus Meets Zacchaeus

On the way to Jerusalem, Jesus and the crowd following Him passed through Jericho. The Jews of Jesus' time called Jericho a little paradise. Springs supplied water to irrigate the flat, fertile fields around the city. Travelers on the caravan route between Damascus and Arabia stopped at Jericho, making it an important trading city. Rose gardens and plantations of balsam trees (raised for their sweet-smelling oil) perfumed its air when the sun went down.

While Jesus was at Jericho, He healed a blind man named Bartimaeus. He also met a rich publican who had climbed a tree to see Him.

for sure. None of the Gospels seem to have been written from a totally chronological viewpoint, so it is sometimes difficult to determine the order of events. This is true with some events covered in this lesson.

Edersheim maintains that Jesus probably traveled from Ephraim to Galilee, where He met His mother and the other women who were in Jerusalem at the time of His crucifixion. A number of other pilgrims traveled with them to Jerusalem. (Compare Mark 15:40, 41.) However, some commentators disagree with this supposition and place some of the events covered in this lesson earlier. For instance, some harmonies of the Gospels place the healing of the ten lepers (Luke 17) at the same time as the sending out of the seventy (Luke 10). While this is possible, it seems unlikely that Luke would record the two concurrent events this far apart. It also seems quite unlikely that the Galilean women who traveled with Jesus to the Passover would have traveled with Jesus and His disciples ever since they left Galilee half a year earlier. It seems more logical that Jesus returned to Galilee before going to Jerusalem for the last time.

Truths to Amplify

- Jesus truly came to this earth to serve. James and John and their mother thought a place of special honor was a worthy goal. Jesus taught them that true greatness means serving others and denying self.

- Jesus had God's will in mind when He waited two days before going to Bethany. From the human viewpoint, it was probably difficult for Him to wait while His friends suffered and questioned His motives. But by waiting He brought more glory to God than He would have by going sooner. Doing what is best for a person's spiritual good, even when he does not understand the purpose, is love and service in its highest form.

- Jesus did all things for God's glory. He knew how upset the ruling Jews would become as a result of His raising Lazarus from the dead. To perform such an awesome miracle so near Jerusalem when the leaders were already seeking His life was like signing His own death warrant. Yet He moved steadily ahead with God's will and plan. As the Passover neared, He could have remained in hiding and avoided the cross. Instead, He openly went up to Jerusalem. Why? Because He knew God's time had come for Him to lay down His life. His actions show that He truly did lay it down of Himself (John 10:18).

Luke 19:1–10

17. Why did the Jews murmur when Jesus went to Zacchaeus's house for a meal? _____
    Zacchaeus was a publican.

18. What did Zacchaeus do which proved that he was sorry for his sins and that he believed Jesus'
    teaching? Zacchaeus said he would give half his goods to the poor and restore fourfold anything he
    had taken unjustly.

Jesus at Bethany

John 11:55–12:11; Mark 14:1–9

The leaders of the Jews hoped to seize Jesus while He was in Jerusalem for the Passover. But they knew that many common people would try to defend Him and that He had often slipped away from them. So they planned to take Jesus secretly. What a surprise when Jesus came publicly to the area with throngs of people around Him!

19. On Jesus' arrival at Bethany, the people prepared a feast for Him in the house of Simon the leper.
    How did Mary show her devotion to Jesus?
    a. Mary took a pound of ointment   .
    b. With this she anointed Jesus' feet and head   .
    c. She also wiped His feet with   her hair   .

Note: Do not confuse this account of Mary anointing Jesus with the incident mentioned in Luke 7:36–50. The one in Luke 7 is in a different setting, even though parts of the two incidents are similar.

20. Judas complained that Mary had wasted this expensive ointment. But Jesus said that she had
    done it in preparation for His _____ burial _____, which He knew would take place in less
    than a week. Apparently Mary realized better than the disciples that soon Jesus would lay down
    His life.

B. BIBLE WORD STUDY

🍇 *Fill in the blanks and answer the questions.*

1. a. Bethany was about _____ fifteen _____ _____ furlongs _____ from Jerusalem (John 11:18).
   b. How far is this in modern measure? (Use the tables of measure inside the back cover.) _____
      about 1 ¾ miles (about 2 ¾ km)

2. a. Judas said that the ointment which Mary poured on Jesus was worth _____ three hundred _____
      pence (John 12:5). (Note: *Pence* is a plural form of *penny*.)
   b. How long did a common laborer need to work to earn one penny? (See Lesson 14 if you do not
      remember.) one day
   c. The ointment that Mary used was very costly. About how many days' wages would it have
      equaled in value? three hundred (about one year's wages)

3. Zacchaeus said that he would restore _____ fourfold _____ (four times as much) anything he had
   wrongly taken from anyone (Luke 19:8).

4. When the disciples sought to gain personal greatness, Jesus reminded them that He had come to
   give His life as a _____ ransom _____ (the price paid for someone's release) (Matthew 20:28).

- Number 19 a. This perfume was worth almost as much as an ordinary working man's wages for an entire year! Mary seems to have understood better than most of Jesus' followers that He would die soon, since Jesus said that she had kept the ointment to anoint Him for His burial.
- Number 19 b. John mentions feet and Mark mentions head. Probably this means that she anointed both.
- Number 19 c. This was proof of her genuine love and commitment.

- Because of the insight Mary had gained from Jesus, she was able to anoint Jesus beforehand for His burial. Other women prepared spices after Jesus had died, but by the time they could go to the tomb, Jesus had already risen.

C. THINKING ABOUT BIBLE TRUTHS

Glorifying God

Some of the apostles apparently had secret ambitions for greatness. Perhaps one reason some of them had followed Jesus was for the power and prestige they thought they could gain by being His disciples. But Jesus helped His followers to see that there is a better way to be great—by bringing glory to God rather than to self.

Those who do all for God's glory need to give up their own ambitions and be willing to suffer for Him. They must recognize that God often receives more glory from their lives during trying times than when everything goes well for them.

1. Martha and Mary agonized over the sickness and death of their brother. They could not understand why Jesus took so long to come. Jesus understood their sorrow and sympathized with them, yet He calmly waited two days before starting for Bethany. He even told His disciples that He was glad He had not been at Bethany to keep Lazarus from dying! (John 11:15). Why was it better in the end that Jesus had waited rather than doing what Mary and Martha wanted? Raising Lazarus after he had been dead four days brought greater glory to God than healing him would have. It also strengthened the faith of the disciples and others.

2. What did Martha (and others) need to do before she could see the glory of God? (John 11:40)
She needed to believe (that Jesus is the Resurrection and the Life).

3. Jesus required His disciples to forsake all that they had (Luke 14:33). This does not mean that they had no personal belongings, but rather that they could hold nothing back for themselves. Jesus tested the rich young ruler's love and commitment by telling him to sell all his possessions and give the money to the poor. Why did he fail the test? (Compare Matthew 6:24 and Matthew 19:20–22.) His love for his possessions was greater than his love for God.

4. Jesus told His disciples not to look for important earthly positions in His kingdom. What big misunderstanding did the disciples have about the kind of kingdom Jesus was preparing to set up? (See Luke 19:11 and Acts 1:6.)
They thought that Jesus would immediately set up an earthly kingdom.

Lesson 20. Jesus—Steadfast in a Gathering Storm   **157**

D. LEARNING MORE ABOUT BIBLE TIMES

Phylacteries

The Jews of Jesus' time bound boxes filled with Scripture verses around their heads and arms. They got the idea from Exodus 13:9 and 16. All Jewish men older than thirteen put on these little boxes, called phylacteries, to say their morning prayers.

The Jews tied up the Scripture verses inside the phylacteries with white hairs from cows' tails. They believed that the phylacteries would keep them from danger and ward off evil spirits.

1. One of the Scripture passages contained in the Jews' phylacteries was Deuteronomy 6:4–9. These verses give a number of places where the Jews were to have God's Law. What is the first (and most important) place mentioned in these verses?   <u>"in thine heart"</u>

If time permits, read this passage in unison during class.

2. How did the Jews misunderstand Exodus 13:9?   <u>   </u>
   <u>The Jews took this command literally and sometimes failed to realize its true spiritual meaning.</u>

3. Why did Jesus condemn the scribes and Pharisees for making their phylactery straps wider and more noticeable? (Matthew 23:5)   <u>They were doing this to be seen of men.</u>

4. How does God want us to carry the Scriptures with us today? (See Psalm 119:11 and Colossians 3:16.)   <u>He wants us to carry memorized Scripture passages with us in our minds (hearts).</u>

5. The Jews had a superstitious belief that wearing phylacteries containing Scripture portions would keep them from evil. Read Psalm 121:7 and tell where the Jews should have been looking for protection from evil.   <u>They should have been looking to God.</u>

158

Chapter Four Review

A. ORAL REVIEW

 Be sure you know the answers to these questions. Answer as many as you can from memory. If you need help, you may check the reference given in brackets.

Who >>

1. Who did the people think Jesus might be? [Matthew 16:13, 14]
2. Who said, "Thou art the Christ, the Son of the living God"? [Matthew 16:16]
3. Who appeared with Jesus at His Transfiguration? [Matthew 17:3]
4. Who was expelled from the synagogue after Jesus healed him? [John 9:24, 34]

What >>

5. In what direction did Jesus tell the blind man of Bethsaida to look? [Mark 8:25]
6. What did Jesus say that He would build upon the confession Peter made? [Matthew 16:18]
7. What did Jesus tell His disciples to rejoice about? [Luke 10:20]
8. During the Feast of Tabernacles, a priest poured out a pitcher of water at the altar. What did Jesus say He would cause to flow from those who believe on Him? [John 7:37–39]
9. What reason did Jesus give for the blindness of the man He healed at Jerusalem? [John 9:1–3]
10. What did Jesus say at the Feast of Dedication that caused the Jews to pick up stones to kill Him? [John 10:30, 31]
11. What effect did the raising of Lazarus have on the Jewish rulers at Jerusalem? [John 11:46, 53]
12. What proved that Zacchaeus sincerely repented? [Luke 19:8]
13. What reason did Jesus give for Mary's act of anointing Him with ointment? [John 12:7]

When >>

14. When did Satan speak through Peter? [Matthew 16:21–23]
15. When did Jesus tell Peter to fish with a hook? [Matthew 17:24–27]
16. When did Jesus weep with a group of mourners? [John 11:33–35]

How >>

17. How did Jesus teach the disciples a lesson in humility? [Mark 9:36, 37]
18. How did Jesus respond when the people of a village refused to receive Him? [Luke 9:51–56]
19. How did the man who had been born blind try to convince the Pharisees that Jesus could not be a sinner? [John 9:30–33]
20. How did the man born blind respond when He learned that Jesus is the Son of God? [John 9:35–38]
21. How did Lazarus's death serve a good purpose? [John 11:4]
22. How does a person become great in the kingdom of God? [Matthew 20:25–27]

1. Elias (Elijah), Jeremias (Jeremiah), John the Baptist, or one of the prophets
2. Peter
3. Moses and Elias (Elijah)
4. the man who had been born blind
5. up
6. His church
7. that their names were written in heaven
8. rivers of living water (the Holy Spirit)
9. "that the works of God should be made manifest in him"
10. He said that God was His Father, and that He and His Father are one.
11. They determined to put Jesus to death.
12. He said he would give half his goods to the poor and restore fourfold anything he had taken unjustly.
13. She did it to prepare His body for burial.
14. when Peter rebuked Jesus for saying that He would suffer and die
15. when they needed tribute money
16. when He saw the people mourning Lazarus's death
17. He used a child as an example.
18. He refused to retaliate and went to another village.
19. He pointed out that a sinner could not do such a marvelous work, because God does not hear sinners.
20. He (believed and) worshiped Jesus.
21. It brought glory to God and gave proof that Jesus is God's Son.
22. by serving others

B. WRITTEN REVIEW

Match

🍇 *Match these descriptions with the terms on the right.*

__a__	1. Falsely claiming to be God	a. blasphemy
__b__	2. Hanukkah	b. Feast of Dedication
__i__	3. Occasion when Jesus' face shone and His clothing became white	c. Feast of Tabernacles
		d. James and John
__h__	4. Loved possessions more than God	e. Lazarus
__f__	5. Small boxes with Scripture verses inside	f. phylacteries
__g__	6. Gave glory to God	g. Samaritan leper
__c__	7. Temporary booths	h. the rich young ruler
__j__	8. Tax	i. Transfiguration
__d__	9. Wanted to take revenge on enemies	j. tribute
__e__	10. Was dead four days	

Lessons From Jesus' Stories

🍇 *Match each parable or story with its lesson.*

__f__	11. God exalts the humble and abases the proud.	a. the good Samaritan
__d__	12. God welcomes repentant sinners who return to Him.	b. the lost sheep
__c__	13. People can be lost through the carelessness of others.	c. the lost coin
__e__	14. We cannot change our destiny after we die.	d. the prodigal son
__b__	15. People can be lost through their own carelessness.	e. the rich man and Lazarus
__a__	16. All men are our neighbors.	f. the Pharisee and the publican

Why

🍇 *Write complete answers. Answer as many as you can from memory. If you need help, you may check the reference given in brackets.*

17. Why did Jesus send out seventy of His disciples two by two? [Luke 10:1, 9] _____
He sent them to heal the sick and to spread the Gospel.

18. Why did Jesus commend Mary instead of reproving her as Martha requested? [Luke 10:38–42]
Mary had chosen the good part that was needful (listening to Jesus), while Martha's work had become a burden that distracted her from Jesus' teaching.

19. Why were some people at Jerusalem afraid to speak openly about Jesus? [John 7:13; 9:22] _____
They were afraid of the Jewish leaders.

20. Why did the Pharisees criticize Jesus for healing the blind man? [John 9:16] _____
Jesus had healed the blind man on the Sabbath Day.

160 Chapter Four Jesus Ministers in Judea and Perea

Map Review

Match each place in the lettered list with its description, and then label it on the map. Review the lessons and the maps in this workbook if you need help.

a. Bethany   f. Jericho
b. Bethsaida   g. Jerusalem
c. Caesarea Philippi   h. Mt. Hermon
d. Capernaum   i. Perea
e. Galilee   j. Samaria

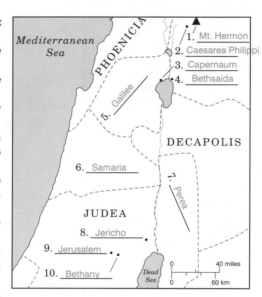

_b_ 21. Here Jesus used spit in healing a blind man.

_c_ 22. Peter confessed Jesus as the Christ at this Gentile city.

_h_ 23. This may have been the place where Jesus was transfigured.

_d_ 24. Peter paid tribute with money he had found in a fish's mouth.

_j_ 25. Some people of this region rejected Jesus because He was headed for Jerusalem.

_g_ 26. Jesus attended feasts at the temple and healed a man born blind.

_i_ 27. Jesus spent His last winter teaching in this region.

_a_ 28. Mary and Martha lived here, and Jesus raised Lazarus from the dead.

_e_ 29. The ten lepers whom Jesus healed lived in this region or in Samaria.

_f_ 30. Jesus met Zacchaeus at this town.

"I am the vine, ye are the branches" (John 15:5).

CHAPTER FIVE

Jesus Completes His Work

Jesus Returns to Jerusalem
Jesus' Final Public Discourses
Jesus' Last Days With His Disciples
The Lamb of God
"Behold, I Am Alive for Evermore"

And they sung a new song, saying,
Thou art worthy to take the book,
and to open the seals thereof:
for thou wast slain, and hast redeemed us to God
by thy blood out of every kindred, and tongue,
and people, and nation. . . .
Blessing, and honour, and glory, and power,
be unto him that sitteth upon the throne,
and unto the Lamb for ever and ever.
Revelation 5:9, 13

Harmony of the Gospels

For important events and teachings covered in Chapter Five

Event or Teaching	Matthew	Mark	Luke	John	Location	Day
Lesson 21. Jesus Returns to Jerusalem						
Jesus rides into Jerusalem on a donkey.	21:1–11[1]	11:1–11	19:29–38	12:12–16	Mt. of Olives	Sunday
The Pharisees protest.	—	—	19:37–40	12:17–19	Mt. of Olives	Sunday
Jesus weeps over Jerusalem.	—	—	19:41–44	—	Mt. of Olives	Sunday
Jesus curses a barren fig tree.	21:18, 19	11:12–14	—	—	Near Bethany	Monday
Jesus cleanses the temple again.	21:12–17	11:15–19	19:45–48	—	Temple courts	Monday
The fig tree is withered away.	21:19–22	11:20–26	—	—	Near Bethany	Tuesday
Lesson 22. Jesus' Final Public Discourses						
The parable of the laborers in the vineyard[2]	20:1–16	—	—	—		
The parable of the two sons	21:28–32	—	—	—	Jerusalem	Tuesday
The parable of the wicked husbandmen	21:33–46	12:1–12	20:9–19	—	Jerusalem	Tuesday
The marriage of the king's son	22:1–14	—	—	—	Jerusalem	Tuesday
Jesus answers and asks questions.	22:15–46	12:13–37	20:20–44	—	Jerusalem	Tuesday
Jesus condemns the scribes and Pharisees.	23:1–39	12:38–40	20:45–47	—	Jerusalem	Tuesday
Lesson 23. Jesus' Last Days With His Disciples						
Jesus foretells future events.	24:1–51	13:1–37	21:5–36	—	Mt. of Olives	Tuesday
The parable of the ten virgins	25:1–13	—	—	—	Mt. of Olives ?	Tuesday
The parable of the talents	25:14–30	—	—	—	Mt. of Olives ?	Tuesday
The Jewish rulers conspire with Judas against Jesus.	26:1–5, 14–16	14:1, 2, 10, 11	22:1–6	—	Jerusalem	Tuesday or Wed.?
Jesus eats the Passover with His disciples.	26:17–25	14:12–21	22:7–18	13:1	Jerusalem	Thursday
Jesus serves the first Communion.	26:26–29	14:22–25	22:19, 20	—	Jerusalem	Thursday
Jesus washes His disciples' feet.	—	—	—	13:2–17	Jerusalem	Thursday
Lesson 24. The Lamb of God						
Jesus prays in the Garden of Gethsemane.	26:36–46	14:32–42	22:39–46	—	Mt. of Olives	Thursday
Jesus is betrayed and arrested.	26:47–57	14:43–53	22:47–54	18:2–12	Mt. of Olives	Friday
Jesus is tried by the Jews and denied by Peter.	26:57–27:1	14:53–15:1	22:54–71	18:13–27	Caiaphas's house	Friday
Jesus is tried before Pilate (and Herod).	27:11–30	15:2–19	23:1–25	18:28–19:16	Judgment hall	Friday
Jesus is crucified at Calvary.	27:31–56	15:20–41	23:26–49	19:17–37	Calvary	Friday
Jesus is buried in a new tomb.	27:57–66	15:42–47	23:50–56	19:38–42	Near Calvary	Friday
Lesson 25. "Behold, I Am Alive for Evermore"						
Women find the tomb empty.	28:1–10	16:1–11	24:1–11	20:1, 2	Jesus' tomb	Sunday
Peter and John run to see the tomb.	—	—	24:12	20:3–10	Jesus' tomb	Sunday
Jesus appears on the way to Emmaus.	—	16:12, 13	24:13–35	—	Near Emmaus	Sunday
Jesus appears to His disciples.	—	16:14	24:36–49	20:19–25	Jerusalem	Sunday
Jesus appears to Thomas.	—	—	—	20:26–29	Jerusalem	After 8 days
Jesus appears in Galilee. (1 Corinthians 15:6)	28:16–20	16:15–18	—	21:1–25	Galilee	During 40 days
Jesus ascends into heaven. (Acts 1:1–12)	—	16:19, 20	24:50–53	—	Bethany	After 40 days

---

[1] Passages given in italics are used in the lesson.

[2] Jesus gave this parable on the way to Jerusalem. It is grouped here with other parables.

163

Lesson 21. Jesus Returns to Jerusalem

In the previous chapters you have studied some of Jesus' wonderful works and many of the truths that He taught. You have seen how quickly men changed their opinion of Jesus. First He was unknown, then popular, and then despised by the general population in Judea and Galilee. You have also seen how the Jewish leaders turned against Him because He did not fit their idea of what the Messiah would be.

In this chapter, you will study the end of Jesus' ministry and what the Jews finally did with their Messiah, the Son of God.

Jesus had accomplished much during His three years of ministry. But as He approached the last week of His earthly life, some things remained for Him to do. The Pharisees needed to be warned again. The disciples needed more instruction. They also needed assurance that

Jesus was still in control, even though their world seemed to be falling apart. Most important, the world needed a Saviour. Being that Saviour would be Jesus' greatest work.

Jesus, who knew very well that He must suffer and die, faced His last week calmly. Though His human body shrank from the pain that lay ahead, He submitted Himself to His Father's will. He faced death as He had always faced life—secure in the knowledge that He was one with His Father and that His Father was working through Him.

In this lesson you will study about one more upsurge of popular favor toward Jesus. However, the people still were expecting an earthly king for their Messiah, and Jesus did not fulfill their expectation. Within a few days a mob would be shouting, "Crucify Him!"

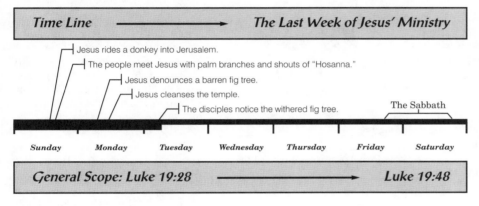

Time Line ⟶ **The Last Week of Jesus' Ministry**

Jesus rides a donkey into Jerusalem.
The people meet Jesus with palm branches and shouts of "Hosanna."
Jesus denounces a barren fig tree.
Jesus cleanses the temple.
The disciples notice the withered fig tree.
The Sabbath

Sunday   Monday   Tuesday   Wednesday   Thursday   Friday   Saturday

General Scope: Luke 19:28 ⟶ **Luke 19:48**

Using the Time Line

1. What two full days of the week does this lesson cover? Sunday, Monday
2. On what day of the week did Jesus cleanse the temple? Monday

Lesson 21

Oral Review

1. Name the New Testament books in order. [L. 1] **Matthew, Mark, Luke, John, Acts, Romans, 1 & 2 Corinthians, Galatians, Ephesians, Philippians, Colossians, 1 & 2 Thessalonians, 1 & 2 Timothy, Titus, Philemon, Hebrews, James, 1 & 2 Peter, 1, 2, & 3 John, Jude, Revelation**

2. Define *Messiah*. What Greek word has the same meaning? [L. 2] **the Anointed One; Christ**

3. Why did Jesus have authority to cleanse the temple? [L. 5] **He is the Son of God.**

4. What did the people in Nazareth try to do to Jesus? [L. 6] **They tried to throw Him over the brow of a hill.**

5. How did the Roman centurion of Capernaum prove his faith in Jesus? [L. 11] **He asked Jesus to heal his servant without coming to his house.**

6. What did Jesus mean when He warned His disciples to beware of the leaven of the Pharisees and Sadducees? [L. 15] **He meant that they should avoid their false doctrine.**

7. What parable illustrates God's willingness to welcome repentant sinners home? [L. 19] **the parable of the prodigal son**

164   Chapter Five   Jesus Completes His Work

A. ANSWERS FROM THE BIBLE

Jesus' Triumphal Entry Into Jerusalem

Just before the events covered in this lesson, Jesus had spent the Sabbath at Bethany, where He had attended a feast with Mary, Martha, and Lazarus. The town of Bethany was located on the eastern slope of the Mount of Olives, within easy walking distance of Jerusalem.

On Sunday Jesus started for Jerusalem on foot with His disciples. By now people in Jerusalem had heard that Jesus was coming to the city (John 12:12). Many people from other regions and countries, who had come for the Passover, wanted to see Jesus (John 11:55, 56). As the word spread that He was on His way, they hurried out of the city to meet Him.

 To complete these exercises, first study the Bible passages that are given. Fill in the short blanks with words. Whenever possible, use exact words from the Bible. Write complete answers for the questions with long blanks. For multiple-choice questions, circle the letter of the correct answer.

Matthew 21:1–11

1. On the way to Jerusalem, Jesus sent two disciples into the village of Bethphage. What did He tell them to bring?   an ass (donkey) and its colt

2. How did Jesus fulfill an Old Testament prophecy on His way to Jerusalem?
   The Old Testament (Zechariah 9:9) had prophesied that Israel's King would come riding on the colt of an ass, bringing salvation. Jesus fulfilled this prophecy by riding the donkey's colt into the city.

3. What was remarkable about the colt on which Jesus rode? (See Mark 11:2.)   The colt had never been ridden, but it let Jesus ride it.

4. What three things did the multitude do to show their respect and love for Jesus?
   a.   They cast their garments in the way.
   b.   They cut down branches from the trees and strawed them in the way.
   c.   They cried, "Hosanna to the son of David."

5. Many people in Judea and Galilee had previously turned away from Jesus. What prompted the multitude's interest in Him now? (See John 12:17, 18.)
   They had heard how Jesus had raised Lazarus from the dead.

The Pharisees Protest

Evidently some of the Pharisees had joined the multitude that went to meet Jesus. They were horrified when the crowd began to proclaim Jesus as the Messiah. Because they did not know what else to do, they appealed directly to Jesus, hoping that He would refute what the people were saying.

Luke 19:37–40

6. Why did the Pharisees not want the multitudes to praise Jesus?
   a. They did not want the people to be deceived.
   b. They were afraid the Sadducees would kill Jesus if they heard the people.
   c. They were jealous of His popularity.

- Also compare Isaiah 62:11.

- In Old Testament times, animals that had never been used were considered especially suited for religious purposes. See Numbers 19:2, Deuteronomy 21:3, and 1 Samuel 6:7.

- Note that these shouts of praise were part of the Hallel, which the Jews chanted regularly at feasts. See comments on page 139 of the pupil's book.

---

8. Why did the disciples not want Jesus to return to Judea when Lazarus became sick? [L. 20] **They were afraid of the Jews.**

In This Lesson

Scope: Matthew 21:1–22; Mark 11:1–26; Luke 19:29–48; John 12:12–19

Focus

- Jesus openly revealed Himself to the crowds gathered at Jerusalem for the Passover.
   —He rode into Jerusalem on a donkey, while a multitude greeted Him as king.
   —The Pharisees protested against the cries of the multitudes, but He said that if they held their peace, the stones would cry out.
   —He wept over Jerusalem and foretold its destruction.
   —He denounced a barren fig tree and used it to teach His disciples a lesson in faith.
   —He cleansed the temple, healed openly there, and accepted the children's praises.
   —The Jewish leaders wanted to arrest Him, but they could do nothing against Him because His time had not yet come.

7. What did Jesus say would have happened if the multitude had stopped praising Him? _____
   The stones would have cried out.

John 12:19

The Pharisees probably made the comment in this verse about the same time that they asked Jesus to rebuke the multitude.

8. What had the Jewish leaders come to realize? _____
   They could do nothing to stop Jesus' powerful influence upon the people.

Jesus Weeps Over Jerusalem

As Jesus approached Jerusalem, He looked over the city and began to weep. He did not weep for Himself, even though He knew that the Jews and Romans would kill Him within a few days. Instead, He wept for the Jews who had rejected Him and would perish at the fall of Jerusalem.

Terrible things happened when the Romans destroyed Jerusalem about forty years later. The devastation was so great that Titus, the Roman general in charge of taking the city, is said to have spread his hands toward heaven and called on God to be his witness that it had not been his desire to cause such extreme suffering.

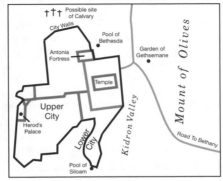

Jerusalem at the Time of Christ

Luke 19:41–44

9. Why was Jerusalem destroyed? _____
   The Jews would not accept Jesus as their Messiah when He came to them.

   _____
   _____
   _____

The People Wonder Who Jesus Is

The people of Jerusalem were moved when they saw Jesus and the multitude entering the city.

Matthew 21:10, 11

10. The people of the city wanted to know what was happening. Who did the multitude say that Jesus is? "Jesus the prophet of Nazareth of Galilee"
    _____

11. This time the multitude did not identify Jesus as the Messiah and King of Israel, even though they had called Him this earlier. Why might they have changed what they said about Him? (Choose three possible reasons.)
    (a.) They may have been afraid of the Jewish leaders in Jerusalem.
    (b.) They may have been disappointed that Jesus had wept over Jerusalem instead of marching in and taking control.
    (c.) They might not have fully understood their earlier exclamations and still thought of Him as a man.
    d. Jesus had told them not to tell anyone in Jerusalem what they knew about Him.

• We cannot be sure of the reasons, but any of these three might have been part of it. For whatever reason, the multitude held back from wholly supporting Jesus as the Messiah, even though in the emotion of the moment they had declared that He was King just shortly before.

Objectives

• Students should know
  —how Jesus fulfilled an Old Testament prophecy during His triumphal entry into Jerusalem. (*He rode into Jerusalem on a donkey's colt, bringing salvation.*)
  —what words of praise the crowd proclaimed while Jesus rode into Jerusalem on a donkey. (*"Hosanna to the son of David"*)
  —who protested when the multitudes praised Jesus during His triumphal entry. (*the Pharisees*)
  —why Jesus wept over Jerusalem. (*He knew what dreadful things were going to happen to the Jews because of their rejection of Him.*)
  —why Jesus cleansed the temple. (*The Jews had made it a den of thieves.*)
  —how Jesus cleansed the temple. (*He cast out all that sold and bought, and He overthrew the tables of the moneychangers and the seats of those that sold doves.*)
  —the meaning of *hosanna.* (*"Save now!"* or *"Save, I pray!"*)

166 Chapter Five Jesus Completes His Work

Jesus Desires Fruit

On Sunday evening, after the triumphal entry, Jesus went back to Bethany. He returned to Jerusalem on Monday morning.

Mark 11:12–14

12. Jesus was hungry as He traveled toward Jerusalem, so He was pleased to see a _____fig tree_____ with _____leaves_____ beside the road ahead.

From a distance the tree appeared to have fruit, even though it was not the normal time for figs to ripen.

13. When Jesus came to the tree, He found nothing but _____leaves_____ on it. This tree probably reminded Him of the Jews who appeared righteous but produced no fruit for God. He said to the tree, "No man eat _____fruit_____ of thee hereafter for ever."

Jesus Cleanses the Temple

Jesus spent much time at the temple during this week. The Jewish leaders had been looking for a chance to arrest Him, but they were afraid that the people would rise up against them if they seized Jesus in public. They would have no power to take Jesus until God allowed them to do so.

Matthew 21:12–16

14. What did Jesus do when He entered the temple? __He cast out all that sold and bought, and over-__
__threw the tables of the moneychangers and the seats of those that sold doves.__

15. What did God intend His house to be? __the house of prayer__

16. What did Jesus say the Jews had turned the temple into? __a den of thieves__

17. Jesus also healed the _____blind_____ and the _____lame_____ that came to Him.

Perhaps the multitude that had greeted Jesus the day before had included children. Fear of the Jewish leaders had very likely silenced many of the adults, but the joyful children could not be quieted so easily. They openly sang their praises to Jesus in the temple courts.

18. How did the chief priests and scribes feel about Jesus' wonderful works and the children's praise? __They were sore displeased.__

19. How did Jesus feel about the children's praise? __He was pleased with it.__

A Lesson From a Fig Tree

Jesus spent Monday night at Bethany again before returning to Jerusalem with His disciples on Tuesday morning. As they passed the fig tree, Peter was amazed to see that it had dried up from the roots.

Mark 11:20–24

20. Jesus used the fig tree to teach His disciples a lesson in
   (a.) having faith in God.   b. bearing fruit.   c. rebuking evil.

- There is an interesting parallel between Jesus denouncing the fig tree and cleansing the temple. Since fig trees have leaves only when they produce fruit, the fig tree was outwardly indicating that it had fruit when it had none. The people were busy getting the temple ready for the Passover, but it was full of thieves and robbers rather than spiritual fruit. Jesus condemned both for the same reason. Our churches will receive the same curse if we do not live up to what we profess.

- See the note for number 5 in Part C.

Truths To Amplify

- It is easy to see that God timed the events of the last week before Jesus' death. This was Passover week, with its many types that pointed to Jesus. Visitors had come from far and near. Although they could not have guessed it, thousands of them would become witnesses to the last great event in Jewish history and to the first great event in the history of the Christian church. Jesus could not have completed His work at a more opportune time.

B. BIBLE WORD STUDY

Choose the best meaning for the word or phrase in italics as it is used in the verse. (This will not always be the dictionary meaning of the word or phrase. You may need to consult a Bible dictionary or the Greek definitions in a large concordance for some of them.)

1. Jesus rode into Jerusalem on the colt of an *ass* (Matthew 21:5).
   (a.) a donkey
   b. a mule

2. The multitudes that followed Jesus to Jerusalem shouted, "*Hosanna* to the son of David" (Matthew 21:9).
   a. derived from a Greek word meaning "praises of God"
   (b.) derived from Hebrew words that literally mean "Save now!" or "Save, I pray!"

3. Jesus came to the fig tree to see if *haply* he might find some figs to eat (Mark 11:13).
   (a.) perhaps; possibly
   b. happily; gladly

4. Jesus foretold that the enemies of Jerusalem would *cast a trench* around the city (Luke 19:43).
   a. dig a ditch
   (b.) build a wall of wooden stakes

5. Jesus also prophesied that the enemies of Jerusalem would *compass the city round* (Luke 19:43).
   a. pass by the city
   (b.) surround or encircle the city

6. The people who saw Jesus raise Lazarus from the dead *bare record* that it had happened (John 12:17).
   a. wrote down what happened
   (b.) told others the story was true

Discuss this in class. The Greek words indicate that this is the proper meaning in this case.

C. THINKING ABOUT BIBLE TRUTHS

The Paradox of Christ's Actions

This lesson shows Jesus responding to situations in ways that may seem opposite. On Sunday He rode a donkey into the city and is described as being meek and lowly. The next day He walked into the temple and drove out the moneychangers and the sellers of doves. The exercises below will help you understand why Jesus' actions were right in both cases.

1. How does the prophet describe Jesus' character in the following verses?
   a. Isaiah 53:7 He would be patient and would not retaliate.
   b. Isaiah 40:11 He would be loving, gentle, and kind to others.

2. Describe Jesus' actions in the following verses.
   a. Matthew 4:23, 24 He was compassionate and caring.
   b. John 11:33–35 He was sympathetic.

The exercises above show Jesus as we usually think of Him. But Jesus did not always respond this way.

Sample answers. The exact wording may vary.

3. How did Jesus respond in the following verses?
   a. Mark 3:5 <u>He became angry.</u>
   b. John 2:13–17 <u>He zealously cleansed the temple.</u>
4. a. Jesus never became upset when people mistreated Him or spoke evil of Him. What was Jesus responding to in Mark 3:5 and John 2:13–17? <u>sin</u>

   b. How did Jesus tell His disciples to treat those who mistreated them? (See Matthew 5:44.)
      <u>"Love your enemies, bless them that curse you, do good to them that hate you, and pray for them</u>
      <u>which despitefully use you, and persecute you."</u>
5. How does the fact that Jesus is both God and man help to explain the seeming paradoxes of His actions and responses? (For a clue, read Romans 12:19, 20.) <u>(Sample answer) As God, Jesus had</u>
   <u>the right to execute vengeance against evildoers. But because He came as the Son of man to seek</u>
   <u>and to save the lost, He usually dealt in mercy rather than in judgment.</u>

Discuss this question in class. Make clear to the students that these incidents from Jesus' life do not justify carnal anger or violence. Jesus never sinned, and all that He did was perfect. As noted above, Jesus' forceful reactions were always in response to sin and were never personal retaliation. In these cases Jesus was using His authority as God to judge and deal with sin. We do not have the authority to deal with sin in the same way that He did. We must act as He taught His followers to respond.

D. LEARNING MORE ABOUT BIBLE TIMES

Money in Bible Times

In the beginning, people did not use money. They traded goods to get what they needed. But early men soon discovered that trading goods for precious metals was handier. Gold, silver, and copper were the first metals used to buy and sell.

1. a. How did people measure these metals?
      (See Genesis 23:16.) <u>by weighing them</u>

   b. What unit of measure is mentioned in this verse? <u>the shekel</u>

Eventually precious metals were formed into disks, bars, and rings of standard weights. This made them easier to measure. The people of Lydia first invented uniform coins. Later the Persians conquered Lydia and adopted the use of coins.

2. What two coins are mentioned in Mark 12:42?

   <u>mite</u>   <u>farthing</u>

Roman, Greek, and Jewish money had come into common use in Palestine by Jesus' time. Only Jewish coins could be used at the temple. This made money changing a profitable business. (Moneychangers charged about 10 percent for their services.)

3. Give two occasions when Jesus took notice of money in the temple at Jerusalem. (Review this lesson, and see Mark 12:41–44.)   Jesus drove out the moneychangers, and He took notice of the widow who gave all she had into the treasury.

4. Jesus said, "Ye cannot serve _____God_____ ____and____ _____mammon_____ [money]" (Matthew 6:24).

5. Paul said, "The (a) _____love_____ of money is the (b) _____root_____ of all evil: which while some (c) _____coveted_____ after, they have . . . pierced themselves through with many (d) _____sorrows_____" (1 Timothy 6:10).

170

Lesson 22. Jesus' Final Public Discourses

The Gospels give more details about the last week of Jesus' ministry than about any other period of His life. (The Gospel of John devotes almost nine of its twenty-one chapters to it.) The previous lesson covered the events that took place on Sunday and Monday of that last week. This lesson covers most of Tuesday.

Tuesday was a busy day for Jesus. It seems to have been the last day of His public ministry, and He had a number of things that He wanted to do. During this day Jesus talked once more with the self-righteous Jewish leaders, spending some time with the chief priests, the elders, the Pharisees, the Herodians, and the Sadducees.

Jesus talked very frankly to the Jewish leaders. His words to them are some of the strongest in the Bible, but He said what He did because of His deep love for these deceived men. Later some of the priests and Pharisees turned from their sins to become Christians (Acts 6:7; 15:5).

Perhaps some of them did so because of the warnings Jesus gave them.

On Tuesday evening, with the public part of His work finished, Jesus paused before leaving the temple. Looking past the crowds that had listened to His final condemnation of the Pharisees, He lamented, "O Jerusalem, Jerusalem, thou that killest the prophets, and stonest them which are sent unto thee, how often would I have gathered thy children together, even as a hen gathereth her chickens under her wings, and ye would not!"

Was Jesus' mission a failure? Was He defeated as He left Jerusalem? Was His rejection by the Jewish nation the end of God's plan? If Jesus had been merely a human leader, He probably would have felt that He had failed. But Jesus was not merely human. He is the Son of God, and He knew that God's plan for Him was very close to its climax. Victory was in sight!

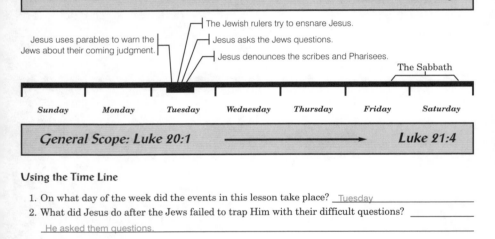

Time Line ⟶ **The Last Week of Jesus' Ministry**

The Jewish rulers try to ensnare Jesus.

Jesus uses parables to warn the Jews about their coming judgment.

Jesus asks the Jews questions.

Jesus denounces the scribes and Pharisees.

The Sabbath

Sunday   Monday   Tuesday   Wednesday   Thursday   Friday   Saturday

General Scope: Luke 20:1 ⟶ **Luke 21:4**

Using the Time Line

1. On what day of the week did the events in this lesson take place? _Tuesday_
2. What did Jesus do after the Jews failed to trap Him with their difficult questions? _____
   He asked them questions.

Lesson 22

Oral Review

1. Who was to be blessed by the coming of the Messiah? [L. 2] **all the families of the earth**
2. How did Jesus find strength to do His work? [L. 8] **He spent much time in prayer.**
3. What did the Gentiles of Decapolis do when they saw Jesus' miracles? [L. 15] **They glorified the God of Israel.**
4. Who appeared with Jesus on the Mount of Transfiguration? [L. 16] **Moses and Elias (Elijah)**
5. Why did the rich young ruler decide not to follow Jesus? [L. 20] **He loved his possessions too**

much to obey Jesus' command to sell all that he had and give his money to the poor.

6. What effect did the raising of Lazarus have upon the Jewish leaders? [L. 20] **They determined to put Jesus to death.**
7. What words of praise did the multitude proclaim as Jesus rode into Jerusalem on a donkey? [L. 21] **"Hosanna to the son of David"**
8. How did Jesus cleanse the temple? [L. 21] **He cast out all that sold and bought, and He overthrew the tables of the moneychangers and the seats of those that sold doves.**

A. ANSWERS FROM THE BIBLE

The last parables that Jesus gave publicly were spoken to people walking with Him to Jerusalem or listening to Him in the temple. In these parables Jesus is giving His audience a view of time and history as God sees it. Each one points to the end of time and warns the audience of coming judgment. Like many parables, these can probably have several interpretations or lessons taken from them, but the following exercises focus on only one lesson for each.

The Laborers in the Vineyard

Jesus gave this parable as He went toward Jerusalem the last time. It is included with the parables that He gave on the last Tuesday of His ministry because it has a similar message.

In this parable the householder is God, and the laborers are God's people. The evening is the end of time, and the wages are the rewards that God will give to His faithful servants.

Matthew 20:1–16

1. Some of the laborers worked for twelve hours, some for nine hours, some for six hours, and some for three hours. Others worked for only one hour. What is strange about the wages that the laborers received?   They all received the same pay, no matter how long they had worked.

2. Which of the following statements best explains an important lesson that this parable teaches?
   a. God does not like to see people standing idle in the marketplace.
   b. It is wise to wait to serve God until later in life.
   c. God rewards His people for their commitment to Him, not for the amount of work they do.
   d. God expects some people to work harder for Him than other people to gain the same reward.

The Two Sons

Jesus gave this parable on Tuesday after the chief priests and elders questioned His authority.

In this parable the father is God. The second son represents the Jewish leaders, such as the Pharisees, who claimed to be doing God's will but were actually rebelling against Him. The first son represents the publicans and sinners who recognized their sinfulness and turned to God in true repentance.

Matthew 21:28–32

3. What made the first son do what his father asked, even though at first he had refused to obey?
   He repented.

4. Which of the following statements best explains a lesson that this parable teaches?
   a. God is more pleased by words than He is by actions.
   b. What we do is even more important than what we say we will do.
   c. The publicans and harlots were always more godly than the Pharisees were.
   d. God wants all of His people to work in vineyards.

The Wicked Husbandmen

In this parable the owner of the vineyard was God, the husbandmen were the Jewish leaders, the servants sent by the owner were God's prophets, and the son was Jesus. This parable contains a pointed warning to the Jewish leaders about their rebellion against God. The Jewish leaders understood the parable, but they were afraid to arrest Jesus in public.

Be sure the students realize that no one can do enough for God to earn a reward. Salvation and eternal life are actually gifts, not wages. It makes sense for all His workers to receive the same amount, since none are worthy of any wages, no matter how long or well they have labored.

In This Lesson

Scope: Matthew 20:1–16; 21:23–23:39; Mark 12:1–44; Luke 20:1–47

Focus

- Jesus used parables and questions to show the Jewish leaders the serious consequences of rejecting Him.
  —The Pharisees and the Sadducees tried to trap Jesus with difficult questions. (By His answers, Jesus not only silenced His enemies but also taught them truths that they were overlooking.)
  —Jesus commended one scribe for showing careful thought and good intentions.
  —Jesus asked questions that the Jews could not answer.
- Jesus denounced the scribes and Pharisees for their hypocrisy and treachery. (Be sure the students understand that Jesus did this because He loved their souls, and not because of a carnal attitude toward them.)

Objectives

- Students should know which parable teaches
  —that God rewards us for our deeds, not for our empty promises. (*the parable of the two sons*)
  —that God will judge those who are unfaithful to the trust that He gives them. (*the parable of the*

Mark 12:1–12

5. a. What did Jesus tell the Jews that God was going to do with the unfaithful husbandmen? _____
       He would destroy the husbandmen.

   b. What would He do with the vineyard?   He would give the vineyard to others.

6. Which of the following statements best explains a lesson that this parable teaches?
   a. God would not have allowed Gentiles to be saved if the Jews had not rejected Jesus.
   b. Jesus was in danger of losing the inheritance that God had meant for Him to have.
   c. Since the Jews as a nation had been unfaithful to their trust, no Jews would be saved.
   (d) Since the Jewish leaders had been unfaithful, God was planning to judge them.

The Marriage of the King's Son

This parable teaches the same lesson as the last one. However, it is more explicit in its details and foretells the fate of the unfaithful Jewish leaders. In this parable the king is God, the son is Jesus, the servants are the prophets, and the invited guests are the Jewish leaders.

Matthew 22:1–14

7. Why did the invited guests fail to come to the king's feast? (Choose two reasons.)
   (a) They were too busy with other things that they thought were more important.
   b. They were afraid to come.
   c. They did not realize that the king wanted them to come.
   (d) They failed to honor their king and his servants.

The king sent his armies to destroy the rebellious guests and their city. This was fulfilled when the Romans destroyed Jerusalem with a great slaughter.

8. The king sent his servants out into the highways to bid everyone they could find to come to the feast. This shows us that
   a. the way of salvation is not voluntary.
   b. God no longer offers salvation to the Jews.
   c. since the rich people rejected the chance to go to the feast, only poor people can be saved.
   (d) the way of salvation is now available for everyone, whether they are Jews or Gentiles.

The house was filled with guests, but when the king came to see them, he noticed a man without a wedding garment.

9. The man without a wedding garment was bound hand and foot and cast out into outer darkness. This shows that
   (a) the king knew it was the man's own choice not to wear a wedding garment.
   b. every Christian must wear exactly the same kind of special clothing to be saved.
   c. the king did not love the man without the wedding garment as much as the other guests.

Questions From the Jews

Luke 20:20–26

The Jewish leaders were trying hard to find a charge on which to condemn Jesus. They knew from experience

Number 9. Some students may choose b. Explain that while a spiritual church should establish guidelines for simple, modest dress, Christian obedience goes much deeper than the clothing we wear. Choice c is true only in the sense that at the Judgment, God will no longer extend His mercy toward sinners. However, when the man chose not to wear the wedding garment, the king loved him just as much as he loved the other guests. Choice a is the best answer.)

wicked husbandmen)
—that God rewards His people for their faithfulness rather than for the amount of work they do. *(the parable of the laborers in the vineyard)*
—that salvation is now for both Jews and Gentiles. *(the parable of the marriage of the king's son)*
• Students should know
—why the laborers who worked for twelve hours were displeased with their wages. *(The owner paid them the same as he had paid those who had worked for only one hour.)*
—why the invited guests did not come to the marriage feast of the king's son. *(They were too busy with things they thought were more important.*

Also, they failed to honor their king and his servants.)
—what the Pharisees asked Jesus in an attempt to trap Him. *("Is it lawful for us to give tribute unto Caesar?")*
—which group of Jews did not believe in a resurrection. *(the Sadducees)*
—how Jesus proved that the Books of Moses teach the resurrection of the dead. *(He quoted God's words from the burning bush: "I am . . . the God of Abraham, the God of Isaac, and the God of Jacob.")*
—two reasons why Jesus condemned the Pharisees so sternly. *(They wanted the praises of men, and*

that it would be difficult to openly trick Jesus, so they sent some Pharisees and Herodians to pose as honest seekers. These men were to ask Jesus a question that the leaders hoped would get Him into trouble no matter how He answered it.

10. How did the Pharisees plan to make trouble for Jesus if He said they should pay taxes to Caesar?

    a. The Pharisees would have reported Him to the Romans. This would have made the Romans angry with Jesus for being anti-Jewish.

    (b.) The Pharisees would have said that He was against the Jews and favored the Romans. Such a position would have caused the multitudes to be angry with Jesus.

    c. They would have blamed Him for supporting the Sadducees. This would have turned against Him any Pharisees that still supported Him.

11. What would the Jews have done if Jesus had said that one should not pay taxes to Caesar?

    (a.) They would have reported Him to the Romans.

    b. They would have said that He was against the Jews and favored the Romans.

    c. They would have blamed Him for supporting the Sadducees.

12. How did Jesus answer their question?   He asked them whose image was on a penny (denarius). When they replied, "Caesar's," He said, "Render therefore unto Caesar the things which be Caesar's, and unto God the things which be God's."

Luke 20:27–38

The Sadducees accepted only the five Books of Moses (Genesis, Exodus, Leviticus, Numbers, and Deuteronomy). They rejected all the rest of the Old Testament. The five Books of Moses do not speak directly about a resurrection from the dead, so the Sadducees refused to believe that those who die will rise again. They came to Jesus with a story and a question that they thought would force Him to admit that there is no resurrection.

13. What Scripture passage from the Books of Moses did Jesus use to prove that the Sadducees were mistaken?   Jesus quoted God's words from the burning bush: "I am . . . the God of Abraham, and the God of Isaac, and the God of Jacob." God is not the God of the dead, but of the living.

Mark 12:28–34

Not everyone in the crowd that day wanted to trap Jesus. A scribe took note of the good answers that Jesus gave to the Sadducees and decided to ask a question to test Jesus' understanding of the Law. It appears that the scribe's question was a sincere one because of the response he gave to Jesus' answer.

14. What commendation did Jesus give to the scribe, which shows this man had good intentions in asking his question?   Jesus said: "Thou art not far from the kingdom of God."

Questions From Jesus

Matthew 22:41–46

Jesus asked the Pharisees some questions too. But they were not able to answer Him.

15. Why did people fear to ask Jesus any more questions after this?   Jesus answered their questions with such wisdom that those who wanted to argue were left with nothing to say. In return He asked them much harder questions that they did not know how to answer.

- If Jesus had said that one should not pay taxes to Caesar, the Jews could have charged Him with stirring up a rebellion against the Romans. Jesus might have been condemned to death on such a charge. This was the main charge the leaders falsely brought against Jesus when they took Him to Pilate. In reality, the Jews were looking for a Messiah who would do just that—deliver them from the Romans—but they were willing to appear loyal to Caesar to condemn Jesus to death.

Be sure the students notice that "I am" is in the present tense. God can be the God of those who have died only if they still exist somewhere.

- Jesus' question exposed the Pharisees' faulty view of the Messiah. They considered the Messiah to be a man, an earthly king after the lineage of David. The only way that they could have answered Jesus' question was to admit that the Messiah was divine as well as human. This would have completely undercut their argument against Jesus' claims; hence they kept quiet. Nor did they dare ask Him any more trick questions.

they were hypocrites.)

—where Jesus received authority to cleanse the temple and to condemn the Pharisees. (*from God*)

Truths to Amplify

- The Gospels record much more about Jesus' works and teachings during the last week before His death than they record about any other period in His life. Twenty chapters of the Gospels are devoted to this week. This shows the importance God places on these events and teachings.

- Jesus' last public discourses reveal His love for all men. He took time to give His enemies a last warning of what the consequences of their sin would be unless they repented.

- Jesus' denouncement of the Pharisees gives us a solemn warning to avoid drifting from godly obedience to dead formalism. If we love God and His Word, we will apply Scriptural principles in practical, everyday life, but we dare not allow external practices to replace salvation and holiness of heart. Jesus said, "Except your righteousness shall exceed the righteousness of the scribes and Pharisees, ye shall in no case enter into the kingdom of heaven" (Matthew 5:20).

Jesus Condemns the Pharisees

Matthew 23:1–12

Jesus talked to the Pharisees many times during His ministry. He explained many things to them, but they turned against Him and refused to listen. At various times Jesus warned His disciples to avoid their errors. In this chapter Jesus pronounced the judgment of God on the Pharisees for their rebellious attitudes. After Jesus' death, some Pharisees evidently saw their error and became Christians (Acts 15:5).

16. In the first twelve verses of this chapter, Jesus analyzed the Pharisees for the common people. What seems to have been one of the Pharisees' *greatest* problems?

  a. They wanted other people to look up to them and obey them.

  b. They were too zealous in keeping the Law of Moses.

  c. They failed to keep the Sabbath Day holy.

Matthew 23:25–28

17. In a number of the woes that Jesus pronounced on the Pharisees, He called them hypocrites. This was because

  a. the Pharisees pretended to love Jesus but actually hated Him.

  b. the Pharisees cleaned the inside of their cups and graves but refused to make the outside attractive.

  c. the Pharisees tried to appear righteous outwardly, but their hearts were corrupt with sin.

Matthew 23:29–38

Jesus loved the Pharisees and desired that they turn from their wickedness. In these parting words to them, He called them a generation of vipers and asked them how they expected to escape the damnation of hell. He predicted that they would scourge and kill the prophets, wise men, and scribes that He would send to them, just as their forefathers had done. Because of their rebellion, God would hold them accountable for all the righteous blood that had been shed upon the earth, and the Jewish nation in Palestine would become desolate.

18. How do we know that Jesus would have liked to spare the Pharisees from their horrible fate if they had let Him do so?   Speaking to the city of Jerusalem, Jesus said, "How often would I have gathered thy children together, even as a hen gathereth her chickens under her wings, and ye would not!"

B. BIBLE WORD STUDY

Circle the letter of the ending that best explains the meaning of the word or words in italics.

1. When the king heard how the invited guests had treated his servants, he was *wroth* (Matthew 22:7). In other words, he was very

  a. afraid.

  b. pleased.

  c. angry.

2. The Pharisees loved to be addressed by the title *Rabbi*, which means (Matthew 23:8)

  a. "my master."

  b. "my beloved one."

  c. "my holy one."

3. Jesus likened the Pharisees to *whited sepulchres* (Matthew 23:27). Literally, this meant they were like
   a. clothing that had been bleached in the sunshine.
   b. graves that had been painted white.
   c. an old building that was crumbling.

4. Jesus told the Pharisees that their house would be left to them *desolate* (Matthew 23:38). This meant that their dwelling place would be
   a. lonely and uninhabited.
   b. defiled by evil men.
   c. full of their enemies.

5. Spies sent by the chief priests *feigned* themselves just men (Luke 20:20). They
   a. cheated the just.
   b. were good men at heart.
   c. pretended to be good.

6. Jesus told His disciples to *render unto Caesar* that which was Caesar's (Luke 20:25). He wanted His disciples to
   a. use wisely for Caesar.
   b. give to Caesar.
   c. save up for Caesar.

C. THINKING ABOUT BIBLE TRUTHS

Jesus' Authority

At the beginning and at the end of His ministry, Jesus drove the moneychangers and other sellers out of the temple. He used strong language in denouncing the scribes and Pharisees. He taught new doctrines that had not been heard in Israel before. It is no wonder that the priests came to Jesus and asked Him what authority He had for doing these things.

Mark 11:27–33

1. When the Jewish leaders questioned Jesus about His authority, what question did He ask them in return?   "The baptism of John, was it from heaven, or of men?"

2. Most of the Jews believed that John the Baptist was   a prophet   .

3. John the Baptist was the forerunner of Jesus and had   baptized   Him before Jesus started His ministry.

4. Jesus was trying to do more than just silence the Jewish leaders with His answer. He wanted to help them see the truth. If they had admitted that John received his authority from God, what would they actually have been saying about Jesus' authority?   It was from God as well.

5. The Jewish leaders did not want to recognize the authority of John, but they did not want to deny it either. Why?   They were afraid of the people because the people thought John was a prophet.

• Remember that John had proclaimed Jesus as the Lamb of God.

176 Chapter Five Jesus Completes His Work

D. LEARNING MORE ABOUT BIBLE TIMES

The Pharisees: From Obedience to Disobedience

The group known as Pharisees had begun several hundred years before Jesus' time. The first Pharisees were men who insisted on keeping all the Law of God, even when most other Jews were abandoning parts of it. But over the years, the Pharisees added many rules of their own to God's Law, and gradually they lost their love for God.

1. By Jesus' time the Pharisees had become proud, legalistic, and hypocritical. What did Jesus say about them in Matthew 23:13? <u>The Pharisees had shut up the kingdom of heaven. They themselves did not enter, and they also kept others from entering.</u>

The Pharisees studied much, and they knew long portions of the Scriptures from memory. They put much effort into teaching their children.

2. How did the well-educated Pharisees feel about those who had less education? (John 7:46–49) <u>The Pharisees looked down on the less educated and called them cursed.</u>

The Pharisees went to great lengths to keep the Law of Moses. They made many additional laws as a precaution to keep them from breaking the laws actually given in the Scriptures.

3. What was the result of the Pharisees' careful attention to detail? (Matthew 23:23) <u>Because of their attention to detail, the Pharisees came to ignore the more important matters of the Law.</u>

Early in their history the Pharisees became interested in mission work. They traveled long distances by land and sea to make converts.

4. What did the Pharisees make out of their converts? (Matthew 23:15) <u>They caused their converts to become twice as bad as themselves.</u>

The Pharisees were the first Jews to gather in homes and synagogues throughout the country to read the Scriptures and pray. They realized that prayer was more important to God than sacrifice.

5. Matthew 6:5 is probably referring to the Pharisees. How did the Pharisees of Jesus' time pray? <u>They prayed in public to be seen of men.</u>

Some of the Pharisees' teachings were true. The Pharisees believed that the dead will rise to live forever. They believed in the coming of a Messiah, in the inspiration of the Scriptures, and in the need of doing good works such as giving alms. Outwardly they appeared righteous, but Jesus could see directly into their sinful hearts. He knew that they did their "good" works only to impress people.

6. What word did Jesus use most often to describe them? <u>hypocrites</u>

177

Lesson 23. Jesus' Last Days With His Disciples

It was probably toward evening on Tuesday when Jesus left the temple for the last time. His public ministry was now finished. He had done what He could for the Jews and their leaders. They would now need to face the consequences of their decisions by themselves.

As Jesus and His disciples left the temple that day, the disciples pointed out the beauty of the temple buildings to Jesus. But Jesus told them that the temple would be destroyed. Not one stone would be left upon another. This announcement must have troubled the disciples. They did not understand.

How could the true worship of God continue in a world without the temple? To faithful Jews, the destruction of the temple would have seemed terrible. Yet their faith in Jesus was so great that they did not dare to doubt what He said. But when and how would it happen? Where would Jesus be when it took place?

These questions and others filled their minds as they climbed the Mount of Olives. Jesus taught His disciples many things that Tuesday evening.

The Gospels are silent about what Jesus and His disciples did on Wednesday, unless Judas met with the chief priests on that day. It is not certain when this meeting took place.

On Thursday evening Jesus ate His last Passover with His twelve disciples. He told them, "With desire I have desired to eat this passover with you before I suffer" (Luke 22:15). The Passover was a Jewish feast that pointed back to Israel's deliverance from Egypt. Indirectly, it also pointed forward to Jesus' death.

That evening Jesus also conducted the first Communion service, the Christian ceremony that would remind His followers of His suffering and death. All of God's message to man would focus on what Jesus would do the next day.

See the notes at the bottom of page 186.

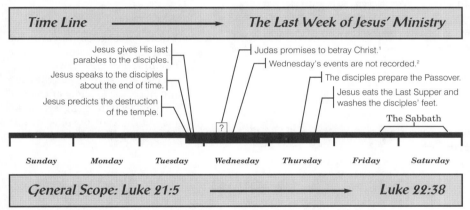

Time Line ⟶ **The Last Week of Jesus' Ministry**

Jesus gives His last parables to the disciples.

Jesus speaks to the disciples about the end of time.

Jesus predicts the destruction of the temple.

Judas promises to betray Christ.[1]

Wednesday's events are not recorded.[2]

The disciples prepare the Passover.

Jesus eats the Last Supper and washes the disciples' feet.

The Sabbath

?

| Sunday | Monday | Tuesday | Wednesday | Thursday | Friday | Saturday |

General Scope: Luke 21:5 ⟶ **Luke 22:38**

[1] It is not certain when Judas met with the chief priests and promised to betray Christ.
[2] Jesus gave His last recorded parables two days before the Passover (Matthew 26:2).

Using the Time Line

1. Which event on the time line is the most difficult to assign to a certain day? _____
   <u>Judas promises to betray Christ.</u>

2. For which day of this week do we have no information about what Jesus did? <u>Wednesday</u>

Lesson 23

Oral Review

1. How did it come about that Jesus was born in Bethlehem rather than in Nazareth, where Mary and Joseph lived? [L. 3] **Mary and Joseph needed to go to Bethlehem for the Roman census, since they were of the line of David**.

2. What did Jesus mean when He said, "The sabbath was made for man, and not man for the sabbath"? [L. 8] **God meant the Sabbath for man's refreshment, not as a burden to him.**

3. In the parable of the sower, what did the seed represent? the ground? [L. 12] *the seed:* **God's Word;** *the ground:* **the hearts of those who hear God's Word**

4. How did Jesus teach His disciples that they should be more humble? [L. 17] **He set a child in the midst of them and told them to become like children.**

5. What did Jesus tell His disciples to do to become great in the kingdom of God? [L.20] **serve others**

6. Why did Jesus weep over Jerusalem? [L. 21] **He knew what dreadful things were going to happen to the Jews because of their rejection of Him.**

7. In the parable of the marriage feast, why did the

A. ANSWERS FROM THE BIBLE

Questions From the Disciples

The disciples were troubled by the things they had heard Jesus tell the Jews. He had prophesied the desolation of the temple and the city of Jerusalem, and He had told the Jews that they would not see Him again until they would say, "Blessed is he that cometh in the name of the LORD." The disciples must have realized that something dramatic was about to happen, even if they did not understand all the warnings that Jesus had been giving them. They wanted to know more about these questions that were weighing on their minds.

Matthew 24:1–3

1. What were the two questions that the disciples asked Jesus?
   a. "When shall these things be?"
   b. "What shall be the sign of thy coming, and of the end of the world?"

Warnings for the Disciples

In these verses Jesus warned His disciples of some things Christians would face before He returned. Jesus knew how easy it would be for false teachers to deceive those who were not established in the truth or who were impatient for Him to return before God's time.

Matthew 24:4–14

2. What warning did Jesus give His disciples before He began to tell them about future events? (Note that Jesus mentioned this danger again in 24:11, 24.)   "Take heed that no man deceive you."

3. In this passage Jesus predicted all but one of the following events. Draw a line through the one that He did *not* mention. (Note that at least some of these events were to take place before the time of the end. Most of them have been at least partly fulfilled.)
   a. Many people would be deceived by false Christs and false prophets.
   b. There would be many wars and uprisings among nations.
   c. Earthquakes would occur in many places.
   d. Christians would be hated by all nations.
   e. Sin would abound and cause many Christians to fall.
   f. All professing Christians would be saved in the end.
   g. The Gospel of the kingdom would be preached to all the world before the end of time.

- These verses seem to cover the entire scope of history from the beginning of the church. Jesus specifically states that they are not necessarily signs of the end of the world, but rather should be considered normal events during the time of the church.

The Destruction of Jerusalem

Luke 21:20–22

These verses are similar to Matthew 24:15–18, but Luke specifically refers to the destruction of Jerusalem.

4. What did Jesus tell the Christians of Judea to do when they saw the armies surrounding Jerusalem?   He told them to flee to the mountains immediately.

The verses above seem to have been fulfilled at the destruction of Jerusalem in A.D. 70. History tells us that when the Roman army first surrounded Jerusalem, they departed again for several months. During this time the Christians fled as Jesus had told them to do. It is said that no Christians remained in Jerusalem when the Roman armies returned and destroyed the city.

invited guests fail to come? [L. 22] **They were too busy with things they thought were more important. (They also failed to honor their king and his servants.)**

8. Which parable teaches that God rewards us for our deeds and not for our empty promises? [L. 22] **the parable of the two sons**

Notes

Refrain from using this lesson to give a detailed exposition of your personal views on prophecy. Instead, keep your discussion centered on what the Bible actually says. Men's opinions on eschatology differ and fluctuate, but God's Word on the subject is always accurate and unchanging.

Also avoid implying that Christians can be assured of being taken out of the world before they face hardships or persecutions. The troubles and sorrows Jesus predicted in the first part of Matthew 24 have affected the world and Christians throughout the church age, and it is quite possible that they will become more intense as the end draws near. Emphasize that Christians can trust God for grace to overcome whatever persecutions or hard times they may face in the future.

Be careful to treat this lesson factually rather than emotionally. Bible class should not become a time when the teacher tries to place students under

Signs of the End

Many people have asked the same questions that the disciples asked Jesus at the beginning of Matthew 24. They would like to know what signs will indicate that the end of time is near. Most of all they would like to know when the end is going to be.

However, Jesus did not tell the disciples when the end would come. He told them that only God knew the day and the hour. But He did tell them some things that would happen at the end of time. These verses give some of these signs. No one knows how all these things will take place or how near the end they will be. Those who think they can wait to prepare for Christ's coming until they see signs of the end will be caught unprepared.

Matthew 24:29–35

5. All except one of the following are mentioned in these verses as signs of the end. Draw a line through the one that is *not* given.

a. Jesus will send His angels to gather the Christians.

b. ~~Fig trees will produce more leaves than usual.~~

c. The people on earth will see Jesus coming and will mourn.

d. The powers of heaven will be shaken.

e. The sign of the Son of man will appear in heaven.

f. The stars will fall from heaven.

g. The sun and the moon will be darkened.

The End

Although no one knows when the end of time will be, we do know that the end will come sometime and that not everyone will be ready for it. This passage also shows clearly that some people will be ready and waiting.

Matthew 24:40–42

6. These verses state that two people will be working together in a field when Jesus returns, but only one will be taken. The same thing will happen to two women preparing food. What does this show us? (Choose two answers.)

a. Jesus will give those who are not ready to meet Him a second chance.

(b.) People will be busy with their normal activities when Jesus returns.

(c.) There will be no advance warning when Jesus returns.

d. Only farmers and cooks will be ready to meet Jesus when He returns.

7. God has not said when Jesus will come again. Because of this

a. Christians need to figure out the date of His return for themselves.

(b.) Christians need to be ready for His return at all times.

c. Christians do not need to be concerned about His return.

Jesus' Last Parables for the Disciples

After telling His disciples some things about the end of the world, Jesus gave them two parables that taught lessons about being ready.

Matthew 25:1–13

8. What were the virgins waiting for?   the coming of the bridegroom

---

conviction. However, do not avoid plain Bible truths either. Present the facts as the Bible gives them. The Holy Spirit can use these truths to speak to the students as He chooses.

In This Lesson

Scope: Matthew 24:1–26:5; 26:14–29; Mark 13:1–14:2; 14:10–25; Luke 21:5–22:38; John 13:1–38

Focus

• Jesus spent Tuesday evening with His disciples on the Mount of Olives, telling them many things they needed to know about the future and the end times. These teachings included

—warnings about tribulations the disciples would face.

—a description of the coming destruction of Jerusalem and the temple.

—signs of the end times and of Christ's return.

—the parable of the ten virgins.

—the parable of the talents.

• Judas made an agreement with the chief priests to deliver Jesus to them for thirty pieces of silver.

9. Half of the ten virgins were wise and half of them were foolish.
   a. Why did Jesus call five of the virgins wise?   _They took extra oil with them in case they ran out._

   b. Why did Jesus call the other five virgins foolish?   _____
   They did not take enough oil with them, so their lamps went out.

10. What lesson did Jesus teach with the parable about the ten virgins?
    (a.) His followers must be ready at all times for His coming.
    b. His followers will know the exact time of His coming by the signs that He has given.
    c. His followers will have time to make final preparations for His coming after they see the signs of the end.

Matthew 25:14–30

11. How did the lord of the servants decide how many talents to give to each servant?   _____
    He gave the talents according to the ability of each servant.

12. a. What did the men with five talents and two talents do with their money?   _____
    They doubled their money by buying and selling.

    b. According to the lord's rebuke in Matthew 25:26, why did the man with one talent fail to use it?
    He was wicked and slothful.

13. What lesson did Jesus teach in the parable of the talents?
    a. Christians with few talents are more accountable than those with many talents.
    b. Jesus expects Christians to become rich in earthly goods while they wait for His return.
    (c.) Christians should make good use of the abilities God gives them.

Judas's Agreement With the Chief Priests

While Jesus was busy teaching His disciples, the Jewish leaders were busy planning how they could kill Him. They had turned against Jesus soon after He had started His ministry, and by now their feelings toward Him had grown into murderous hatred. To their delight, one of Jesus' disciples offered to help them achieve their evil purpose.

Matthew 26:1–5, 14–16

14. Why did the Jews not want to arrest Jesus in public or during the Passover?   _____
    The Jewish leaders did not want to stir up the crowds who had gathered for the Passover.

The chief priests paid Judas thirty pieces of silver (the legal price of a slave) out of the temple treasury. This money was normally to be used to buy sacrifices for the temple.

15. How did the Jewish leaders know that Judas was willing to betray his Master?   _____
    He went to the chief priests and asked what they would give him if he delivered Jesus to them.

The First Communion Service

The Bible does not say what Jesus did the day before the Passover. When the day had come to prepare the Passover meal, Jesus sent several of His disciples to Jerusalem to get it ready for Him and the twelve. Part of this preparation included going to the temple to have the Passover lamb killed.

Jesus and His disciples ate the Passover meal together that evening for the last time. Jesus also added a new ceremony, probably after the regular meal was over. Like the Passover meal, Communion has a deep spiritual meaning.

• Jesus did not condemn the virgins for sleeping. That is the normal thing to do at night. While we wait for Christ to return, we should be involved in the normal activities of life. However, we dare not let our normal duties distract us from being ready for Christ's return.

• The man's excuse was that he was afraid (apparently of losing the lord's money). Human reasoning might sympathize with his fear, but the lord saw that his heart was lazy and corrupt.

• Notice that God had other plans, and that Jesus was arrested and crucified right over the time of the feast.

Objectives
• Students should know
  —what warning Jesus gave His disciples before He told them about the future. (*Take heed that no man deceive you.*)
  —what Jesus told the Christians to do when they saw armies around Jerusalem. (*flee to the mountains*)
  —some signs Jesus gave of the end. (*examples: stars falling from heaven, sun and moon darkened, powers in heaven shaken*)
  —when Jesus' followers need to be ready for His coming. (*at all times*)
  —why Jesus called half of the ten virgins wise and the others foolish. (*The five wise ones carried extra oil, but the foolish ones did not.*)
  —what lesson Jesus taught by the parable of the talents. (*Christians should make wise use of the talents God gives them.*)
  —who agreed to deliver Jesus to the Jewish leaders. (*Judas Iscariot*)
  —why Jesus wants His followers to observe Communion. (*to remind them of His suffering and death*)
  —why Peter did not want Jesus to wash his feet. (*He did not understand what Jesus was teaching.*)
  —what lesson Jesus taught by washing His disciples'

Luke 22:14–20

16. Before passing the bread and the cup to His disciples, Jesus mentioned
    - (a) the suffering He was about to experience.
    - b. the need to examine oneself.
    - c. the wolves that would scatter the flock.
    - d. the disciples' desire to be the greatest.

17. Jesus said that the bread He broke was
    - a. the fellowship of His sufferings.
    - b. Communion.
    - c. the New Testament in His blood.
    - (d) His body.

18. Christians observe Communion
    - a. to celebrate the Jewish Passover.
    - (b) in remembrance of Christ's suffering and death.
    - c. to show the world that they are followers of Jesus.

The First Feet-Washing Service

While Jesus and His disciples were together for the Last Supper, Jesus did something that startled the disciples—He poured water into a basin and washed their feet. This ceremony, like Communion, had a spiritual significance that the disciples did not understand until later.

John 13:2–17

19. At first Peter did not want Jesus to wash his feet. But when Jesus said that this would mean having no part with Him, Peter asked Him to also wash his hands and head. This shows that Peter
    - a. was not willing to obey Jesus.
    - b. wanted to wash Jesus' feet.
    - (c) did not understand Jesus' teaching.

20. What did Jesus want His disciples to do? (Choose two answers.)
    - (a) follow His example and wash one another's feet
    - b. be better accepted by the Jews than He was
    - c. wash the feet of their enemies
    - (d) learn how to humbly serve one another in love

B. BIBLE WORD STUDY

🍇 *Choose the ending that best explains the meaning of each italicized word or phrase.*

1. When Jesus told the disciples about the coming *desolation* of Jerusalem (Luke 21:20), He was predicting that Jerusalem would be
   - a. inhabited by the Romans.
   - (b) left totally in ruins and without inhabitants.
   - c. established as a Christian city.

2. The literal meaning of the word *talent* as used in the parable of the talents is (Matthew 25:15)
   - (a) a unit of money weighing about 75 pounds.
   - b. the ability to perform a certain task well.
   - c. a region of a country ruled by the king's servant.

- If time permits, discuss the meaning of the bread and of the cup in the Communion service, and the significance of the feet-washing ceremony.

- Some people believe that Jesus and His disciples ate the Last Supper the day before the Passover and that Jesus died at the time the Passover lambs were being killed. John 18:28 and 19:14 could support this view. However, Matthew 26:17–20, Mark 14:12–17, and Luke 22:7–14 all seem to indicate that Jesus ate the regular Passover at the normal time. The Passover lambs had to be killed at the temple (Deuteronomy 16:5, 6), and it seems very unlikely that this could have been done a day early. The Bible sometimes uses "Passover" and "Feast of Unleavened Bread" interchangeably. (See Ezekiel 45:21 and Luke 22:7 for examples.) It is possible that John 18:28 and 19:14 use "Passover" in this broader sense. Since both viewpoints have some evidence in their favor, it is difficult to be sure which is correct.

- Number 17. Point out that Jesus could not have meant that the bread changed to His physical body, since He was present with them at the time. Rather, the bread represented His body.

feet. (*the need to humbly serve one another*)

—the literal definition of *talent*. (*a unit of money weighing about 75 pounds*)

—how many years passed between Jesus' prediction that Jerusalem would be destroyed and its fulfillment. (*forty*)

Truths to Amplify

- In the last week before His crucifixion, Jesus was more concerned about preparing His disciples for what was coming than He was about Himself. Students can benefit from this example of unselfishness.

- Jesus did not promise that the Christian life would be an easy one. This is vividly portrayed in Matthew

24. The students should recognize that the time of peace and prosperity that God's people are enjoying in North America today is highly unusual. Few Christians in history have lived during times such as this. The peace and prosperity that North Americans enjoy could end very quickly.

- The destruction of Jerusalem marked the end of Old Testament Palestine. The Jews faced severe judgment for rejecting their Messiah.

- Since no one knows when the end of time will be, Jesus' followers need to always be ready.

3. The lord of the servants said the servant with one talent should have given it to the *exchangers* (Matthew 25:27). In other words, he should have given it to people who
   a. would have hidden it in a safe place for him.
   b. would have given him rich goods in return.
   c. would have paid him for the use of it.

4. The lord could have received *usury* for his money (Matthew 25:27). This means the exchangers would have
   a. kept the money safe.
   b. paid interest on the money.
   c. made sure the money was used properly.

5. Jesus said that there would be *gnashing of teeth* in outer darkness (Matthew 25:30). This means that those cast into outer darkness will
   a. have their teeth broken.
   b. be bitten by something in the dark.
   c. grind their teeth in pain.

6. Before washing the disciples' feet, Jesus *girded* himself with a towel (John 13:4). That is, Jesus
   a. covered His feet with a towel.
   b. tied the towel around His waist.
   c. dried Himself with the towel.

C. THINKING ABOUT BIBLE TRUTHS

God Brings Judgment

God cannot tolerate sin. A nation that becomes sinful will eventually face God's judgment. Because God is merciful, He withholds His judgment as long as He can. We can see this in the judgment of Jerusalem and other cities mentioned in the Bible.

1. Read Jonah 1:2. What was the city of Nineveh like?   It was a very wicked city.

2. Read Jonah 3:2–4. What was God planning to do to Nineveh?
   He planned to destroy it within forty days.

3. Read Jonah 3:5–10. Why did God change His mind about judging Nineveh at this time?
   The people of Nineveh repented of their sins.

Within a hundred years after Jonah's preaching, God did bring judgment on Nineveh because they returned to their sins. This time they did not receive a second chance. The city of Nineveh was destroyed so completely that for many years people thought it had never existed.

4. Read Matthew 23:34–37. Why was God planning to judge Jerusalem?
   The Jews were wicked, and they refused to repent.

5. Jerusalem was destroyed about forty years after Jesus prophesied its desolation. Why might God have waited this long before bringing judgment upon Jerusalem and the Jews?
   (Sample answer) He gave them a chance to repent under the preaching of the Christians.

D. LEARNING MORE ABOUT BIBLE TIMES

Jewish History After Christ

The Jewish nation lasted almost forty years after Christ's death and resurrection. But things did not go well with the Jews after they rejected the Messiah. When Jerusalem finally fell in A.D. 70, many Jews were killed, and the Jewish way of life as they had known it came to an end.

Herod Agrippa

Herod Agrippa I was the grandson of Herod the Great, the king who had tried to destroy Jesus when He was born. Agrippa was appointed ruler of Galilee in A.D. 37, and in A.D. 41 he also became king over Samaria and Judea. Agrippa I is mentioned several times in Acts 12, where he is called *Herod* or *Herod the king*.

1. Herod Agrippa was an ardent supporter of the Jewish religion. In Acts 12:1–4 he killed _____James_____ and put _____Peter_____ into prison to please the Jews.

Acts 12:20–23 tells how Herod Agrippa I died after accepting praise from the people of Caesarea, who called him a god. This was in A.D. 44. After his death, Palestine was again placed under the rule of Roman governors.

The King Agrippa who is mentioned in Acts 25 was the son of Herod Agrippa I and is sometimes called Agrippa II. He was a ruler under the Romans from A.D. 52 to 70, but he never ruled over Judea and Jerusalem. He joined the Romans in destroying the Jews in A.D. 70.

Jewish Unrest

From A.D. 44 to 64, three different Roman governors ruled Judea in succession. They were Felix, Festus, and Albinus (al BY nuhs). During most of this time, widespread lawlessness prevailed in Judea. It appears that Felix was a corrupt ruler. He paid a band of robbers to kill the Jewish high priest, against whom he had a grudge.

2. The apostle Paul was captured in Jerusalem while Felix ruled, and was tried by him. What did Felix want from Paul, which shows what kind of person Felix was? (See Acts 24:24–26.) _____

   He wanted Paul to give him money (a bribe) to let him go free.

Soon after this, Felix was replaced by Festus. During this time the Jewish priests were at war with each other because of a disagreement over the division of the tithes. All Judea was in turmoil as the various factions hired assassins to murder their enemies. At the same time, bandits still roamed the country and the Zealots promoted outright rebellion against Rome.

3. With the Jews in such a state of upheaval, it is understandable why Paul did not want to be sent to Jerusalem for a trial during Festus's reign. What did Paul request instead? (Acts 25:9–12) _____

   He appealed to Caesar for a trial.

Florus, the last governor of the Jews, was appointed in A.D. 64. This ruler appears to have been even worse than the Roman governors before him. Besides encouraging the bandits of Judea, Florus incited the Jews to riot in Jerusalem so that he could rob the temple during the tumult. He seems to have purposely tried to provoke the Jews into outright rebellion by his oppressive policies.

In A.D. 66 the Jews rose against the Romans. They massacred the troops stationed in Jerusalem and took over the city. When the Roman ruler of Syria heard about this, he brought an army to Jerusalem to recapture it. However, while he was in the process of attacking the walls, he suddenly withdrew as if in fear. The Jews attacked the Romans as they retreated, winning a temporary victory over them. The Christians in Judea (along with some upper-class Jews) used this opportunity to flee across the Jordan River to Pella, where they remained in safety.

The Destruction of Jerusalem

For a short time the Jews ruled themselves. But this only brought more trouble, since three different Jewish parties fought among themselves for power. Vespasian, the Roman general who was sent to overthrow the Jews, conquered Galilee and most of Judea. Then he gathered his army at Caesarea in preparation to attack Jerusalem. Nero, the emperor of Rome, was overthrown while Vespasian was at Caesarea, and the army proclaimed Vespasian emperor in his place. Vespasian left his son Titus in charge of conquering the Jews while he returned to Rome.

Titus surrounded Jerusalem during the Passover, when it was full of visitors. According to Josephus, an eyewitness of the destruction, two to three million people were trapped in the city. Many people starved to death, and many others were killed in the turmoil within the city. Had the Romans waited long enough, the Jews might have destroyed themselves. The Romans destroyed the outer walls, the city, and finally the temple, where the last of the Jews had gathered to defend themselves. It was a terrible time. Many Jews were brutally killed, and the city was completely destroyed. Josephus says that over a million Jews lost their lives at Jerusalem during the siege.

Later the Romans plowed up the city to make it difficult for the Jews to return to it. All that remained was part of a wall and several towers to show people where Jerusalem had once been.

4. What had Jesus said would happen to the temple? (Matthew 24:1, 2) _____

   Every stone would be thrown down.

5. This judgment of God fell on the Jews about forty years after Jesus told the Pharisees that God would hold them accountable for all the righteous blood shed in Jerusalem. According to Jesus' words, when was this judgment to take place? (Matthew 23:34–36) _____

   The judgment was to fall on the generation He was speaking to.

Jesus' words came to pass with terrible accuracy. God gave the Jews as much time as He could to turn back to Him, but finally judgment fell. It is noteworthy that the war which brought about the destruction of the temple and the end of the Jewish nation lasted for about three and a half years. This was the same length of time that Jesus had walked among them. Thus God allowed the Jews to take their own way and rule themselves for as long as their rejected Messiah had been with them. The turmoil and the bitter end of their nation should have shown them the fallacy of their dreams.

- The Roman general Titus had not intended to destroy the temple, but his soldiers set it on fire without orders. It is said that the gold which covered the walls melted and ran between the cracks in the stones. To get the gold, the Romans dismantled the temple, fulfilling this prophecy.

- It seems that God, in His mercy, delayed the fulfillment of this prophecy as long as possible. A generation is usually considered to be a few years less than forty, but probably some of the people who heard Jesus speak that day were still alive when the prophecy was fulfilled. One has to wonder how many people in Jerusalem thought back to Jesus' words during those fateful days.

The Wailing Wall—a section of the wall of the temple courtyard still standing today

185

Lesson 24. The Lamb of God

The period covered by this lesson begins late Thursday night or very early Friday morning of the last week of Jesus' ministry. Jesus had led eleven of His disciples to the Garden of Gethsemane after eating the Last Supper with them.

The Israelites had celebrated their first Passover just before they left Egypt. Each family had killed a lamb and sprinkled its blood upon their door frames. The Lord had passed over their houses that night. Wherever He had seen the blood, He had left the house in peace. Wherever He had not seen the blood, He had killed the first-born son.

The Passover was a picture of Jesus and His work. Jesus is the Lamb of God. Like the Passover lamb, He died as a sacrifice. Today when people repent and believe on Him, His blood is sprinkled upon their hearts (in a figure) and cleanses them of sin.

Although the chief priests did not realize it, the Passover that year was the most important one in history. After Jesus offered Himself, there would no longer be any need for the old Jewish sacrifices. Within forty years the temple would be destroyed and the Jewish sacrifices would cease.

John the Baptist had called Jesus "the Lamb of God." But none of His followers seemed to understand that Jesus was going to offer Himself as the ultimate sacrifice for the sins of the world.

Part A is longer than usual in this lesson and will require extra class and study time. Because of the importance of this section, it would be better to allot extra time than to reduce the size of the assignment. The other sections of the lesson are somewhat shorter than average to partly compensate for this.

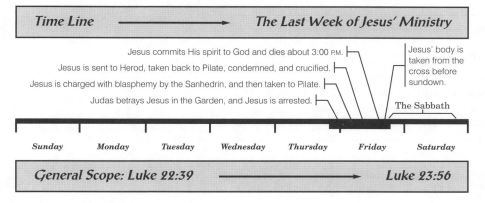

Using the Time Line

🍇 *Number the following events in the order that they happened.*

 4 Jesus is condemned at the insistence of the Jewish leaders and then crucified.

 2 Jesus is questioned by the Jewish council and then taken to the Romans.

 1 Judas leads Jesus' enemies to Him.

 3 Pilate sends Jesus to Herod, but Herod sends Him back to Pilate.

Lesson 24

Oral Review

1. What two things were miraculous about John the Baptist's birth? [L. 4] **His birth was foretold by an angel, and his parents were too old to have children.**

2. Jesus told Nicodemus that He had come to ——— the world rather than to condemn it. [L. 5] **save**

3. What reason did Jesus give for Lazarus's sickness and death? [L. 20] **It was "for the glory of God, that the Son of God might be glorified thereby."**

4. Define *hosanna*. [L. 21] **"Save now!" or "Save, I pray!"**

5. Why were the laborers who worked for twelve hours upset with their master when he paid them their wages? [L. 22] **He paid them the same wages that he paid to the ones who had worked for only one hour.**

6. What question did the Pharisees ask Jesus that they hoped would get Him into trouble no matter how He answered it? [L. 22] **"Is it lawful to give tribute to Caesar?"**

7. When do Jesus' followers need to be ready for His return? [L. 23] **at all times**

A. ANSWERS FROM THE BIBLE

Jesus' Agony in the Garden

During the Last Supper, Jesus revealed to the disciples that one of them would betray Him. After this Satan entered into the heart of Judas, and Judas left to find the Jewish leaders and help them capture Jesus. Meanwhile, Jesus told the other disciples that they would all be offended because of Him. Peter replied that he would never be offended, but Jesus said that he would deny Him three times before the cock crowed twice. Jesus also spoke His last words of comfort to the disciples. Then He led them to the Garden of Gethsemane and spent time there in fervent prayer, preparing Himself for the ordeal that lay just ahead.

Matthew 26:30–46

1. As the Son of God, Jesus was fully aware that God wanted Him to give His life as a sacrifice. But He was also a man, with a normal human desire to live. What words did Jesus pray that show how difficult it was for Him to face His coming suffering and death? _____

   "O my Father, if it be possible, let this cup pass from me: nevertheless not as I will, but as thou wilt."

2. What proves that the disciples did not realize how severe a trial Jesus was passing through? ____

   They slept while He was praying.

Matthew 26:51–57

Evidently this garden was a place where Jesus and His disciples frequently went, since Judas knew where to find them. Sometime during the night, the band of soldiers arrived to arrest Jesus. Judas approached Him and kissed Him to show the soldiers which man to arrest.

3. Peter tried to defend his Master by fighting with a sword, but Jesus told him to put it up. What did Jesus tell him to show that He was choosing to allow the soldiers to arrest Him? _____

   "Thinkest thou that I cannot now pray to my Father, and he shall presently give me more than twelve legions of angels?"

Jesus' Trial Before the Jewish Leaders

Jesus went quietly with the mob while the disciples fled into the night. Friendless and alone, He allowed the mob to do with Him what they would. This was the moment the Jewish leaders had been waiting for, and they made the most of it.

Matthew 26:58–75

4. On what charge did the Jewish leaders condemn Jesus to death?   on the charge of blasphemy

5. a. Why did Peter follow Jesus? _____

   Peter followed Jesus "to see the end" (to see what would be done to his Lord).

   b. What did Peter do that he had said he would never do?   He denied Jesus three times.

6. What caused Peter to remember Jesus' words?   the crowing of a rooster (because Jesus had said that Peter would deny Him three times before the cock crowed)

This question may be difficult for some students. Discuss it in class to be sure they understand why the Jewish leaders condemned Jesus. Also note that they used a different accusation when they took Him to Pilate.

- Luke 22:61 adds that Jesus turned and looked at Peter.

8. What was the literal meaning of *talent* in Jesus' time? [L. 23] **a unit of money weighing about 75 pounds**

In This Lesson

Scope: Matthew 26:30–27:66; Mark 14:26–15:47; Luke 22:39–23:56; John 18:1–19:42

Focus

- As the Lamb of God, Jesus endured mental anguish, betrayal by a friend, false accusation, an unjust trial, mockery and shame, and the excruciating pain of crucifixion.
  —Jesus experienced extreme agony in Gethsemane while His disciples slept. As a man, He shrank from suffering and death, but He surrendered to His Father's will.
  —Judas led a band of soldiers to the Garden and betrayed Jesus with a kiss. Peter tried to defend Jesus with a sword, but Jesus rebuked him.
  —During the night, the Jewish leaders condemned Jesus on the charge of blasphemy. Peter denied Jesus three times while he was waiting "to see the end."
  —The Jews brought Jesus to Pilate on the charge that He claimed to be a king and was a threat to the Roman government. Both Pilate and Herod declared Jesus innocent, but Pilate finally agreed

Jesus' Trial Before Pilate

The Jewish leaders had charged Jesus with blasphemy, but they could not legally put Him to death. They knew that the Romans would not consider blasphemy against the Jewish God to be a crime worthy of death. So they brought Jesus to Pilate on the charge that He claimed to be a king and was a threat to the Roman government (Luke 23:2).

John 18:33–38

7. When Pilate asked Jesus if He was the king of the Jews, Jesus answered, "Thou sayest it," which meant "yes" (Luke 23:3). How is Jesus' kingdom different from a Roman kingdom? _____
   Jesus' kingdom is not of this world (and His servants do not fight carnal battles).

8. Jesus told Pilate that everyone who is of the truth hears His voice. What did Pilate ask then? ___
   "What is truth?"

Jesus did not try to answer the many charges that the Jewish leaders brought against Him, but Pilate told them that he had found no fault in Jesus. When Pilate learned that Jesus was from Galilee, He sent Him to Herod Antipas, who was also in Jerusalem at that time. Pilate probably hoped that this would free him from the responsibility of trying Jesus.

At first Herod was glad to see Jesus. He hoped that Jesus would perform a miracle for him. But Jesus did not show off His power or answer Herod's questions, so Herod mocked Him and sent Him back to Pilate.

Matthew 27:15–25

The Roman rulers apparently had a custom of releasing one Jewish prisoner each year to the people. Pilate hoped to persuade the multitude to ask for Jesus' release. While he was waiting for their answer, he received a message from his wife warning him not to have anything to do with condemning this righteous man.

9. a. Whom did the chief priests persuade the people to ask for instead of Jesus?
   Barabbas

   b. What did they demand that Pilate do with Jesus?   "Let him be crucified."

10. Pilate washed his hands and said he was innocent of shedding Jesus' blood. The Jews answered,
    " His blood be on us, and on our children   ."

John 19:7–16

Pilate still believed that Jesus was innocent. He decided to have Jesus scourged, or severely beaten, in an attempt to satisfy the crowd and make them feel sorry for Jesus. However, the chief priests and officers only repeated the demand that Jesus be crucified. In an attempt to make their case against Jesus stronger, they added the accusation upon which they had condemned Him by their law—"He made himself the Son of God." This charge made Pilate even more afraid to condemn Jesus, and he asked Him from where He had come.

11. At first Jesus did not answer Pilate. What did Jesus say when Pilate pointed out that he had authority to release Him or to crucify Him?   "Thou couldest have no power at all against me,
    except it were given thee from above: therefore he that delivered me unto thee hath the greater sin."

_____

Once again Pilate tried to release Jesus. This time the Jewish leaders, who normally hated being under Roman rule, tried to appear loyal to the emperor. They declared that Pilate would be working against Caesar if he released someone who claimed to be a king.

Pilate had withstood the Jews throughout the trial to this point, but he was not willing to risk being called a traitor to save Jesus.

12. Pilate made one last appeal by asking, "Shall I crucify your King?" What did the chief priests answer?   "We have no king but Caesar."

_____

- Pilate could not completely free himself from the guilt of condemning an innocent man. He could have refused to consent to Jesus' death, but he was not willing to risk his position to save Jesus. However, by accepting responsibility for Jesus' blood, the Jews brought upon themselves the terrible judgment that Jesus had predicted in Matthew 23:34–36; 24:1, 2.

- This shows how desperate the leaders had become in their efforts to have Jesus killed. Under normal circumstances, no Jew would have acknowledged Caesar as his only king. To do so was to deny the Messiah, which is exactly what these leaders were doing.

to crucify Him after the Jewish leaders declared that no friend of Caesar would release a potential rival to his throne.
—Jesus was crucified with two thieves. After suffering on the cross for six hours, He committed His spirit to God and laid down His life.
—Joseph of Arimathaea and Nicodemus laid Jesus' body in Joseph's new tomb.

Objectives
- Students should know
  —who cut off the ear of the high priest's servant. (*Peter*)
  —how we know that Jesus could have prevented

His enemies from arresting Him. (*He said that He could have asked God for more than twelve legions of angels.*)
—what charge the Jewish leaders used to condemn Jesus when they tried Him. (*blasphemy*)
—what the Jews answered when Pilate said that he was innocent of Jesus' blood. (*"His blood be on us, and on our children."*)
—who denied Jesus three times before the rooster crowed twice. (*Peter*)
—who asked, "What is truth?" (*Pilate*)
—what Pilate wrote on the sign that was placed on Jesus' cross. (*"Jesus of Nazareth the King of the Jews"*)

Jesus' Crucifixion at Calvary

Mark 15:15–23

13. After trying in vain to release Jesus, (a) _____Pilate_____ finally delivered Jesus to the soldiers to be (b) _____crucified_____. Jesus and two thieves, each bearing his own cross, were led in a procession through the stone streets of Jerusalem and outside the city walls to a place called Calvary. Four soldiers were assigned to each condemned man.

14. Jesus had been awake all night. First He had prayed in the Garden of Gethsemane, and then He had stood before Annas, Caiaphas, Pilate, and Herod to be judged. His captors had hurried Him around from one trial to another, and the soldiers had mistreated and scourged Him. Jesus' inner determination to do God's will was still as strong as ever, but His body was so weak that _____Simon_____ of Cyrene was compelled to carry His cross.

15. Before the soldiers nailed Jesus to the cross, they offered Him (a) _____wine_____ mixed with (b) _____myrrh_____ to drink. But when Jesus tasted it, He refused to drink it. He wanted to be able to think and speak clearly to the end. Jesus' prayer for those who crucified Him was, "Father, forgive them; for they know not what they do" (Luke 23:34).

John 19:19–22

16. Above Jesus' head, a sign prepared by Pilate gave His name and accusation. It was written in the (a) _____Hebrew_____, _____Greek_____, and _____Latin_____ languages, and it read: (b) "_Jesus of Nazareth the King of the Jews_____."

17. The Jews did not want those who passed by to think of Jesus as their king, so they asked Pilate to change the sign to "_____He said_____, I am King of the Jews." But Pilate replied, "What I have written I have written."

Luke 23:39–43

18. The two thieves crucified with Jesus apparently joined the chief priests, soldiers, and others in mocking Jesus (Matthew 27:44). But one of the two saw his mistake and reproved the other. Jesus rewarded his faith by saying, "_Verily I say unto thee, To day shalt thou be with me in paradise_____."

John 19:25–27

19. _____John_____, "the disciple whom Jesus loved," stood near the cross, with Mary the mother of Jesus and some other women. Jesus wanted this disciple to care for Mary as his own mother. (If you need help, review Part D in Lesson 9).

Matthew 27:45–49

20. It was now midday, but suddenly the sun disappeared and a strange darkness fell upon all the land. The darkness lasted for _____three_____ hours.

21. About the ninth hour (3:00 P.M.), Jesus, suffering in both body and soul, cried out, "Eli, Eli, lama sabachthani?" This meant, "_My God, my God, why hast thou forsaken me_____?"

22. About the same time, Jesus said, "I thirst" (John 19:28). Someone ran and filled a sponge with _____vinegar_____ for Him to drink.

- It is surprising that Pilate tried as hard as he did to release Jesus. Pilate was not noted for caring much about unfortunate Jews. Perhaps this was God's way of showing the Jews beyond doubt that Christ's blood was on *their* hands. They would never be able to blame the Romans for killing Jesus.

- Some people believe that Jesus was crucified on Thursday rather than on Friday. If this is correct, Jesus was in the grave more nearly three full days and nights. However, He would have risen on the fourth day instead of the third, and we would need to conclude that Friday was a special Sabbath. The wording of the Gospels seems to indicate that the women rested only one Sabbath Day before going to the tomb.

—who said, "Truly this was the Son of God." (*the centurion who was at Jesus' crucifixion*)

—who buried Jesus' body. (*Joseph of Arimathaea and Nicodemus*)

—what happened to the veil of the temple when Jesus died. (*It was torn from top to bottom.*)

Truths to Amplify

- Jesus' death completed the Old Testament era, and His resurrection initiated the New Testament era.
- With some help, seventh grade students should be able to see that the animal sacrifices, the priesthood, the special feasts, and the Old Testament Law all pointed to Jesus. One type especially suited for students to consider is the lamb that Abraham found to sacrifice in Isaac's place.

- The Bible clearly states that Jesus gave His life; no man had the power to take it from Him (John 10:18). Although He was led as a lamb to the slaughter, Jesus did not die as a helpless victim. Rather, as the Lord of life, He temporarily submitted to death so that He could offer eternal life to man.

23. Many of those who stood by misunderstood Jesus' cry to God. They mocked, "Let be, let us see whether _____Elias (Elijah)_____ will come to save him."

Jesus' Death on the Cross

24. Soon after this Jesus said, (a) "__It is finished_____" (John 19:30). He also cried with a loud voice, "Father, (b) __into thy hands I commend my spirit__ _____" (Luke 23:46).

25. Jesus' human body died as other men die. But His death was so unusual that the centurion in charge exclaimed, "__Truly this was the Son of God__ _____" (Matthew 27:54).

26. With evening coming on, the soldiers broke the thieves' legs to hasten their deaths. But Jesus was already dead, so they _____pierced_____ His side (John 19:34).

Jesus' Burial in a New Tomb

John 19:38–41

27. _____Joseph_____ of Arimathaea and Nicodemus took the body of Jesus and laid it in a newly cut tomb that was nearby.

B. BIBLE WORD STUDY

Match the following meanings with the words on the right.

_e_	1. To hit with the fist (Matthew 26:67)	a. scourge
_a_	2. To whip severely (Matthew 27:26)	b. malefactor
_d_	3. A mixture of sour wine and water (Matthew 27:34)	c. rail
_c_	4. To speak harshly and bitterly to; revile (Luke 23:39)	d. vinegar
_b_	5. An evildoer; criminal (John 18:30)	e. buffet

C. THINKING ABOUT BIBLE TRUTHS

How Did Jesus Die?

The Roman centurion who watched Jesus die saw that He was different from most persons who were crucified. Usually condemned persons had to be dragged to their crosses while they screamed and kicked in resistance. They raged at their tormentors with the bitterest hatred and clung to life as long as it lasted. Jesus was different— so different that the centurion was convinced that He was indeed the Son of God.

1. Read Luke 23:33, 34. Did Jesus hate those who were putting Him to death? How do you know?
   No. Instead of cursing them, He prayed, "Father, forgive them, for they know not what they do."

2. Read John 10:17, 18; 19:31–33. Jesus died before the two thieves who were crucified with Him. What do these verses tell us about His death? _____
   He gave His life voluntarily; the Jews and Romans did not take it.

- Number 24 b. This is a quotation from Psalm 31:5.

- Number 1. The Greek indicates the use of fists.

- This still did not lessen the sin of those who condemned Him to death.

D. LEARNING MORE ABOUT BIBLE TIMES

The Sanhedrin (For class discussion)

Seventy-one Jewish leaders met regularly in Jerusalem. They formed the Sanhedrin (san HEHD rihn), the governing body of the Jews. Sitting in a semicircle, the Sanhedrin judged persons accused of violating Jewish law.

Two clerks recorded what was said at a Sanhedrin trial. One wrote everything said in favor of the person being judged, and the other wrote everything said against him. Then the seventy-one men voted to decide whether to convict or acquit the person. Voting began with the youngest so that no one would be influenced by an older man.

A man could not normally be sentenced to death on the same day he was found guilty. If he was condemned to die, someone was to walk before him on the way to his execution shouting, "This man has been found worthy of death. If anyone knows anything to clear him, let him come forward and declare it."

1. The regular procedures of the Sanhedrin were meant to protect an innocent person who had been unjustly accused. But at Jesus' trial, the members of the Sanhedrin deliberately set out to find Him guilty of a crime deserving the death sentence. What kind of witness did the Sanhedrin seek while Jesus was on trial? (Matthew 26:59) __false witnesses__

The Veil of the Temple

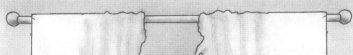

Made of finely twined blue, purple, and scarlet linen, the veil of the temple separated the holy place from the most holy place. According to ancient Jewish writers, two veils hung at the entrance of the most holy place. Each veil measured 60 feet long and 30 feet wide, and was as thick as the palm of a man's hand.

2. Hebrews 10:20 compares Jesus' body to the veil of the temple. Like the temple veil, Jesus stood between God and man while He lived in His human body. What happened to the temple veil when Jesus died? (Matthew 27:51)   It was torn in two from top to bottom.

3. The temple veil kept men from freely coming into God's presence (Hebrews 9:7, 8). But when Jesus gave His body and blood as the perfect sacrifice, God tore the veil to show that He had provided a new way for man to have fellowship with Him. According to Hebrews 10:19, where can Christians freely enter by the blood of Jesus?   Christians can enter "into the holiest."

- Because Jesus' blood removes our sins rather than just covering them, we can have direct fellowship with God without needing to go through an earthly priest.

The Torn Veil

There's a hush in the holy of holies
    And a stagnant pall of despair;
No odor of dew and raindrops
    In the dark and the musty air;
No light in that inner sanctum,
    No life where the law is stored;
Like a hand that is clenched, it is keeping
    The holy within its hoard.
The curtain, heavy and ancient,
    Hangs in onerous folds,
Hiding the sacred ark
    That the Word of Jehovah holds.

Then a cry from a cross: " '*Tis finished*,"
    And its echo becomes a quake
That convulses the earth with a shiver,
    And the temple's foundations shake;
One long, deliberate r-r-rip,
    And the curtain is torn in two!
And a light bursts into the gloom
    With an atmosphere fresh and new.
The "letter that killeth" is vanquished
    By the "spirit that giveth life."
There's a hush in the holy of holies . . .
    But it's sweet now, and free of strife.

—Margaret Penner Toews
From *Five Loaves and Two Small Fish*

192

Lesson 25. "Behold, I Am Alive for Evermore"

It was over.

By sunset on Friday evening, Jesus' body was lying in a borrowed tomb, dead. The Bible does not record what the disciples did on the Sabbath. Unlike the Jewish leaders, the disciples did not seem to remember that Jesus had said He would rise again.

Then Sunday dawned with its earth-shaking events. News of Jesus' resurrection began trickling through Jerusalem early in the morning. The soldiers guarding the tomb were the first to find out, and they ran to tell the news to the chief priests.

The Jewish leaders were shocked at this manifestation of God's power. They immediately took steps to limit the damage they knew this would do to their cause. But it was already too late. Jesus was forever beyond their power.

He had risen!

If Jesus had stayed in the grave, the world would soon have forgotten Him. His good teachings would have been lost, His disciples would have returned to their fishing, and the Jewish leaders would have regained their power over the Jews.

But Jesus arose!

The disciples and many other people saw Jesus after His resurrection. They heard Him speak, they ate with Him, and they walked with Him along the roads of Palestine. All those who saw Jesus knew that He had risen from the dead, and that He is indeed the Messiah, the Saviour of the world.

There would be no church and no Christians today if Jesus had not risen.

Praise God, the Lord is risen indeed!

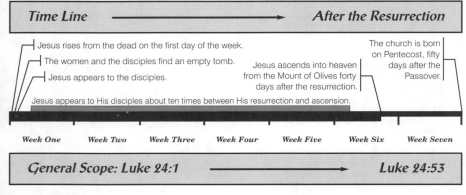

Time Line ──────────────➤ **After the Resurrection**

Jesus rises from the dead on the first day of the week.

The women and the disciples find an empty tomb.

Jesus appears to the disciples.

Jesus ascends into heaven from the Mount of Olives forty days after the resurrection.

The church is born on Pentecost, fifty days after the Passover.

Jesus appears to His disciples about ten times between His resurrection and ascension.

Week One   *Week Two*   *Week Three*   *Week Four*   *Week Five*   *Week Six*   *Week Seven*

General Scope: Luke 24:1 ──────────➤ **Luke 24:53**

Using the Time Line

1. How many days after the resurrection was Jesus' ascension?   <u>forty days</u>
2. How many days after the Passover was the day of Pentecost?   <u>fifty days</u>

A. ANSWERS FROM THE BIBLE

The four Gospels give four interesting accounts of Jesus' resurrection, each slightly different. We do not know how all the details fit together. Was there one group of women, or two? Did Mary Magdalene come first by herself, or did she come with the rest? These details are not as important as the fact that the four different accounts all speak of one true event.

• Do not be misled by reference books that reflect negatively on the Gospel of John. This Gospel gives different details than the other Gospels, but that does not mean that it is

Lesson 25

Oral Review

1. What three things did Satan tempt Jesus to do in the wilderness? [L. 5] **turn stones to bread, jump from the pinnacle of the temple, and worship him**
2. What does the Lord's Prayer mean when it says, "Forgive us our debts, as we forgive our debtors"? [L. 10] **God will not forgive our sins if we refuse to forgive others for the wrongs they do against us.**
3. What did Jesus use to feed a crowd of five thousand? of four thousand? [L. 14, 15] **five (barley) loaves and two fish; seven loaves and a few small fish**
4. According to the parable of the Good Samaritan, who is our neighbor? [L. 19] **any person who is in need of our help**
5. What warning did Jesus give His disciples before telling them about the future? [L. 23] **"Take heed that no man deceive you."**
6. What did Jesus tell the Christians of Judea to do when they saw armies surrounding Jerusalem? [L. 23] **He told them to flee to the mountains immediately.**
7. How do we know that Jesus could have prevented His enemies from arresting and crucifying Him?

If you and your classmates were each to write about an unusual day at school, would all your accounts be the same? Not very likely. Each of you would describe details that you remembered best or considered most significant. Someone who was not present would not learn everything from one account, but he could learn more by comparing all of them.

In the same way, we can learn much about the events surrounding Jesus' resurrection by comparing the Gospels, even though we still do not understand exactly how everything happened. God inspired each Gospel writer to describe certain details so that we can learn all we need to know about these important events.

The Empty Tomb

Jesus' body lay quietly in the tomb over the Sabbath. The Jewish guard outside had nothing to do. But very early on Sunday morning, the guards received the greatest shock of their lives. First they felt a great earthquake. Then they saw a powerful angel descend from heaven, roll back the stone that sealed the door, and sit on it. The angel's appearance was like lightning and his clothing as white as snow. The guards were so frightened that they became as dead men. When they regained their senses, the tomb was empty and deserted. They hurried into the city to inform the Jewish leaders about what had happened. Meanwhile, Jesus' friends had no idea that His body was no longer in the tomb. Faithful women were preparing to perform their final acts of love for Him.

Mark 16:1–11; John 20:1–18

1. What did Mary Magdalene and the other women want to do at Jesus' tomb? _____
   The women wanted to anoint Jesus' body with spices.

2. What did the women see inside the tomb? two angels in white clothes

3. What was the reaction of the disciples when the women told them what they had seen? (See Luke 24:10–12.) They thought that the women were just telling idle tales. (They did not believe.)

4. What did Peter and John see in the tomb? the linen clothes in which Jesus' body had been wrapped and the napkin which had covered his face

5. To whom did Jesus first appear? Mary Magdalene

6. What were the disciples doing when Mary Magdalene told them that she had seen the Lord? ____ mourning and weeping

Jesus Appears to His Disciples

It seems that the women among Jesus' friends had more faith in Him than the apostles did. Perhaps that is why He appeared to Mary Magdalene first, and why the women saw angels at the tomb but the disciples did not. Even when the women told the disciples what they had learned, the disciples did not believe.

Luke 24:13–35

🍇 *For exercises 7–12, draw a line through the incorrect word or phrase, and then write that part of the sentence correctly on the blank.*

7. Two disciples walking to Emmaus were talking about ~~what they would do now since Jesus was no longer with them~~. the things that had happened the past few days.

8. When Jesus came upon the two disciples, He acted as if He ~~knew all about their discussion.~~ ____ did not know what they were talking about.

9. Beginning ~~with the books of prophecy,~~ Jesus explained His death and resurrection to the two disciples. at Moses and all the prophets,

inaccurate or that it contradicts the others. John probably wrote his Gospel a number of years after the others were written. Perhaps John felt a need to give details that the other writers had left out. God inspired each writer to meet a particular need, and together they provide a balanced account of Jesus' life, death, and resurrection. We should view John's Gospel as an effort not to supplant, but to supplement the other Gospels.

- Mark mentions only one angel.

- We should not be too hard on the apostles for their lack of faith. We would probably have reacted in a similar fashion. Use this lesson to promote faith in the students rather than to reproach those who should have had more faith.

[L. 24] **He said that He could call for twelve legions of angels. (He also said no one could take His life, but that He would lay it down Himself.)**

8. What did Pilate write on the sign that was placed on Jesus' cross? [L. 24] **"Jesus of Nazareth the King of the Jews" (The wording varies slightly in different Gospels.)**

In This Lesson

Scope: Matthew 28; Mark 16; Luke 24; John 20, 21; Acts 1:1–14

Focus
- Early on Sunday morning, Jesus rose triumphantly from the dead.
  —The guards and the chief priests at least partially realized what had happened, but they agreed to spread a false report.
  —The women and the disciples discovered that Jesus' body was missing from the tomb. Angels appeared to the women, telling them that Jesus had risen.

194   Chapter Five   Jesus Completes His Work

10. The two invited Jesus to stay with them for the night. They recognized Jesus when He took bread, blessed it, broke it, and ~~began to eat~~. _gave it to them._

11. The two disciples went to ~~Galilee~~ that night and found the disciples gathered together. _____
    Jerusalem

12. The disciples said, "The Lord is risen indeed, and hath appeared to ~~Mary Magdalene~~." _Simon._

John 20:19–25

After the two disciples returned from Emmaus, Jesus appeared in the midst of the group. Thomas was not with them at this time.

13. a. Why did the disciples shut the doors of the place where they had gathered? _____
       They were afraid of the Jews.

    b. On what day of the week did Jesus appear to this group of His disciples? _____
       the first day of the week

14. What did Thomas say when the other disciples told him that they had seen the Lord? _____
    "Except I shall see in his hands the print of the nails, and put my finger into the print of the nails, and
    thrust my hand into his side, I will not believe."

• This was still the day of Jesus' resurrection.

John 20:26–29

One week later, the disciples were gathered again with the doors shut. This time Thomas was with them. When Thomas saw Jesus, he no longer felt the need to touch His wounds. He exclaimed, "My Lord and my God."

15. Jesus was glad that Thomas finally believed in His resurrection. However, whom did Jesus say would receive greater blessings than those who believed after seeing Him? _____
    "they that have not seen, and yet have believed"

Jesus Talks to Peter

The New Testament mentions about ten times that Jesus appeared to His followers after the resurrection. Jesus used these appearances to further prepare the apostles for the time when He would return to heaven. During these forty days the disciples traveled back to Galilee, where they met Jesus on a mountain. One time Jesus was seen by over five hundred people at once (1 Corinthians 15:6).

The disciples did not seem to understand that Jesus was preparing them to carry on the work of His kingdom. Peter became restless with the inaction and decided to go fishing. Some of the other disciples went with him. When they returned to shore, Jesus was there waiting for them.

John 21:15–17

16. After they finished eating, Jesus talked with Peter.
    a. How many times had Peter denied Jesus? (See Mark 14:72.) _three times_
    b. How many times did Jesus ask Peter if he loved Him? _three times_

17. What commission did Jesus give to Peter during this conversation? _____
    Jesus told Peter to feed His sheep and lambs.

• You might want to discuss the possible connection between these two incidents.

The Ascension of Jesus

Forty days after the resurrection, the disciples gathered with Jesus for the last time. He had finished His work on earth, and now it was time for Him to return to His Father. But before He left, He gave them some final instructions. He promised to send the Holy Spirit in His stead. The Holy Spirit would guide them in the tremendous task of establishing the church on earth.

—The disciples refused to believe that Jesus had risen until He revealed Himself to them.
—Jesus revealed Himself to His followers at different times between His resurrection and ascension. (See notes on the next page.)

Objectives
• Students should know
  —why the women went to the tomb on Sunday morning. (*to anoint Jesus' body with spices*)
  —what the women saw when they entered the tomb. (*two angels in white clothes*)
  —who was the first person to see Jesus after His resurrection. (*Mary Magdalene*)

—what Jesus used to explain His death and resurrection to two disciples walking to Emmaus. (*the Books of Moses and all the prophets*)
—who said he would not believe that Jesus had risen until he saw and touched His wounds. (*Thomas*)
—what Jesus did in the presence of His disciples to prove that His body had risen. (*He ate fish and honeycomb, and He told them to touch Him.*)
—how many times Jesus asked Peter if he loved Him. (*three*)
—what Jesus' last command was to His apostles. (*He told them to be witnesses for Him in Jerusalem, Judea, Samaria, and unto the uttermost part of the earth.*)

Acts 1:1–14

18. What did Jesus promise that the Holy Spirit would give the disciples? power

19. What last instruction did Jesus give the disciples before leaving them? They were to be witnesses
    of Him in Jerusalem, Judea, Samaria, and unto the uttermost part of the earth.

20. What promise did the two angels give the disciples? Jesus would return as they had seen Him go.

This passage ends with the interesting note that Jesus' mother and His brothers were with the disciples in the upper room. Apparently the brothers of Jesus had come to believe that He is the Messiah. In 1 Corinthians 15:7 the apostle Paul states that Jesus had appeared to James. This may have been the apostle James, but it seems more likely that it was the Lord's (half) brother James, who later became the leader of the church at Jerusalem. Perhaps Jesus' appearance to James had led His brothers to believe in Him.

B. BIBLE WORD STUDY

1. Many people called Jesus *rabbi* (master or teacher). But after His resurrection, Mary called Him *Rabboni*. This word is used only twice in the New Testament—once in John 20:16, where the word is given in its original form, and once in Mark 10:51, where its English equivalent is used. What does *Rabboni* mean? (Compare the two verses where it appears.) Lord

2. Emmaus lay *threescore furlongs* from Jerusalem (Luke 24:13). Use the tables of measure inside the back cover to find the distance between Emmaus and Jerusalem. about 7 miles (about 11 km)

3. Jesus *expounded* the Scriptures to the disciples who were walking to Emmaus (Luke 24:27). To *expound* means to

   a. quote.   (b.) explain.   c. recite.

4. Jesus gave His apostles the authority to *remit* sins (John 20:23). This means that in His Name they could

   (a.) forgive sins.   b. punish sins.   c. overlook sins.

5. In the same verse Jesus also gave His apostles the authority to *retain* sins. This means that in His Name they could

   a. punish unbelievers for their sins.

   b. deliver people from their sins.

   (c.) hold people responsible for their sins.

C. THINKING ABOUT BIBLE TRUTHS

Faith in the Resurrection

At first the apostles found it difficult to accept the fact of the resurrection. Thomas stands out as the doubter of the group and is often known as Doubting Thomas. However, it is of little value for us to condemn Thomas. The question that we face is this: Do we have enough faith to believe in the resurrection, or are we doubters too?

John 20:24–29

1. What did Thomas say he would need to do before he could believe in the resurrection? _____
   He insisted that he would need to touch Jesus' wounds to believe that Jesus was really alive.

• *Unger's Bible Dictionary* states that *Rabboni* means "My Lord, My Master." Other references may differ slightly, but *Rabboni* carried a higher level of honor than *Rabbi*.)

• You may want to mention to the students that this power was bestowed on the church, along with the responsibility to keep the church pure by judging sin in the lives of its members. Only God can actually forgive or condemn, but the church must use God's Word to identify sin, to administer discipline as necessary, and to receive repentant offenders back into fellowship.

—what promise the angels gave the disciples after Jesus had ascended into heaven. (*Jesus would someday return as He had left.*)

Truths to Amplify

• The Lord is risen indeed! Many have denied this and claimed that Jesus only appeared in a vision or that He was not dead in the first place. But through faith we know that He did rise from the dead as the Gospels portray.

• Because of their lack of faith in what Jesus had told them, the disciples were slow to believe in the resurrection. Our lack of faith can lead us into problems too.

• Jesus ascended to heaven, and He will someday return to earth in a similar way.

Notes

• It is difficult to determine the exact order of events on the day of Jesus' resurrection. The following list is probably as accurate as any.

   —Mary Magdalene and the other women go to the tomb early on Sunday morning to embalm Jesus' body.

   —The women meet angels in the empty tomb and quickly return to the apostles to tell them what the angels had said.

   —The apostles do not believe, but Peter and John

2. Thomas believed without doing what he had said. What made him believe? _____
   He saw Jesus face to face.

3. Jesus pronounced a blessing on those who ___believe without seeing Him___

   _____.

4. What group of people have believed in Jesus' resurrection without seeing Him for themselves?
   all true Christians except those who saw the resurrected Christ

D. LEARNING MORE ABOUT BIBLE TIMES

Proofs of Jesus' Resurrection (For class discussion)

Jesus "shewed himself alive after his passion [sufferings] by many infallible proofs" (Acts 1:3). He could have appeared to all the Jews, but many of them were not ready to receive Him by faith. Their hearts were so hard that they would not have been persuaded, "though one rose from the dead" (Luke 16:31). Instead, Jesus revealed Himself openly to "witnesses chosen before of God," who in turn gave testimony that He is risen indeed (Acts 10:41).

The Jewish leaders were the first to deny that Jesus rose from the dead. They spread the rumor that His disciples had stolen the body. However, their actions show that they were convinced that He had risen.

Some people think the disciples just saw a vision of Jesus after His death. But this does not explain what happened to Jesus' body; neither would a mere vision have been likely to convince the disciples that Jesus' body had risen. Perhaps Thomas thought the disciples had seen a vision of Christ. But when he personally came face to face with Him, Thomas needed no further proof. The same is true for all those who personally know Jesus today.

🍇 *This section deals with three important proofs of Jesus' resurrection. Other proofs could also be mentioned. Think about these questions, and be prepared to discuss them in class.*

Proof 1: Jesus' body left the sealed, guarded tomb, and no one can account for it except by His resurrection.

1. Could the disciples have easily stolen Jesus' body from a sealed tomb with a heavy stone at the entrance without waking the soldiers guarding it? ___no___

2. What would the chief priests have done to the soldiers if they had actually thought the soldiers had allowed the disciples to take the body? (See Acts 12:18, 19.) ___They would have had them killed.___

   _____

3. If the Jews or the Romans had known where Jesus' body was, what would they have done when the apostles began to preach openly that Jesus had risen? _____
   They would have presented Jesus' body to prove the disciples wrong and to silence them forever.

   _____

Proof 2: The apostles' earnestness in spreading the news of Jesus' resurrection, in spite of persecution, proves that they were thoroughly convinced that Jesus had risen from the dead.

Jesus rebuked His apostles for not believing in His resurrection sooner. However, their initial doubt shows that they were not convinced by mere hearsay or by a vision.

- It would have been foolish for anyone to try rolling back the heavy stone in the soldiers' presence. Even if the soldiers had fallen asleep, they would have stayed close to the tomb, where any disturbance would have awakened them. Anyone attempting to steal the body would have needed to kill the soldiers first, and that clearly was not done.

- The Jewish leaders probably wished they could kill the soldiers to prevent any possibility of their spreading the news. But since they could not dare let the soldiers testify at a trial, they silenced them with money. This gave them an explanation for the empty tomb, along with "witnesses" to "prove" it. The glaring inconsistency in this official report is that the "witnesses" were admitting to a serious neglect of duty for which they were not punished. The leaders' request that the tomb be made sure had backfired on them.

run to the tomb. They see the empty tomb but no angels. John believes when he sees the grave clothes, but he still does not seem to understand.
—Mary Magdalene returns in bewilderment to the tomb by herself and meets Jesus in the Garden.
—Mary returns to the apostles to tell them that she met Jesus and talked with Him, but they still do not believe.
—Jesus appears to two disciples as they travel to Emmaus.
—Jesus appears to Peter.
—The two from Emmaus return to Jerusalem. The disciples there doubt their story but report that Jesus had appeared to Peter.

—Jesus appears suddenly in their midst as they talk. The disciples show by their fear that they still do not really believe. Jesus rebukes them for their unbelief and asks for some food to eat, to prove that He is not just a spirit. Thomas is absent from the gathering.

4. What did Jesus do to prove to the disciples that His body had risen, and that they were not seeing a vision or a spirit? (Luke 24:39–43) He told them to touch Him, and He ate fish and honeycomb.

5. How does Thomas's insistence on proof before he would believe help to confirm Jesus' resurrection? He would not have been convinced by a mere vision of Jesus.

6. On the day of Pentecost, the apostles risked their lives to preach Jesus' resurrection in the very city where Jesus had been condemned about fifty days before. What would the apostles most likely have done if they had thought that Jesus was still dead?
They probably would have dispersed and quietly gone back to their old lives.

7. At one time Paul persecuted the church. Suddenly he turned around and became the church's greatest missionary. What had Paul seen that changed his mind? (1 Corinthians 15:3–8)
He had seen the risen Christ (on the way to Damascus).

Proof 3: Through the New Birth, believers around the world, throughout the church age, have experienced the power of the resurrected Christ in their own hearts.

8. What proof of Jesus' resurrection do believers have that unbelievers do not? (John 14:16, 17)
the Spirit of God, who dwells within Christians

"You ask me how I know He lives? He lives within my heart!"

198

Chapter Five Review

A. ORAL REVIEW

 Be sure you know the answers to these questions. Answer as many as you can from memory. If you need help, you may check the reference or lesson numbers given in brackets.

>>

Who

1. Who protested when the multitudes praised Jesus during His triumphal entry into Jerusalem? [Luke 19:39]
2. Who gave Jesus the authority to cleanse the temple and to condemn the Pharisees? [Lesson 22]
3. Who agreed to deliver Jesus to the Jewish leaders? [Matthew 26:14, 15]
4. Who cut off the ear of the high priest's servant? [John 18:10]
5. Who asked, "What is truth?" [John 18:38]
6. Who said, "His blood be on us, and on our children"? [Matthew 27:25]
7. After Jesus died, who said, "Truly this was the Son of God"? [Matthew 27:54]
8. Who buried Jesus' body? [John 19:38, 39]
9. Who was the first person to see Jesus after He rose from the dead? [Mark 16:9]
10. Who said he would not believe that Jesus had risen until he saw and touched His wounds? [John 20:25]

What >>

11. What is the meaning of *hosanna*? [Lesson 21]
12. What question did the Pharisees ask Jesus, which they hoped would get Him into trouble no matter how He answered? [Luke 20:21, 22]
13. What warning did Jesus give His disciples before He began telling them about future events? [Matthew 24:4]
14. What did Jesus tell the Christians of Judea to do when they saw armies surrounding Jerusalem? [Luke 21:20, 21]
15. What lesson did Jesus teach in the parable of the talents? [Lesson 23]
16. What is the purpose of Communion? [Luke 22:19]
17. What lesson did Jesus teach by washing His disciples' feet? [Lesson 23; John 13:12–17]
18. What did Jesus tell Peter that showed He could have prevented the soldiers from arresting Him? [Matthew 26:53]
19. What was the charge on which the Jewish leaders condemned Jesus when they tried Him? [Matthew 26:63–66]
20. What did Pilate write on the sign that was placed on Jesus' cross? [John 19:19]
21. What did Jesus mean when He said, "Eli, Eli, lama sabachthani"? [Matthew 27:46]
22. What happened to the veil of the temple when Jesus died? [Matthew 27:51]
23. What did Jesus do in the presence of His disciples to prove that His body had risen, and that they were not seeing a vision or a spirit? [Luke 24:39–43]

1. the Pharisees
2. God
3. Judas
4. Peter
5. Pilate
6. the Jews
7. the centurion in charge of the crucifixion
8. Joseph of Arimathaea and Nicodemus
9. Mary Magdalene
10. Thomas
11. "Save now!" or "Save, I pray!"
12. "Is it lawful for us to give tribute unto Caesar?"
13. "Take heed that no man deceive you."
14. He told them to flee immediately to the mountains.
15. God expects us to make good use of the abilities He gives.
16. It reminds Christians of Jesus' suffering and death.
17. God wants us to humbly serve one another in love. (Jesus washed His disciples' feet as an example for us to follow.)
18. He could have asked God to send more than twelve legions of angels.
19. blasphemy
20. "Jesus of Nazareth the King of the Jews"
21. "My God, my God, why hast thou forsaken me?"
22. It was torn into two pieces from top to bottom.
23. He told them to touch Him, and He ate fish and honeycomb.

24. What was Jesus' last command to the apostles? [Acts 1:8]
25. What promise did the angels give the disciples after Jesus had ascended into heaven? [Acts 1:10, 11]

How   >>

26. How did Jesus fulfill an Old Testament prophecy during His triumphal entry into Jerusalem? [Matthew 21:4, 5]
27. How did Jesus prove to the Sadducees that the Books of Moses teach the resurrection? [Luke 20:37, 38]
28. How many years passed between Jesus' prophecy concerning the destruction of Jerusalem and its fulfillment? [Lesson 23]
29. How many times did Peter deny Jesus before the rooster crowed? [Matthew 26:75]
30. How many times did Jesus ask Peter if he loved Him? [John 21:15–17]

B. WRITTEN REVIEW

When

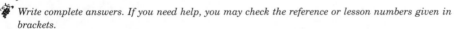 *Write the day of the week when each event took place. Use the time lines in this chapter if you need help.*

Sunday	1. Jesus rides a donkey into Jerusalem.
Monday	2. Jesus denounces a barren fig tree.
Monday	3. Jesus cleanses the temple.
Tuesday	4. Jesus warns the Jews with parables.
Tuesday	5. The Jewish rulers try to trap Jesus with a trick question.
Tuesday	6. Jesus tells the disciples about end-time events.
Thursday	7. Jesus eats the Passover supper with His disciples.
Friday	8. Jesus is arrested and tried by the Sanhedrin.
Friday	9. Jesus is tried and condemned by Pilate.
Friday	10. Jesus dies and His body is buried.
Saturday	11. Jesus' body lies in a borrowed grave this entire day.
Sunday	12. Jesus rises from the dead.

Why

Write complete answers. If you need help, you may check the reference or lesson numbers given in brackets.

13. Why did Jesus weep over Jerusalem? [Luke 19:41–44] He knew the terrible destruction that would come upon the city because of the Jews' rejection of Him.
14. Why did Jesus cleanse the temple? [Matthew 21:12, 13] The Jews had made it a den of thieves with their (dishonest) buying and selling.
15. Why did the invited guests fail to come to the marriage feast of the king's son? [Matthew 22:3–6; Lesson 22] They were too busy with other things that they considered more important. (Also, they failed to honor their king and his servants.)

24. "Ye shall be witnesses unto me both in Jerusalem, and in all Judaea, and in Samaria, and unto the uttermost part of the earth."
25. Jesus would return someday in the same way He had left.
26. He fulfilled Zechariah 9:9 by riding into Jerusalem on a donkey's colt.
27. He quoted God's words from the burning bush: "I am . . . the God of Abraham, the God of Isaac, and the God of Jacob."
28. about forty years
29. three
30. three

Number 8. Jesus may have been arrested before midnight on Thursday.

Chapter Five   Jesus Completes His Work

200   Chapter Five   Jesus Completes His Work

16. Why did Jesus condemn the Pharisees so sternly? (Give two reasons.) [Matthew 23:5–7, 28] _____
    They wanted other people to look up to them, and they were hypocrites.
    _____

17. Why were five of the ten virgins called foolish and the other five called wise? [Matthew 25:3, 4]
    The foolish virgins did not carry extra oil, and the wise ones did.
    _____

18. Why did Peter object when Jesus wanted to wash his feet? [Lesson 23] _____
    He did not understand what Jesus was trying to teach (and he felt unworthy to have Jesus wash his feet).

19. Why did the women go to the tomb on Sunday morning? [Mark 16:1] _____
    to anoint Jesus' body with spices
    _____

Signs of the End

20. Which two of the following are signs of the end? [Lesson 23]
    a. the destruction of Jerusalem
    (b.) stars falling from heaven
    c. leaves growing on fig trees
    (d.) the sun and moon becoming dark

Lessons From Parables

Match each lesson with the parable that teaches it. If you need help, review Lesson 22.

c	21. God rewards us for our deeds, not our empty promises.	a. the laborers in the vineyard
d	22. God will judge those who are unfaithful to the trust that He gives them.	b. the marriage of the king's son
		c. the two sons
a	23. God rewards people for their faithfulness, not for the amount of work that they do.	d. the wicked husbandmen
b	24. Salvation is now offered to all people.	

"I am the vine, ye are the branches" (John 15:5).

CHAPTER SIX

God Calls a New People

The Church Is Born

The Gospel Spreads Throughout Palestine

The Gospel Spreads Through Asia

The Gospel Spreads to Europe

"I Have Fought a Good Fight"

For as many as are led by the Spirit of God, they are the sons of God.
For ye have not received the spirit of bondage again to fear;
but ye have received the Spirit of adoption, whereby we cry, Abba, Father.
The Spirit itself beareth witness with our spirit, that we are the children of God:
And if children, then heirs; heirs of God, and joint-heirs with Christ;
if so be that we suffer with him, that we may be also glorified together.
Romans 8:14–17

The Book of Acts

Important events covered in Chapter Six

Event	Reference	Location	Date A.D.[1]
Lesson 26. The Church Is Born			
Matthias is ordained to take Judas's place.	1:15–26	*Jerusalem (upper room)*	*30*
The Holy Spirit is poured out on the day of Pentecost.	2:1–13	*Jerusalem*	*30*
Peter preaches; 3,000 repent; the church is founded.	2:14–47	*Jerusalem*	*30*
Peter and John heal a lame man in Jesus' Name.[2]	3:1–26	*Jerusalem (temple)*	
The Jewish leaders threaten the apostles.	4:1–31	*Jerusalem*	
Lesson 27. The Gospel Spreads Throughout Palestine			
Ananias and Sapphira lie to the Holy Ghost.	5:1–11	*Jerusalem*	
The apostles are imprisoned; an angel releases them.	5:17–42	*Jerusalem*	
The church ordains seven men to help the apostles.	6:1–6	*Jerusalem*	
Stephen preaches to the Jews and is stoned by them.	6:8–7:60	*Jerusalem*	
Philip teaches the Samaritans and an Ethiopian.	8:4–40	*Samaria; desert road*	
God instructs Peter to take the Gospel to Cornelius.	10:1–11:18	*Joppa; Caesarea*	
Lesson 28. The Gospel Spreads Through Asia			
Saul is converted after meeting Jesus.	9:1–22	*Damascus*	*37[3]*
Saul escapes from Damascus and from Jerusalem.	9:23–30	*Damascus; Jerusalem*	
The church at Antioch sends out Barnabas and Saul.	13:1–3	*Antioch*	*47[4]*
Paul's First Missionary Journey	13:4–14:28	*Cyprus; Asia Minor*	*47, 48*
Paul rebukes Barjesus.	13:6–13	*Paphos, on Cyprus*	
The Lycaonians reverence Paul and later stone him.	14:8–20	*Lystra*	
Lesson 29. The Gospel Spreads to Europe			
Paul's Second Missionary Journey	15:36–18:22	*Asia Minor; Europe*	*50–53*
Paul and Silas respond to the Macedonian call.	16:6–10	*Troas*	
Paul casts a demon out of a girl; Paul and Silas are put in prison.	16:16–40	*Philippi*	
Paul preaches at Athens and Corinth.	17:15–18:18	*Athens; Corinth*	
Paul's Third Missionary Journey	18:23–21:17	*Asia Minor; Europe*	*53–57*
The silversmiths of Ephesus stir up a riot against Paul.	19:23–41	*Ephesus*	
Eutychus falls from a window; Paul restores him to life.	20:6–12	*Troas*	
Paul bids farewell to the elders of Ephesus.	20:17–38	*Miletus*	
Paul is arrested at Jerusalem.	21:18–22:29	*Jerusalem*	*57*
Lesson 30. "I Have Fought a Good Fight"			
Paul is taken to Caesarea after his life is threatened.	23:12–35	*Jerusalem; Caesarea*	*57*
Paul testifies before Felix, Festus, and King Agrippa.	24–26	*Caesarea*	*57–59*
Paul is shipwrecked on his voyage to Rome.	27:1–44	*Mediterranean Sea*	*59*
Paul performs miracles on the island of Melita.	28:1–10	*Melita*	*59–60*
Paul arrives at Rome and teaches the Jews.	28:11–31	*Rome, under house arrest*	*60*
Paul finishes his course with joy.	(2 Timothy 4:6–8)	*Rome, in prison*	*67, 68[5]*

---

[1] All dates are approximate. Dates given for this period can vary by several years, depending on the method used to determine them.

[2] The events recorded in Acts 3–10 are difficult to date. Probably all of them took place between A.D. 30 and 44.

[3] The dating of Paul's conversion depends on which of his visits to Jerusalem is described in Galatians 2:1.

[4] Herod Agrippa I (the Herod of Acts 12:23) died in A.D. 44. Paul's first missionary journey was apparently made after Herod's death.

[5] Some sources date Paul's death as early as A.D. 64.

203

Lesson 26. The Church Is Born

During much of the Old Testament period, God worked primarily through the Jews as a nation. God made a special covenant with Abraham, Isaac, and Jacob. Through their descendants He revealed His Word and sent His Son.

It is true that God has always accepted Gentiles who have had true faith in Him. God brought Rahab and Ruth into the godly line, and He blessed men, such as Naaman, who believed in His power and submitted to His will. These God-fearing Gentiles found more favor with God than did the unbelieving Jews of their time. Nevertheless, the Jews were God's chosen family, and it was difficult for Gentiles of Old Testament times to share in the special blessings of God's people.

This changed after Jesus' ascension. No longer was it important to belong to a certain earthly family. Instead, God called out true believers to become His spiritual family, the church. The first believers were all Jews, but God soon revealed that He would receive believing Gentiles into His new chosen family without requiring them to become Jews.

God's people were no longer a nation, but a church made up of true believers from all nations. Natural relationships no longer determined whether a person could claim God's special blessings. Everyone had an equal privilege to become a part of God's people.

In this chapter you will study the beginning of the church. About two thousand years have passed since then, but you can still see results of this beginning in your own church.

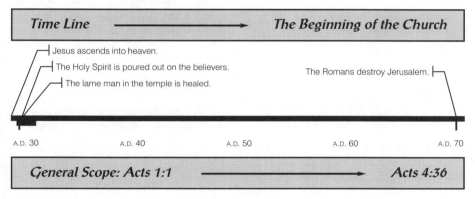

Time Line ⟶ **The Beginning of the Church**

- Jesus ascends into heaven.
- The Holy Spirit is poured out on the believers.
- The lame man in the temple is healed.
- The Romans destroy Jerusalem.

A.D. 30   A.D. 40   A.D. 50   A.D. 60   A.D. 70

General Scope: Acts 1:1 ⟶ **Acts 4:36**

Using the Time Line

1. How many years passed between Jesus' ascension and the destruction of Jerusalem? <u>about forty years</u>
2. What very important event took place soon after Jesus' ascension? <u>The Holy Spirit was poured out on the believers.</u>

A. ANSWERS FROM THE BIBLE

Before Jesus returned to heaven, He commanded the apostles to remain in Jerusalem until they were baptized with the Holy Spirit. After the ascension, the apostles returned to Jerusalem and spent their time in an upper room with others of Jesus' disciples. About 120 believers waited together for the fulfillment of Jesus' promise.

Lesson 26

Oral Review

1. Name three important districts of Palestine. [L. 1] **Galilee, Samaria, Judea**
2. How did Peter, James, and John make their living before Jesus called them to be disciples? [L. 6] **They were fishermen.**
3. How does following the Golden Rule help us to treat others as we should? [L. 10] **Generally we want others to treat us kindly and fairly, so we will treat others this way if we follow this rule.**
4. Why did the Pharisees ask Jesus for a sign from heaven? [L. 15] **They wanted to find fault with Him.**
5. What effect did the raising of Lazarus have on the people who witnessed it? [L. 20] **Many of them believed on Jesus and became His followers.**
6. How did Jesus fulfill an Old Testament prophecy during His triumphal entry into Jerusalem? [L. 21] **He fulfilled Zechariah 9:9 by riding into Jerusalem on the colt of an ass (donkey), bringing salvation.**
7. How did Jesus show the Sadducees that the Books of Moses taught the resurrection? [L. 22] **He quoted God's words from the burning**

The New Apostle

Judas's place among the twelve apostles was empty. While the 120 disciples waited in the upper room for the outpouring of the Holy Spirit, they decided to replace him. The Lord showed them whom He had chosen for this work.

🍇 *To complete these exercises, first study the Bible passages that are given. Fill in the short blanks with words. Whenever possible, use exact words from the Bible. Write complete answers for the questions with long blanks. For multiple-choice questions, circle the letter of the correct answer.*

Acts 1:15–26

1. From what group of men was the new apostle chosen?   from the men who had accompanied
   Jesus' disciples from the baptism of John until Jesus' ascension

2. Of the two men appointed, how did the apostles determine which one was the Lord's choice? ____
   They cast lots, and the lot fell upon Matthias.

The Day of Pentecost

The day of Pentecost was fifty days after the Passover and about a week after Jesus' ascension. In the Old Testament it was known as "the feast of harvest" or "the day of the firstfruits." On this day the Jews dedicated their harvest to God and brought freewill offerings to the temple. They also remembered the giving of the Law of Moses.

God chose this day to bring the Christian church into existence. He wrote His new laws upon the hearts of the believers and began the great harvest of souls into His kingdom.

Acts 2:1–13

3. What three signs accompanied the outpouring of the Holy Spirit? (See 2:2–4.)
   a. A sound from heaven as of a rushing mighty wind filled the house.
   b. Cloven tongues like fire sat on each of the disciples.
   c. The disciples began to speak in other languages.

4. It appears that the disciples went out into the streets soon after the outpouring of the Spirit and started telling people about the wonderful works of God.
   a. Why was the day of Pentecost an ideal time for the Spirit to enable the disciples to speak in many languages at Jerusalem?   Visitors from many countries had come for Pentecost.

   b. In what two ways did the onlookers react to the marvelous things that were happening? _____
      Some people were amazed, but others mocked.

The more God and His work are exalted, the more the enemies of God oppose God's people. When the disciples of Jesus spoke in different languages, some people accused them of being drunk.

5. Peter said that it was too early in the day to be drunk. Which statement below gives another reason why drunkenness was not a sensible explanation for what had happened to the disciples?
   a. The disciples were too poor to buy enough wine to make 120 people drunk at the same time.
   b. Drunk people talk nonsense, but the disciples were talking in understandable languages.

Peter's Sermon

When Peter heard what the crowds were saying, he realized that someone needed to tell them what was taking place. The Holy Spirit moved him to preach a sermon, and he pointed out to the crowd that the Old Testament prophets had predicted the things that were happening.

- Acts 1:15–26 illustrates a number of principles for choosing leaders. The leaders of a unified group of believers recognized the need for an additional leader, and they stated a Scriptural basis for choosing one. After considering the qualifications for this office, the group nominated two from among themselves. Then they humbly submitted the final choice to God through the use of the lot.

- Probably most of them understood at least some Greek, but it was a special blessing for them to hear the Gospel in their mother tongues.

---

bush: "I am . . . the God of Abraham, the God of Isaac, and the God of Jacob."

8. Why does Jesus want His followers to observe Communion? [L. 23] **to remind them of His suffering and death**

In This Lesson

Scope: Acts 1:1–4:31

Focus

- The church was born on the day of Pentecost.
  —While the disciples waited for the Holy Spirit, God revealed through the lot that Matthias was to take Judas's place as an apostle.

—The Holy Ghost came upon the believers on the day of Pentecost. Three thousand souls responded to Peter's message, and they were added to the church through baptism.

—Through Jesus' power, Peter and John healed a lame man at the temple. This opened another opportunity for Peter to preach, and many more souls believed.

—The Jewish leaders arrested Peter and John for preaching in the temple, but they feared to harm them because the miracle was widely known. The apostles' words and actions before the council proved that they had been with Jesus.

Acts 2:14–21, 36–40

6. It was dangerous to speak publicly about Jesus in Jerusalem. Only seven weeks had passed since the Jews had crucified Jesus. How had Peter changed since receiving the Holy Spirit? _____
   Peter had become zealous for Jesus, preaching boldly in spite of personal danger.

7. What reason did Peter give to explain why the disciples were speaking in other languages? _____
   God had poured out His Spirit on His servants (as He had prophesied through Joel).

8. What had Joel prophesied concerning all those who would call on the Name of the Lord? _____
   They would be saved.

9. a. According to 2:37, what happened to the people when they heard Peter speak? _____
   They were pricked in their hearts.

   b. What did Peter tell them they should do? repent and be baptized

The Birth of the Church

Peter's sermon had dramatic results. The Holy Spirit moved mightily among the people, and many believed in Jesus that day. The new church was experiencing a powerful beginning.

Acts 2:41–47

10. About (a) ___three thousand___ people who repented and believed were (b) ___baptized___ .

11. The baptized converts continued steadfastly in the apostles' (a) ___doctrine___ and (b) ___fellowship___ , in breaking of (c) ___bread___ , and in (d) ___prayers___ .

12. The first Christians sold their (a) ___possessions___ and (b) ___goods___ , and distributed them to all men as every man had (c) ___need___ .

13. According to Acts 4:34, what was the result of the Christians' willingness to share their possessions with each other? None of them lacked anything they needed.

A Miracle in the Temple

Some time later, Peter and John went to the temple one afternoon. Here they met a lame man begging at the gate. As a result of this encounter, many more people became believers.

Acts 3:1–14

14. Peter asked the lame man to look at him. The lame man expected Peter and John to give him (a) ___money (alms)___ , but Peter said he had no silver or gold. Instead, Peter told him to (b) " rise up and walk ."

15. How did Peter make it clear to the lame man that he was not doing the miracle by his own power?
    He said, "In the name of Jesus Christ of Nazareth rise up and walk."

16. When the people saw the lame man (a) ___walking___ and (b) ___leaping___ and (c) ___praising God___ , they were filled with (d) ___wonder___ and (e) ___amazement___ .

17. Peter made use of the opportunity to speak to the crowd about ___Jesus___ .

• Probably most of the first converts who were baptized into the early church were devout Jews who had a knowledge of the Scriptures and had been worshiping God under the Old Testament Law. Many may have heard Jesus' teachings. They quickly responded after hearing the Gospel message and seeing evidence of the Holy Spirit's power working through the apostles.

Other answers are also possible.

Objectives

• Students should know
   —how the believers determined who should be ordained in Judas's place. (*They chose two men, and then they cast lots to determine which one was God's choice.*)
   —what the believers began to do after they were filled with the Spirit. (*speak in other languages*)
   —which Old Testament prophet had foretold the outpouring of the Holy Spirit. (*Joel*)
   —what Peter told the people to do after they were convicted on the day of Pentecost. (*repent and be baptized*)
   —how many believers were added to the church on the day of Pentecost. (*about three thousand*)
   —how the early church at Jerusalem provided for the needs of its members. (*Those who had possessions sold them, and the money was distributed according to everyone's needs.*)
   —what the lame man did after Peter and John healed him. (*walked, leaped, and praised God*)
   —what part of the apostles' message especially upset the Jewish leaders. (*their preaching about the resurrection through Jesus' power*)
   —the definition of *remission*. (*forgiveness; pardon*)
   —the name of the large outer temple court that anyone could enter. (*the court of the Gentiles*)

The Apostles' Testimony

It was impossible to deny that a miracle had taken place. The people of Jerusalem recognized the man who had been lame for more than forty years. As a result, many believed Peter's message. But the Jewish leaders were upset at the preaching and arrested Peter and John.

Acts 4:1–13

18. The opposition to Peter and John's preaching came from the priests, the captain of the temple, and the Sadducees.

   a. What part of the apostles' message was especially displeasing to them? _____

      The apostles were preaching through Jesus the resurrection from the dead.

   b. Why would this point have upset the Sadducees more than some other teachings of the apostles? _____

      The Sadducees denied that there was a resurrection from the dead.

19. How did Peter's and John's life and speech show that they had been with Jesus? _____

   Peter and John boldly testified about Jesus, even though they were "unlearned and ignorant men."

B. BIBLE WORD STUDY

Choose the ending that best explains the meaning of the words in italics.

1. The people were *confounded* when they heard the disciples speak in many languages (Acts 2:6). In other words, they were
   (a.) astonished and bewildered.   b. angry and upset.   c. eager and excited.

2. When Peter preached on the day of Pentecost, those who heard him were *pricked in their hearts* (Acts 2:37). This means
   a. they felt physical pain in their hearts.
   (b.) they felt guilty because of their sins.
   c. they became upset at what Peter was saying to them.

3. When Peter explained to the multitude how to find *remission* of sins (Acts 2:38), he was telling them how to
   a. acknowledge their sins.
   b. be able to pay for their sins.
   (c.) find forgiveness or pardon for their sins.

4. Peter told the multitude to save themselves from this *untoward generation* (Acts 2:40). By this he meant they should separate themselves from
   a. Jews who had stopped attending temple services.
   b. anyone who was young and uncooperative.
   (c.) the disobedience and corruption of the people around them.

5. The new converts served God with *singleness of heart* (Acts 2:46). This means that they
   a. decided they would never get married.
   (b.) served God sincerely, putting Him first in all things.
   c. were afraid to disobey the apostles.

Truths to Amplify

- The disciples displayed many faults during the years of Jesus' ministry. Sometimes they were faint-hearted. Sometimes they were proud and tried to determine who would be the greatest. Even during Jesus' trial, death, and resurrection, the disciples failed in numerous ways. But after Pentecost, they suddenly changed. Instead of denying Jesus, Peter now spoke boldly about Him to as many people as he could. Instead of hiding behind closed doors, the disciples went everywhere preaching the Gospel.

    What made the difference? The transforming power of the Holy Spirit in their lives! Only those who have experienced the New Birth can comprehend this change.

6. The lame man expected Peter and John to give *alms* to him (Acts 3:3). He thought they would
   a. give him some money.　　　b. have some medicine for him.　　c. heal him of his affliction.

7. While Peter and John were preaching, the guard came and *put them in hold* (Acts 4:3). In other words, they
   a. told them to stop talking.　　　b. put them in prison.　　　c. beat them with rods.

C. THINKING ABOUT BIBLE TRUTHS

Facing Opposition

Christians have faced opposition ever since the church began. This opposition comes in various ways, but every generation has faced it in one form or another. However, most opposition to truth comes in one of two forms.

1. Read 2 Corinthians 11:14. Sometimes Satan attacks the church in the form of *an angel of light*. Which of the following statements best describes this method?
   a. Satan appears in churches as an angel and openly tries to persuade Christians to disobey God. Those who think he is an angel listen to him and are deceived into sin.
   b. Satan works through false teachers who appear to be good, righteous people. Some Christians are deceived by these false teachers and accept their false doctrine.

2. Read 1 Peter 5:8. This verse says that Satan attacks the church as *a roaring lion*. Which of the following statements best describes this method?
   a. Satan sends ungodly people to threaten, hurt, imprison, or kill Christians. This frightens some Christians into giving up their faith.
   b. Satan sends ungodly people to tempt Christians by telling them that they are missing much fun by following God. Some Christians are snared by the love of pleasure and lose their faith.

3. Sometimes Satan uses one method, and at other times he uses the other method in his attempt to destroy the church. He can also use both methods at the same time. Revelation 2:13, 14 mentions both of them.
   a. Which verse describes Satan working as an angel of light? ___verse 14___
   b. Which verse describes Satan working as a roaring lion? ___verse 13___

4. a. Try to find an example from church history or from the Bible illustrating how Satan attacks the church as a roaring lion. Briefly describe the event. _____
   (Individual answers) _____
   _____
   _____

   b. Try to find an example from church history or from the Bible illustrating how Satan attacks the church as an angel of light. Briefly describe the event. _____
   (Individual answers) _____
   _____
   _____

5. Which method did Satan use against the disciples in this lesson? ___He attacked as a roaring lion.___
   _____

D. LEARNING MORE ABOUT BIBLE TIMES

Herod's Magnificent Temple

Read the following information and complete the exercises.

Visitors to Jerusalem in New Testament times never failed to be impressed by the temple. Josephus writes that its white marble structure, trimmed in gold, glistened like a snow-capped mountain in the sun.

Herod's temple was enormous. He spent many years building the temple mount and the buildings upon it. Ten thousand workmen labored under the direction of one thousand priests. They used a thousand carts to haul great stones from surrounding quarries. Retaining walls of rectangular stones lined the mount on which the temple stood. On the outside, these walls were more than 100 feet high in places. The low spots inside the walls had been filled in to make the area level for the temple courts and buildings. Many huge, costly stones were used in building the walls and the temple. According to Josephus, some stones were as much as 45 cubits (60 feet) long, 5 cubits (7½ feet) high, and 6 cubits (9 feet) wide. Some of the large stones from the foundation of the wall have been found in modern times.

East and west of the temple mount, bridges crossed the valleys and led to the gates. On the southwest corner was a great set of steps leading to the lower city. Porticos (porches with roofs supported by columns) surrounded the outer court. The south porch, called the Royal Portico, was larger and more splendid than those on the other sides.

Three courts surrounded the temple itself: the court of the Gentiles, where anyone could enter; the court of women, where both Jewish men and women could enter; and finally the inner court, where only priests and Jewish men worshiped God.

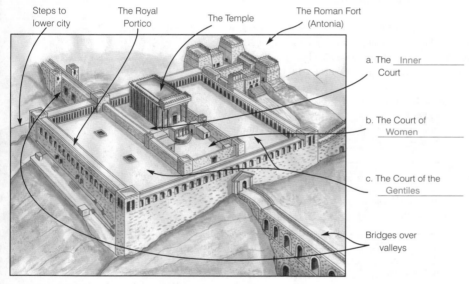

Steps to lower city   The Royal Portico   The Temple   The Roman Fort (Antonia)

a. The __Inner__ Court

b. The Court of __Women__

c. The Court of the __Gentiles__

Bridges over valleys

"Walk about Zion, and go round about her: tell the towers thereof.
Mark ye well her bulwarks, consider her palaces" (Psalm 48:12, 13).

1. Label the three courts in the diagram.

2. The Beautiful Gate of the temple was probably the eastern gate, leading into the women's court. Whom did Peter and John meet here? (Acts 3:2–7)   the lame man

3. Jesus and the apostles often taught in Solomon's Porch, which was part of the portico that surrounded the temple courtyard. It may have been the eastern portico, or it may have been another name for the Royal Portico. Why did a crowd gather in Solomon's Porch while Peter and John were at the temple? (Acts 3:11)   They saw that Peter and John had healed the lame man.

4. At the northeast corner of the temple courtyard stood the Roman fort (castle). Which apostle was saved from a mob by a band of soldiers who ran down the steps from the fort? (Acts 21:30–32)
Paul

The Destruction of the Temple

Less than one hundred years after King Herod rebuilt the temple, the Romans destroyed it. They burned and smashed the magnificent buildings on the mount. They broke down the bridges and completely destroyed the place where the temple had stood. Only the lower level of the retaining wall between the western bridge and the great southwestern staircase was left to show people where the temple had stood. This section is now called the Wailing Wall or Western Wall. (See the photograph on page 184.) The Jews paid dearly for their rebellion against God.

210

Lesson 27. The Gospel Spreads Throughout Palestine

We may think that most Jews were like the Pharisees and Sadducees who opposed Jesus. However, there were many Jews in Palestine and in other countries who feared God and sincerely desired to serve Him. It was partly because of these Jews that the early church grew so rapidly. Since these devout Jews were already following God to the best of their knowledge, they were open to the Holy Spirit's call to become part of the new church.

Thousands of these God-fearing Jews, long tired of the hypocrisy and narrow-mindedness that had overtaken their religion, rejoiced to hear the Gospel. Included in this multitude of believers was a great company of priests (Acts 6:7). The Gospel message, accompanied by special miraculous signs, became more powerful every day.

It is true that many Jews rejected the Gospel and turned against the early Christians. Still, many who felt no special attraction to the Gospel must have found it difficult to argue against the facts. Thousands had seen the darkness and had felt the earthquake the day Jesus died. The supernatural tearing of the temple veil could not have been kept a secret, especially among the priests. And most Jews around Jerusalem had very likely heard rumors about Jesus' resurrection.

This lesson shows how the Gospel moved beyond Jerusalem into the surrounding regions. In light of everything Jesus had said and done in Palestine, it is not surprising that the Gospel spread rapidly there.

- To avoid making this lesson too full, the events mentioned in Acts 12 are not covered. This passage could be used in a devotional period.

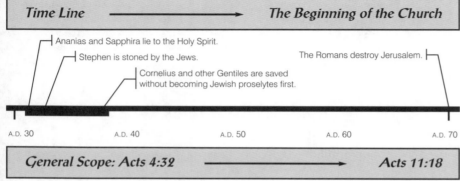

Time Line ⟶ **The Beginning of the Church**

| Ananias and Sapphira lie to the Holy Spirit. |
| Stephen is stoned by the Jews. |
| The Romans destroy Jerusalem. |
| Cornelius and other Gentiles are saved without becoming Jewish proselytes first. |

A.D. 30   A.D. 40   A.D. 50   A.D. 60   A.D. 70

General Scope: Acts 4:32 ⟶ **Acts 11:18**

Note: We do not know exactly when the events covered in this lesson happened. Herod Agrippa I died in A.D. 44, and the events in this lesson probably took place before then. (See Acts 12:23.)

Using the Time Line

1. Which event on the time line shows that Satan was still bringing opposition to the church from without? _Stephen is stoned by the Jews._

2. Which event shows that Satan was starting to bring opposition from within the church? _____
   Ananias and Sapphira lie to the Holy Spirit.

Lesson 27

Oral Review

1. To what two people did the angel Gabriel appear? Where did he appear to each? [L. 2] **Gabriel appeared to Zacharias in the temple at Jerusalem; he appeared to Mary in Nazareth.**

2. When a sick man was lowered through the roof, what did Jesus do to prove to the Jews that He could forgive sins? [L. 7] **He healed him.**

3. Why did Jesus teach in parables? [L. 12] **so that only those who believed would understand**

4. People had various ideas about who Jesus was.

Who did Peter say Jesus is? [L. 16] **the Christ, the Son of the living God**

5. What was the charge on which the Jewish leaders condemned Jesus when they tried Him? [L. 24] **blasphemy**

6. What promise did the angels give the disciples after Jesus had ascended into heaven? [L. 25] **He will return in a manner similar to the way He had left.**

7. When the people were pricked in their hearts on the day of Pentecost, what did Peter tell them to do? [L. 26] **repent and be baptized**

8. Define *remission*. [L. 26] **forgiveness, pardon**

A. ANSWERS FROM THE BIBLE

Ananias and Sapphira—a Couple Who Lied to the Spirit

Among the first believers, it became a common display of love to sell one's possessions and give the proceeds to the church. This money was used in caring for the needy. The Bible does not record that the early church ever required this sacrifice of its members. Rather, it seems to have been a totally voluntary gesture.

Acts 5:1–11

1. Verse 1 tells us that Ananias and Sapphira sold a possession.
   a. What possession did they sell? a piece of land
   b. What did they decide to do with the money they received?
      They decided to give part of the money to the church and to keep part of it.
2. What might have motivated them to pretend that they were giving all the money they had received? (Individual answers)

3. Which of the following statements best summarizes the sin of Ananias and Sapphira?
   a. They were guilty of lying because they pretended to give all the money when they gave only part of it.
   b. They were guilty of stealing because they kept money for themselves that really belonged to God.
   c. They were guilty of murder because they each helped cause the other's death by their mutual support.
4. Ananias and Sapphira's sin was a tragedy among the early believers. In spite of this, how did God's swift judgment on their sin work for the good of the church?
   Many people feared God when they saw what had happened to Ananias and Sapphira.

Peter and John—Leaders Who Obeyed God

The church continued to grow rapidly during this time. People from surrounding cities soon realized that God had given special powers to the apostles, and they came flocking to Jerusalem to be healed. This greatly upset the Jewish leaders. They had hoped to eliminate Jesus' threat to their system by persuading Pilate to crucify Him. Now they discovered that the threat was multiplied in the apostles and their new followers, for the Gospel message exposed them as murderers of the Messiah. They decided to take action against the new movement and its leaders before the threat became even greater. But God worked a miracle for the apostles that clearly showed the Jewish leaders how little power they had over Jesus' followers.

Acts 5:17–41

5. What miracle did God perform for the apostles in this passage?
   He sent an angel to release them from prison.
6. The Jewish leaders had commanded the apostles to stop preaching about Jesus, but the apostles had continued to preach the Gospel anyway. What good reason did the apostles give for disobeying the Jewish leaders? "We ought to obey God rather than men."

Discuss with the students some reasons why Ananias and Sapphira might have done what they did. Did they want the praise of men? Were all the "best" people selling their land, and they wanted the glory that would go with such a sacrifice? And further, how might we be guilty of similar sins?

A careful reading of verses 3 and 4 makes it clear that the sin was in the lying, not in keeping the money. Peter said plainly that the land and the money were theirs (not God's). He did not rebuke them for keeping part of the money, but for false representation.

Be sure the students understand this. Some people have tried to use this account as a basis for teaching that God requires His people to practice a community of goods. That is an incorrect interpretation of this passage. Community of goods is not necessarily wrong, and it might even be desirable in certain situations, but the Bible does not require it.

Be sure students understand that the apostles were not rebelling against authority, but instead they were obeying God rather than men when the decrees of men opposed the commands of God.

In This Lesson

Scope: Acts 4:32–8:40; 9:32–11:18

Focus

- The Gospel spread throughout Palestine despite opposition from within and without the church.
  —Ananias and Sapphira lied to the Holy Ghost and were struck dead because of it.
  —The Jewish leaders arrested the apostles, but an angel freed them from prison. After finding the apostles preaching in the temple again, the leaders took counsel to kill them, but Gamaliel advised them to refrain.
  —The church ordained seven deacons to care for

material needs among the members.
  —The Jews rose up against Stephen and stoned him.
  —Philip ministered to the Samaritans and to the Ethiopian eunuch.
  —The Holy Spirit directed Peter to Cornelius. The Jews were surprised to see the Holy Spirit fall on the believing Gentiles just as He had fallen on them.

7. The Jewish leaders were so upset by Peter's answer that they decided to kill the apostles. Then Gamaliel, an important teacher among them, gave the council some advice.

a. What did Gamaliel say would happen to the new movement if God was not with it? _____
   It would come to nothing.

b. What warning did Gamaliel give the Jewish leaders?   If the movement was of God, they would
   not be able to overthrow it, because they would be fighting against God.
   _____

8. The Jewish leaders heeded Gamaliel's words and let the apostles go, but first they beat them and gave them another warning. How did the apostles respond to the beating and threats? _____
   They rejoiced that God considered them worthy to suffer shame for Him.

Stephen—the First Martyr

Even though the Jewish leaders had listened to Gamaliel's advice, Satan was still busy stirring up opposition against the new church. These verses describe how the church faced problems from inside as well as outside. The Grecians of Acts 6:1 were Greek-speaking Jews.

Acts 6

9. a. What problem did the church face from within?   The Grecians (Greek-speaking Jews) felt that
      their widows were being neglected by the Hebrews (Hebrew-speaking Jews).

   b. What solution did the apostles propose to take care of this need?   They said seven men should
      be appointed by the group to make sure that such needs were properly cared for.

   c. What would we call these seven men today? (See 1 Timothy 3:8–13.)   deacons

10. Stephen was one of the men chosen by the congregation at this time.

    a. How does this passage describe Stephen?
       He was a man full of faith and power who did great wonders and miracles among the people.

    b. Why were the unbelieving Jews frustrated in their dispute with Stephen? _____
       They were not able to resist the wisdom and spirit by which he spake.

11. How did those of the synagogue of the Libertines manage to turn the people against Stephen?
    The Libertines said they had heard Stephen speak blasphemous words against Moses and against
    God. (They also set up false witnesses.)

Acts 7:54–60

Stephen's enemies brought him before the council (Sanhedrin) for judgment. There he preached a powerful sermon that portrayed how God had worked with the Jews since the time of Abraham (Acts 7:1–53). He also showed the Jews how they and their fathers had resisted and rejected God by their actions. Stephen's words pierced deep into the men's hearts, and they seethed with rage against him.

12. What vision did Stephen see that upset the Jews even more? _____
    He saw heaven opened and Jesus standing on the right hand of God.

13. The Jewish Sanhedrin had no authority from the Romans to execute criminals. It may have been the Jews from the synagogue of the Libertines who led out in mobbing Stephen. However, it does not seem that the Sanhedrin tried to protect him. How did the mob kill Stephen? _____
    They stoned him to death.

- This Gamaliel is mentioned in Acts 22:3 as Paul's teacher.

- Gamaliel's reasoning that a movement will prosper only if it is of God was valid in the case of the apostles, but this is not always true. Some false teachers, such as Muhammad, have gained large followings. Nevertheless, truth will ultimately triumph, and those who fight against it will be found fighting against God. "If God be for us, who can be against us?" (Romans 8:31).

Objectives

- Students should know
  —what sin Ananias and Sapphira committed. (*They lied to the Holy Spirit.*)
  —on what occasions the apostles refused to obey the Jewish leaders. (*when the leaders commanded them to stop preaching about Jesus*)
  —who advised the Jewish leaders not to kill the apostles. (*Gamaliel*)
  —what the apostles did after they were beaten and threatened. (*They rejoiced to be counted worthy to suffer for Jesus and continued to preach.*)
  —why the church chose seven men to help the apostles. (*The Grecian widows were not being properly cared for.*)
  —what Stephen's last words were. (*"Lord, lay not this sin to their charge."*)
  —who preached the Gospel to the Samaritans. (*Philip*)
  —why Philip left Samaria in the midst of a revival. (*God sent him south to help an Ethiopian eunuch.*)
  —how God prepared Peter for Cornelius's request for help. (*by sending a vision and telling him to go with the men whom Cornelius had sent*)
  —how Peter knew that Cornelius and his friends had received the Holy Spirit. (*They spoke with tongues.*)

Lesson 27. The Gospel Spreads Throughout Palestine **213**

14. a. What were Stephen's last words? "Lord, lay not this sin to their charge."

___

    b. What does this show us about Stephen? Like Jesus, he was concerned about those who killed

    him, and he desired their salvation. (He was forgiving.)

___

Philip—a Missionary for God

After the martyrdom of Stephen, the persecution quickly spread. Many men and women were put into prison, and many Christians left Jerusalem to avoid the persecution. Philip, another of the seven deacons appointed earlier, traveled to Samaria and preached there.

Acts 8:4–8, 26–40

15. How did the people of Samaria respond to Philip's ministry? They gave heed to him (and had great joy).

___

___

16. Why did Philip leave Samaria? ___
An angel told him to go to the desert between Jerusalem and Gaza.

___

17. Philip must have thought it strange to leave Samaria during the great revival there, but God saw someone else who needed help.

    a. Whom did Philip meet in the desert? an Ethiopian eunuch

    b. Where did this man probably take the Gospel? to Ethiopia

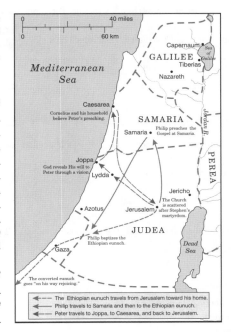

Cornelius—a Gentile Convert

Even during persecution, the church continued to grow. Acts 9 describes the conversion of Saul, the raising of Dorcas by Peter, and the growth of the church throughout Judea, Galilee, and Samaria. Up to this time all the converts had been either Jews or Jewish proselytes (Gentiles who had been converted to Judaism). But God did not intend for the new church to be composed only of Jews. When the time was right, He sent Peter to Cornelius.
Note: You will study the conversion of Saul in the next lesson.

Acts 10:1–27, 34, 35, 44–48

18. An angel told Cornelius to send for Peter. While the messengers were traveling, God sent an unusual vision to Peter to prepare him to accept the Gentiles.

    a. Why did Peter object to eating the animals in the sheet, in spite of his hunger and God's command to kill and eat? They were unclean animals that Jews were not to eat.

___

    b. What lesson was God trying to teach Peter by the vision? God would now accept the Gentiles
even though they had been considered unclean before this time. (After God had cleansed something, it was no longer unclean.)

—what Peter meant when he said that God is no respecter of persons. (*God does not accept or reject people on the basis of who they are.*)

Truths to Amplify

• Lying and other sins against God's Spirit and His church are very serious. God brought swift judgment upon Ananias and Sapphira as a warning to all who are tempted to corrupt the church for personal advantage. Although judgment usually does not fall so swiftly, unrepented sin will always bring the same consequences in the end.

• Prompt church discipline and careful attention to the needs of members can help prevent problems from becoming major hindrances to the church.

19. Cornelius was a Gentile who worshiped God, but evidently he had not become a Jewish proselyte. How did God show Peter that he should baptize Cornelius and his friends, even though they were Gentiles?   The Holy Spirit fell on them while Peter was speaking to them, and they spoke in tongues.

Acts 11:1–4, 18

20. The Jewish Christians in Jerusalem voiced disapproval when they heard that Peter had visited Gentiles and preached to them.
    a. How did they respond after Peter had told them the whole story? (See Acts 11:18.) _____
       They held their peace and glorified God.
    b. What conclusion did the believers reach about the Gentiles? _____
       God had granted repentance to the Gentiles.

B. BIBLE WORD STUDY

Circle the letter of the ending that best shows what each italicized word means in the context of the verse. Use a dictionary or Bible dictionary if you need help.

1. Sapphira was *privy* to Ananias's plans (Acts 5:2). In other words, she
   a. was against his plans.
   b. was surprised at his plans.
   (c.) knew about his plans.

2. The high priest called the *senate* together to decide what to do with the apostles (Acts 5:21). This included
   (a.) the Sanhedrin and the elders of Israel.
   b. the Jewish rulers and the Roman governor.
   c. the Pharisees and the Essenes.

3. The Jews *suborned* men to speak against Stephen (Acts 6:11). This means that they
   a. forced the men to tell the truth about Stephen.
   b. forbade the men to witness against Stephen.
   (c.) persuaded the men to tell lies about Stephen.

4. Peter fell into a *trance* on the rooftop (Acts 10:10). He was
   a. sick and partly delirious.
   (b.) unaware of his surroundings, even though he was partly awake.
   c. sleeping and had a dream.

5. God is no *respecter of persons* (Acts 10:34). This means that He does not
   (a.) accept or reject people on the basis of who they are.
   b. love those who have rejected Him.
   c. have respect for Gentile people.

6. The Gentiles *prayed* Peter to *tarry* with them for several days (Acts 10:48). This means they
   a. worshiped Peter so that he would stay with them for a while.
   b. thought Peter was a god who could bless them.
   (c.) begged him to wait a few days before starting for home.

C. THINKING ABOUT BIBLE TRUTHS

Responding to Persecution

1. Read Acts 8:3, 4. Persecution is never pleasant, but sometimes it has good results. What took place in these verses as a result of the persecution in Jerusalem? _____
   The Christians who were scattered abroad preached the Gospel everywhere they went.
   _____

2. Read Hebrews 11:35–38. Persecution is not new for God's people. List some of the sufferings mentioned in these verses, which the Old Testament saints endured. >> _____
   They were tortured.
   They faced trials of cruel mockings and scourgings (beatings).
   They were bound and placed in prison.
   They were stoned, sawed apart, tempted, and killed with the sword.
   They wandered about dressed in animal skins, being destitute, afflicted, and tormented.
   They wandered in deserts, mountains, dens, and caves.

   Sample answers. Students should have some of these.

3. Read John 15:20 and 2 Timothy 3:12.
   a. Should God's people expect to be persecuted? _yes_ _____
   b. Why or why not? _Jesus was persecuted, so His followers should also expect to be persecuted._
      (Christians should not expect to be treated differently than Jesus was.)

4. Read the following passages, and write the instruction each gives about reacting to persecution.
   a. Matthew 5:10–12 _____
      Those who are persecuted for Jesus' sake should rejoice and consider themselves blessed.
   b. Matthew 5:44 _We are to pray for those who persecute us._
      _____
   c. Matthew 10:23 _When we are persecuted in one city, we should flee to another one._
      _____
   d. Romans 12:14 _We should bless those who persecute us._
      _____

5. Read 1 Timothy 2:1, 2. Sometimes people today think persecution would solve many problems in the church. Some even pray that the church would be persecuted. However, what do these verses tell us we should pray for instead of persecution? _____
   They tell us to pray that we might live a quiet and peaceable life in all godliness and honesty.
   _____

   Discuss this question in class. God's people will receive opposition. If Christians maintain the right attitude in persecution, God can use the opposition to strengthen and purify the church. However, these verses indicate that God's people should not ask for opposition. Church problems are caused by carnality, not the lack of persecution. Some of the church's worst problems have arisen during times of persecution.

D. LEARNING MORE ABOUT BIBLE TIMES

Palestine Under Military Control

After the Romans took charge of Palestine, the Jews lived with a new military presence. Roman soldiers stood watch at their street corners, paraded through their cities, and drilled on the pavement of the Fortress Antonia, right beside the temple. The main base for the Roman army in Palestine was in Caesarea, but some Roman soldiers were always stationed in Jerusalem. Roman soldiers had the right to make anyone carry their equipment for one mile.

During New Testament times, the Roman army was divided into legions that numbered up to six thousand men. Each legion was normally divided into ten divisions, or cohorts, of about six hundred men. Each of these divisions was under the command of a chief captain.

1. On what occasion did a chief captain in Jerusalem save the apostle Paul's life? (Acts 21:30, 31) _____
   when a mob of angry Jews seized Paul in the court of the temple
   _____

2. In our English Bibles, a cohort is referred to as a band. To what band did Cornelius belong? (Acts 10:1)   the Italian band
_____

Each cohort was divided into three maniples. Maniples were divided further into two groups called centuries. Centuries originally numbered one hundred men and were commanded by centurions.

3. On what occasion did a Roman centurion exclaim that Jesus was truly the Son of God? _____
   at Jesus' crucifixion
_____

A Roman soldier was outfitted in armor similar to that worn by the man in the sketch. He usually carried a dagger, a double-edged sword, and a javelin (short spear). Various passages in the Bible use a soldier's dress or equipment to illustrate spiritual truths.

4. What items of a soldier's normal equipment does the writer of Ephesians 6:13–18 use as illustrations?   belt (girdle), breastplate, footwear, shield, helmet, sword
   _____
   _____

217

Lesson 28. The Gospel Spreads Through Asia

In the last lesson you saw how God spoke to the Jewish church through the conversion of Cornelius. This opened the way for many other Gentiles to become part of the church.

At that time, the city of Antioch was the third largest city in the Roman Empire. Here the first Gentile church was born. Its members apparently talked so much about Christ that people began calling them Christians.

Another important step toward bringing the Gospel to the Gentiles took place when Saul was converted. Saul had hated Christians and had led the first major persecution against the church. He had approved the stoning of Stephen and had stormed from house to house in Jerusalem, arresting every Christian he found. According to his own testimony, he caused some of those he arrested to be put to death.

But terrible as Saul's deeds were, God saw that Saul did not realize that he was working against Him. This lesson shows how God helped Saul to see his mistake and change from a violent persecutor of the Christians into a zealous missionary to the Gentiles.

Throughout their long history, the Israelites had known about God but had never freely shared this knowledge with their Gentile neighbors. But after God revealed that Gentiles could be saved through faith in Jesus, things were different. The Christians went everywhere, preaching God's Word to anyone who would hear. Missionaries such as Paul and Barnabas started churches wherever a group of believers turned to the Lord.

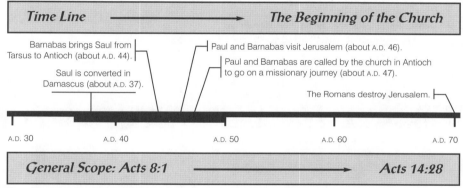

Time Line ——————→ **The Beginning of the Church**

Barnabas brings Saul from Tarsus to Antioch (about A.D. 44).

Paul and Barnabas visit Jerusalem (about A.D. 46).

Paul and Barnabas are called by the church in Antioch to go on a missionary journey (about A.D. 47).

Saul is converted in Damascus (about A.D. 37).

The Romans destroy Jerusalem.

A.D. 30   A.D. 40   A.D. 50   A.D. 60   A.D. 70

General Scope: Acts 8:1 ——————→ **Acts 14:28**

Note: The dates for events in Paul's life are approximate.

Using the Time Line

1. About how many years passed between Paul's conversion and his call to be a missionary? _____
   about ten years
2. Which event on the time line can be dated accurately? The Romans destroy Jerusalem.

Lesson 28

Oral Review

1. What name of Jesus refers to His humanity? to His deity? [L. 3] **Son of man; Son of God**
2. Why were the Pharisees very upset when Jesus healed on the Sabbath? [L. 8] **He was ignoring their Sabbath laws.**
3. In what way is the kingdom of heaven like the pearl of great price in the parable? [L. 12] **We need to give up everything to be part of God's kingdom, just as the man in the parable needed to sell everything he had to buy the pearl.**
4. Why did Martha become upset with her sister Mary? What did Jesus tell Martha? [L. 17] **Martha complained that Mary had left her to do all the work. Jesus told Martha that she was too concerned about serving and that Mary was doing what was most important.**
5. Who said he would not believe that Jesus had risen until he saw and touched His wounds? [L. 25] **Thomas**
6. What did the people in the upper room begin to do when they were filled with the Spirit? [L. 26] **They began to speak in other tongues (languages).**
7. What are two main ways that Satan attacks the

A. ANSWERS FROM THE BIBLE

Saul's Conversion

Seldom is there a bigger change in a man than the change that took place in Saul's life. In this passage we see what kind of person Saul was before his conversion and how God brought his ambitious plans to a sudden halt.

Acts 7:54–8:3; 9:1–9

1. How did Saul take part in Stephen's death? _____
   Saul consented to Stephen's death and watched over the clothing of those who stoned him.

2. Why did Saul persecute the church? (See Galatians 1:13, 14.) _____
   Saul was "exceedingly zealous of the traditions of [his] fathers."

3. Jesus revealed Himself to Saul in an unusual way on the road to Damascus. However, He did not force Saul to become a Christian.
   a. How did Jesus get Saul's attention? _____
      He caused a bright light from heaven to shine on Saul, and He called Saul's name.
   b. How did Saul's reaction prove that his attitude toward Jesus had changed? _____
      Saul responded, "What wilt thou have me to do?" (Before this he had done all he could to destroy
      Jesus' work. Now he was calling Him Lord and asking what he should do.)

4. Describe the contrast between the way Saul left Jerusalem and the way he entered Damascus.
   When Saul left Jerusalem, he was proud and angry. When he came to Damascus, he was humble and
   ready to do what God wanted him to do.

Acts 9:10–22

The Saul who reached Damascus was greatly changed from the proud, angry man who had left Jerusalem. Blind and humbled, he needed to be led by the hand into the city. His original mission in Damascus was forgotten. Now Saul was primarily interested in what God wanted him to do.

5. What did Saul do during his three days of blindness? _He prayed (and fasted)._

6. a. Why was Ananias afraid to go to Saul? _____
      He had heard that Saul persecuted Christians and that he had come to Damascus for that purpose.

   b. What reason did Jesus give Ananias for going anyway? _____
      Jesus said that He had chosen Saul to bear His Name before Gentiles, kings, and Jews.

7. Soon Saul was preaching about Jesus in the local synagogues. Why did this astonish the Jews so much? _They knew that he had come to Damascus to arrest Christians, but instead he was preaching
   about Jesus.

Saul Flees for His Life

Saul soon left Damascus and went to Arabia for three years (Galatians 1:15–18). Here he spent time studying the Old Testament Scriptures and learning more about God's plan for the New Testament church. After this he returned to Damascus and preached the Gospel to the Jews there. He was such a powerful influence for Christianity in Damascus that the Jews held a council to determine how to deal with him.

Note that Saul evidently believed he was serving God by persecuting the Christians. Discuss with the students how God honored Saul's sincere desire to serve Him by revealing greater truth to him. God will always reveal Himself to the sincere seeker.

---

church? [L. 26] **as an angel of light (deception from within), and as a roaring lion (persecution from without)**

8. What were Stephen's last words? [L. 27] **"Lord, lay not this sin to their charge."**

In This Lesson

Scope: Acts 8:1–3; 9:1–31; 13:1–14:28

Focus

• Saul was converted after seeing a vision on the way to Damascus.
   —He became as zealous in preaching the Gospel as he had formerly been in persecuting the church.

—Saul escaped from Damascus and Jerusalem when the unbelieving Jews tried to kill him.

• After praying and fasting, the church at Antioch sent out Barnabas and Saul on their first missionary journey.
   —Barnabas and Saul (who was hereafter called Paul) preached the Gospel and performed miracles on the island of Cyprus and in Asia Minor. Both Jews and Gentiles believed, but the unbelieving Jews stirred up persecution against the missionaries.
   —As Paul and Barnabas returned home, they visited the churches they had started and ordained elders in every church.

Acts 9:23–31

8. What did the Jews decide to do with Saul?   They decided to kill him.

9. How did Saul manage to escape from the Jews?
   The Christians lowered Saul over the city wall in a basket.

10. After his escape from Damascus, Saul traveled to Jerusalem and tried to join the disciples there.
    Why were the Christians at Jerusalem afraid of him at first?
    They did not believe that he actually was a Christian.

11. How did Saul finally manage to establish fellowship with the Jerusalem church?
    A man called Barnabas believed him and introduced him to the apostles.

Saul's former friends at Jerusalem were now his enemies. When he began to preach boldly about Jesus, they tried to kill him, just as he had once tried to destroy the church at Jerusalem. According to Saul's later testimony in Acts 22:17–21, he did not want to run away from his enemies. He probably felt that he deserved to suffer the same fate he had brought on others. But God instructed him to leave. He had other work for Saul to do. The Christians in Jerusalem took Saul to Caesarea and sent him back to Tarsus, his hometown.

12. a. What did the churches experience after Saul went to Tarsus?
       The churches had rest, were edified, and multiplied.

    b. (Challenge question) Why would the church have experienced less opposition after Saul left?
       (Sample answer) Probably the fact that Saul had once been a leader of the persecutors turned
       them against him. His presence fired up the persecution. After he left, the object of the enemies'
       personal antagonism was gone.

The First Missionary Journey

   Saul spent a number of years in Tarsus. During this time he preached the Gospel in the regions of Syria and Cilicia. While he was ministering there, the Gentile church in Antioch was born. The church at Jerusalem sent Barnabas to Antioch to oversee the new church. From Antioch, Barnabas went to Tarsus and brought Saul back to help him. The church in Antioch became a strong witness for Christ. It was this church that sent Barnabas and Saul on their first missionary journey. You can follow the course of this journey on the map in the last section of this lesson.

Acts 13:1–13

13. What did the believers at Antioch do to discern God's will?   They fasted and prayed.

14. Barnabas and Saul started their first missionary journey by sailing to the island of Cyprus. Here
    they met two men in the city of Paphos. One man was a Jew called Barjesus, or Elymas. He was a
    false prophet and magician who tried to withstand them. The other man was a local government
    official called Sergius Paulus. (Note that from this time on, Saul is called Paul.)
    a. What happened to Barjesus? Why?
       He was struck blind because he tried to withstand the work of God.
    b. How did Sergius Paulus respond when he heard Paul's message and saw God's judgment on
       Barjesus?   He believed (and was astonished at the doctrine of the Lord).

- Acts 9:31 might also be a general reference to the period of rest the church enjoyed after the conversion of Saul, the most zealous persecutor of Christians.

- Josephus states that Antioch "deserves the place of the third city in the habitable earth that was under the Roman empire, both in magnitude and other marks of prosperity" (Wars 3:2:4). The two greater cities were Rome and Alexandria.

- Soon after Paul and Barnabas started churches, they ordained local elders to guide the believers. Many of these early leaders were probably Jews or proselytes who had a knowledge of the Old Testament Scriptures before they were converted. (See 2 Timothy 3:15.) If God had not scattered the Jews throughout much of the world, it might have taken Paul and Barnabas much longer to establish stable churches among the Gentiles.

Objectives
- Students should know
  —how Saul participated in Stephen's death. (*He consented to it and kept the clothing of those who stoned Stephen.*)
  —what happened to Saul on the road to Damascus. (*He saw a light from heaven that blinded him. After falling to the ground, he heard Jesus speak to him.*)
  —who helped Saul at Damascus. (*Ananias*)
  —why Saul fled from Damascus and from Jerusalem. (*The unbelieving Jews tried to kill him after his conversion.*)

  —who sent Barnabas and Saul on their first missionary journey. (*the church at Antioch, under the direction of the Spirit*)
  —who tried to turn Sergius Paulus away from the faith. (*Barjesus, also known as Elymas*)
  —what the people of Lystra attempted to do for Paul and Barnabas. (*offer sacrifices to them*)
  —what the people of Lystra did to Paul after the unbelieving Jews stirred them up. (*stoned him*)
  —how Paul and Barnabas provided leadership for the churches they had started. (*They ordained elders in every church.*)

220   Chapter Six   God Calls a New People

Acts 14:1–20

Paul and Barnabas traveled on to Perga, and here John Mark, Barnabas's nephew, left them and returned to Jerusalem. From Perga they traveled to Antioch (in Pisidia), where they preached in the synagogue to the Jews. When the Jews turned against Paul and Barnabas, they preached to the Gentiles, and many turned to Christ. But the Jews stirred up opposition against Paul and Barnabas and drove them out.

From Antioch, Paul and Barnabas traveled to Iconium, Lystra, and Derbe. In Iconium many people believed, but again the missionaries were forced to leave because of persecution. In Lystra Paul was stoned and left for dead.

15. Why did the people of Lystra want to offer a sacrifice to Paul and Barnabas? _____

   They thought they were gods after Paul healed a lame man.

   _____

16. a. Why did the people of Lystra stone Paul? _____

      Some Jews from Iconium and Antioch stirred them up against Paul and Barnabas.

   b. The people of Lystra thought Paul was dead, but what happened? _____

      He rose up and went into the city. The next day he traveled on to Derbe.

Acts 14:21–28

From Lystra, Paul and Barnabas traveled on to Derbe. Here they preached to many people. Derbe was the turnaround point for this trip. On their way home, Paul and Barnabas stopped in the cities where they had started churches and helped to establish them more firmly in the faith.

17. Paul and Barnabas encouraged the new believers in each church as they returned home. What two specific things did they teach?

   a. They encouraged them to continue in the faith.

   b. They taught that we must enter the kingdom of God through much tribulation.

18. Paul and Barnabas were concerned that the churches they had founded would be able to continue even after they left. How did they provide leadership for the churches? _____

      They ordained elders in every church.

After returning home to Antioch, Paul and Barnabas gathered the church together to tell how God had worked through them in Asia and had brought many Gentiles to the faith.

B. BIBLE WORD STUDY

🍇 *Choose the ending that best defines the word or phrase in italics as it is used in the verse.*

1. Saul *made havock* (today spelled *havoc*) of the church (Acts 8:3). He was trying to
   a. confuse the church.
   (b) destroy the church.
   c. belittle the church.

2. Saul was *haling* men and women to prison (Acts 8:3). This means that he
   (a) dragged them.
   b. ordered them.
   c. accompanied them.

3. Jesus said that Saul was His *chosen vessel* to take the Gospel to the Gentiles (Acts 9:15). Saul was Jesus'
   a. ship.   (b) instrument.   c. follower.

- Iconium is now the large Turkish city of Konya. Archaeologists have confirmed that Iconium was one of the oldest urban centers in the world. It was an important city in Roman times, and it rose to even greater prominence under the Byzantines. After its capture by the Seljuk Turks, it became a world center of learning and the arts. Located in a narrow, fertile valley near the Taurus Mountains, Konya is becoming a tourist resort today.

- Lystra and Derbe have long ago disappeared. Lystra was apparently the hometown of Timothy (Acts 16:1, 2), although some people believe he was from Derbe (see Acts 20:4).

- Note the practice of ordaining a plural ministry to serve together.

Truths to Amplify

- God can save the worst enemies of the cross if they are willing to acknowledge their sin and repent. Paul experienced the conversion that he later taught: "If any man be in Christ, he is a new creature: old things are passed away; behold, all things are become new" (2 Corinthians 5:17).

- Paul's and Barnabas's willingness to suffer for Christ was a key to their effectiveness. When they were persecuted, they moved on if necessary, yet they continued to preach the Gospel wherever they went. Paul re-entered Lystra after the people had stoned him there, and he did not leave for Derbe until the next day. Later he returned to all the cities that he had visited, ordaining elders in each church.

Do we love God's kingdom enough to give our lives in His service?

4. When Saul came to Jerusalem, he *assayed* to join himself unto the disciples (Acts 9:26). He
   a. feared to join them.
   b. attempted to join them.
   c. looked forward to joining them.

5. Herod the *tetrarch* ruled part of Palestine (Acts 13:1). A tetrarch ruled
   a. one-fourth of a province.
   b. three-fourths of a province.
   c. one-half of a province.

6. A *sorcerer* named Barjesus opposed Barnabas and Saul (Acts 13:6). Sorcerers are people who
   a. accept bribes.
   b. teach false doctrine.
   c. use Satan's power.

7. Sergius Paulus was a *prudent* man (Acts 13:7). This means that he was a man who
   a. was often sick.
   b. had understanding.
   c. was proud.

C. THINKING ABOUT BIBLE TRUTHS

Fulfilling the Great Commission

The early church took the Great Commission very seriously. During the first hundred years of the church, the Christians spread the Gospel to most parts of the world known to them. The Great Commission is still an important teaching for the church today. Jesus expects His people to go to all the world with the message of salvation.

Matthew 28:19, 20; Acts 1:8

1. The disciples were to go to all the world, teaching and baptizing those who would listen to them.
   a. What were they to teach those who believed? _____
      to observe all the things that He had commanded them
      _____

   b. Why is it so important for new believers to be taught these things? _____
      They cannot remain Christians very long if they disobey God.

2. The Christian missionaries faced much opposition in some places they went. Where did they get the strength they needed to continue preaching the Gospel? _____
   They received their power from the Holy Spirit.

3. In early church times, missionaries often served on the mission field for life and never went home again. What reasons can you think of for this? _____
   (Sample answers. Accept other answers that show clear thinking.)
   Travel was slow, difficult, and dangerous.
   Persecution sometimes hindered the Christians from traveling.
   Long-term missionaries can provide stability for a growing church.

• Long-term missionaries still can provide stability for a growing church. However, God calls some missionaries to spread the Gospel quickly over large areas, as Paul and Barnabas did. It is important for churches to follow the Spirit's direction and for individuals to be willing to give long- or short-term service as God leads.

222   Chapter Six   God Calls a New People

D. LEARNING MORE ABOUT BIBLE TIMES

Paul's First Missionary Journey

This map shows the approximate route that Paul and Barnabas took on their first missionary journey, along with the main cities that they visited.

🍇 *Place the following letters at their correct places on the map to show where each event took place. The events are given in the order they happened.*

A. The church sends out Paul and Barnabas (Acts 13:1–4).

B. Barjesus is smitten with blindness (Acts 13:6–11).

C. John Mark leaves Paul and Barnabas and returns to Jerusalem (Acts 13:13).

D. Paul is invited to preach in a synagogue (Acts 13:14–41).

E. The people try to worship Paul and Barnabas, but later they stone Paul (Acts 14:8–20).

If the students do not write in their workbooks, they should either trace the map or do these exercises together in class, discussing the name and the location of the city where each event took place.

Travel by Land in Bible Times

Because of the difficulties of travel, people of Bible times preferred to stay near home. Most people made trips only when necessary for business or trade, for government affairs, or for important religious feasts. Pleasure trips were almost unknown. In this section you will see some difficulties Jesus and His apostles faced in their journeys.

Roads

Read Isaiah 40:3–5. Roads in the Middle East were poor in Old Testament times. Wooden-wheeled vehicles bumped mercilessly across long, stony stretches of rough road, or bogged down in mud. Before an important man such as a king or some other high-ranking government official arrived, workers repaired the roads. These verses compare the preparations for Jesus' coming to improving a road through the desert.

1. What types of road building and repair does the prophet mention? __making a straight highway in the desert, filling in holes and low places in the road (every valley shall be exalted), leveling out bumps in the road (every mountain and hill shall be made low), straightening the road, smoothing out the rough places__

The Persians built the first good roads through the Middle East. Wider, better chariot paths connected the far-flung provinces of their empire. But it still took three months to travel from Sardis, a city at the western end of their royal road, to Susa, their capital city.

2. a. Using a Bible atlas, find the approximate length of the Persian royal road that ran from Sardis to Susa. (Look in a Bible atlas for a map of the Persian Empire that shows the Persian royal road. *The Moody Atlas of Bible Times* and *Baker's Bible Atlas* both show this.) about 1,600 miles

   b. How many days would it take to travel this distance today at 500 miles a day? about three days

• For more information on travel in Bible times, see *The New Manners and Customs of Bible Times*.

Allow reasonable variation.

• It might interest the students to notice that we travel as far in a day as they did in a month!

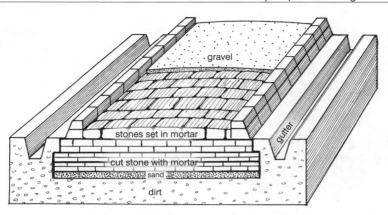

Cross Section of a Roman Roadbed

The Romans were the first to build excellent roads on a large scale in the Middle East. Most Roman roads were four layers deep and had drainage ditches on either side. The Roman network of roads included 50,000 miles of highways that reached from Spain to Arabia, and another 200,000 miles of secondary roads. Still, it took fifty-four days for couriers to travel from Rome to Caesarea in Palestine.

The Roman roads and bridges were so well built that some of them are still in existence today.

3. **On what road was the apostle Paul blinded by a light from heaven? (Acts 9:1–3)** _____

    on the road from Jerusalem (Palestine) to Damascus

The sketch on the right shows some ways that people traveled or sent messages in Bible times. Jesus and His apostles usually walked. Camels were used for desert travel.

Chariot   Oxcart Courier   Foot travel   Donkey

Common Means of Travel and Transportation

Accommodations for Travelers

There were no quiet motels or convenient restaurants for travelers in Bible times. People carried food with them on their journeys. At night they slept on the upper floors of noisy inns. Donkeys, mules, horses, and oxen stayed in open courtyards below.

4. **Many inns of Bible times were rough, sinful places. Where did Jesus tell His disciples to stay while they were on preaching trips? (Matthew 10:11–12)** _____

    in houses of the worthy (respectable) people of the towns they entered

_____

5. What choice did early Christians have other than staying in rowdy inns? (See 1 Peter 4:9; Hebrews 13:2.) _____

The early Christians stayed in one
another's homes while traveling.

_____

_____

_____

Courtyard of a Typical Inn

Hindrances to Travel

At special toll booths, travelers paid taxes on the goods they carried, a fee for each wheel or axle on their vehicles, and a certain amount for every person in their group. They were required to do this every time they entered a new taxation area.

It was also the custom for people meeting each other on the road to stop and ask each other's names, where they were going, how many children they had, and so forth. All this took time and made travel even slower.

Travel in Bible times was also dangerous. Bandits and highwaymen lived in the hills and made a living by robbing travelers. Because of these dangers, most people traveled in groups or caravans.

The apostle Paul traveled unusual distances for his time. One person calculated that the total distance of his trips recorded in the Bible is over 13,400 air miles (21,600 km). The actual distance would have been much greater because the distance by road from one place to another is often much farther than a straight line drawn on a map. Furthermore, Paul quite likely made some journeys that the Bible does not record.

6. The apostle Paul faced many dangers in his journeys. Read 2 Corinthians 11:26 and list three perils that he faced while traveling. _the sea (waters), the wilderness, and robbers_

_____

- However, people were expected to move on and not stay longer than two or three days at one place. See Proverbs 25:17.

- The other perils mentioned were not necessarily perils associated with traveling.

225

Lesson 29. The Gospel Spreads to Europe

In the last lesson you saw how the church reached out to the lost in Asia. There some Jews and many Gentiles responded to the call of the Gospel. But the command of Jesus was to go into all the world, and in this lesson you will see Paul reaching beyond Asia into Europe for the first time. Here he found other people who joyfully accepted the Gospel.

Even though Paul and Barnabas were great men of God, they were still human. They had a sharp disagreement before leaving on a second missionary journey. Barnabas wanted to take his nephew, John Mark, with them again. But Paul

did not think this was wise, since John Mark had deserted them on their first journey. Because of this, Barnabas took Mark and left for Cyprus, his homeland, and Paul took Silas with him.

But the spreading of the Gospel was not man's work. The Holy Spirit decided when and where it should be preached. Sometimes the Spirit told the Christians to go. At other times He told them to wait. As the early Christians learned to listen to the Holy Spirit, the church grew and prospered.

This lesson covers the second and third missionary journeys of Paul.

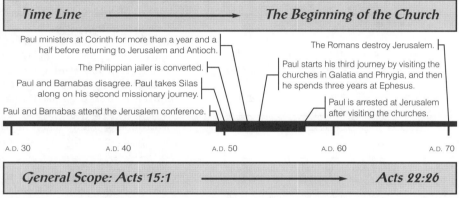

Note: The dates for events in Paul's life are approximate.

Using the Time Line

1. About when did the Jerusalem conference take place? _about A.D. 50_
2. About what year was Paul arrested? _about A.D. 57_

A. ANSWERS FROM THE BIBLE

The Second Missionary Journey

After the disagreement between Paul and Barnabas, they decided to go on separate trips. Barnabas and John Mark went to Cyprus, while Paul took Silas and traveled north through Syria and Cilicia. Paul had preached in Cilicia before coming to Antioch, and he probably had Christian friends to visit. He may have visited his home in Tarsus, as shown on the first map in this lesson. From here he retraced his way through Lystra, Derbe, and

Lesson 29

Oral Review

1. What message did John the Baptist preach? [L. 4] **"Repent ye: for the kingdom of heaven is at hand."**
2. Name the twelve disciples. [L. 9] **Simon Peter, Andrew, James, John, Philip, Bartholomew, Matthew, Thomas, James the son of Alphaeus, Simon Zelotes, Judas the brother of James, Judas Iscariot**
3. What reason did Jesus give for the blindness of the man whom He healed at Jerusalem? [L. 18] **"that the works of God should be made**

manifest in him"
4. In the parable of the marriage feast of the king's son, why did the invited guests not come to the feast? [L. 22] **They were too busy with things that they thought were more important. (Also, they failed to honor their king and his servants.)**
5. What sin did Ananias and Sapphira commit? [L. 27] **They lied to the Holy Spirit.**
6. How did Peter know that Cornelius and his Gentile friends had received the Holy Spirit? [L. 27] **They spoke with tongues (just as the Jewish believers had done on the day of Pentecost).**

Iconium, encouraging the churches he had started on his previous journey. At Lystra, Paul asked Timothy to join them. You can follow the course of this second missionary journey on the first map in the last section of this lesson.

The Macedonian Call

Paul wanted to preach the Gospel in many places, but at least twice the Holy Spirit stopped the group from going where Paul intended. Finally, while they were at Troas, the Holy Spirit revealed to Paul what the next step on the trip was to be.

Acts 16:5–34

1. How did God reveal to Paul where they were to go from Troas? _____
   A man of Macedonia spoke to Paul in a vision, asking him to come and help them.

2. Often Paul made his first contacts in a new place by preaching in the Jewish synagogue. However, no mention is made of a synagogue in Philippi. Perhaps not enough Jews lived in Philippi to establish one.
   a. How did Paul make contact with the few people of Philippi who believed in God? _____
      He joined a group of worshipers who had gathered by a river on the Sabbath.

   b. Who believed the message that Paul brought?   Lydia and her household

3. While Paul and Silas were in Philippi, a demon-possessed slave girl started following them, telling people that Paul and Silas were servants of the most high God. After many days of this, Paul finally cast the demon out of her.
   a. Why were the girl's masters upset with what Paul had done?   The masters could no longer
      make money from the girl's fortunetelling after the demon was cast out.

   b. What did the slave girl's masters do about their loss? _____
      They dragged Paul and Silas to the magistrates.

4. It appears that no official inquiry was made into Paul and Silas's doings. Instead, the magistrates and the crowd mobbed them, beat them, and threw them into prison.
   a. The discomfort of the stocks and the pain from their bruises may have been what kept Paul and Silas awake that night. What did they do at midnight?   They prayed and sang praises to God.
   b. What happened while they did this? _____
      There was a great earthquake that opened the prison doors and set the prisoners free.

5. In those days, a jailer was put to death if he allowed his prisoners to escape. When the Philippian jailer saw that the prison doors were open, he assumed that the prisoners had fled. He drew his sword to kill himself, but Paul stopped him. What question did the jailer ask Paul and Silas? ____
   "Sirs, what must I do to be saved?"

6. The Philippian jailer and his whole household were baptized that night. Some people use this incident to support the baptism of babies or immature children. However, what does 16:34 say which shows that all the members of the household were old enough to understand and receive the Gospel?   They all believed in God.
   _____

- It is possible that some Christians had already reached Europe before Paul and Silas received the Macedonian call. Since Rome was the capital of the Roman Empire, it seems quite likely that Christianity might have reached there earlier than many other areas. Jews from Rome were present at Jerusalem when the Holy Spirit was poured out (Acts 2:10). However, Paul's second missionary journey was the church's first organized mission effort to Europe. That part of Europe probably had almost no previous knowledge of Christianity.

- You might want to discuss with the students why the jailer asked such a seemingly unrelated question. Did he have prior knowledge of God? Had he heard of the message Paul and Silas were preaching, or of the slave girl's cry? Had he been listening to Paul and Silas's songs and prayers? We do not know, but something convicted him.

- Also note that Acts 16:32 says the missionaries preached to all in the house.

7. Who sent Barnabas and Saul on their first missionary journey? [L. 28] **the church at Antioch (through the leading of the Holy Spirit)**

8. How did Paul and Barnabas provide leadership for the churches that they helped to start? [L. 28] **They ordained elders in every church.**

In This Lesson

Scope: Acts 15:1–22:26

Focus

- Paul and Silas left Antioch on Paul's second missionary journey.
  —After passing through Asia Minor, Paul received a call from Macedonia.
  —In Philippi, Paul and Silas were thrown into prison after casting a demon out of a slave girl.
  —After God opened the prison with an earthquake, the Philippian jailer was converted.
  —Paul and his companions preached at Thessalonica, Berea, Athens, and Corinth.

- Paul returned to Jerusalem and Antioch and then began his third missionary journey.
  —Paul ministered in Ephesus for two years. While he was there, the silversmiths stirred up a riot against the Christians.
  —Paul visited the churches of Macedonia and Greece. On his return trip, he stopped at Troas,

Paul in Thessalonica and Berea

In the morning, the Philippian magistrates decided to release Paul and Silas. When the rulers learned that the missionaries were Roman citizens, they came in person to release Paul and Silas, and begged them to leave the city. After bidding the believers farewell, Paul and Silas traveled on to Thessalonica. Here they found a Jewish synagogue.

Acts 17:1–15

7. According to verse 4, some of the Jews in Thessalonica believed, along with a large number of the Greeks. This success was the cause of the next problems that Paul and Silas faced.

   a. Why did the Jews try to attack Paul and Silas? _____
     They were moved with envy at the missionaries' success.

   b. What three things did they accuse Paul and Silas of doing? _turning the world upside down,_
     doing contrary to Caesar's decrees, and saying that Jesus is king instead of Caesar

8. The Thessalonian believers sent Paul and Silas to Berea to escape the Jews. In Berea the missionaries again went into the Jewish synagogue and preached. What did the Berean Jews do that showed them to be more noble than most of the Thessalonian Jews? _They received the Word with_
readiness of mind and searched the Scriptures to see if what Paul and Silas preached was the truth.

Paul in Athens

In spite of the good response Paul and Silas received in Berea, trouble soon started. When the Thessalonian Jews heard of the success of the Gospel at Berea, they went there to stir up the people against Paul and Silas. The believers took Paul to Athens to escape the resulting turmoil. While Paul waited there for Timothy and Silas to join him, he preached in the synagogue and in the marketplace.

Athens was a city of philosophers. When these men heard of Paul's teachings, they brought him to their gathering place on Mars Hill and asked him to explain the doctrines he taught.

Acts 17:16–34

9. Paul had seen an altar in Athens dedicated to "The Unknown God." How did Paul use this altar to present Christ to the philosophers of Athens? _____
     He said he would declare to them the God that they were ignorantly worshiping.

Paul in Corinth

Only a few people of Athens believed the Gospel. Most people there did not have enough faith in God to accept the doctrine of the resurrection. Paul did not wait for Timothy and Silas, but moved on to Corinth, where they finally caught up with him again.

The missionaries found many people at Corinth who were interested in the Gospel. As usual, they first preached in the Jewish synagogue, but again the Jews opposed the work.

Acts 18:1–16

10. When the Jews refused the message of salvation, what did Paul tell them? _____
     Their blood would be on their own heads, and he would go to the Gentiles from then on.

11. What encouragement did Paul receive from the Lord while he was in Corinth? _____
     The Lord told Paul not to be afraid to speak, for He was with him, and no one would be able to harm
     him at Corinth.

where Eutychus fell from a window, and at Miletus, where he bade farewell to the Ephesian elders.

—Paul's third journey ended at Jerusalem, where the Jews tried to kill him. The Romans rescued him and held him in prison for trial.

Objectives

• Students should know
  —how Paul knew he should go to Macedonia. (*He had a vision of a man asking him to come.*)
  —why Paul and Silas were thrown into prison at Philippi. (*Paul cast an evil spirit out of a slave girl, making her unprofitable to her masters.*)

  —how God delivered Paul and Silas from prison. (*by sending an earthquake*)
  —what good came from Paul and Silas's imprisonment at Philippi. (*The jailer and his household were saved.*)
  —what the Jews of Berea did when they heard Paul and Silas's preaching. (*They searched the Scriptures daily to see if their teaching was true.*)
  —where Paul saw an altar to "The Unknown God." (*at Athens*)
  —where Demetrius stirred up a riot against Paul. (*at Ephesus*)
  —who fell out of a window at Troas while Paul was preaching. (*Eutychus*)

228   Chapter Six   God Calls a New People

12. Sometime later the Jews seized Paul and took him before Gallio, the deputy of that region. Why did Gallio refuse to judge Paul?   He did not want to be a judge of religious questions.

Paul was in Corinth for more than a year and a half. From there he traveled to Ephesus, where he again preached in the synagogue. However, he did not stay there long, because he wanted to go to Jerusalem for the next feast. From Jerusalem he returned to Antioch in Syria.

The Third Missionary Journey

After a short stay at Antioch, Paul started on his third missionary journey. He had promised the Ephesian church that he would return if it was the Lord's will, and that is where he headed. His journey took him through Galatia and Phrygia, where he visited the churches that he had established earlier.

Silas is not mentioned on this journey, but Timothy was with Paul for at least part of the trip. Apparently Luke, the author of Acts, was also with him during the last part of the journey, since he uses the pronoun *we* when talking of Paul's traveling party. A number of other brethren from various places in Asia and Europe also traveled with Paul at times.

Paul in Ephesus

Ephesus was an important city at the time the apostle Paul ministered there. The governor of the Roman province of Asia lived there, and many important trade routes of Asia passed through it. Ephesus was also the religious capital of the province, and the site of the temple of the goddess Diana. Because of the prominence of this city, everything of importance that happened there became known throughout the province of Asia. Thus, through Paul's preaching at Ephesus, the Bible tells us that "all they which dwelt in Asia heard the word of the Lord Jesus, both Jews and Greeks" (Acts 19:10). This is probably one reason why Paul stayed in Ephesus for two years.

Many people turned to Christ at Ephesus. But as in other places, success also brought opposition. Some people in Ephesus felt threatened by the new religion.

Acts 19:8–12, 21–41

13. For what two reasons were Demetrius and the other silversmiths of Ephesus upset with the success of Paul's preaching?   Their craft was endangered by the success of Christianity, and they feared that the goddess Diana would be despised and destroyed.

• Their loss of income was probably their primary concern.

14. The silversmiths stirred up a riot that swept through the city. Finally, after the mob had shouted for about two hours, the town clerk managed to quiet the crowd. What did he say the silversmiths should have done if they thought they were being wronged?   They should have taken the matter to the deputies and let them settle it in a lawful assembly.

Paul Returns to Jerusalem

After the riot, Paul left Ephesus and traveled into Macedonia, strengthening the churches there. He spent three months in Greece, probably visiting Corinth again. His life was threatened as he prepared to sail back home to Syria, so he retraced his steps through Macedonia, as shown on the second map in this lesson. At Troas he preached to the Christians, who had assembled for Communion and worship.

Acts 20:6–16

15. What happened to Eutychus while Paul was preaching at Troas?   He went to sleep and fell out of a window on the third floor.

16. Why did Paul bypass Ephesus on his way to Jerusalem?   He was trying to save time so that he could be at Jerusalem for Pentecost.

—where the Romans rescued Paul from the Jews. (*at Jerusalem*)

Truths to Amplify

• Jews scattered throughout the Roman Empire became the first recipients of the Gospel message. But in every city, the Gospel spread beyond the boundaries of Judaism to transform Gentiles who believed. People of Lycaonia, Phrygia, Greece, and now Latins in Europe all became part of the body of Christ.

• Paul taught that all true believers, whether Jew or Gentile, are "Abraham's seed, and heirs according to the promise." The meaning of passages such as Galatians 3:28, 29; Ephesians 2:11–14; and Colossians 3:9–11 becomes clear in light of the context in which Paul wrote these epistles.

Paul's Arrest

Paul must have sensed that trouble lay ahead. When he called for the elders of Ephesus to meet him at Miletus, he told them that the Holy Spirit had revealed that bonds and afflictions awaited him. He did not expect to ever see them again.

Paul landed at Tyre on his way to Jerusalem. At Caesarea a prophet called Agabus warned him that if he went to Jerusalem, he would be bound by the Jews and handed over to the Gentiles. Paul's friends tried to persuade him not to go to Jerusalem, but he would not change his mind.

When Paul reached Jerusalem, he met with James and the elders. They asked him to take part in a purification ceremony at the temple with four other Jewish Christians. This would prove to people in Jerusalem that he was still faithful to the Law of Moses. While Paul was in the temple, some Jews from Asia recognized him.

Acts 21:27–40

17. a. How did the Jews of Asia begin an uproar against Paul in Jerusalem? _____

They cried out that Paul taught against the Jews, the Law, and the temple, and that he had polluted the temple by bringing Greeks into it.

b. Why did they think that Paul had polluted the temple? They had seen Paul with Trophimus, an Ephesian, in the city; and they supposed that Paul had brought him into the temple.

The Romans rescued Paul from the rioters, who were intent on killing him just as rioters had killed Stephen about twenty-five years before. While Paul was being taken to the Roman fortress, he asked the chief captain for permission to address the people. He told them the story of his conversion to Christianity, and they listened until he said that God had called him to go to the Gentiles.

Acts 22:22–29

The chief captain was confused. He could not understand why the mob was so determined to kill Paul, so he told his men to scourge Paul in an attempt to make Paul tell why the crowd was so angry with him.

18. Why did the chief captain change his mind about scourging Paul? _____

Paul told him that he was a Roman citizen. It was illegal to beat an uncondemned Roman citizen.

B. BIBLE WORD STUDY

 Choose the best ending to explain the meaning of each italicized word or phrase.

1. In Philippi, Paul met a girl with a *spirit of divination* who practiced *soothsaying* (Acts 16:16). This girl had
   a. a demon that enabled her to predict the future.
   b. a charming personality that helped her to comfort the grieving.
   c. an unusual ability to heal the sick.

2. When Paul and Silas were cast into prison, their feet were fastened in *stocks* (Acts 16:24). Their feet were
   a. bound together with ropes.   b. chained to each other.   c. fastened in a wooden frame.

3. Paul reasoned from the Scriptures in the Jewish synagogues, *alleging* that Christ arose from the dead (Acts 17:3). He was
   a. explaining how Christ rose from the dead.
   b. showing why Christ rose from the dead.
   c. confirming that Christ rose from the dead.

230   Chapter Six   God Calls a New People

4. Some of the Jews *consorted* with Paul and Silas (Acts 17:4). These Jews
   a. joined themselves to Paul and Silas.
   b. disputed with Paul and Silas.
   c. plotted against Paul and Silas.

5. The unbelieving Jews persuaded some *lewd fellows of the baser sort* to set the city in an uproar and to attack the house where they thought Paul was staying (Acts 17:5). These people were
   a. loud and boisterous men.
   b. wicked men of the lowest class.
   c. large, muscular men.

6. The authorities of Thessalonica *took security* of Jason and those with him (Acts 17:9). This means Jason and the others needed to
   a. pay money to guarantee their future good behavior.
   b. leave the city immediately to avoid being put into prison.
   c. promise that they would not attend any more Christian services.

7. The Epicureans and Stoicks (today spelled *Stoics*) whom Paul met at Athens were *philosophers* (Acts 17:18). Philosophers are men who
   a. try to hinder those who preach the truth.
   b. seek wisdom through human reasoning.
   c. have little or no training or education.

C. THINKING ABOUT BIBLE TRUTHS

A Warning for the Church

When the apostle Paul met with the Ephesian elders on his way back from his third missionary journey, he felt sure it would be his last opportunity to speak to them. He warned the elders about some of the things that would happen to the church after he was gone. Even before Paul died, some of the churches he had established were turning away from the truths that he had taught them.

Acts 20:28–38

1. What did Paul say would happen after his departing? _____
   Grievous wolves would enter in among them, not sparing the flock.

2. a. From where else would troublemakers come?   of their own selves _____

   b. What would these men do? _____
    They would speak perverse things and draw away disciples after them.

3. Paul commended the Ephesian elders to God and to His Word. What would the Word do for them if they heeded it?   It would build them up and give them an inheritance. _____

4. Read 2 Timothy 1:15, which Paul wrote to Timothy near the end of his life. What does this verse show us about his prophecy to the Ephesian elders? _____
   It was starting to be fulfilled even before he died.

- Opposition would come from outside the church.

- Opposition would come from within the church.

5. About thirty years after Paul died, the apostle John wrote the Book of Revelation. Revelation 2 and 3 contain messages that Jesus gave to John for the seven churches in Asia.

   a. What had happened to the church at Ephesus by this time? (Revelation 2:4) _____

      The people had left their first love.

   b. What did Jesus tell them they would need to do? "Repent, and do the first works."

D. LEARNING MORE ABOUT BIBLE TIMES

Paul's Second Missionary Journey

Write the letter of each event listed below on the map beside the city where it happened.

A. Timothy joins Paul and Silas (Acts 16:1).

B. Paul has a vision of a man asking for help (Acts 16:8–10).

C. Paul and Silas are put into prison (Acts 16:12, 19–40).

D. The Jews study the Bible daily (Acts 17:10–12).

E. Paul preaches on Mars Hill (Acts 17:16–34).

F. Gallio refuses to judge Paul (Acts 18:1, 12–17).

Derbe could also be considered correct for A (See Acts 20:4).

232   Chapter Six   God Calls a New People

Paul's Third Missionary Journey

Write the letter of each event listed below on the map beside the city where it happened.

A. A silversmith starts a riot against Paul (Acts 19:23–41).

B. Eutychus falls out the window while Paul is preaching (Acts 20:6–12).

C. Paul bids farewell to the Ephesian elders (Acts 20:17–38).

D. Agabus prophesies that Paul will be bound in Jerusalem (Acts 21:8–14).

E. Paul preaches to a Jewish mob who had tried to kill him (Acts 21:17–22:23).

233

Lesson 30. "I Have Fought a Good Fight"

You have studied the apostle Paul's conversion, his three missionary journeys, and his arrest in Jerusalem. In this lesson you will study his trip to Rome. The Bible gives more details of his life than you will study in this course. However, considering that Paul was a Christian for about thirty-five years, our knowledge of his life is quite limited.

We do know that Paul did an unusual amount of traveling. As you read in Lesson 28, he probably traveled more than 13,400 miles (21,600 km). Since in many cases the actual distances he traveled would have been greater than they appear to be on a map, the real figure may be much larger. When we consider the dangerous and difficult conditions under which Paul often traveled, we realize that this was an amazing feat of endurance. Only a person fully dedicated to Christ's work could have persevered through all the trials Paul faced.

The Bible does not record the end of Paul's life. However, it seems quite likely that Paul was released after his first imprisonment and arrested again later. History records that he gave his life for his faith.

The apostle Paul's zeal should challenge us to be faithful. After his conversion, he gave his whole life in God's service. At the end he could truly say, "I have fought a good fight, I have finished my course, I have kept the faith: henceforth there is laid up for me a crown of righteousness" (2 Timothy 4:7, 8).

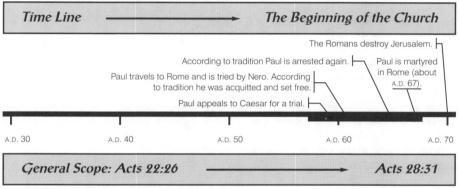

Time Line ⟶ The Beginning of the Church

The Romans destroy Jerusalem.

According to tradition Paul is arrested again.

Paul is martyred in Rome (about A.D. 67).

Paul travels to Rome and is tried by Nero. According to tradition he was acquitted and set free.

Paul appeals to Caesar for a trial.

A.D. 30   A.D. 40   A.D. 50   A.D. 60   A.D. 70

General Scope: Acts 22:26 ⟶ Acts 28:31

Note: The dates for events in Paul's life are approximate.

Using the Time Line

1. The Book of Acts ends with Paul waiting for his first trial before Nero. According to the time line, at approximately what date does the Book of Acts end? about A.D. 60 (Answers may vary slightly.)

2. According to the time line, what probably happened to Paul after the events recorded in the Book of Acts? He was probably released for a few years and then arrested again. After his second arrest he was condemned and executed.

Lesson 30

Oral Review

1. What did John the Baptist say when he learned that Jesus was becoming more popular than he was? [L. 5] **"He must increase, but I must decrease."**

2. What did Jesus mean by the statement, "Ye cannot serve God and mammon"? [L. 10] **We cannot serve God if we allow the desire for material things to control us.**

3. What did Jesus teach that caused many people to turn away from Him? [L. 14] **He told them that He is the Bread of Life that came down from heaven.**

4. In the parable of the prodigal son, who was lost besides the younger son? [L. 19] **the elder son**

5. Why did Jesus call half of the ten virgins wise and the other half foolish? [L. 23] **The five wise ones had taken extra oil, but the five foolish ones had not.**

6. What happened to Saul on the road to Damascus? [L. 28] **He saw a light from heaven that blinded him. After falling to the ground, he heard Jesus speak to him.**

7. How did Paul know that he should go to Macedonia? [L. 29] **In a vision, he saw a man asking**

A. ANSWERS FROM THE BIBLE

Paul in Danger

The chief captain hardly knew what to do with Paul after he learned that Paul was a Roman citizen. The day after Paul's arrest, the chief captain called for the Jewish leaders and brought Paul before them. However, the council became so violent that the Romans were forced to rescue Paul again.

The Jews were determined to take advantage of Paul's captivity and stop his missionary efforts once for all. They devised a plan to kill him. However, God was not finished with Paul yet.

Acts 23:12–24

1. How did the Jews plan to kill Paul?   They planned to ask the Romans to bring Paul to the council again. They would then lie in wait to kill him.

2. How did God cause the plan to fail?   He caused the plan to become known to Paul's nephew, who told it to Paul and to the chief captain. The chief captain sent Paul to Caesarea by night under heavy guard.

Paul Before Felix

Evidently the chief captain felt that Paul's case was too complicated for him to deal with. He decided to send him to Felix, the governor, and let him decide what to do with Paul. Since their plan to kill Paul had failed, the Jews now needed to accuse him at a trial. However, they were still determined not to let Paul escape death.

Acts 24:1–25

3. What accusations did the Jews bring against Paul at his trial before Felix?   They said that he was a pestilent fellow, a mover of sedition, and a ringleader of the sect of the Nazarenes. They also accused him of profaning the temple.

4. The Jews tried to appear as innocent as possible to the governor. By stating that they were planning to judge Paul according to Jewish law, they implied that the chief captain had interfered with a lawful process when he took Paul from them. In reality, what had the Jews been preparing to do to Paul when the chief captain interfered?   They were preparing to kill him.

5. It seems that Felix did not want to give a judgment either for or against Paul. How did he put off Paul's accusers?   He told them that he wanted to wait until the chief captain came so that he could learn more about the case.

Paul Before Festus

Apparently Felix never gave a ruling on Paul's case, even though he knew he was innocent. He gave Paul some liberties, yet he kept him in prison, hoping that Paul would pay money for his freedom. Two years later, when a new governor was appointed, Felix left Paul bound as a favor to the Jews. The Jews immediately approached Festus, the new governor, and tried to persuade him to bring Paul back to Jerusalem to be judged.

him to come and help the people of Macedonia.

8. At what city did Demetrius and other silversmiths stir up a riot against Paul? [L. 29] **Ephesus**

In This Lesson

Scope: Acts 22:26–28:31

Focus

- When the Jews in Jerusalem plotted to kill Paul, the chief captain sent him to Caesarea.
  - —Paul was tried by Felix, who did not give a verdict.
  - —During his trial before Festus, Paul appealed to Caesar to avoid being sent for trial at Jerusalem.
  - —Paul gave his testimony to King Agrippa and Bernice.
- Paul traveled to Rome by ship with a group of prisoners.
  - —After encountering a violent storm, the ship was wrecked on the island of Melita
  - —Paul was allowed to stay in his own rented house as a prisoner in Rome. From there, he called for the Jews and preached the Gospel to them.
- Paul was probably released and then arrested again before giving his life as a martyr.

Acts 25:1–12

6. a. Why did Festus ask Paul to go to Jerusalem for his trial?   He wanted to please the Jews.

   b. Every Roman citizen had the right to a trial before Caesar himself if he thought he was being treated unfairly. Why did Paul appeal to Caesar at this point?
   It was the only way he could be sure that he would not be sent to Jerusalem to be judged. (He knew that if he went to Jerusalem, the Jews would probably kill him.)

Paul Before King Agrippa

When Paul appealed to Caesar, Festus had no choice but to honor his request. However, Festus was not sure how to handle the case, for he felt foolish sending a prisoner to Caesar without any charges against him. Evidently he did not consider the Jewish accusations to be valid.

When King Agrippa and his wife came to visit, Festus gathered a group to hear Paul speak. Festus hoped that they might help him to formulate an accusation. Apparently King Agrippa was glad for an opportunity to hear Paul speak.

Acts 26:1–28

7. Why was Paul glad for the opportunity to present his case before King Agrippa?
   King Agrippa was an expert in the customs and questions of the Jews.

8. Paul recounted his conversion experience to the group.
   a. How did Festus react to Paul's story?   He said that Paul had lost his mind from much learning.

   b. How did King Agrippa respond?   He said, "Almost thou persuadest me to be a Christian."

The council was not much help to Festus. King Agrippa agreed that Paul was innocent. The Bible does not say what accusation Festus sent to Rome.

Paul's Trip to Rome

Shortly after Paul's defense before Agrippa, he was sent with a group of prisoners being taken to Rome. Evidently Luke traveled with Paul, since he uses the word *we* in referring to Paul's traveling companions.

Acts 27

9. The centurion in charge of the prisoners was apparently responsible to find transportation for the group. They traveled in whatever ships were available at the time.
   a. Why did Paul think they should not go farther than the port called Fair Havens?
      It was a dangerous time of the year to travel by sea.
   b. Why did the centurion not listen to Paul?   The master and owner of the ship thought it was safe to continue, and the port was not a very suitable place to spend the winter.

10. The ship had not gone far before the bad weather that Paul had warned them about came upon them. The storm was so violent that the men on board lost all hope of being saved. However, what message of hope did Paul receive from God during the storm?
    God said that Paul and all those with him would be saved, but they would be cast up on an island.

- It is difficult to know whether Agrippa was serious or whether he was just mocking Paul. You might want to discuss this with the class.

Objectives
- Students should know
  —how Paul's nephew helped to prevent the Jews from killing Paul. (*He told their plot to Paul and to the chief captain.*)
  —which Roman rulers Paul testified to while he was imprisoned at Caesarea. (*Felix, Festus, and Agrippa*)
  —who said, "Almost thou persuadest me to be a Christian." (*King Agrippa*)
  —what message of hope God gave to Paul during a severe storm. (*God would save all those on the ship.*)
  —why the barbarians of Melita thought Paul was a

god. (*He was not harmed when a poisonous snake bit him.*)
  —where Paul lived during his first imprisonment at Rome. (*in his own rented house*)
  —why Paul could face imprisonment and death calmly. (*He had fought a good fight, finished his course, and kept the faith. He was looking forward to a crown of life.*)

Truths to Amplify
- "All things work together for good to them that love God" (Romans 8:28). Paul's imprisonment and trials gave him the opportunity to testify before a number of important government officials. Paul also

236   Chapter Six   God Calls a New People

11. a. Why did the soldiers want to kill the prisoners after the ship ran aground near land? _____
    so that they would not escape

    b. Why did the centurion refuse to let them kill the prisoners?   He wanted to save Paul's life.

Acts 28:1–20

   God's promise to Paul was fulfilled exactly. Everyone on the ship was saved, but the ship was lost. On the island where they were shipwrecked lived some barbarians, who treated the refugees very kindly.

12. a. Why did the barbarians think that Paul must have been a murderer? _____
    A poisonous snake bit him, even though he had survived the shipwreck.

    b. Why did they change their minds?   The snake bite did not harm him.

13. What other miracles did Paul perform on the island? _____
    He healed the father of the chief man of the island. He also healed many others who had diseases.

14. a. The rest of the trip to Rome went smoothly. What favor did Paul receive in Rome that was unusual for a prisoner? (See also 28:30.) _____
    He was allowed to dwell in his own private house and receive visitors there.

    b. How does this show God's overruling power at work on behalf of the church? _____
    God made it possible for Paul to continue his labors for the church, even as a prisoner.

15. Whom did Paul call together soon after he arrived in Rome?   the chief (leaders) of the Jews

   The Jewish leaders spent a day with Paul while he explained the Christian beliefs to them. As usual, some of them believed; but many did not.

   The Book of Acts ends with the apostle under guard in his own rented house, awaiting trial before Nero. According to tradition, Paul was acquitted at this first trial and was set free.

After the Book of Acts

   There is some difference of opinion about what Paul did after the events recorded in the Book of Acts. Although the Bible does not specifically say what happened, Paul's epistles give us some clues. Most scholars think that 2 Timothy was written during a later imprisonment, since its description of Paul's circumstances is much different from the description given in Acts 28:16, 30, 31.

16. The epistles to Philemon and to the Philippians were probably written during Paul's first imprisonment. In both of them he expresses his confidence that he would be released shortly and that he would be able to visit those to whom he was writing. According to Romans 15:24, 28, where else did Paul hope to go?   Spain

17. a. Paul gave a few details about his second imprisonment and trial in 2 Timothy 4:10, 11, 16. What made this imprisonment harder for him to bear than the one described in Acts 28:30?
    In the imprisonment described in 2 Timothy, almost all of Paul's friends forsook him and he had to
    stand alone. Acts 28:30 describes a house arrest, which allowed his friends to visit.

    b. What did Paul ask Timothy to do in 2 Timothy 4:9, 21? _____
    He asked him to come to Rome before winter.

   We do not know whether Timothy was able to fulfill Paul's last request. According to history, Paul was brought to trial before Nero again that summer and was condemned. He was beheaded and buried in Rome in an unknown

wrote many of the New Testament books while in prison.

- Paul lived within the will of God; therefore he could face persecution, shipwreck, or whatever other danger he encountered, with the assurance that God would take care of him. This lesson shows that he was just as willing to die as he was to live. Though it ends with Paul's death, teach the lesson with a note of triumph. It is a great triumph when a Christian faces the last enemy in victory.

grave. And so the great apostle and missionary passed from earthly life to his eternal reward. If we are faithful, we will meet him there someday.

Map Work

🍇 *Place the letter of each event at the place on the map where it took place. If the exact place is not given in the Bible, place the letter in the approximate area.*

A. Paul is kept in prison for several years before appealing to Caesar (Acts 23:33–24:27).

B. The centurion refuses to winter at this place (Acts 27:8–12).

C. The ship runs into a storm at sea (Acts 27:14–20).

D. The ship is wrecked, but everyone on the ship escapes to land (Acts 27:39–28:1).

E. Paul is imprisoned in his own rented house (Acts 28:16, 30).

B. BIBLE WORD STUDY

🍇 *Choose the ending that gives the best meaning for the italicized word as it is used in this lesson.*

1. Felix sent for Paul and *communed* with him because he hoped that Paul would give him some money (Acts 24:26). Felix and Paul

   (a.) talked together.   b. ate together.   c. observed Communion together.

2. The master of the ship wanted to keep going because the port was not *commodious* to winter in (Acts 27:12). The port was not

   a. close to the sea.   (b.) a suitable place to stay.   c. open to the public.

3. Paul warned them that they would lose the *lading* of the ship if they ventured farther (Acts 27:10). In other words, they would lose

   a. their rigging.   (b.) their cargo.   c. the seamen.

4. The ship was caught in a great *tempest* (Acts 27:18). This storm was a

   (a.) violent windstorm.   b. tornado.   c. tidal wave.

5. The shipwrecked sailors were cast up on an island inhabited by *barbarians* (Acts 28:4). This means that the people were

   a. cannibals.   b. Greeks.   (c.) foreigners.

6. Paul was bitten by a *viper* on the island of Melita (Acts 28:3). This animal was a

   a. deadly spider.   (b.) poisonous snake.   c. scorpion.

C. THINKING ABOUT BIBLE TRUTHS

"I Am Now Ready to Be Offered"

The apostle Paul was not afraid to die. He had faced death many times before in his life. Sometimes God had to tell him to leave a place that was not safe for him. To him death was the doorway to God's presence, not something to be dreaded.

Philippians 1:20–24

1. It is natural for human beings to fear death. But in these verses Paul stated that he had a desire to depart (die). Why did he feel this way? _____

   He was ready to die, and he knew that his life after death would be far better than his earthly life was.

2. In spite of Paul's desire to depart and be with Christ, he was also willing to live for a while longer. Why did he think it would be better for him not to die at that time? _____

   He was needed by the churches.

2 Timothy 4:6–8

Paul wrote these words while he was in prison, waiting to be sentenced to death. He did not show any signs of fear or regret. Rather, he was already looking beyond the suffering that he expected to experience to a better life after death. He had earnestly done the work that God had called him to do. Now he was ready to rest.

3. What was the apostle looking forward to?   crown of righteousness from God

4. Paul made a very significant statement in this passage. He said: "I am now ready to be offered. . . . I have fought a good fight, I have finished my course, I have kept the faith." In light of this statement, why was Paul able to face death so steadfastly? _____

   (Sample answers) He had done the work God asked of him. He had remained faithful.

5. Paul did not have an easy life. He traveled thousands of miles, often on foot, through dangerous territory. He faced many hardships and persecutions. Yet he did not falter or allow any of these trials to hinder his faithfulness to God. What should his example inspire us to do? _____

   (Individual answers)

- You might want to discuss with the students why some people fear death.

Discuss this question in class if possible. Encourage your students to maintain a lifetime goal of having Paul's testimony at the end of their lives.

D. LEARNING MORE ABOUT BIBLE TIMES

The Work of the Apostles

Jesus had special work for the apostles to do. He spent much time with them while He was on earth, teaching them the truths that laid the foundation for Christian doctrine. On the day of Pentecost, they also received the Holy Spirit to give them further direction for their work. The apostles were a chosen group of leaders who were given the special work of helping to establish the church. The office of apostle no longer exists today.

Spreading the Gospel

At first the apostles stayed in Jerusalem, even after the other Christians were scattered by persecution. However, there is no indication in the last part of the Book of Acts that they were still in Jerusalem. According to early church writers, the apostles traveled to many parts of the world to preach the Gospel.

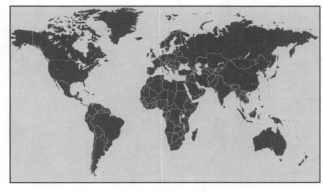

One writer suggested that it appears that the apostles divided the known world among themselves. Then each went his separate way and preached Christ in the area to which he was assigned. We do not know if this is actually how they decided where each one should go, but we do know that Christ had commanded them to go into all the world, and that the Holy Spirit led them according to His will.

There are very few Christian writings other than the New Testament that give information about the first seventy-five years of the church. Since the Bible gives only certain details, we do not know how far the Gospel was taken during this time. However, by the end of the first century, the Gospel had spread into most of the known world, and the church had grown remarkably. The early church took seriously their responsibility to spread the Gospel. All the apostles but John were killed as martyrs for Christ, and John would have been martyred too if God had not spared him.

1. Read Matthew 24:14; 28:19; and Acts 1:8.
   a. How far were the apostles to go with the Gospel message? _____
      "unto the uttermost part of the earth"
   b. What did Christ say would happen before the end of time? _____
      The Gospel must be preached to the whole world.

2. Most of the apostles made the ultimate sacrifice by dying as martyrs for the cause of the Gospel. What did Jesus tell Peter would happen to him when he was old? (See John 21:18.) He would stretch forth his hands, and others would put clothes on him and carry him where he did not want to go.

- According to tradition, Peter was crucified.

Establishing the Church

The New Testament church did not exist before the Holy Spirit came on the day of Pentecost. The apostles had the responsibility of establishing the church and guiding it in its early years. Through Christ's ministry on earth and the direction of the Holy Spirit, the apostles received direct revelation from God to lay the foundation of the church and to start it in the right direction.

240   Chapter Six   God Calls a New People

3. Read Matthew 16:18, 19. In these verses Jesus gave Peter the keys of the kingdom of heaven. Other verses such as Mark 16:14–16 and John 20:21–23 show that Jesus gave this authority to all the apostles. They were to use these "keys" to keep the church pure and free from sin.

a. What power did the apostles receive from Jesus with these "keys"? _____
   the power to bind or loose

b. The apostle Paul used the power that Jesus had given the apostles. What did Paul instruct the Corinthian church to do to a sinner in their midst? (See 1 Corinthians 5:3–5.) _____
   He said to deliver him to Satan. (He instructed them to excommunicate the sinner.)

c. After the church was established, the "keys" passed from the apostles to the church. The office of apostle was not needed after this. How does the church use the power of these "keys" today? (See 1 Corinthians 5:13; 2 Thessalonians 3:6, 14.) _____
   It restricts membership to those who are faithful.

Writing the Scriptures

The Old Testament Scriptures were of great value, but the church needed more instruction than the Old Testament offered. The Gospels partly served this purpose by preserving the record of Jesus' life and teachings, but even that was not enough. The church needed practical instruction in many areas of everyday Christian living.

The Holy Spirit used the apostles to give this instruction, first by preaching and then by writing. The Spirit inspired the apostle Paul to write most of the New Testament epistles, but other apostles and leaders also wrote. As questions arose in the churches Paul had established, the believers asked Paul what they should do. Many of his answers form parts of the New Testament.

Most New Testament teaching is very practical. It was written in response to real problems faced by real people. God used this method to ensure that the teachings of the apostles would live beyond the memory of their oral teaching.

4. Read 2 Peter 1:12–15. In these verses, Peter told his readers that he knew he would die soon and that he wanted to help them remember his teachings after his death. According to 2 Peter 3:1, what is one method that he used to help them to remember?   He wrote down the teachings.

5. Read 2 Peter 3:15, 16. What word does Peter use to describe the writings of the apostle Paul and other men of God?   Scriptures

The apostles are dead, yet they still speak to us through their writings. The New Testament was an important part of their ministry to the early church, and it is still the major foundation of the church today. The power of the New Testament is immeasurable. Thousands have found salvation because God led the apostles and their helpers to write His message to the church. In the next workbook of this series, you will study more of the New Testament books.

🍇 *Review the names of the New Testament books. You will need to know them for the final test.*

- You may want to mention to the students that this power was bestowed on the church, along with the responsibility to keep the church pure by judging sin in the lives of its members. Only God can actually forgive or condemn, but the church must use God's Word to identify sin, to administer discipline as necessary, and to receive repentant offenders back into fellowship.

- It is generally thought that Mark based his writings on Peter's teaching, just as Luke probably based his on Paul's. If so, Peter had a direct influence on the writing of the second Gospel.

241

Chapter Six Review

A. ORAL REVIEW

 Be sure you know the answers to these questions. Answer as many as you can from memory. If you need help, you may check the reference or lesson numbers given in brackets.

Who >>

1. Who advised the Jewish leaders to refrain from killing the apostles? [Acts 5:33–40]
2. Who brought great joy to the Samaritans by preaching the Gospel to them? [Acts 8:5–8]
3. Whom did God send to help Saul after Saul was blinded on the way to Damascus? [Acts 9:10–18]
4. Who tried to turn Sergius Paulus away from the faith? [Acts 13:6–8]
5. Who said, "Almost thou persuadest me to be a Christian"? [Acts 26:28]

What >>

6. What did the believers in the upper room begin to do after they were filled with the Holy Spirit? [Acts 2:4]
7. What Old Testament prophet had foretold that God would pour out His Spirit? [Acts 2:16–21]
8. What did the lame man do after Peter and John healed him in Jesus' Name? [Acts 3:8]
9. What part of the apostles' message especially upset the Jewish leaders? [Acts 4:1, 2]
10. What are two main ways that Satan attacks the church? [Lesson 26]
11. What is the meaning of *remission*? [Lesson 26]
12. What was the name of the large temple court that anyone could enter? [Lesson 26]
13. What sin did Ananias and Sapphira commit? [Acts 5:4, 5; Lesson 27]
14. What did the apostles do after the Jewish leaders beat them and threatened them? [Acts 5:40–42]
15. What need prompted the early church to choose seven men to help the apostles? [Acts 6:1]
16. What were Stephen's last words? [Acts 7:60]
17. What part did Saul take in putting Stephen to death? [Acts 7:58; 8:1]
18. What happened to Saul on the road to Damascus? [Acts 9:3–9]
19. What did Peter mean when he said that God is no respecter of persons? [Acts 10:34, 35; Lesson 27]
20. What did the people of Lystra attempt to do after Paul healed a lame man? [Acts 14:8–13]
21. What did the people of Lystra do to Paul after the unbelieving Jews stirred them up? [Acts 14:19]
22. What good came from Paul and Silas's imprisonment at Philippi? [Acts 16:27–34]
23. What did the Jews of Berea do when they heard Paul and Silas preach? [Acts 17:10, 11]
24. What Roman rulers did Paul testify to while he was imprisoned at Caesarea? [Acts 24:22; 25:1, 6; 26:1]
25. What message of hope did God give to Paul while he was on a ship during a severe storm? [Acts 27:21–26]

B. WRITTEN REVIEW

 Write the answers to these questions. Do as many as you can from memory. If you need help, you may check the reference given in brackets.

1. Gamaliel
2. Philip
3. Ananias
4. Barjesus (Elymas the sorcerer)
5. King Agrippa
6. They began to speak with other tongues (languages).
7. Joel
8. He walked, leaped, and praised God. (He also entered the temple with Peter and John.)
9. their preaching through Jesus the resurrection from the dead
10. as an angel of light (deception from within), and as a roaring lion (persecution from without)
11. forgiveness; pardon
12. the court of the Gentiles
13. They lied to the Holy Spirit.
14. They rejoiced to be counted worthy to suffer for Christ (and they continued to preach).
15. The Grecians were murmuring that their widows were being neglected.
16. "Lord, lay not this sin to their charge."
17. He consented to his death and kept the clothes of those who stoned him.
18. He saw a light from heaven that blinded him. After falling to the ground, he heard Jesus speak to him.
19. God does not accept or reject people on the basis of who they are.
20. offer sacrifices to Paul and Barnabas
21. stoned him
22. The jailer and his household believed and were baptized.
23. They searched the Scriptures daily to see if the teaching was true.
24. Felix, Festus, and Agrippa
25. All those on the ship would be saved.

242   Chapter Six   God Calls a New People

Why

1. Why did the apostles refuse to obey the Jewish leaders on certain occasions? [Acts 4:19, 20; 5:29]
   God had commanded them to preach, so they could not obey men who told them to stop.

2. Why did Philip leave Samaria in the midst of a revival? [Acts 8:26–29] _____
   God sent him to help an Ethiopian eunuch.

3. Why were the Jews astonished when Saul began preaching about Jesus? [Acts 9:19–21] _____
   He was preaching the message that he had formerly opposed.

4. Why did Saul need to flee from Damascus and from Jerusalem? [Acts 9:23–25, 29, 30] _____
   The unbelieving Jews tried to kill him after his conversion.

5. Why did the barbarians of Melita think that Paul was a god? [Acts 28:3–6] _____
   He was not harmed when a poisonous snake bit him.

6. Why could Paul face his imprisonment and death calmly? [2 Timothy 4:6–8] He had fought a
   good fight, finished his course, and kept the faith. He had a crown of life to look forward to.

How

7. How did the believers determine who should be ordained in Judas's place? [Acts 1:23–26] _____
   They chose two men, and then they cast lots to determine which one was God's choice.

8. How many believers were added to the church on the day of Pentecost? [Acts 2:41] _____
   about three thousand

9. How did the early church provide for the needs of its members? [Acts 2:44–46; 4:34, 35] _____
   Those who had possessions sold them, and the money was distributed according to everyone's need.

10. How did the apostles' lives show that they had been with Jesus? [Acts 4:13] _____
    They testified boldly about Jesus, even though they were considered unlearned and ignorant.

11. How did God prepare Peter for Cornelius's request for help? [Acts 10:9–20] _____
    He showed Peter unclean animals in a vision and told him to rise and eat. (He also told him to go with
    the men who were coming to seek him.)

12. How did Peter know that Cornelius and his Gentile friends had received the Holy Spirit? [Acts
    10:44–46] They spoke with tongues (just as the Jewish believers had done on the day of Pentecost).

13. How did Paul and Barnabas provide leadership for the churches they had helped to start? [Acts
    14:23] They ordained elders in every church.

14. How did God deliver Paul and Silas from the prison at Philippi? [Acts 16:26] _____
    He sent an earthquake that opened the doors and released the prisoners' bands.

15. How did Paul's nephew help prevent the Jews from carrying out their plot to kill Paul? [Acts 23:12–22] He told their plans to Paul and to the chief captain.

Map Review

 Match each place on the right with its description, and then label it on the map. Review the maps in Lessons 28–30 if you need help.

i	16. This was Saul's hometown.	a. Antioch
a	17. The church in this large city sent out Barnabas and Saul.	b. Athens
j	18. Paul saw a vision of a man from Macedonia calling for help. Later, Eutychus fell out of a window here.	c. Caesarea
		d. Corinth
g	19. After helping a slave girl, Paul and Silas were thrown into prison.	e. Ephesus
b	20. Paul preached on Mars Hill.	f. Jerusalem
d	21. Gallio refused to judge Paul.	g. Philippi
e	22. Demetrius and other silversmiths stirred up a riot against Paul.	h. Rome
f	23. A Jewish mob tried to kill Paul at the temple.	i. Tarsus
c	24. Paul was kept in prison several years before he appealed to Caesar.	j. Troas
h	25. Paul was kept under house arrest while awaiting trial before Nero.	

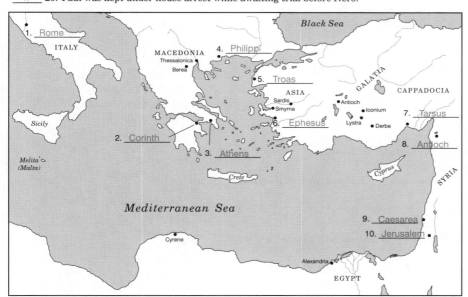

244

Reviewing What You Have Learned

 This exercise reviews some of the important facts you have studied this year. Be sure you know the answers to these questions before taking the final test. Try to answer as many as you can from memory. If you need help, you may check the references or lesson numbers in brackets.

Chapter One—Jesus Comes to Minister >>

1. Name the twenty-seven New Testament books in order. (Be sure you know the correct spellings.) [Lesson 1]
2. Name three important districts of Palestine. [Lesson 1]
3. To what two people did the angel Gabriel appear? Where did he appear to each? [Luke 1:11, 12, 26–28]
4. Define *Messiah*. What Greek word has the same meaning? [Lesson 2]
5. How did a heathen ruler's decree help to fulfill a prophecy about Jesus' birth? [Luke 2:1–5]
6. What name of Jesus refers to His humanity? to His deity? [John 1:49, 51]
7. What was John the Baptist's message? [Matthew 3:2]
8. How did God the Father and God the Holy Spirit manifest themselves at Jesus' baptism? [Matthew 3:16, 17]
9. How did Jesus overcome Satan's temptations? [Matthew 4:4, 7, 10]
10. Why did Jesus have authority to cleanse the temple? [John 2:16]
11. Jesus told Nicodemus that He had come to —— the world rather than to condemn it. [John 3:17]
12. What did John the Baptist say when he learned that Jesus was becoming more popular than he was? [John 3:30]

Chapter Two—Acceptance and Rejection >>

13. How did Peter, James, and John make their living before Jesus called them to be disciples? [Mark 1:16–20]
14. How did synagogue worship differ from temple worship? [Lesson 6]
15. Why did Jesus always tell evil spirits to be quiet when they testified that He was the Son of God? [Lesson 7]
16. How do we know that prayer was important to Jesus? [Mark 1:35; Luke 6:12]
17. Why were the Pharisees so upset when Jesus healed on the Sabbath? [Lesson 8]
18. When did the Jewish Sabbath begin? When did it end? [Lesson 8]
19. What did Jesus mean when He said, "The Sabbath was made for man, and not man for the sabbath"? [Mark 2:27; Lesson 8]
20. Why was Jesus criticized when He went to Levi's house for a feast? [Mark 2:15–17]
21. Name the twelve disciples. [Luke 6:14–16]
22. What does the Lord's Prayer mean when it says, "Forgive us our debts, as we forgive our debtors"? [Matthew 6:12, 14, 15; Lesson 10]
23. What did Jesus mean by the statement, "Ye cannot serve God and mammon"? [Lesson 10]
24. How does following the Golden Rule help us to treat others as we should? [Matthew 7:12; Lesson 10]

1. Matthew, Mark, Luke, John, Acts, Romans, 1 & 2 Corinthians, Galatians, Ephesians, Philippians, Colossians, 1 & 2 Thessalonians, 1 & 2 Timothy, Titus, Philemon, Hebrews, James, 1 & 2 Peter, 1, 2, & 3 John, Jude, Revelation
2. Galilee, Samaria, Judea
3. Gabriel appeared to Zacharias in the temple at Jerusalem; he appeared to Mary in Nazareth.
4. the Anointed One; Christ
5. Caesar required everyone to register in his ancestral city. Joseph took Mary to Bethlehem, the city of David, where Jesus was born.
6. Son of man; Son of God
7. "Repent ye: for the kingdom of heaven is at hand."
8. God the Father said, "This is my beloved Son, in whom I am well pleased." The Holy Spirit descended upon Jesus in the form of a dove.
9. He quoted from the Scriptures.
10. He is the Son of God.
11. save
12. "He must increase, but I must decrease."
13. They were fishermen.
14. Sacrifices were offered at the temple but not at synagogues.
15. He did not need or want Satan's help.
16. At times He rose early in the morning (or stayed up all night) to pray.
17. He was ignoring their Sabbath laws.
18. It began at sunset on Friday and ended at sunset on Saturday.
19. God meant the Sabbath for man's refreshment, not as a burden to him.
20. Levi was a publican and was considered a sinner.
21. Simon Peter, Andrew, James, John, Philip, Bartholomew, Matthew, Thomas, James the son of Alphaeus, Simon Zelotes, Judas the brother of James, Judas Iscariot
22. It means that God will not forgive our sins if we refuse to forgive others for the wrongs they do against us.
23. We cannot serve God if we allow the desire for material things to control us.
24. Generally we want others to treat us kindly and fairly, so we will treat others this way if we follow this rule.

Final Review

This review is intended for class discussion or as a self-study review before the final test. It could also be used for extra review throughout the school year.

Chapter Three—Jesus Ministers to Jews and Gentiles >>

25. How did the Roman centurion prove his faith in Jesus? [Matthew 8:8]
26. Why did Simon the Pharisee love Jesus less than did the woman who washed Jesus' feet? [Luke 7:40–48; Lesson 11]
27. Why did the scribes and Pharisees always become upset when Jesus forgave someone's sins? [Mark 2:6, 7; Lesson 11]
28. What lesson does the parable of the sower teach? [Matthew 13:18–23; Lesson 12]
29. In the parable of the sower, what does the seed represent? the ground? [Matthew 13:19; Lesson 12]
30. Why did Jesus teach in parables? [Matthew 13:10–13]
31. How did Jairus show his faith in Jesus? [Mark 5:22, 23, 36, 40]
32. Why could Jesus not do as many miracles in Nazareth as He did in other places? [Mark 6:5, 6]
33. What did Jesus use to feed the five thousand? [Mark 6:41]
34. Who continued to follow Jesus after many people turned away? [John 6:67–69]
35. What did Jesus teach His disciples by healing the daughter of a Gentile woman? [Lesson 15]
36. What did the Gentiles of Decapolis do when they saw Jesus' miracles? [Matthew 15:30, 31]

Chapter Four—Jesus Ministers in Judea and Perea >>

37. People had various ideas about who Jesus was. Who did Peter say Jesus is? [Matthew 16:16]
38. What did Jesus say He would build upon Peter's confession? [Matthew 16:18]
39. Who appeared with Jesus at His Transfiguration? [Matthew 17:3]
40. In what did Jesus tell His disciples to rejoice? [Luke 10:20]
41. What did Jesus tell Martha when she became upset with her sister Mary? [Luke 10:41, 42]
42. Why were some people at Jerusalem afraid to speak openly about Jesus? [John 7:13; 9:22]
43. What is the meaning of *blasphemy*? [John 10:33; Lesson 18]
44. According to the parable of the Good Samaritan, who is our neighbor? [Lesson 19]
45. In the parable of the Pharisee and the publican, why did God forgive the publican but not the Pharisee? [Lesson 19; Luke 18:14]
46. What did Jesus say was the purpose of Lazarus's sickness and death? [John 11:4]
47. Why did the rich young ruler decide not to follow Jesus? [Matthew 19:21, 22]
48. What did Jesus tell His disciples to do to become great in the kingdom of God? [Matthew 20:25–27]

Chapter Five—Jesus Completes His Work >>

49. How did Jesus fulfill an Old Testament prophecy during His triumphal entry into Jerusalem? [Matthew 21:4, 5]
50. Why did Jesus weep over Jerusalem? [Luke 19:41–44]
51. In the parable of the marriage of the king's son, why did the invited guests not come to the king's feast? [Matthew 22:3–6]
52. How did Jesus show the Sadducees that the Books of Moses teach the resurrection? [Luke 20:37, 38]
53. What warning did Jesus give His disciples before He began to tell them about future events? [Matthew 24:4]

25. He asked Jesus to heal his servant without coming to his house.
26. The woman saw herself as a great sinner, and Simon did not see his need; therefore he was not forgiven.
27. They knew that only God could forgive sins, and they did not want to admit that Jesus was God.
28. People respond to the Gospel in different ways.
29. God's Word; the hearts of those who hear God's Word
30. so that only those who believed would understand
31. Jairus asked Jesus to heal his daughter and trusted Jesus even after he heard that his daughter had died.
32. The people of Nazareth did not believe in Him.
33. five (barley) loaves and two fish
34. Jesus' twelve disciples
35. He loved Gentiles as well as Jews. (Whoever has true faith, whether Jew or Gentile, will receive God's blessings.)
36. They glorified the God of Israel.
37. Peter said, "Thou art the Christ, the Son of the living God."
38. His church
39. Moses and Elias (Elijah)
40. that their names were written in heaven
41. He told her that she was too concerned about serving. Mary had chosen the good part, and it would not be taken away.
42. They feared the Jewish leaders.
43. falsely claiming to be God
44. any person who is in need of our help
45. The publican acknowledged his sin and begged for mercy, but the Pharisee was proud and did not see his need for repentance.
46. "for the glory of God, that the Son of God might be glorified thereby"
47. He loved his possessions too much to obey Jesus' command to sell all that he had and give his money to the poor.
48. serve others
49. He fulfilled Zechariah 9:9 by riding into Jerusalem on the colt of an ass (donkey), bringing salvation.
50. He knew the terrible destruction that would come upon the city because of the Jews' rejection of Him.
51. They were too busy with other things that they considered more important. (Also, they failed to honor their king and his servants.)
52. He quoted God's words from the burning bush: "I am . . . the God of Abraham, the God of Isaac, and the God of Jacob."
53. "Take heed that no man deceive you."

54. When do Jesus' followers need to be ready for His return? [Matthew 24:42, 44]

55. Why does Jesus want His followers to observe Communion? [Luke 22:19]

56. What did Jesus tell Peter that showed that He could have prevented the soldiers from arresting Him? [Matthew 26:53]

57. What was the charge on which the Jewish leaders condemned Jesus at His trial? [Matthew 26:63–66]

58. Who said he would not believe that Jesus had risen until he saw and touched His wounds? [John 20:24, 25]

59. What promise did the angels give the disciples after Jesus had ascended into heaven? [Acts 1:10, 11]

60. What did Jesus do in the presence of His disciples to prove that His body had risen, and that they were not seeing a vision or a spirit? [Luke 24:39–43]

Chapter Six—God Calls a New People   >>

61. When the people were pricked in their hearts on the day of Pentecost, what did Peter tell them to do? [Acts 2:37, 38]

62. How did the apostles' lives show that they had been with Jesus? [Acts 4:13]

63. What are two main ways that Satan attacks the church? [Lesson 26]

64. What were Stephen's last words? [Acts 7:60]

65. What happened to Saul on the road to Damascus? [Acts 9:3–9]

66. How did Peter know that Cornelius and his Gentile friends had received the Holy Spirit? [Acts 10:44–46]

67. Who sent Barnabas and Saul on their first missionary journey? [Acts 13:1–3]

68. How did Paul and Barnabas provide leadership for the churches they had helped to start? [Acts 14:23]

69. How did Paul know that he should go to Macedonia? [Acts 16:9]

70. What did the Jews of Berea do when they heard Paul and Silas's preaching? [Acts 17:10, 11]

71. What Roman rulers did Paul testify to while he was imprisoned at Caesarea? [Acts 24:22; 25:1, 6; 26:1]

72. Why could Paul face his imprisonment and death calmly? [2 Timothy 4:6–8]

54. at all times

55. to remind them of His suffering and death

56. "Thinkest thou that I cannot now pray to my Father, and he shall presently give me more than twelve legions of angels?"

57. blasphemy

58. Thomas

59. Jesus would someday return in a manner similar to the way He had left.

60. He ate fish and honeycomb, and He told them to touch Him.

61. repent and be baptized

62. They testified boldly about Jesus, even though they were considered unlearned and ignorant.

63. as an angel of light (deception from within), and as a roaring lion (persecution from without)

64. "Lord, lay not this sin to their charge."

65. He saw a light from heaven that blinded him. After falling to the ground, he heard Jesus speak to him.

66. They spoke with tongues (just as the Jewish believers had on the day of Pentecost).

67. the church at Antioch (under the Spirit's direction)

68. They ordained elders in every church.

69. In a vision, he saw a man asking him to come to Macedonia and help them.

70. They searched the Scriptures daily to see if their teaching was true.

71. Felix, Festus, and Agrippa

72. He had fought a good fight, finished his course, and kept the faith. He was looking forward to a crown of life.

God Visits His Chosen Family
Chapter One Test

Name _____ Date _____ Score _____

A. *Match. You will not need all the choices.*   *(10 points)*

d	1. Hebrew name that means "the Anointed One"	a.	Caesar Augustus
k	2. Came from the East to see Jesus	b.	Jesus
a	3. Helped fulfill a prophecy concerning the place of Jesus' birth	c.	Herod the Great
f	4. Received a message from God that broke a long silence	d.	Messiah
i	5. Was compared to Elijah	e.	Son of man
j	6. Means "God with us"	f.	Zacharias
c	7. Pretended that he wanted to worship Jesus	g.	Herod Antipas
e	8. Refers to Jesus' humanity	h.	Christ
b	9. Was a name given to the Messiah because "he shall save his people from their sins"	i.	John the Baptist
		j.	Emmanuel
g	10. Had John the Baptist beheaded	k.	The wise men

B. *Fill in the blanks, or underline the correct words.*   *(11 points)*

11. _____Mary_____ said, "Be it unto me according to thy word."
12. _____Jesus_____ said, "Wist ye not that I must be about my _____Father's_____ business?"
13. Nathanael said, "Can there any good thing come out of _____Nazareth_____?"
14. God sent His Son so that "the world through him might be _____saved_____."
15. John the Baptist said, "He must _____increase_____, but I must _____decrease_____."
16. Jesus grew up among (Gentiles, Greek Jews, <u>Galileans</u>).
17. Jesus quoted ____the Scriptures____ to overcome Satan's temptations.
18. Jesus' disciples (followed, <u>believed on</u>, were afraid of) Him when they saw His power to turn water into wine.
19. Jesus had authority to cleanse the temple because He is the Son of _____God_____.

C. *Give complete answers.*   *(12 points)*

20. How did the Old Testament saints know about the Messiah? _____
    God foretold the Messiah's coming through His Old Testament prophets.
    _____

21. What was John the Baptist's message? "Repent ye: for the kingdom of heaven is at hand."
    _____
    _____

22. a. What did John the Baptist eat? He ate locusts and wild honey.

    b. What did he wear? He wore clothes made from camels' hair, and a leather belt.

23. a. What was heard at the baptism of Jesus? Those who were present heard "a voice from heaven, saying, This is my beloved Son, in whom I am well pleased."

    b. What did John and Jesus see? They saw "the Spirit of God descending like a dove" upon Jesus.

D. *Write the names of the New Testament books, using the correct order and spelling.*   *(21 points)*

Gospels
24. Matthew
25. Mark
26. Luke
27. John

Book of History
28. Acts

Pauline Epistles
29. Romans
30. 1 & 2 Corinthians
31. Galatians
32. Ephesians
33. Philippians
34. Colossians
35. 1 & 2 Thessalonians
36. 1 & 2 Timothy
37. Titus
38. Philemon

General Epistles
39. Hebrews
40. James
41. 1 & 2 Peter
42. 1, 2, & 3 John
43. Jude

Book of Prophecy
44. Revelation

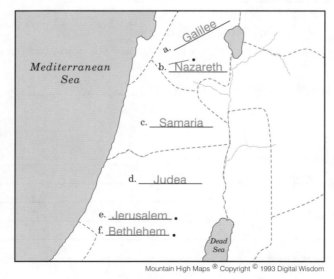

Mountain High Maps ® Copyright © 1993 Digital Wisdom

Palestine at the Time of Christ

E. *Write the following names in the proper places on the map.*   *(6 points)*

45. Judea
46. Bethlehem
47. Nazareth
48. Samaria
49. Galilee
50. Jerusalem

Total Points: 60

God Visits His Chosen Family
Chapter Two Test

Name _____   Date _____   Score _____

A. *Match. You will not use all the sentence endings.*   *(8 points)*

<u>i</u> 1. The Galilean nobleman	a. confessed that he was a sinful man after Jesus performed a miracle.
<u>c</u> 2. Peter's mother-in-law	
<u>b</u> 3. The leper	b. went to the priest after being healed.
<u>g</u> 4. The man sick with the palsy	c. showed hospitality after being healed.
<u>d</u> 5. Matthew	d. was a publican before meeting Jesus.
<u>a</u> 6. Peter	e. is a messenger of good news.
<u>h</u> 7. A disciple	f. did not think Jesus could forgive sins.
<u>e</u> 8. An apostle	g. was forgiven before being healed.
	h. is one who follows and learns.
	i. asked Jesus to heal his son.

B. *Write* true *or* false.   *(8 points)*

<u>true</u>   9. Jesus moved to Capernaum after the people of Nazareth rejected Him.

<u>false</u>   10. The unclean spirits refused to acknowledge Jesus as the Son of God.

<u>true</u>   11. The Jewish Sabbath began Friday evening and ended Saturday evening.

<u>true</u>   12. The Pharisees were more guilty of breaking God's Sabbath laws than Jesus' disciples were.

<u>true</u>   13. Jesus was accused of being a friend of publicans and sinners.

<u>false</u>   14. Jesus preached the Sermon on the Mount to those who had rejected Him.

<u>false</u>   15. A person who prays loud enough for others to hear is guilty of using vain repetitions.

<u>true</u>   16. When Jesus said, "Forgive us our debts, as we forgive our debtors," He meant that God will not forgive us if we refuse to forgive others.

C. *Fill in the blanks, or underline the correct word.*   *(10 points)*

17. Jesus found strength to do His work by spending much time in _____prayer_____.

18. At the beginning of the Sermon on the Mount, Jesus gave ten points known as the _____Beatitudes_____.

19. Jesus said that it was lawful to do _____good_____ on the Sabbath.

20. Jesus had the authority to say what was lawful on the Sabbath because He was _____Lord_____ of the Sabbath.

21. The prophet _____Isaiah (Esaias)_____ foretold that the Gentiles would trust in Jesus.

22. A person sick of the _____palsy_____ has lost some or all of his ability to move or feel.

23. During His early ministry, Jesus preached the Gospel in many synagogues of (<u>Galilee</u>, Decapolis, Samaria).
24. God wants us to give our alms in _____<u>secret</u>_____.
25. We can lay up _____<u>treasures</u>_____ in heaven by seeking the things of God rather than the things of this earth.
26. The people were astonished that Jesus taught as one having _____<u>authority</u>_____, and not as the scribes.

D. *Write complete answers.*   *(12 points)*

27. Why were the people of Nazareth offended by Jesus' stories of Elijah and Naaman?_____
    <u>Jesus showed by these stories that believing Gentiles receive more of God's blessings than unbeliev-</u>
    <u>ing Jews do.</u>

28. What Jewish worship ceremony, performed at the temple, was not practiced at the synagogues?
    <u>Sacrifices were offered at the temple but not at synagogues.</u>

29. What did Jesus mean by the following statements?
    a. "The sabbath was made for man, and not man for the sabbath." _____
       <u>God made the Sabbath for man's refreshment, not as a burden to him.</u>

    b. "Ye cannot serve God and mammon." _____
       <u>We cannot serve God if we allow the desire for material things to control us.</u>

30. These are two Old Testament commands that Jesus changed in the Sermon on the Mount. Give the changes that He made to them.   (Wording of answers may vary.)
    a. "An eye for an eye, and a tooth for a tooth." <u>Changed to: "Resist not evil: but whosoever shall</u>
       <u>smite thee on thy right cheek, turn to him the other also."</u>

    b. Love thy neighbour, and hate thine enemy." <u>Changed to: "Love your enemies, bless them that</u>
       <u>curse you, do good to them that hate you, and pray for them which despitefully use you, and per-</u>
       <u>secute you."</u>

E. *Write the names of Jesus' twelve disciples.*   *(12 points)*
(Answers for 31–42 may be in any order.)

31. Simon Peter	37. Matthew
32. Andrew	38. Thomas
33. James	39. James the son of Alphaeus
34. John	40. Simon Zelotes
35. Philip	41. Judas the brother of James
36. Bartholomew	42. Judas Iscariot

Total Points: 50

God Visits His Chosen Family
Chapter Three Test

Name _____ Date _____ Score _____

A. *Match the descriptions on the left with the items or persons on the right.*   *(10 points)*

g   1. Asked Jesus for a sign from heaven
e   2. Asked Jesus to leave
i   3. Expressed gratitude for the forgiveness
      Jesus had given
h   4. A Gentile who begged help of Jesus
a   5. A girl
f   6. Had a daughter who died
c   7. Means "multitude"
d   8. Poisonous weeds
j   9. Was healed by touching Jesus
b   10. Yeast

a. damsel
b. leaven
c. legion
d. tares
e. the Gadarenes
f. Jairus
g. the Pharisees
h. the Syrophoenician woman
i. the woman who washed Jesus' feet
j. the woman with an issue

B. *Fill in the blanks.*   (Count ½ point for each answer in number 15.) *(10 points)*

11. Jesus raised a widow's son back to life near the city of _____Nain_____.
12. In the parable of the sower, the seed represented the _____Word_____ of God.
13. Jesus did not do many miracles in Nazareth because of the people's _____unbelief_____.
14. The _____Sea of Galilee_____ is also called the Lake of Gennesaret.
15. Jesus fed the five thousand with _____five_____ loaves and _____two_____ small fish.
16. After Jesus fed the five thousand, the people wanted to make Him _____king_____.
17. Jesus walked on the water during the fourth _____watch_____ of the night.
18. The Pharisees rejected the _commandment (Word)_ of God in order to keep their traditions.
19. The true bread from heaven is _____Jesus_____.
20. The Gentiles of Decapolis glorified the _____God_____ of Israel when they saw Jesus' miracles.

C. *Circle the letter of the correct answer.*   *(2 points)*

21. Which of the following parables teach that a person must be willing to give up everything to be part of the kingdom of heaven?
   a. the parable of the sower and the parable of the net
   b. the parable of the mustard seed and the parable of the leaven
   c. the parable of the pearl of great price and the parable of the hidden treasure
   d. the parable of the tares and the parable of the seed growing secretly

22. Which of the following items represents the world in the parable of the tares?
    a. the weedy grain field
    b. the tares
    c. the enemy
    d. the leaven of the Pharisees

D. *Write complete answers.*   (*12 points*)

23. How did the Roman centurion whose servant was sick prove that he had great faith in Jesus?
    He asked Jesus to heal his servant without coming to his house.

24. Why did the scribes and Pharisees find fault with Jesus for forgiving sins?
    They knew that only God could forgive sins, and they did not want to acknowledge Jesus as God.

25. Why did Jesus teach in parables? Jesus taught in parables so that only those who believed in Him
    would understand His teaching. (Jesus taught in parables so that those who only wanted to find fault
    would not understand His teaching.)

26. How did the man called Legion serve Jesus after Jesus cast the devils out of him?
    He went home and told about the great things Jesus had done for him.

27. What teaching of Jesus caused many people to turn away from Him?
    His teaching that He is the Bread of Life that came down from heaven turned many people away.

28. What did Jesus teach His disciples by taking time to help Gentiles?
    Jesus taught his disciples to love Gentiles as well as Jews. (Whoever has true faith, whether Jew or
    Gentile, will receive God's blessings.)

E. *Match the letters on the map with the names below.* (*6 points*)

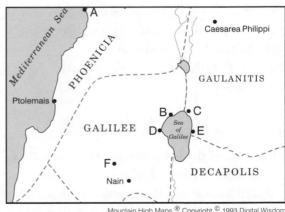

Mountain High Maps ® Copyright © 1993 Digital Wisdom

C   29. Bethsaida
B   30. Capernaum
E   31. Gergesa
D   32. Magdala
F   33. Nazareth
A   34. Tyre

Total Points: 40

God Visits His Chosen Family
Chapter Four Test

Name _____ **Date** _____ **Score** _____

A. *Match. You will not use all the choices.* *(8 points)*

_e_	1. Appeared at Jesus' Transfiguration	a. the blind man whom Jesus healed
_g_	2. Could no longer change their destinies	
_c_	3. Was compared to rivers of living water	b. a child
_d_	4. Died so that "the Son of God might be glorified thereby"	c. the Holy Spirit
		d. Lazarus (Mary and Martha's brother)
_f_	5. Like the elder brother in the parable of the prodigal son	
_h_	6. Returned to glorify God	e. Moses and Elijah
_a_	7. Worshiped Jesus after learning that He is the Son of God	f. the Pharisees
		g. the rich man and Lazarus
_b_	8. Used by Jesus as an example of humility	h. the Samaritan leper
		i. Zacchaeus

B. *Write* true *or* false. *(5 points)*

____true____ 9. When Jesus was transfigured, His face shone as the sun and His clothing became as white as the light.

____true____ 10. Peter found tribute money for Jesus and himself in the mouth of a fish.

____false____ 11. Jesus told His disciples that they should rejoice more in the great power that He had given them than in anything else.

____false____ 12. The main lesson taught by the parable of the prodigal son is that people can be lost through the carelessness of others.

____true____ 13. When Lazarus was raised, many of the Jews who were present believed in Jesus.

C. *Fill in the blanks.*   (Count ½ point for each answer in number 14.) *(5 points)*

14. Some people thought Jesus might be John the Baptist, ____Elijah (Elias)____, Jeremiah, or one of the ____prophets____.

15. The blind man at Jerusalem was born blind so that "the works of ____God____ should be made manifest in him." (Give credit for *Jesus* unless you have emphasized the exact quotation in class.)

16. After Jesus raised Lazarus from the dead, the Jewish leaders resolved to ____kill____ Jesus.

17. Jesus told His disciples that those who ____serve____ others are the greatest in the kingdom of heaven. (Partial credit could be given for *death*.)

18. Jesus said that Mary anointed His feet in preparation for His ____burial____.

D. *Write the names of those who made the following statements.*   *(5 points)*

<u>   Peter   </u>   19. "Thou art the Christ, the Son of the living God."

<u> God the Father </u>   20. "This is my beloved Son, in whom I am well pleased; hear ye him."

<u> James and John </u>   21. "Wilt thou that we command fire to come down from heaven, and consume them?" (Give two names.)

<u> the man born blind </u>   22. "We know that God heareth not sinners: but if any man be a worshipper of God, and doeth his will, him he heareth."

<u>   Zacchaeus   </u>   23. "If I have taken any thing from any man by false accusation, I restore him fourfold."

E. *Write complete answers.*   *(10 points)*

24. Why did Jesus need to rebuke Peter soon after He had commended him? <u>Jesus recognized Satan's influence in Peter when Peter began to rebuke Him for talking about needing to suffer and die.</u>

25. What did Jesus say at the Feast of Dedication that caused the Jews to try to stone Him? <u>He said that God was His Father, and that He and His Father are one.</u>

26. In the parable of the Good Samaritan, what commandment of God did the Samaritan obey that the priest and the Levite ignored? <u>"Thou shalt love thy neighbour as thyself."</u>

27. In the parable of the Pharisee and the publican, why was the publican justified rather than the Pharisee? <u>The publican confessed his sin and asked for forgiveness, but the Pharisee proudly proclaimed his "good" works and failed to see his need for repentance.</u>

28. Why did the rich young ruler decide not to follow Jesus? <u>He loved his possessions too much to obey Jesus' command to sell all that he had and give his money to the poor.</u>

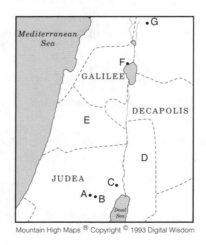

F. *Match the letters on the map with the names below.*   *(7 points)*

<u> B </u>   29. Bethany

<u> G </u>   30. Caesarea Philippi

<u> F </u>   31. Capernaum

<u> C </u>   32. Jericho

<u> A </u>   33. Jerusalem

<u> D </u>   34. Perea

<u> E </u>   35. Samaria

Total Points: 40

God Visits His Chosen Family
Chapter Five Test

Name _____ **Date** _____ **Score** _____

A. *Match. You may use names more than once or not at all.*   *(8 points)*

___e___ 1. Asked Jesus to tell the multitudes to stop singing Hosanna

___a___ 2. Were called wise because they carried extra oil

___e___ 3. Were strongly condemned by Jesus for their hypocrisy

___d___ 4. Tried to defend Jesus from the mob by using his sword

___d___ 5. Was brought to his senses when a rooster crowed

___c___ 6. Helped to bury Jesus' body

___b___ 7. Was the first person to meet Jesus after His resurrection

___h___ 8. Heard Jesus expound Old Testament prophecies concerning His death and resurrection

a. five virgins
b. Mary Magdalene
c. Nicodemus
d. Peter
e. Pharisees
f. Sadducees
g. twelve disciples
h. two disciples who went to Emmaus

B. *Match each statement with the person(s) who said or wrote it. You may use names more than once or not at all.*   *(10 points)*

___g___ 9. "Except I shall see in his hands the print of the nails, . . . I will not believe."

___b___ 10. "God is not the God of the dead, but of the living."

___c___ 11. "His blood be on us, and on our children."

___f___ 12. "Jesus of Nazareth the King of the Jews"

___b___ 13. "My God, my God, why hast thou forsaken me?"

___e___ 14. "Thou shalt never wash my feet."

___a___ 15. "Truly this was the Son of God."

___d___ 16. "What will ye give me, and I will deliver him unto you?"

___f___ 17. "What is truth?"

___b___ 18. "Ye also ought to wash one another's feet."

a. a Roman centurion
b. Jesus
c. the Jews
d. Judas
e. Peter
f. Pilate
g. Thomas
h. the two thieves

C. *Fill in the blanks. The longer blanks require more than one word.*   *(6 points)*

19. The Jewish leaders condemned Jesus on a charge of _____blasphemy_____.

20. When Jesus died, the _____veil of the temple_____ was torn in half.

21. Jesus fulfilled an Old Testament prophecy by riding a donkey into _____Jerusalem_____.

22. Jesus warned His disciples to "take heed that no man _____deceive_____ you."

23. After His resurrection, Jesus asked Peter three times if he _____loved_____ Him.

24. Jesus said that the Jews had made the temple a _____den of thieves_____.

D. *Circle the letter of the best answer.*   *(4 points)*

25. Which parable teaches that God rewards His people for their faithfulness rather than for the amount of work that they do?
    (a) The Laborers in the Vineyard   c. The Wicked Husbandmen
    b. The Two Sons   d. The Marriage of the King's Son

26. The Pharisees tried to trap Jesus by asking Him
    a. where He received authority to cleanse the temple.
    (b) whether it was lawful to pay taxes to Caesar.
    c. what signs would appear before the end of the world.

27. Since God has not revealed when the end of the world will be, Jesus' followers need to
    a. figure out for themselves when it will be.
    b. study the Bible to see when it will be.
    (c) be ready for it at all times.

28. Why did God allow the Romans to make Jerusalem a desolation?
    a. The disciples had doubted Jesus' resurrection.
    (b) The Jews had rejected Jesus as the Messiah.
    c. God was rewarding the Romans because they did not want to crucify Jesus.

E. *Write complete answers for these questions.*   *(12 points)*

29. What lesson did Jesus teach His disciples with the parable of the talents? _____
    God's children should make wise use of the abilities He has given them.
    _____

30. In the parable of the marriage feast, why did the invited guests refuse to come? _____
    They were too busy with things that they considered more important. (They also failed to honor the
    king and his servants.)

31. How do we know that Jesus could have prevented His enemies from arresting and crucifying Him?
    (Sample answers) Jesus could have called for twelve legions of angels to protect Him, but He did not.
    He said that no man could take His life, but He would lay it down. Just before He died, He committed
    His spirit to God with a loud voice.

32. What are Christians to remember when they participate in a Communion service? _____
    They should remember Jesus' suffering and death.
    _____

33. What did Jesus do in the presence of His disciples to prove that His body had risen? _____
    He ate food and told them to touch Him.
    _____

34. What promise did the angels give the disciples after Jesus had ascended? _____
    Jesus will come again just as He left.
    _____

Total Points: 40

God Visits His Chosen Family
Chapter Six Test

Name _____ **Date** _____ **Score** _____

A. *Match. You may use names more than once or not at all.* *(10 points)*

<u> f </u> 1. Prophesied that the Holy Spirit would be sent   a. Ananias and Sapphira

<u> i </u> 2. Preached to the Jews on the day of Pentecost   b. Barjesus

<u> a </u> 3. Lied to the Holy Spirit   c. Barnabas

<u> j </u> 4. Taught the Samaritans and an Ethiopian eunuch   d. Demetrius

<u> i </u> 5. Was the first to take the Gospel to the Gentiles   e. Eutychus

<u> b </u> 6. Tried to turn Sergius Paulus away from the faith   f. Joel

<u> g </u> 7. Was stoned at Lystra   g. Paul

<u> d </u> 8. Started a riot at Ephesus   h. Paul's nephew

<u> e </u> 9. Fell out of a window while Paul was preaching   i. Peter

<u> h </u> 10. Helped to save Paul from a Jewish plot   j. Philip

                                                                         k. Stephen

B. *Write* true *or* false. *(5 points)*

<u> false </u> 11. The apostle Paul was ordained by lot to take Judas Iscariot's place.

<u> false </u> 12. The largest court of the temple, which anyone could enter, was called the court of women.

<u> true </u> 13. The apostles rejoiced that they were counted worthy to suffer for Jesus.

<u> true </u> 14. Paul saw an altar dedicated to "The Unknown God" at Athens.

<u> false </u> 15. Paul testified before all of the following Roman rulers: Felix, Festus, Agrippa, Gallio, and Nero.

C. *Fill in the blanks.* *(5 points)*

16. On the day of Pentecost, about <u> three thousand </u> believers were added to the church.

17. Saul was converted after Jesus revealed Himself to him near the city of <u> Damascus </u>.

18. The church at <u> Antioch </u> sent Barnabas and Saul on their first missionary journey.

19. Paul and Barnabas <u> ordained </u> <u> elders </u> in every church that they had started.

20. In a vision, Paul saw a man from <u> Macedonia </u> who asked for help.

D. *Write the names of those who said the following things.* *(4 points)*

<u>   Stephen   </u> 21. "Lord, lay not this sin to their charge."

<u> the Philippian jailer </u> 22. "Sirs, what must I do to be saved?"

<u>   Agrippa   </u> 23. "Almost thou persuadest me to be a Christian."

<u>   Paul   </u> 24. "I have fought a good fight, I have finished my course, I have kept the faith."

E. *Write complete answers.*   *(10 points)*

25. What are the two main ways that Satan attacks the church?   Satan attacks the church as an angel
    of light (deception from within), and as a roaring lion (persecution from without).
    _____

26. How did the early church at Jerusalem provide for the needs of its members? _____
    Those who had possessions sold them, and the money was distributed according to everyone's need.
    _____

27. Why did the apostles refuse to obey the Jewish leaders on certain occasions? _____
    God had commanded them to preach, so they could not obey men who told them to stop.
    _____

28. What did the apostles do that proved they had been with Jesus? _____
    They testified boldly about Jesus, even though they were considered unlearned and ignorant.
    _____

29. How did the Jews of Berea make sure that Paul's teaching was true? _____
    They searched the Scriptures daily to see if the teaching was true.
    _____

F. *Match the letters on the map with the names below.*   *(6 points)*

E   30. Antioch
C   31. Corinth
D   32. Ephesus
F   33. Jerusalem
B   34. Philippi
A   35. Rome

Mountain High Maps ® Copyright © 1993 Digital Wisdom

Total Points: 40

God Visits His Chosen Family
Final Test

Name _____   **Date** _____   **Score** _____

A. *Match. You will not use all the choices.*   (*10 points*)

__d__	1. Means "the Anointed One"	a. Gentiles of Decapolis
__k__	2. Refers to Jesus' humanity	b. Jairus
__j__	3. Refers to Jesus' deity	c. Levi
__f__	4. Added many Sabbath rules and other laws to God's Law	d. Messiah
__c__	5. A publican who became one of Jesus' disciples	e. mammon
__g__	6. Asked Jesus to heal his servant without coming to his house	f. Pharisees
		g. a Roman centurion
__b__	7. Asked Jesus to heal his daughter	h. a rich young ruler
__a__	8. Glorified the God of Israel	i. Sadducees
__h__	9. Loved his possessions more than God	j. Son of God
__i__	10. Did not believe in the resurrection	k. Son of man

B. *Write* true *or* false.   (*10 points*)

_____false_____ 11. The three most important districts of Palestine were Judea, Samaria, and Macedonia.

_____true_____ 12. Jesus refused to let evil spirits testify that He is the Son of God.

_____true_____ 13. The scribes and Pharisees realized that when Jesus forgave sins, He was claiming to be God.

_____true_____ 14. Jesus taught that God will forgive only those who forgive others.

_____false_____ 15. Jesus taught in parables so that everyone could understand the truth.

_____true_____ 16. In the parable of the sower, the seed represents God's Word.

_____false_____ 17. Jesus told Martha that serving others was the most important thing a person could do.

_____false_____ 18. Christians observe Communion in remembrance of Jesus' resurrection and ascension.

_____true_____ 19. Paul and Barnabas ordained elders in every church that they had established.

_____false_____ 20. The Jews of Berea failed to recognize the importance of the Holy Scriptures.

C. *Fill in the blanks.*   (Count ½ point for each answer in number 23.) (*8 points*)

21. Jesus told Nicodemus that He had come to _____save_____ the world.

22. The Sabbath began at sundown on _____Friday_____ evening.

23. Jesus fed the five thousand with _____five_____ loaves and _____two_____ fish.

24. Jesus said that He would build His _____church_____ on the confession that He is the Christ.

25. The parable of the Good Samaritan teaches that any person in need of our help is our
_____neighbor_____ .

26. The Jewish leaders condemned Jesus on a charge of _____blasphemy_____ .

27. On the day of Pentecost, Peter told the multitude to _____repent_____ and be baptized.

28. Under the direction of the Holy Spirit, the church at _____Antioch_____ sent Barnabas and Saul on their first missionary journey.

D. *Write the names of the people who said the following things. You may use some names more than once.*   *(7 points)*

John the Baptist	29. "He must increase, but I must decrease."
Jesus	30. "It is written, Thou shalt worship the Lord thy God, and him only shalt thou serve."
Peter	31. "Thou art the Christ, the Son of the living God."
Jesus	32. "Take heed that no man deceive you."
Thomas	33. "Except I shall see in his hands the print of the nails, . . . I will not believe."
Stephen	34. "Lord, lay not this sin to their charge."
Paul	35. "I have fought a good fight, I have finished my course, I have kept the faith."

E. *Write complete answers.*   *(12 points)*

36. How did God the Father and God the Holy Spirit manifest themselves at Jesus' baptism? _____
God the Father said, "This is my beloved Son, in whom I am well pleased." The Holy Spirit descended upon Jesus in the form of a dove.

37. How does following the Golden Rule help us to treat others as we should? _Generally we want_
others to treat us kindly and fairly, so we will treat others this way if we follow this rule.

38. Why did Simon the Pharisee love Jesus less than did the woman who washed Jesus' feet? _The_
woman saw herself as a great sinner, and Simon did not see his need; therefore he was not forgiven.

39. How did Lazarus's death serve a good purpose? _It brought glory to God by revealing Jesus' power_
to raise the dead. (Many of the Jews that witnessed Lazarus's resurrection believed on Jesus.)

40. How did Jesus prove to His disciples that His body had risen, and that they were not seeing a vision or a spirit? _He ate food, and He told them to touch Him._

41. How could the Jewish leaders tell that the apostles had been with Jesus? _____
They testified boldly about Jesus, even though they were considered unlearned and ignorant.

F. *Write the names of the New Testament books, using the correct order and spelling.*   *(21 points)*

Gospels	Pauline Epistles	General Epistles
42. _____ Matthew _____	47. _____ Romans _____	57. _____ Hebrews _____
43. _____ Mark _____	48. 1 & 2 _____ Corinthians _____	58. _____ James _____
44. _____ Luke _____	49. _____ Galatians _____	59. 1 & 2 _____ Peter _____
45. _____ John _____	50. _____ Ephesians _____	60. 1, 2, & 3 _____ John _____
Book of History	51. _____ Philippians _____	61. _____ Jude _____
46. _____ Acts _____	52. _____ Colossians _____	**Book of Prophecy**
	53. 1 & 2 _____ Thessalonians _____	62. _____ Revelation _____
	54. 1 & 2 _____ Timothy _____	
	55. _____ Titus _____	
	56. _____ Philemon _____	

G. *Write the names of Jesus' twelve disciples.*   *(12 points)*

(Answers for 63–74 may be in any order.)

63. _____ Simon Peter _____	69. _____ Matthew _____
64. _____ Andrew _____	70. _____ Thomas _____
65. _____ James _____	71. _____ James the son of Alphaeus _____
66. _____ John _____	72. _____ Simon Zelotes _____
67. _____ Philip _____	73. _____ Judas the brother of James _____
68. _____ Bartholomew _____	74. _____ Judas Iscariot _____

Total Points: 80

Index of Special Features

Miscellaneous Special Features